THE POLITICS OF CONGRESSIONAL ELECTIONS

FIFTH EDITION

Gary C. Jacobson
University of California, San Diego

New York • San Francisco • Boston
London • Toronto • Sydney • Tokyo • Singapore • Madrid
Mexico City • Munich • Paris • Cape Town • Hong Kong • Montreal

For Marty and Karen

Publisher: Priscilla McGeehon
Senior Acquisitions Editor: Eric Stano
Marketing Manager: Megan Galvin-Fak
Production Manager: Eric Jorgensen
Project Coordination, Text Design and Electronic Page Makeup: UG / GGS Information
Services, Inc.
Cover Design Manager: Nancy Danahy
Cover Design: Keithley & Associates
Cover Photo: Tony Stone Images
Manufacturing Buyer: Roy Pickering
Printer and Binder: Courier-Stoughton
Cover Printer: Phoenix Color Corp

Library of Congress Cataloging-in-Publication Data

Jacobson, Gary C.
     The politics of congressional elections / Gary C. Jacobson.—5th ed.
         p. cm.
     Includes bibliographical references and index.
     ISBN 0-321-07069-0
     1. United States. Congress—Elections.   I. Title.

 JK1976.J27 2000
 324.973—dc21   00-031490

Please visit our website at http://www.awl.com

ISBN 0-321-07069-0

12345678910—CRS—03020100

CONTENTS

LIST OF TABLES

LIST OF FIGURES

PREFACE

This book, like the previous four editions, is about congressional election politics, broadly understood. In writing it, I have tried to keep in mind that elections are means, not ends in themselves. What happens during campaigns or on election days is, of course, fascinating and important, and I do not neglect congressional candidates, campaigns, and voters. But campaigns and elections are more than curious rituals only because they reflect deeper structural patterns and currents in American political life and help determine how—and how well—we are governed. A considerable part of the book is therefore devoted to tracing the connections between the electoral politics of Congress and other important political phenomena. Examining congressional election politics in this way inevitably raises fundamental questions about representation and responsibility, and these are the central normative concerns of the book. My intent here, then, is to offer a systematic account of what goes on in congressional elections and to show how electoral politics reflect and shape other basic components of the political system, with profound consequences for representative government.

Research on congressional elections continues to thrive, and, as before, it will quickly become clear to the reader how much I have learned from the work and ideas of other scholars. Information on congressional voters, candidates, and campaign finances becomes richer with each passing election as well; we now have the 1988–1992 Senate Election Study to go along with the indispensable American National Election Studies (NES). These developments, along with the remarkable upheavals produced by the congressional elections of the early 1990s and the precarious Republican hold on Congress continue to make thinking and writing about congressional elections an intellectual pleasure.

I remain deeply indebted to the many friends and colleagues who have guided and stimulated my thinking about congressional election politics. The genesis of this book was my work as a member of the Committee on Congressional Election Research of the Board of Overseers of the National Election Studies, which designed the congressional component included in the American National Election Studies since 1978. Everyone I worked with on the committee has contributed to it in some way: Alan Abramowitz, David Brady, Heinz Eulau, Richard Fenno, John Ferejohn, Morris Fiorina, Barbara Hinckley, Malcolm Jewell, Jack Katosh, James Kuklinski, Thomas Mann, David Mayhew, Warren Miller, Glenn Parker, Barbara Sinclair, Michael Traugott, Raymond Wolfinger, and Gerald Wright.

Since then, a continuing association with the NES Board has helped keep me in touch with other scholars who have contributed in various ways to my understanding of congressional elections and politics: Larry Barrels, Richard

Brody, Stanley Feldman, William Flanigan, Charles Franklin, Edie Goldenberg, Mary Jackman, Stanley Kelley, Rod Kiewiet, Donald Kinder, David Leege, Douglas Rivers, Steven Rosenstone, Gina Sapiro, Merrill Shanks, Walter Stone, Mark Westlye, and John Zaller. I also wish to thank the many political scientists who used the earlier editions in their teaching and have let me know what they liked and disliked about the book.

I am grateful to all of my colleagues at U.C. San Diego for providing an environment wonderfully conducive to scholarly work. Samuel Kernell read and commented on several chapters and has shared some of the research reported in the book. I have also enjoyed instructive and stimulating conversations with Nathaniel Beck, Amy Bridges, Peter Cowhey, Gary Cox, Elizabeth Gerber, Richard Kronick, David Laitin, Skip Lupia, John Mendeloff, Mathew McCubbins, and Samuel Popkin. Mo Fiorina, Herbert Jacob, Burdett Loomis, Tom Mann, and Steve Rosenstone read the entire manuscript of the first edition, and their service continues to register in this one. Jon Bond, Priscilla Southwell, Darrell West, Lynda Powell, Melissa R. Michelson, Bradford S. Jones, and eight anonymous scholars reviewed previous editions with an eye to improving this one; the book is clearly better for their suggestions and probably the worse for my not having heeded more of them. I am obliged to Denise Gimlin, Edward Lazarus, Del Powell, and David Wilsford for helping to gather some of the data analyzed in Chapter 6. Greg Bovitz, Mike Dimock, Tommy Kim, and Jeff Lazarus helped in various important ways (whether they know it or not) to this revision. David Epstein supplied me with some timely data. They have all earned my thanks.

Part of the research reported here was supported by a grant from the National Science Foundation (SES-80-7577), for which I am most grateful. Some of the data used in this book were made available by the Inter-University Consortium for Political and Social Research. The data for the 1978–1998 American National Election Studies and the 1988–1992 Senate Election Study were originally collected by the Center for Political Studies of the Institute for Social Research, the University of Michigan, under grants from the National Science Foundation. Neither the original collectors of the data nor the Consortium bear any responsibility for the analyses and interpretations presented here, and the same, of course, holds for anyone else I have mentioned.

Since the last edition of this book, the scholarly community has mourned the death of Warren Miller. Without his intellectual and entrepreneurial contributions to the study of congressional elections, this book would be inconceivable. I feel fortunate to be among the many scholars whose careers were profoundly affected by Warren and his work. I am deeply grateful, and I shall miss him.

Gary C. Jacobson
San Diego
December 16, 1999

CHAPTER ONE

Introduction

Elections touch the core of American political life. They provide ritual expression of the myth that makes political authority legitimate: We are governed, albeit indirectly, by our own consent. Elections are also the focus of thoroughly practical politics. They determine who will hold positions of real power in the political system and, by establishing a framework in which power is pursued, profoundly affect the behavior of people holding or seeking power. The mythical and practical components of elections meet at the point where electoral constraints are supposed to make leaders responsive and responsible to the public. How comfortably they fit together has deep consequences for the entire political system. Almost any important development in American political life will be intertwined with the electoral process.

Congressional elections in particular are intimately linked to many basic phenomena of American politics. In countless ways, obvious and subtle, they affect the performance of Congress and, through it, the entire government. At the same time they reflect the changing political landscape, revealing as well as shaping its fundamental contours.

The basic questions to be asked about congressional elections are straightforward: Who gets elected to Congress and how? Why do people vote the way they do in congressional elections? How do electoral politics affect the way Congress works and the kinds of policies it produces? What kind of representation do congressional elections really provide? Every answer has further implications for the workings of American politics; and many of them must be traced in order to grasp the deeper role of congressional elections in the political process.

To explain what goes on in congressional elections and to understand how they are connected in myriad ways to other aspects of American political life are the broad purposes of this book. It also has a more pointed intention: to use a careful examination of the complex, multifaceted business of electing Congress to help understand why politicians in Washington have found it so difficult to fashion measured solutions to pressing national problems.

A central theme in earlier editions of this book was that political incapacity and stalemate were fostered by an electoral process that gave senators and representatives every reason to be individually responsive but little reason to be collectively responsible. In the 1990s, the chickens of collective irresponsibility came home to roost. First, the 1992 elections brought the highest turnover of House seats in fifty years. Then the 1994 elections put Republicans in control of both Houses of Congress for the first time in forty years. They have held onto their majorities for two more elections under conditions of increasing partisan polarization, epitomized by their failed attempt to impeach and remove

Bill Clinton from the White House. The elections of the 1990s and the politics they embody raise many new questions and open many new possibilities, so this edition gives considerable attention to the changes in the electoral politics of Congress observed over the past decade and their implications for the first election of the new millennium.

Congressional elections are complex events. The sources of this complexity are many. An important one is the number of different perspectives from which congressional elections can be examined. Consider the alternative ways the question, "How's the congressional election going?" might be answered. A candidate or campaign manager would immediately begin talking about what was going on in the district, who was ahead, what groups were supporting which candidate, how much money was coming in, what issues were emerging. A national party leader—the president, for example—would respond in terms of how many seats the party might gain or lose in the House and Senate and what this might mean for the administration's programs. A private citizen might grumble about the hot air, mudslinging, and general perfidy of politicians, or might scarcely be aware that an election was taking place.

Similarly, political scientists and other people who study congressional elections do so from a variety of research orientations. Some study voters: Why do people vote the way they do? Indeed, why do they vote at all? Others study candidates and campaigns: Who runs for Congress, and why? What goes on in campaigns? How is money raised and spent—and what difference does it make? Or they explore the aggregate results of congressional elections: What accounts for the changes in the distribution of House and Senate seats between the two parties? Still others are interested in representation: How are the activities of members of Congress, and the performance of Congress as an institution, connected with what goes on in elections? These and other questions are deserving of individual attention. But it is no less essential to understand how they are all interrelated.

People involved in congressional elections are at least implicitly aware of the connections between the different levels of analysis. Voters are interested primarily in the candidates and campaigns in their state or district, but at least some are conscious of the broader political context and may, for example, adapt their congressional voting decision to their feelings about presidential candidates. Presidents worried about the overall makeup of the Congress are by no means indifferent to individual races and sometimes involve themselves in local campaigns. Candidates and other congressional activists are mindful of national as well as local political conditions they believe influence election outcomes; and, of course, they spend a great deal of time trying to figure out how to appeal effectively to individual voters.

Scholars, too, are fully aware that, although research strategies dictate that the congressional election terrain be subdivided into workable plots, no aspect of congressional elections can be understood in isolation. It is essential to integrate various streams of investigation for any clear account of what is going on. This is no simple task. One difficulty is quite familiar to students of the social sciences: how to connect the accounts of individual behavior to large-scale social phenomena. The problem is one of coordinating the micro- and macro-level accounts of political behavior (there are middle levels, too, of course). But it turns out to be a most fruitful problem. Its solution is a rich source of insight into congressional election processes and their consequences.

The approach taken in this book is to examine congressional elections from several perspectives while attending throughout to the interconnections among them. Chapter 2 sets out the legal and institutional context in which congressional elections take place. This formal context is easily taken for granted and overlooked, but it is, on reflection, fundamental. The very existence of congressional elections depends on this structure, and it shapes them in a great many important ways. The chapter also surveys briefly the rich variety of social, economic, and ethnic mixes that are found among states and congressional districts, for this diversity underlies many distinctive aspects of congressional election politics.

The third and fourth chapters examine, respectively, congressional candidates and campaigns. The pervasive effects of incumbency inject a theme common to both of these chapters. The resources, strategies, and tactics of candidates vary sharply, depending on whether a candidate is an incumbent, a challenger to an incumbent, or running for an open seat where neither candidate is an incumbent. They also differ between House and Senate candidates in each of these categories. The strategies of candidates in different electoral situations and the consequences of varying strategies are explored. So are the roles of campaign money, organization, campaign activities and tactics, and the local political context. Campaigns both reflect and work to reinforce candidates' assumptions about the electorate, and they are also closely linked to the behavior in office of those elected.

Chapter 5 deals with voting in congressional elections. Knowing who votes and what influences the voting decision are valuable pieces of information in their own right, but such knowledge is even more important as a means for understanding what congressional elections mean, what they can and cannot accomplish. The way voters react is tied closely to the behavior of candidates and the design and operation of campaigns—and to what members of Congress do in office.

Chapter 6 looks upon congressional elections as aggregate phenomena. When all the individual contests are summed up over an election year, the collective outcome determines which party controls the Congress and with how large a majority. It also strongly influences the kinds of national policies that emerge; it is at this level that the government is or is not held responsible. Congressional elections clearly respond to aggregate political conditions. But aggregate outcomes are no more than the summation of individual voting decisions in the districts to election results across all districts. The path that leads from aggregate political conditions to individual voting decisions to aggregate congressional election outcomes is surprisingly complicated; candidates' strategies turn out to provide a critical connecting link. The points in this chapter are illustrated by brief reviews of each biennial election from 1980 to 1990, with considerably more detailed accounts of the crucial 1992, 1994, 1996, and 1998 elections.

Finally, of course, congressional elections are important for how they influence the behavior of elected leaders and therefore the success or failure of politics. In fact, the knowledge that they are elected officials is the key to understanding why members of Congress do what they do in office. Not only that they are elected, but how they are elected matters. How candidates mount campaigns and how voters choose between them has a crucial effect on what members of Congress do with their time and other resources and with the quality, quantity, and direction of their legislative work. Electoral necessities enhance or restrict in predictable ways the influence of individuals, groups, parties, congressional leaders, and presidents. And all of these things affect the performance of Congress as a policy-making institution. These arguments are developed in the seventh chapter.

The final chapter assesses Congress as a representative institution. It argues that the evolution of electoral politics during the postwar era produced a system that encouraged individual responsiveness but collective irresponsibility, weakening government's capacity to deal effectively with pressing national problems. Members of Congress avoided collective punishment for government's failures until divided partisan control of the government ended with the 1992 elections. The Democrats' victory exposed them to the full force of popular wrath in 1994, costing them majority control of both houses. The chapter examines how the Republican takeover of Congress resurrected divided government, although in an unfamiliar form, put radical reforms of Congress on the agenda, and exacerbated the growing partisan polarization in both Congress and the electorate. The Republicans' attempt to impeach and remove Clinton, and the public's reaction to it, were, I argue, products of this new configuration of political forces. The chapter concludes by considering how these forces may be combined to shape electoral politics in the year 2000 and beyond.

CHAPTER TWO

The Context

The ascendant importance of individual candidates and campaigns that characterized the electoral politics of Congress from the 1960s through the 1980s has been challenged in the 1990s by the growing influence of national and partisan forces. Nonetheless, congressional campaigns continue to be largely candidate-centered affairs. Even when national issues have an unusually powerful effect on the results, as in 1994, their effects vary widely according to how they are exploited locally. Although national parties have recently expanded their efforts to recruit and finance candidates, most serious congressional aspirants operate, out of choice or necessity, as individual political entrepreneurs. The risks, pains, and rewards of mounting a campaign are largely theirs. Most instigate their own candidacies, raise most of their own resources, and put together their own campaign organizations. Their skills, resources, and strategies have a decisive effect on election outcomes. Voters, for their part, though showing signs of growing partisan loyalty, continue to be influenced strongly by their assessments of the particular candidates running in the state or district.

The focus on individual candidacies has important implications for every aspect of the political process to which congressional elections are relevant. Many are spelled out in subsequent chapters. This chapter traces some of the roots of candidate-centered electoral politics. It examines the constitutional, legal, and political contexts in which congressional elections take place, for they are fundamental sources of the present system, and it cannot be understood apart from them.

THE CONSTITUTIONAL FRAMEWORK

Whether or not to have an elected legislature was never a question during the Constitutional Convention that met in Philadelphia in 1787. The influence of British parliamentary tradition and colonial experience—all thirteen colonies had legislatures with at least one popularly elected house—was decisive. Beyond question, the new government would have one. But not much else about it was certain. Delegates disagreed about how the legislative branch would be organized, what its powers would be, and how its members would be selected.

The matter of selection involved several important issues. The most crucial was the basis of representation: How were seats in the legislature to be apportioned? Delegates from large states naturally preferred representation according to population; otherwise, their constituents would be underrepresented. Those from smaller states were convinced that their interests would be in jeopardy if only numbers counted, so they proposed equal representation for each state. The controversy coincided with another unsettled and unsettling issue: Was it to be a national government representing a national citizenry, or was it to be a federal government representing sovereign states?[1]

The conflict was resolved by a quintessential political deal. General sentiment was strongly in favor of a bicameral legislature,[2] and this made a solution easier. Each side got what it wanted. Seats in one chamber, the House of Representatives, would be apportioned by population; each state's representation would be determined by its share of the population as measured in a decennial census (Article I, Section 2). In the other chamber, the Senate, states would enjoy equal representation, each choosing two senators (Article I, Section 3).

This "great compromise," as it has been called, opened the way to resolving another dispute. At issue was the extent of popular participation in electing officials in the new government. Most delegates were skeptical of democracy as they conceived it, but to varying degrees. A bicameral legislature allowed different levels of popular involvement in choosing members of Congress. Representatives were to be "popularly"[3] chosen in frequent elections. Biennial elections were the compromise choice between the annual elections proposed by many delegates and the three-year term advocated by James Madison.[4] Broad suffrage and short terms were meant to ensure that one branch of government, the House, remained as close as possible to the people.

The Senate, in contrast, was designed to be much more insulated from momentary shifts in the public mood. The term of office was set at six years (another compromise; terms of three, four, five, six, seven, and nine years had been proposed.)[5] Continuity was enhanced by having one-third of the Senate's membership elected every two years. Senators, furthermore, were to be chosen by state legislatures rather than by voters. The Senate could thus act as a stable and dispassionate counterweight to the more popular and radical House, protecting the new government from the volatility thought to be characteristic of democracies. Its structure could also embody the elements of state sovereignty that remained.[6]

The opposition to popular democracy embodied in the indirect election of senators (and the president) diminished during the nineteenth century. Restrictions on suffrage were gradually lifted, and more and more offices came to be filled by popular election. The Civil War effectively settled the issue of national sovereignty. By the beginning of this century the constitutional method of choosing senators had come to be viewed by most Americans as undemocratic and corrupting, and it was replaced, via the Seventeenth Amendment, ratified in 1913, by popular election. Members of both houses of Congress are now chosen in elections in which nearly every citizen past his or her eighteenth birthday is eligible to vote.[7]

Congressional Districts

The Constitution itself apportioned seats among states for the first Congress (Article I, Section 3). Following the initial census in 1790, membership of the House was set at 105, with each state given one seat for each 33,000 inhabitants. Until 1911, the House grew as population increased and new states were added. Congress sought to limit the politically painful reductions in representation faced by states suffering unfavorable population shifts by adding seats after each decennial census. Eventually a point was reached where further growth could seriously impair the House's efficiency. Membership was set at 435 after the 1910 census, and strong opposition developed to any further increase.

A crisis thus arrived with the 1920 census results. Large population shifts between 1910 and 1920 and a fixed House membership would mean that many states—and members of Congress—would lose seats. Adding to the turmoil was the discovery by the census that, for the first time, a majority of Americans lived in urban rather than rural areas. Reapportionment was certain to increase the political weight of city dwellers and reduce that of farmers. The result was an acrimonious stalemate that was not resolved until 1929, when a law was passed establishing a permanent system for reapportioning the 435 House seats after each census; it would be carried out, if necessary, without additional legislation.[8]

The new system took effect after the 1930 census. Because twenty years had passed since the last apportionment, unusually large shifts occurred. California's delegation went from eleven to twenty; other big gainers were Michigan (+4), Texas (+3), and New York, Ohio, and New Jersey (+2 each). Twenty-one states lost seats; Missouri lost three and four other states lost two.[9] Subsequent shifts have not been so dramatic, but the beginning of each decade still ushers in a period of heightened uncertainty and anxiety among congressional incumbents.

Anxiety is not misplaced. In 1992, redistricting gave thirty-five incumbents the choice of retiring or facing another incumbent in the primary or general election. Some retired; nine ended up losing contests to other incumbents. As in past decades, the new distribution of House seats reflected population shifts since the previous census, redistributing power among states and regions. States in the East and Midwest lost a total of seventeen seats to states in the South and West, which together had controlled a bare majority—218 of 435 seats—in the House during the 1980s. After the 1990 census, this majority increased by another seventeen seats, with California (+7), Florida (+4), and Texas (+3) the big winners, and New York (−3), Illinois, Michigan, Ohio, and Pennsylvania (all −2) the big losers.[10]

At first federal law fixed only the number of representatives each state could elect; other important aspects of districting were left to the states. Until 1842, single-member districts were not required by law, and a number of states used multi-member or at-large districts. Thereafter, apportionment legislation usually required that states establish contiguous single-member districts and, in some years, required that they be of roughly equal populations and even "compact" in shape. Such requirements were never, when ignored by map makers, successfully enforced. Single-member districts became the overwhelming norm, but districts composed of "contiguous and compact territory . . . containing as nearly as practicable an equal number of inhabitants," in the words of the 1901 reapportionment act, did not.[11]

Many states continued to draw districts with widely differing populations. In 1930, for example, New York's largest district (766,425) contained nearly nine times as many people as its smallest (90,671). As recently as 1962, the most populous district in Michigan (802,994) had 4.5 times the inhabitants of its least populous (177,431).[12] Rural populations were usually overrepresented at the expense of people living in cities and suburbs. The Supreme Court's 1964 ruling in *Wesberry* v. *Sanders* (376 U.S. 1), however, applied the principle of one person-one vote to congressional districts, and since then, malapportioned districts have, under the watchful eye of the courts, become extinct.

The Court's rulings have indeed given more equal weight to each citizen's House vote, but they have also reinforced some less desirable aspects of the congressional election system. Drawing district lines with an eye to numbers rather than to natural political communities increases the number of districts composed of people with nothing in common save residence in the district. District boundaries are even less likely than before to coincide with the local political divisions—cities, counties, state legislative districts—around which parties are organized. So a greater number of congressional aspirants become political orphans, left to their own organizational devices. More will be said later about the irrelevance of local parties to most congressional candidates; the structure of House districts is clearly one of its sources.

Partisan Gerrymandering

The requirement of equal district populations has also encouraged another old political custom: gerrymandering. District boundaries are not politically neutral. Parties controlling state governments are naturally tempted to draw district lines designed to maximize the number of seats the party can win, given the number and distribution of its usual voters. The idea is to concentrate the opposing party's voters in a small number of districts which that party can win by large margins, thus "wasting" many of its votes, and to create as many districts as possible where their own party has a secure, though not overwhelming, majority.[13] Forced by the Court's strict standard of equality to ignore community boundaries in drawing districts, legislators are freer to pursue naked partisan advantage. The use of computers allows precise integration of partisan with egalitarian objectives.[14]

Partisan gerrymanders are easier to calculate than to carry out, however. Arrangements that might add to a party's share of seats often conflict with other political necessities, particularly the protection of incumbents unwilling to increase their own electoral risks to improve their party's collective welfare.[15] Voters more attuned to candidates than to parties often frustrate partisan schemes.[16] But state legislatures still try, when the opportunity arises, to draw lines favoring their party's House candidates. The redistricting activity that followed the 1980 census offers some examples of what can happen.

Indiana Republicans, in full control of the state government, executed the most flagrant Republican gerrymander. Their intentions were undisguised: "They [the Democrats] are going to have to face the political reality that we are going to do everything we can to hurt them," said the chairman of the state senate's Elections Committee, Charles E. Bosma.[17] It was no idle threat. Bosma's committee produced one new district that contained the homes of three Democratic incumbents. Two Democrats had their districts chopped up and redistributed to four new districts. All five of the Democrats planning to seek reelection had to move their place of residence to have any chance at all;

the remaining Democrat gave up and decided to run for statewide office. The Democrat's 6-5 majority was expected to become a 4-6 or 3-7 minority after the 1982 election (Indiana lost a seat through reapportionment).[18]

It did not work out quite that way. All of the Democratic incumbents who sought reelection won; the only losing incumbent from Indiana was a Republican. The split after 1982 was 5-5, and Democrats picked up three more seats during the decade, taking an 8-2 majority into the 1994 election, when Republicans finally won control (6-4) of Indiana's delegation. Moreover, Indiana's example inspired Democrats to retaliate, notably in California, where many more seats (forty-five in the 1980s) were at stake. The California gerrymander, designed by U.S. Representative Philip Burton, helped Democrats to exploit the strongly pro-Democratic tide running in 1982 to raise their majority in the California House delegation from 22-21 to 28-17. The Burton plan was overturned by referendum and so was only in effect for 1982, but its replacement was no less friendly to Democrats, who retained a 27-18 majority through the next three elections.

Republicans blamed the Democrats' more skillful gerrymandering for their failure to realize the sizable gain they had expected from the shift of House seats to states in the South and West after 1980.[19] In fact, it cost them at most three or four seats.[20] Ironically, the Republican National Committee, mindful of basic arithmetic, supported a suit brought by Indiana Democrats challenging the constitutionality of the partisan gerrymander. California's congressional Democrats, facing a similar lawsuit filed by California Republicans, sided with the Indiana Republicans.[21] In 1986, the Supreme Court declared that partisan gerrymandering could be unconstitutional if it were sufficiently egregious, but that the Indiana gerrymander was not flagrant enough to be set aside. Neither, the Court decided in a 1989 case, was the California gerrymander.

The Court has yet to reveal just what would make a partisan gerrymander unfair enough to be unconstitutional. Despite the absence of clear standards, however, the prospect of constitutional challenges probably restrained partisan gerrymandering after the 1990 census; whatever the reason, there is little evidence of systematic partisan bias in the district lines drawn for the 1990s.[22] However, a different kind of gerrymandering became far more common—and controversial.

Racial Gerrymandering

In a 1986 decision (*Thornburg* v. *Gingles*), the Supreme Court had construed the Voting Rights Act to require that legislative district lines not discriminate, even unintentionally, against racial minorities. The decision was widely interpreted as requiring map makers to design districts in which racial ethnic minorities comprised a majority of voters wherever residence patterns made this feasible. Assiduous pursuit of this goal, backed by modern computer technology, produced some of strangest looking districts on record.

Gerrymandering often produces bizarrely shaped districts; the term itself comes from a cartoon depicting an odd, salamander-like creature suggested by a district drawn under the administration of Elbridge Gerry, an early governor of Massachusetts. Perhaps the most audacious modern example of partisan gerrymandering was the 6th District of California as drawn in 1982 by Philip Burton for his brother, John (who surprised everyone by retiring from Congress before he could enjoy it). The district was composed of three sections connected only by the waters of the San Francisco Bay; two parts of one section were linked only by a narrow strip of land underlying some railroad yards.

Racial gerrymandering after 1990 inspired some equally creative artwork; the 12th District of North Carolina, for example, stitched together African-American communities in several of the state's larger cities using Interstate 85 (northbound lanes in one county, southbound lanes in another) as the thread. Racial gerrymandering was far more effective than partisan gerrymandering typically is; the 1992 elections raised African-American representation in the House from twenty-five to thirty-eight, Hispanic representation, from ten to seventeen. In 1993, however, a more conservative Court ruled (in *Shaw* v. *Reno*) that bizarrely shaped districts designed to concentrate minority voters might violate the constitutional rights of white voters. The Court went further in 1995 (*Miller* v. *Johnson*), striking down Georgia's districting on the ground that any mapping in which race was the "predominant factor" violated the Constitution's guarantee of equal protection.[23] Subsequent court decisions forced the modification of racially gerrymandered districts in Florida, Georgia, Louisiana, New York, Texas, and Virginia, but through 1998, every minority incumbent running in a redrawn district won reelection. The only casualty was Cleo Fields, who did not seek reelection after his Louisiana district fell from 55 percent to 28 percent black.[24] The Court's stance works to the disadvantage of Republicans. Minority voters are primarily Democrats; packing them into minority-majority districts helped Republican candidates elsewhere; racial gerrymandering was responsible for as many as ten of the seats Republicans gained in the South in 1992 and 1994.[25]

House districts will be reapportioned and reconfigured once again after the 2000 census, and states in the South and West are projected to gain eight more seats at the expense of states in the Northeast and Midwest. The issue of racial gerrymandering is sure to arise once more. *Shaw* v. *Reno* did not overturn *Thornburg* v. *Gingles*, and the Court decreed in *Hunt* v. *Cromartie* (1999) that race could be considered in drawing districts if the primary motive was to achieve a partisan rather than racial gerrymander (recognizing that blacks are overwhelmingly Democratic in party loyalty).[26] The extent to which racial gerrymandering is now required, permitted, or forbidden remains unsettled, assuring another decade of judicial intervention in the districting process.

States as Electoral Units

For the Senate, "districts" are fixed by state boundaries, and the question of reapportionment never arises. It is easy to find examples of state boundaries that, like House district lines, cut across natural economic units—greater New York City, with suburbs in Connecticut and New Jersey, forms such a unit— and that are sharply divided into distinct and conflicting political regions (Tennessee, for example). But this matters less because states are, after all, important political units for purposes other than Senate elections. Indeed, this is an important basis for some of the differences between House and Senate elections that are spelled out in later chapters.

States compose an odd set of electoral units for another, quite obvious, reason: their great diversity in population. A senator from California represents more than sixty-eight times as many people as a senator from Wyoming. The nine largest states are home to 51 percent of the population but elect only 18 percent of the Senate; the smallest twenty-six states control 52 percent of the Senate but hold only 18 percent of the population.

The potential electoral bias introduced by unequal state populations has only recently begun to receive careful scholarly scrutiny. During the post–Civil War era, it favored Republicans.[27] Since the advent of popular election of Senators, the bias has generally favored whichever party is in the minority nationally: the Democrats between1914 and 1930; the Republicans during the New Deal realignment and from 1956 though 1992. By allowing the minority party to win a share of seats significantly larger than its share of votes, Senate "malapportionment" makes it harder for popular majorities to rule, just as the Framers intended.[28] Indeed, without it, Republicans would not have held the Senate in the early 1980s; they won majority control by taking a disproportionate share of the smaller states, winning twenty-two of thirty-four Senate contests in 1980 while winning less than a majority of Senate votes cast nationwide.[29] The Republican Senate majority that took over after 1994, in contrast, drew almost equally from large, medium, and small states.

ELECTION LAWS

The diversity that once characterized state election laws has gradually given way to substantially greater uniformity, but important differences remain. Congress was given the constitutional power to regulate all federal elections (Article I, Section 4), but was in no hurry to do so. Initially, states were allowed to go entirely their own way. For example, at one time many states elected members of Congress in odd-numbered years; the practice did not entirely end until 1880. The date of federal elections was not fixed as the first Tuesday after the first Monday in November until 1845 (and states could still hold elections on a different date if their constitutions so required). For a time some states required the winner of a congressional election to receive a majority of all votes cast; now all states permit election by plurality, at least in general elections. Restrictions on suffrage once varied from state to state; constitutional amendments, court decisions, and federal laws have now eliminated almost every restriction on suffrage for citizens who have passed their eighteenth birthday.

The trend toward more uniform election laws is not merely of historical interest. A single date for all federal elections encourages national campaigns, party tickets, and coattail effects. Each election is more than an isolated, idiosyncratic event, or at least it can be treated as such by voters. The removal of formal and informal barriers to voting has substantially altered the political complexion of some areas, notably in the Deep South, where formerly excluded black voters are now an important political force. Lowering the voting age to eighteen has made the student vote a key factor in districts encompassing large university towns, such as Ann Arbor, Michigan, and Madison, Wisconsin.

The process of voting itself has undergone important changes. Prior to the 1890s, each local party produced its own ballots, listing only its own candidates, which were handed to voters outside the polling place. The party ballots were readily distinguishable; voting was thus a public act. Because local parties printed the ballots, internal party rivalries were sometimes fought with multiple or competing party ballots, frustrating state party leaders' pursuit of electoral unity and control.[30] The system invited intimidation of voters and other forms of corruption, and it was expensive for the parties to administer. It was replaced in a remarkable burst of reform between 1888 and 1896, when about 90 percent of the states adopted what was called the Australian Ballot (after the country of its origin). An Australian Ballot is produced by the government, lists candidates from all parties, and is marked in the privacy of a voting booth.

Although the Australian Ballot has been blamed for weakening party loyalty by making it easier for voters to vote for different parties' candidates for different offices,[31] in some forms it increased partisan loyalty, at least initially. In states that adopted the *party column* ballot, which lists candidates by party, ticket splitting diminished. Beyond using the party column format, the ballot could foster straight-ticket voting by allowing voters to mark a single spot (or pull a single lever on a voting machine) to vote for all the party's candidates. On the other hand, where states adopted the *office bloc* ballot, which lists candidates by office, ticket splitting was facilitated. The search for partisan advantage led some states to switch back and forth between the two forms depending on which party or faction was in power.[32] Differences among ballot types, and their consequences, persist to this day.[33]

Again, variations in formal procedures are politically consequential. The effects of ballot formats that make ticket splitting easier run counter to those of uniform election dates. Easier ticket splitting weakens coattails and other partisan links between candidates. It helps to focus the election on candidates rather than parties.

POLITICAL PARTIES

Without question the most important additions to the institutional framework established by the Constitution have been political parties. The parties, along with the system of presidential elections which inspired their development, are the formal institutions that contribute most to making congressional elections other than purely local festivals and politicians other than purely independent political entrepreneurs. The long-term atrophy of party organizations and weakening of partisan ties from the 1950s through the 1970s thus contributed to the detachment of congressional elections from national political forces and to the rise of candidate-centered campaigns. For the same reason, the recent emergence of more vigorous national party organizations has contributed to a modest but significant reversal of these trends. I will have more to say about this in Chapter 4.

The decline of parties stemmed from a variety of causes; several of the more important ones are discussed later. A fundamental factor, however, is clearly institutional: the rise and spread of primary elections as the method for choosing party nominees for the general election. Nineteenth-century parties nominated candidates in caucuses and, later, conventions. These were often dominated by self-elected party elites; they came under increasing criticism when the United States entered into a period of sectional one-party dominance following the election of 1896. Parties faced with serious competition found it prudent to nominate attractive candidates; without this constraint—with the assurance of victory because of an overwhelming local majority—they could freely nominate incompetent hacks or worse. With the nomination tantamount to election in so many places, the general election, and therefore the voter, seemed increasingly irrelevant.

The direct primary election was introduced as a way to weaken party bosses by transferring the right to choose the party's nominees to the party's voters and to allow people to cast a meaningful vote despite meaningless general elections. It was also an effective method for settling disputes over who was the party's official candidate, which became necessary when states adopted the Australian Ballot. In the South, where one-party dominance was most pronounced, most states eventually established a second, runoff primary between the two candidates receiving the most votes when none wins a majority on the first ballot. Today, election laws in every state provide for primary elections for House and Senate nominations—though the rules governing them vary from state to state—and party leaders are able to control the nomination in very few places.

A few states still hold nominating conventions and require that candidates receive a minimum vote at the convention (20 percent is the usual threshold) to be eligible for the primary ballot. But even this may not give the party much control. In one convention state, Colorado, the eventual Republican nominee for the Senate in 1980, Mary Buchanan, did not win support of 20 percent of the delegates, but she got on the primary ballot anyway, by petition. She defeated three other Republicans, all of whom were preferred by party leaders, then lost the general election.[34]

Scattered modern instances of party control over congressional nominations can still be found. When the congressman who represented Illinois' 5th District (in Chicago) died in 1975, state representative John Fary "was called into Mayor Richard J. Daley's office. At 65, Fary had been a faithful servant of the machine; and he thought the Mayor was going to tell him it was time to retire. Instead, he was told he was going to Congress."[35] He did, declaring on the night of his special election victory, "I will go to Washington to help represent Mayor Daley. For twenty-one years I represented the Mayor in the legislature, and he was always right."[36] When, in 1982, Fary ignored the party's request that he retire, he was crushed in the primary. More recently, Representative Tom Manton filed for reelection, then convened a meeting of Queens, New York, Democratic committeemen to announce that he was retiring and got them to nominate his protégé, Joseph Crowley, as his replacement, before other potential candidates even knew the seat was open. Responding to their complaints, Crowley was unapologetic: "What you're hearing is not so much about the process, but sour grapes. What happened here is simply that I was offered an ice cream cone, and I took it."[37]

Fary's tale and Crowley's surprise treat are noteworthy because they are so atypical. The party organization's influence on congressional nominations varies but is typically feeble. Few congressional candidates find opposition from the local party leaders to be a significant handicap; neither is their support very helpful. The nomination is not something to be awarded by the party but rather a prize to be fought over (when it seems worth taking) by freebooting political entrepreneurs.

Primary elections have largely deprived parties of their most important source of influence over elected officials. Parties no longer control access to the ballot and, therefore, to political office. They cannot determine who runs under the party's label and so cannot control what the label represents. National parties have never had much influence in the nominating process, and this has long been an important barrier to strong party discipline in Congress. American parties lack a crucial sanction available to their European counterparts: the ability to deny renomination to uncooperative members. Now state and local parties typically have few sanctions and little influence. The primary election system also complicates the pursuit of a congressional career. Candidates must be prepared to face two distinct, if overlapping, electorates.

Differences in primary election laws underlie much of the diversity among congressional election processes across states. The date of the general election may be fixed, but primaries are held at any time from March through September. The runoff primary used in ten southern states has already been mentioned; where two-party competition has finally developed, candidates must sometimes win three serious contests to gain office. Some states, notably California and Washington, hold *blanket* primaries, allowing any voter to vote in any party's primary; registered Democrats, for example, may vote in Republican primaries, and registered Republicans may vote in Democratic primaries. Louisiana has a unique system in which candidates of both parties compete in the same primary; if no candidate receives an absolute majority of votes, the top two vote-getters compete in the general election—even if they are from the same party.

Rules governing access to the ballot also differ: some states require only a small fee and virtually anyone can run; others require a larger fee or some minimum number of signatures on a petition. Challenges to incumbents as well as third-party or independent candidacies are thus encouraged or discouraged to differing degrees.[38]

This discussion of the legal and institutional framework of congressional elections has necessarily been brief; filling in all the details would demand volumes. But it is sufficient to alert us to some of the important ways in which reference to the formal context is required to account for the activities of candidates, voters, and other participants in congressional elections.

It is important to remember that the formal context does not arrive mysteriously from somewhere outside the political system. Rules and institutions are consciously created and shaped by politically active people to help them achieve their goals. Rules that encourage members of Congress to pursue their aims independently of their party evolve because voters and politicians value independence. Although in the short view it seems that the formal framework establishes a set of independent parameters to which political actors are forced to adapt, it does not. Rather, the framework itself reflects the values and preferences prevalent among politically active citizens, and it changes as these values and preferences change.

SOCIAL AND POLITICAL CONTEXTS

Rules and customs controlling districting and primary elections may contribute to the large idiosyncratic component of congressional elections, but the contribution is hardly decisive. Idiosyncrasy is deeply rooted in the cultural, economic, and geographical heterogeneity of the United States. A few short examples will suggest the astonishing variety of electoral conditions that would-be candidates must be prepared to face. States and districts vary in:[39]

Geographical size.   Simple geography is an abundant source of variation. House districts are as small as 10 square miles (New York's 11th District) or as large as Alaska's 586,000 square miles, where campaigning by airplane is essential and occasionally fatal.[40] Even Michigan has a district that is more than 450 miles from end to end (the 1st). The range among states is smaller but still enormous. The purely physical problems of campaigning in or representing constituencies differ greatly and can be quite severe.

Population.   Obviously, states vary widely in population, and both districts and states also vary in population density. Imagine the problems faced by California's senators, who are expected to represent nearly 33 million people living more than 2,500 miles from Washington, DC. It is probably no coincidence that in the last fifty years only two of California's senators have won more than two terms. Alaska's senators serve only 587,000 people, but they are even further from the capitol and are scattered over a far larger area. Rhode Island, in contrast, is a "tiny little city state,"[41] compact, with a relatively small population.

Economic base.   Most of the workers in the 9th District of Michigan get their paycheck from auto manufacturers, mainly General Motors; nearly a third of the payroll in South Carolina's 1st District comes directly or indirectly from the Defense Department; 60,000 federal employees live in Maryland's 8th District.[42] Delaware is the home of DuPont, with far greater revenues than the state government. At the other extreme are states and districts with thoroughly heterogeneous local economies.

Income.   According to the 1990 census, the second poorest district in the nation is Kentucky's 5th; its median family income at that time was $17,798. The wealthiest is Maryland's 8th, with a median income of $64,199. The Kentucky district is represented in the House by a Republican; the Maryland district gave Bill Clinton 57 percent of its votes in 1996.

Communications.   Districts such as Kentucky's 6th (Lexington) and Nevada's 1st (Las Vegas) coincide with media markets and are covered efficiently by newspapers and television and radio stations. Compare them with any of the thirty-five or so districts that fall into the New York City media market or to a state such as Wyoming, with multiple media markets. Or consider New Jersey, a state of more than 7.9 million people, all of whom live in media markets centered outside the state (in New York and Philadelphia). Campaigning—and representing—are largely communication. It is easy to see how media market structure determines which tactical options are available to candidates and how easily they can attract public attention.[43] But more subtle influences operate as well. In some districts, for example, a member of Congress is a newsworthy politician; in others, he or she is lost in the crowd.

Ethnicity.   Some districts are overwhelmingly of one racial or ethnic group; 74 percent of the residents of New York's 11th District are African-American; 84 percent in the 33rd District of California are Hispanic. As of 2000, twenty-three districts had African-American majorities and sixteen districts had Hispanic majorities. Other districts are an ethnic patchwork. California's 8th was, in 1990, 13 percent African-American, 16 percent Hispanic, 28 percent Asian; 5 to 10 percent each of the rest reported Italian, Irish, English, and German ancestry.[44] States, too, have very different ethnic mixes: The political importance of Jews in New York, Irish in Massachusetts, and Hispanics in New Mexico are familiar examples.

Age.   The median age in Florida's 13th District (Sarasota) was 47 in 1990; 37 percent of the eligible voters were over 65. Compare this with a district such as Utah's 3rd, where the median age is 24, or with Wisconsin's 2nd, which includes 43,000 university students. Imagine how the dominant political concerns differ among the three.

Political habits.   Some districts have historic traditions of strong loyalty to the candidates of one party or the other; others are characterized by intense two-party competition. Still others seem perversely contrarian; the 12th District of Ohio turned out a Republican incumbent amid the Republican sweep in 1980 and a Democratic incumbent amid the Democratic sweep in 1982. Voter turnout in recent House elections in which both major parties fielded candidates has ranged from under 20 percent to above 80 percent; for Senate elections the range is narrower—from 33 percent to 70 percent—but still striking.

These categories and examples do not begin to exhaust the possibilities, but they are sufficient to make the point: Politically relevant conditions vary enormously across states and districts and are a potent source of localism and idiosyncrasy in the electoral politics of Congress. The problem for each congressional aspirant is to devise a strategy to win and maintain the support of voters in a particular state or district, and it is not surprising that no common formula has been discovered. Nor is it surprising that candidates try to nurture an image of independence. But recognition of the heterogeneity among states and districts cannot explain why political fragmentation and independence increased during the 1960s and 1970s, nor why it has diminished since then.

ENDNOTES

1. See James Madison, Alexander Hamilton, and John Jay, *The Federalist*, ed. Edward Meade Earle (New York: Modern Library, 1937), Nos. 37 and 39.
2. Ten of the thirteen colonies and, of course, Britain, had bicameral legislatures.
3. The Constitution specifies that "Electors in each State shall have the Qualifications requisite for the Electors of the most numerous Branch of the State Legislature" (Article 1, Section 2). Property and other qualifications were, in fact, common in the early years of the nation; universal suffrage was a long time in arriving.
4. *Electing Congress* (Washington, DC: Congressional Quarterly, 1978), p. 135.
5. Ibid.
6. Madison, Hamilton, and Jay, *The Federalist*, No. 62.
7. The exceptions are people in penal and other institutions and, in many states, former felons. Senate seats vacated by retirement, death, or resignation before the end of the term may be filled by gubernatorial appointment until the next regular general election; vacated House seats are filled by special elections.
8. *Congressional Quarterly's Guide to U.S. Elections* (Washington, DC: Congressional Quarterly, 1976), pp. 530-534.
9. Ibid.
10. "Final Count Will Shift Seats to Far West and South," *Congressional Quarterly Weekly Report* 48 (September 1, 1990):2794.
11. *Guide to U.S. Elections*, p. 528.
12. Ibid.
13. Bruce E. Cain, *The Reapportionment Puzzle* (Berkeley: University of California Press, 1984), pp. 148-150.
14. Rob Gurwitt, "Judgment on Gerrymanders Expected from Indiana Case," *Congressional Quarterly Weekly Report* 39 (September 28, 1985):1939.
15. Cain, *Reapportionment*, pp. 151-157.
16. Richard Born, "Partisan Intentions and Election Day Realities in the Congressional Redistricting Process," *American Political Science Review* 79 (1985):317.
17. "Redistricting: Gov. Gerry's Monuments," *Congressional Quarterly Weekly Report* 39 (May 9, 1981):811.
18. "Classic Gerrymander by Indiana Republicans," *Congressional Quarterly Weekly Report* 39 (October 17, 1981):2017-2022.
19. Alan I. Abramowitz, "Partisan Redistricting and the 1982 Congressional Elections," *Journal of Politics* 45 (1983):767-770.
20. Andrew W. Robertson, "American Redistricting in the 1980s: The Effect on Midterm Elections," *Electoral Studies* 2 (1983):113-129.
21. Gurwitt, "Gerrymanders," p. 1940.
22. Richard G. Niemi and Alan I. Abramowitz, "Partisan Redistricting and the 1992 Congressional Elections," *Journal of Politics* 56 (1994):811-817; John W. Swain, Stephen A. Borrelli, and Brian C. Reed, "Partisan Consequences of the Post-1990 Redistricting for the U.S. House of Representatives," *Political Research Quarterly* 51 (1998):945-967.

23. Holly Idelson, "Court Takes a Harder Line on Minority Voting Blocs," *Congressional Quarterly Weekly Report* 53 (July 1, 1995):1944-1946.
24. Michael Barone and Grant Ujifusa, *The Almanac of American Politics 2000* (Washington, DC: National Journal, 1999), p. 697.
25. Kevin A. Hill, "Does the Creation of Majority Black Districts Aid Republicans? An Analysis of the 1992 Congresional Elections in Eight Southern States," *Journal of Politics* 57 (1995):384-401. Professor Hill kindly provided the 1994 update (personal communication). John W. Petrocik and Scott W. Desposato argue that the damage to Democrats from racial gerrymandering was largely indirect (forcing incumbent Democrats to run in new districts with many new constituents) and contingent on the strong pro-Republican tide among white southerners in 1992 and 1994; see their "The Partisan Consequences of Majority-Minority Redistricting in the South, 1992 and 1994," *Journal of Politics* 60 (1998):613-633.
26. Caroline E. Brown, "High Court Upholds Minority Districts," *Congressional Quarterly Weekly Report* 57 (May 22, 1999):1202.
27. An exception may be the years 1876-1892, when Republicans were able to win the Senate more consistently than the House or the White House by winning a disproportionate share of newly admitted, less populous states in the West. See Charles H. Stewart III, "Lessons from the Post-Civil War Era," in *The Politics of Divided Government*, eds. Gary Cox and Samuel Kernell (Boulder, Colorado: Westview Press, 1991).
28. Frances E. Lee and Bruce I. Oppenheimer, "Senate Apportionment: Competitiveness and Partisan Advantage," *Legislative Studies Quarterly* 22 (1997):3-24.
29. John T. Pothier, "The Partisan Bias in Senate Elections," *American Politics Quarterly* 12 (1984):89-100.
30. Lisa A. Reynolds, "Reassessing the Impact of Progressive Era Ballot Reform," (Ph.D. diss., University of California, San Diego, 1995), pp. 23-27.
31. Jerrold G. Rusk, "The Effects of the Australian Ballot Reform on Split Ticket Voting: 1876-1908," in *Controversies in Voting Behavior*, eds. Richard G. Niemi and Herbert F. Weisberg (San Francisco: W.H. Freeman, 1976), pp. 485-486.
32. Reynolds, "Progressive Era Ballot Reform," pp. 77-106.
33. Rusk, "Australian Ballot Reform," pp. 493-509; Angus Campbell, Philip E. Converse, Warren E. Miller, and Donald E. Stokes, *The American Voter* (New York; John Wiley, 1960), p. 276.
34. "The Outlook: Senate, House, and Governors," *Congressional Quarterly Weekly Report* 38 (October 11, 1980):2999.
35. Michael Barone, Grant Ujifusa, and Douglas Matthews, *The Almanac of American Politics 1980* (New York: E.P. Dutton, 1979), p. 246.
36. Alan Ehrenhalt, ed., *Politics in America: Members of Congress in Washington and at Home* (Washington, DC: Congressional Quarterly Press, 1981),p. 333.
37. Barone and Ujifusa, *Alamanac of American Politics 2000*, p. 1117.
38. Stephen Ansolabehere and Alan Gerber, "The Effects of Filing Fees and Petition Requirements on U.S. House Elections, *Legislative Studies Quarterly* 21 (1996):249-264.

39. All of the examples discussed are, unless otherwise noted, taken from Barone and Ujifusa, *Almanac of American Politics 2000*.

40. House Majority Leader Hale Boggs and Alaska Congressman Nick Begich were killed in a plane crash while campaigning in that state in 1972.

41. Barone and Ujifusa, *Almanac of American Politics 2000*, p. 1410.

42. *Congressional Districts in the 1990s* (Washington, DC: Congressional Quarterly, 1993), pp. 349, 669.

43. Richard G. Niemi, Lynda W. Powell, and Patricia L. Bicknell, "The Effects of Congruity between Community and District on the Salience of U.S. House Candidates," *Legislative Studies Quarterly* 11 (1986):190–198.

44. *Congressional Districts in the 1990s*, p. 71.

CHAPTER THREE

Congressional Candidates

Each state or congressional district is a unique electoral arena. Diversity among constituencies underlies the astonishing variety of political forces operating in congressional politics. When attention is shifted to particular states or districts, however, as it is when we examine congressional candidates and campaigns—the subjects of this and the next chapter—the local context becomes a constant rather than a variable factor. Its elements are fixed, at least for the short run. Electoral variation originates elsewhere, in changing political conditions and issues, and in the skills, resources, and strategies of candidates and other participants in electoral politics.

THE INCUMBENCY FACTOR

From the 1950s through the 1980s, the electoral importance of individual candidates and campaigns expanded, while that of party labels and national issues diminished. The emergence of a more candidate-centered electoral process helped one class of congressional candidates to prosper: the incumbent officeholders. Indeed, the electoral advantage enjoyed by incumbents, at least as measured by electoral margins, increased so notably after the mid-1960s that it became the main focus of congressional electoral research for the next quarter century. This research leaves little doubt that incumbency confers major electoral benefits, but it also reveals that these benefits are neither automatic, nor certain, nor constant across electoral contexts. Even during the 1970s and 1980s, when House incumbents were riding their highest, impressive reelection rates and expanded electoral margins seemed ever more dearly bought. The pursuit of reelection absorbed a great deal of time, energy, and money, reflecting members' enduring sense of electoral uncertainty and risk. The electoral upheavals of the early '90s showed that their worry was not misplaced; the advantages of incumbency are far more contingent than the surface evidence might have suggested.

Nonetheless, incumbency stands out as a conspicuous factor in congressional elections from almost any perspective. Most obviously, incumbency is a dominant consideration because incumbents are so consistently successful at winning elections, and everyone involved in politics knows it. At a deeper level, nearly everything pertaining to candidates and campaigns for Congress is profoundly influenced by whether the candidate is an incumbent, challenging an incumbent, or pursuing an open seat. And understanding why—and how—modern incumbents have usually done so well is central to comprehending the strengths and weaknesses of the House as an institution.

The basic picture seems clear enough. The data in Table 3-1 show just how thoroughly incumbents have dominated postwar House elections. Typically, more than 90 percent of the races include incumbents, and more than 90 percent of them win. On the average, fewer than 2 percent of officeholders are defeated in primary elections, and fewer than 7 percent lose general elections. Even in years very unfavorable to one of the parties, a large majority of its House incumbents return. In 1994, the Democrats' worst year since 1946, 84 percent of the House Democrats who sought reelection won. In 1974, a notoriously bad year for Republicans, 77 percent of the Republican incumbents who ran were returned to office.

The story is rather different for Senate incumbents. Though the odds still favor them, senators have not been as consistently successful at winning reelection as have representatives. On average, 78 percent have won reelection during the postwar period; 5 percent lost primaries, 17 percent lost general elections. Moreover, their electoral fortunes fluctuate much more widely from year to year. In 1980, for example, only 55 percent of the incumbent Senate candidates won reelection. In 1986, more incumbent senators than representatives were defeated, even though fourteen times as many of the latter were running. Yet in 1982, 1990, and 1994, Senate incumbents were more difficult to defeat than House incumbents. This is only the first of many instances of greater variability to be observed among Senate elections.

Figure 3-1 displays graphically the fluctuations in the success rates of House and Senate incumbents in elections from 1946 through 1998. The sharp swings in the fortunes of Senate incumbents are clearly visible. House incumbents were much more vulnerable in 1946 and 1948 than in later elections; after 1948, the data show no statistically significant trend, although the high rates of success sustained in elections from 1984 through 1990 and again in 1998 do stand out visually.[1] From 1950 through 1998, then, the reelection prospects of House incumbents showed considerable year-to-year variation but did not increase significantly. This is curious, because by other measures, incumbent electoral performance improved dramatically over these years.

TABLE 3–1   REELECTION RATES OF HOUSE AND SENATE INCUMBENTS, 1946–1998

YEAR	SEEKING REELECTION	DEFEATED IN PRIMARIES	DEFEATED IN GENERAL ELECTION	PERCENTAGE REELECTED
House				
1946	398	18	52	82
1948	400	15	68	79
1950	400	6	32	91
1952	389	9	26	91
1954	407	6	22	93
1956	411	6	16	95
1958	396	3	37	90
1960	405	5	25	93
1962	402	12	22	92

YEAR	SEEKING REELECTION	DEFEATED IN PRIMARIES	DEFEATED IN GENERAL ELECTION	PERCENTAGE REELECTED
House				
1964	397	8	45	87
1966	411	8	41	88
1968	409	4	9	97
1970	401	10	12	95
1972	390	12	13	94
1974	391	8	40	88
1976	384	3	13	96
1978	382	5	19	94
1980	398	6	31	91
1982	393	10	29	90
1984	409	3	16	95
1986	393	2	6	98
1988	408	1	6	98
1990	406	1	15	96
1992	368	19	24	88
1994	387	4	34	90
1996	384	2	21	94
1998	401	1	6	98
Senate				
1946	30	6	7	57
1948	25	2	8	60
1950	32	5	5	69
1952	31	2	9	65
1954	32	2	6	75
1956	29	0	4	86
1958	28	0	10	64
1960	29	0	1	97
1962	35	1	5	83
1964	33	1	4	85
1966	32	3	1	88
1968	28	4	4	71
1970	31	1	6	77
1972	27	2	5	74
1974	27	2	2	85
1976	25	0	9	64
1978	25	3	7	60
1980	29	4	9	55
1982	30	0	2	93
1984	29	0	3	90
1986	28	0	7	75
1988	27	0	4	85
1990	32	0	1	97
1992	28	1	4	82
1994	26	0	2	92
1996	21	1	1	90
1998	29	0	3	90

Sources: Norman J. Ornstein, Thomas E. Mann, and Michael J. Malbin, *Vital Statistics on Congress 1997–1998* (Washington, DC: Congressional Quarterly, 1998), Tables 2–7 and 2–8; data for 1998 compiled by author.

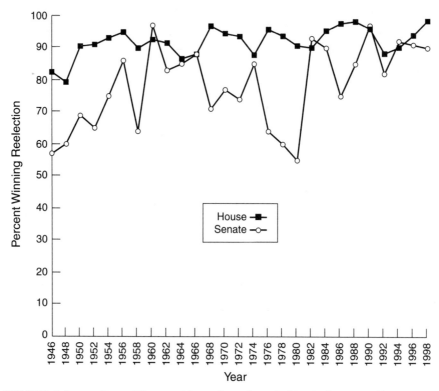

FIGURE 3–1. Success Rates of House and Senate Incumbents Seeking Reelection, 1946-1998
Source: Data in Table 3-1.

Measuring the Value of Incumbency

The most straightforward measure—the mean percentage of the two-party vote won by incumbent House candidates in contested elections from 1946 through 1998—is displayed in Figure 3-2. The average incumbent's vote share rose dramatically from the late '40s to the late '80s, from about 60 percent to about 68 percent. After its peak in 1986 and 1988, it dropped back below 65 percent for the next four elections before rising again to 66 percent in 1998. Even with the dip in the 1990s, it remains significantly above its pre-1968 average.

The incumbent's vote share is an ambiguous measure of the incumbency advantage, however. Some proportion of it reflects the partisan makeup of the district and would go to any candidate with the same party label; conceivably, all an incumbent's votes could fall into this category.[2] The incumbency advantage must therefore be gauged by how much better candidates do running as incumbents than they would do running as nonincumbents. Scholars have taken several approaches to estimating this difference, but all of them support

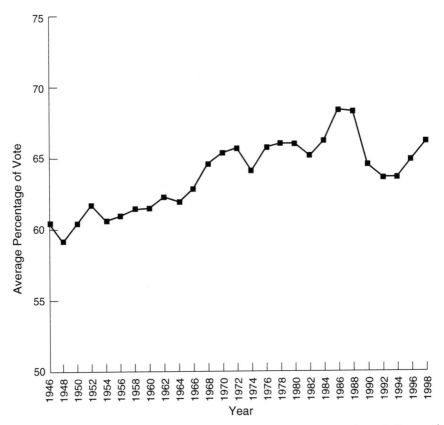

FIGURE 3–2. Average Percent of the Major Party Vote Won by House Incumbents in Contested Elections, 1946–1998
Source: Compiled by author.

the same conclusion: the electoral value of incumbency, measured in votes, increased sharply during the 1960s.

The simplest approach is to look at what happens to the district vote in adjacent elections with and without the incumbent. Thus scholars initially estimated the incumbency advantage by calculating the *sophomore surge* (the average gain in vote share won by candidates running as incumbents for the first time compared to their vote share in the initial election) and *retirement slump* (the average drop in the party's vote from the previous election when the incumbent departs and the seat is thrown open).[3] Averaged together into a single index, they form the *slurge*.[4] More elaborate approaches have sought to refine estimates by eliminating selection bias and other sources of error in the components of the slurge.[5] Although consensus has yet to emerge on which technique is most appropriate, the choice makes little practical difference. All of the indices tell the same basic story.

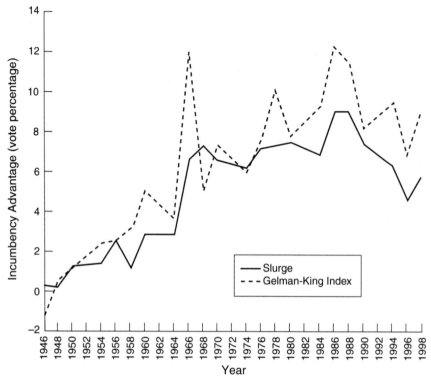

FIGURE 3–3. Incumbency Advantage in House Elections, 1946-1998
Source: Compiled by author.

Figure 3-3 displays the postwar trends in two popular measures, the slurge and Gelman and King's index.[6] Both show the growing value, in votes, of holding a House seat; both show a particularly sharp increase in the mid-1960s, and both show that the incumbency advantage, so measured, has persisted at the higher level into the 1990s. According to the slurge, the value, in votes, of incumbency jumped from an average of 2.1 percent in the 1946-1966 period to 7.0 percent for 1968-1998; according to Gelman and King's index, it jumped from 3.3 percent to 8.5 percent. Both indices show a modest decline in the value of incumbency in the 1990s compared to the 1980s; in 1996 and 1998, the slurge registers its lowest values since 1964.

The value, in votes, of Senate incumbency also increased during the 1960s. Trends in Senate elections are more difficult to detect, because the number of contests is much smaller (thirty-three or thirty-four in most election years) and only a third of the Senate's seats are automatically up in any election year. Still, careful analysis suggests that Senate incumbency, worth a little more than 2 percent of the vote in elections from 1914 (when Senators first became subject to popular election) to 1960, rose to 7 percent for the 1962-1992 period.[7] Why this change did not make Senate elections involving incumbents any less competitive is a question I shall address later.

The Vanishing Marginals

David Mayhew identified and named one effect of the augmented House incumbency advantage: the "vanishing marginals."[8] Increased vote shares meant that fewer incumbents held "marginal" seats—those taken with narrow margins of victory and so thought to be at heightened risk for future losses. Conventionally, seats won with less than some specified share of the two-party vote are designated marginal; 60 percent is the most common break point. Figure 3-4 shows how the proportion of incumbents whose vote lifted them out of the marginal range (60 percent or less) varied over the postwar period. Until 1966, an average of 61 percent of House incumbents won in excess of 60 percent of the vote; the proportion jumped to 73 percent for the 1968-1982 period (the jump that caught Mayhew's eye) and higher still, to 83 percent, for 1984-1988. For the 1990-1998 period, however, it dropped back down to 71

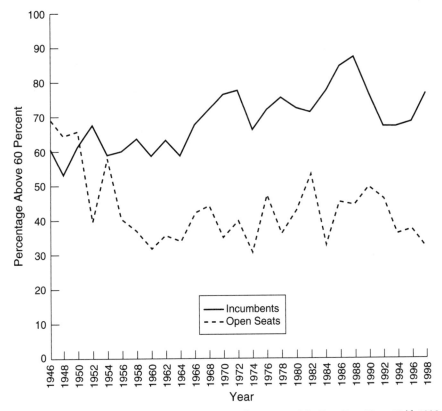

FIGURE 3–4. House Candidates Receiving More Than 60 Percent of the Two-Party Vote, 1946-1998
Source: Compiled by author.

percent. As Mayhew also pointed out (and Figure 3-4 shows), most contests for open seats have remained in the marginal range, so the vanishing marginals were *not* simply the effect of a more general decline in closely contested elections. Incumbency itself had something to do with it.

Scholars who first noticed the rise in the value of incumbency according to these measures understandably took it to signify a decline in electoral competition. With wider margins of safety, fewer incumbents should lose, turnover should decline, and therefore so should the *swing ratio*—the percentage of seats changing hands for a given percentage swing in the national partisan vote.[9] Remarkably, none of these things occurred until more than a decade after they were anticipated, and not for the reasons initially proffered. House incumbents were not significantly less likely to lose in the 1970s than they were in the 1950s. Neither—if marginality is defined correctly—did the number of marginal House seats decline over this period. And seat swings remained nearly as sensitive as before to vote swings.

Measures of marginality are, in essence, estimates of vulnerability. Members of Congress who win with less than some specified share of votes supposedly have a higher risk of defeat in the next election. Such thresholds are arbitrary, however, and make sense only if they are, in fact, stable indicators of vulnerability. Table 3-2, which lists the percentage of incumbents at various margins who lost in the next election, shows that they are not. As the "marginal" incumbents (by the customary 60 percent standard) became safer, nonmarginal incumbents became more vulnerable. Indeed, an incumbent elected in the 1970s with between 60 and 65 percent of the vote was almost as likely to lose in the next election as was an incumbent in the 1950s who had been elected with 55 to 60 percent of the vote (7.9 percent compared with 8.2 percent).

Although the mean incumbent's vote increased by about 5 percentage points during the 1960s, then, incumbents added almost nothing to their electoral se-

TABLE 3–2   INCUMBENTS DEFEATED IN GENERAL ELECTIONS TO THE U.S. HOUSE OF REPRESENTATIVES, BY PREVIOUS VOTE MARGIN AND DECADE (IN PERCENTAGES)

	VOTE MARGIN IN PREVIOUS ELECTION:					
Decade	50.0–59.9%	60.0–64.9%	>65%	Standard Deviation of Vote Swing	Loser's Mean Vote in Prior Election	Losers Who Were Not Marginal
1940s	27.8	4.7	0.6	5.5	54.5	7.1
1950s	13.4	2.2	0.8	5.3	54.1	8.7
1960s	13.2	3.2	1.3	6.6	55.6	16.9
1970s	12.6	7.9	1.8	9.4	58.0	35.2
1980s	8.3	2.4	0.7	8.2	56.1	24.3
1990s	12.3	5.0	0.2	7.2	54.9	17.2

Note: Includes only incumbents who faced major party opponents in stable (nonredistricted) districts. Decades are defined by reapportionment cycles; for example, the 1950s include 1952 through 1960; the exceptions are the 1940s (1946 through 1950) and the 1990s (1992 through 1998).

Source: Compiled by author.

curity in the 1970s because they were little safer with a 65 percent margin than they had been in the 1950s with a 60 percent margin, and their comparative risk at higher margins (above 65 percent) was also greater. Because incumbent defeats did not diminish and marginal seats—correctly defined—did not dwindle, there was no reason to expect the swing ratio to have been significantly lower during this time, and it was not.[10]

How could vote margins increase without adding to House incumbents' security, diminishing competition, or dampening swings? The answer lies in another crucial change first noticed by Thomas E. Mann: an attendant increase in the heterogeneity of interelection vote swings among districts.[11] Consider a hypothetical case. Suppose the average incumbent wins with 55 percent of the vote and the interelection vote swing is normally distributed with a standard deviation of 5 percentage points. This means that, other things equal, an incumbent with the average margin has about a .84 chance of winning in the next election, because .16 of the normal curve falls one standard deviation below the mean (that is, in this case, below 50 percent). Now suppose the average incumbent's vote increases to 60 percent. If the standard deviation of the interelection vote swing does not change, the average incumbent's probability of winning next time jumps to .98, because only .02 of the normal curve falls two standard deviations below the mean. But if the standard deviation increases to 10 percentage points, the incumbent's seat is just as much at risk as it was before.

With this in mind, observe the fourth column in Table 3-2. The table lists the standard deviation of interelection swings in the Democratic vote across incumbent-held House districts averaged by decade. As the average incumbent's vote margin grew, so did the heterogeneity of interelection vote swings. In the 1940s and 1950s, the standard deviation of the swing averaged 5.4; in the 1970s, it averaged 9.4. Vote margins could increase without making incumbents significantly safer because electorates became more volatile and idiosyncratic across districts.[12]

Additional evidence that larger vote margins did not necessarily enhance electoral safety appears in the final two columns of Table 3-2. The fifth column lists the mean vote share losing incumbents had won in the election immediately prior to their defeat. In the earlier decades, the typical loser had won about 54 percent of the vote in the previous election; in the 1970s, the average loser's previous vote was 58 percent. The sixth column lists the percentage of losing incumbents whose previous vote had put them out of the marginal range as it is customarily defined; in the 1970s and 1980s, a sharply higher proportion of losers had held seats by what was once thought to be a safe margin.

In the late 1980s, some of the effects anticipated from the "vanishing marginals" did finally come to pass. Incumbents were reelected at record rates in 1986 and 1988. The swing ratio finally underwent a statistically significant decrease (of about 25 percent).[13] Critics proclaimed the end of electoral competition; President Ronald Reagan, among others, made the invidious observation that there was "less turnover in Congress than in the Supreme Soviet."[14] Incumbency, it seems, had finally overwhelmed all other electoral forces. In retrospect, however, the elections of the late 1980s seem more an aberration than a new norm; all the relevant figures and tables in this chapter show a sharp revival of electoral competition for incumbent-held seats since then. Why did the predicted collapse of competition take so long to happen? Why did competition revive so vigorously in the 1990s?

These questions only begin the list of things we want to know about the nature of the incumbency advantage in congressional elections. Why do incumbents usually do so well? Why do House incumbents do so much better than Senate incumbents? Why did House incumbents' vote margins increase sharply in the mid-1960s and again in the mid-1980s, and then fall in the 1990s? Why did district electorates become more volatile, preventing incumbents from turning wider vote margins into greater electoral security? The answers are crucial to understanding congressional politics as well as congressional elections. They involve a complicated, interlocking set of institutional, behavioral, and contextual elements that we begin to examine in this chapter, but that will take the rest of the book to explicate fully.

SOURCES OF THE INCUMBENCY ADVANTAGE

The Institutional Characteristics of Congress

A good starting point is to consider the institutional characteristics of Congress. David Mayhew, summarizing the results of his close examination of Congress as of the early 1970s, put it succinctly: "If a group of planners sat down and tried to design a pair of American national assemblies with the goal of serving members' reelection needs year in and year out, they would be hard pressed to improve on what exists."[15]

The congressional system that Mayhew described permitted the widest individual latitude for pursuing reelection strategies. For example, a highly decentralized committee and subcommittee structure allowed members to specialize in legislative areas where they could best serve local interests. It also provided most members with a solid piece of legislative turf. The operative norm for writing legislation was similar: something for everyone. Positive-sum distributive politics, represented by the pork barrel and the Christmas tree bill (one with separate little "gifts" for a variety of special interest groups) were much more prevalent than the zero-sum competition for scarce resources. Members deferred to each other's requests for particular benefits for their states or districts in return for deference to their own.

The parties also bowed to the varied electoral needs of members. Party discipline within Congress was lightly applied. In the face of controversial and divisive issues, Mayhew noted, "the best service a party can supply to its congressmen is a negative one: it can leave them alone. And this is in general what the congressional parties do."[16] Party leaders, taking the position that the first duty is to get reelected, encouraged members to "vote the district first"; members happily complied.

The system allowed members to take the "right" positions, make pleasing statements, and bring home the bacon while avoiding responsibility for the collective performance of Congress. It provided a setting for emphasizing individual achievements while insulating members from blame for the general failures and inadequacies of the institution, which were at least in part a consequence of the patterns of individual behavior encouraged by the system itself. This is important, because the public's assessment of Congress' performance was often strongly negative. Ratings of Congress actually declined while House incumbents were increasing their vote margins in the late 1960s and early 1970s. Disdain for Congress did not extend to its individual members; people generally rated their representatives far higher than their Congress.[17]

Members of Congress also voted themselves an astonishing array of official resources that could be used to pursue reelection. These include salary, travel, office, staff, and communication allowances that are now, by a conservative estimate, worth about $1 million per year for House members and up to several times that much for senators (whose allowances vary by state population).[18] All of these perquisites were augmented dramatically in the 1960s and 1970s, with trends flattening out in the 1980s. The expansion of personal staffs of House and Senate members since 1930 is documented in Figure 3-5. The sharpest increase occurred between the 1950s and the late 1970s. The value to members of personal staff was underlined in 1994 when the new Republican House majority voted to slash committee staff by one-third but rejected a proposal to reduce personal staff from eighteen to sixteen.[19] Travel allowances have grown in comparable fashion (see Table 3-3; before travel allowances became so generous, members would, of course, return to their districts on occasion at their own expense).

The growth of other official resources has kept pace. The most important congressional perquisite is the franking privilege, which allows members to use the

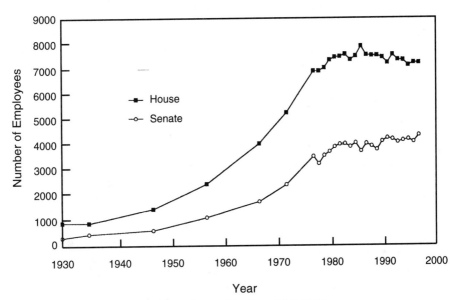

FIGURE 3–5. Personal Staff of House and Senate Members, 1930–1997
Source: Norman J. Ornstein, Thomas E. Mann, and Michael J. Malbin, *Vital Statistics on Congress, 1997–1998* (Washington, DC: Congressional Quarterly Press, 1998), p. 135.

TABLE 3–3   HOUSE MEMBERS' PAID TRIPS TO THEIR DISTRICTS, 1962–2000

YEAR	TRIPS TO DISTRICT
1962	3
1966	5
1968	12
1973	18
1975	26
1977	33
1978 and later	unlimited

Note: Since 1978, travel expenses have been included in an overall lump sum for offices, equipment, supplies, postage, communications, etc., which members may budget as they see fit. The lump sum total for 1997 averaged $901,771 per member.

Sources: Morris P. Fiorina, *Congress: Keystone of the Washington Establishment,* 2nd edition (New Haven: Yale University Press, 1989), p. 61; Norman J. Ornstein, Thomas E. Mann, and Michael J. Malbin, *Vital Statistics on Congress 1997–1998* (Washington, DC: Congressional Quarterly Press, 1994), Table 5–12.

mails free of charge for "official business," which is broadly interpreted to include most kinds of communications to constituents. Figure 3-6 reveals that franked mail grew by more than an order of magnitude between the 1950s and 1980s. Public criticism led both houses to tighten up the rules governing franked mail in 1990, so the volume has fallen substantially from its peak in 1984. Even tighter rules were proposed by Republican reformers in 1994, but reforms were successfully opposed by newly elected members representing large western districts.[20] It is easy to understand members' reluctance to deny themselves such a serviceable tool. Other media have not been overlooked. Facilities for preparing radio and television tapes and films are available to members free of charge. In 1977, members voted themselves unlimited WATS line service for long-distance telephone calls. Most offices are now linked to the Internet.

Changes in Voting Behavior

Obviously, one major advantage of incumbency is control of extensive official resources for reaching and serving constituents. The remarkable expansion of these resources during the 1960s thus offered a ready explanation for larger incumbent vote margins: more vigorous exploitation of ever-expanding communications resources.[21] The accepted ideas about voting behavior in congressional elections lent support to this view. Voters were known to favor candidates with whom they were familiar (that is, whose names they could recall when asked), so more extensive self-advertising by members could be expected to have direct electoral payoffs, assuming that it made them more familiar to voters. Apparently it did not. John Ferejohn showed that the proportion of voters who could recall incumbents' names did not increase between 1958 and 1970; nor did incumbents' familiarity advantage over their challengers grow. He proposed that a change in voting behavior was behind the enlarged incumbency advantage. Voters had become substantially less loyal to political parties during the 1960s and early 1970s. Perhaps they were merely substituting one simple voting cue, incumbency, for another, party.[22]

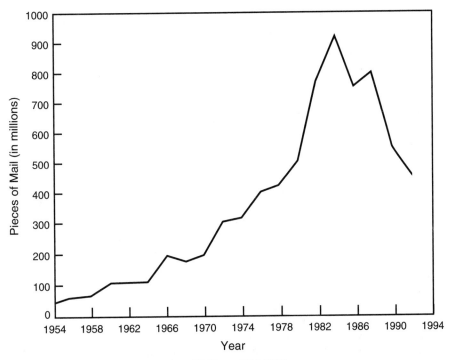

FIGURE 3–6. Election-Year Congressional Mailings, 1954–1992
Source: Norman J. Ornstein, Thomas E. Mann, and Michael J. Malbin, *Vital Statistics on Congress, 1997–1998* (Washington, DC: Congressional Quarterly Press, 1998), p. 172.

This explanation reflected a conception of voters as remarkably uninformed and superficial in their approach to voting decisions. As Chapter 5 will report in greater detail, this view of congressional voters has been challenged by more recent research. And if the congressional electorate is at least modestly more sophisticated and better informed than was once commonly thought, voters' preference for incumbents must arise from something more than the simple fact of incumbency.

Constituency Service

Recognizing this, Morris Fiorina argued that members of Congress had enhanced their own electoral fortunes, not simply by advertising themselves more extensively, but also by changing the focus of their activities and thus the content of the message they sent to voters. Essentially, they created needs, then reaped the rewards of spending more time and energy catering to them. In the decades following World War II, Congress enacted legislation that increased the size and scope of the federal government enormously. Government growth generated an increasing volume of demands from citizens for help in coping with bureaucratic mazes or in taking advantage of federal programs. Members responded to the demand by continually adding to their capacity to deliver assistance. The growth of personal staffs has already been noted. The placement of new staff was equally significant; a disproportionate share went into augmenting their capacity to provide services to constituents. Back in 1972, 13 percent of personal Senate staff and 23 percent of personal House staff worked in district or state offices; by 1997, the proportions had grown to 31 percent and 44 percent, respectively.[23]

The greater demand for services and the greater resources for providing them created more opportunities for building credit with constituents. For electoral purposes, "the nice thing about case work is that it is mostly profit; one makes many more friends than enemies."[24] Casework is also nonpartisan. The party affiliation of the member delivering or that of the constituent receiving the assistance is irrelevant. What counts is the member's ability to deliver services, which increases with tenure in Washington and consequent seniority and familiarity with the administrative apparatus. It is, therefore, perfectly reasonable for voters to prefer candidates on the basis of their incumbency rather than on their party label or policy positions. And it is equally reasonable for members to concentrate on providing services rather than on making national policy as a strategy for staying in office.

Fiorina's thesis is still controversial because the pertinent evidence has been equivocal. The amount of time spent in the district appears to have little effect on the incumbent's vote margin, for example.[25] The value of the pork barrel has also been called into doubt, though the latest research suggests that Democrats, at least, have benefited from delivering local projects.[26] Nor is it fully established that personal and district services persuade voters to prefer incumbents, though again more recent research, including some clever experimental studies, indicate that they do.[27] Part of the analytic problem is that if members work the district harder the more insecure they are, then harder work may be associated with narrower electoral margins, even if it is what keeps the member in office.[28]

As originally proposed, none of these explanations took note of the fact that, despite wider reelection margins, House incumbents kept losing at about the same rate as before until the late 1980s. Once this is recognized, the evidence marshaled on their behalf takes on a rather different cast. For example, it is striking that the steep increase in staff, travel, and communications allowances during the 1960s and 1970s failed to produce any net improvement in incumbents' reelection prospects at the time they were occurring. Not until the late 1980s—well after the growth in official resources had flattened out—did the average incumbent's probability of reelection actually grow, and that change was only temporary. Considered in this light, it appears that incumbents spent a decade running ever harder just to stay in the same place.

Similarly, the idea that incumbents have prospered by exploiting the decline of partisanship among voters needs amendment. The basic argument is that a less partisan, more candidate-oriented electorate favors incumbents. Diminished partisanship means fewer automatic votes against an incumbent, so personal cultivation of the district can pay off in a wider vote margin. But it also means fewer automatic votes for an incumbent and so larger potential vote losses should local electoral circumstances change.[29] A less partisan electorate is more fickle; the vote is less stable from one election to the next, and a wide margin in one election is a weaker guarantee of success in the next.[30]

Although it, too, was proposed as part of an explanation for greater incumbent security, Fiorina's main point, that incumbents' increased emphasis on nonpartisan district services has altered the meaning of the electoral choice, is not necessarily blunted if incumbents' security has been exaggerated. Attention to constituency service plainly does command an enlarged share of the time of members and their staffs.[31] Members elected since the mid-1970s in particular have "exhibited great ingenuity and phenomenal tenacity in 'cultivating' their districts."[32] Fiorina's thesis thus helps explain why first-term House members, once much more vulnerable than more senior incumbents, became considerably more difficult to defeat.

Prior to the changes of the 1960s, new members were often swept into the House on a partisan tide, then swept out again two years later as it receded. Between 1946 and 1966, for example, 20.5 percent of all new House members lost their first reelection bid, a rate of defeat nearly quadruple that of members who had served two or more terms (5.2 percent). Since then, first-termers have held onto newly won seats much more consistently; only 7.3 percent have lost, compared with 3.9 percent of more senior incumbents. Indeed, between 1968 and 1980, the defeat rates of newcomers (5.6 percent) and senior members (4.4 percent) did not differ significantly ($p = .24$). Since then, the greater vulnerability of new members has returned; in the 1980s and 1990s, 9.5 percent of first-termers, but only 3.0 percent of senior members, have lost.

Until the late 1980s, then, declining partisanship and more assiduous cultivation of House districts enhanced the reelection prospects mainly of first-term incumbents. After the first reelection, House members were actually more vulnerable in the 1970s than they had been before the changes of the 1960s. The advent of a more candidate-centered politics did not automatically favor incumbents. A less partisan electorate may make it easier for a representative to develop the kind of personal hold on a district that insulates him or her from external political forces. But a less partisan electorate is also more fickle; support from constituents is easier to lose as well as to win; an easy victory one year does not guarantee reelection next time.

Nor did greater insulation from outside forces reduce uncertainty or risk. The locus of competition merely shifted to the district. The incumbent assumes a larger burden of responsibility for winning reelection. Before the mid-1960s, House members who lost could put much of the blame on forces beyond the district and hence their control. On average, their interelection vote swing was only 4.6 percentage points worse than their party's mean swing. Since 1968, the average loser's vote swing has been 8.7 percentage points worse than his or her party's mean.

The Variability of the Incumbency Advantage

Incumbency remains a powerful advantage, to be sure. But its electoral value is clearly not a constant. It depends in part on what the incumbent does with the resources available and on how hard and shrewdly he or she works to build and maintain support in the district. And this varies among members, although the degree of variation declined during the 1970s and 1980s as those members less inclined to endless pursuit of reelection quit or were weeded out. It depends even more on the kind of opposition the incumbent faces; as we shall see, differences in the skills and resources of challengers are a primary source of variation over time in incumbents' electoral fortunes. And it depends on what competing considerations shape voters' judgments, as the 1992 and 1994 elections made clear (see Chapter 6).

It is safe to assume that incumbents who seek reelection want to stay in Congress. Why do some exploit the resources of office more vigorously than others to this end? The principal reason is that they have other important things to do with their time, energy, and staff. Single-minded pursuit of reelection detracts from work in Washington and therefore from a member's power and influence in Congress and impact on public policy. Reelection is an instrumental, not ultimate, goal. Sometimes opportunities to build support back in the district must be foregone if a member is to share in governing the country. And the longer a member is in office, the more opportunities to influence policy and to gain the respect of others in government. Members very soon find that they have to balance their desire for electoral security against their desire for a successful career in Washington.

One reelection strategy might diminish this tradeoff. For incumbents who stake their electoral futures on their party's performance, cultivating the district could lose some of its urgency. Many of the Republicans taking office for the first time in 1994 initially wedded their fortunes to the party's "Contract with America," dedicating their energies to dismantling welfare and regulatory programs and balancing the budget. Pledged to limiting their stay in Congress, they claimed to want careers that were, in the words of one of them, Steve Largent of Oklahoma, "brilliant but brief."[33] But even members far more interested in revolutionizing government than in lengthy congressional careers do not necessarily pay less attention to their districts. Losing would jeopardize the revolution. Insofar as supporting fundamental change forces members to cast politically dangerous votes, they have all the more reason to please constituents in every other way they can.

Discouraging the Opposition

Casework, trips back to the district, issuing newsletters, and all the other things members do to promote reelection are not aimed merely at winning votes in the next election. They are also meant to influence the perceptions formed by politically active people of the member's hold on the district. The electoral value of incumbency lies not only in what it provides to the incumbent, but also in how it affects the thinking of potential opponents and their potential supporters. Many incumbents win easily by wide margins because they face inexperienced, sometimes reluctant challengers who lack the financial and organizational backing to mount a serious campaign for Congress. If an incumbent can convince potentially formidable opponents and people who control campaign resources that he or she is invincible, he or she is very likely to avoid a serious challenge and so will be invincible—as long as the impression holds.

This is so because politically skilled and ambitious nonincumbents follow rational career strategies; people who control campaign resources make strategically rational decisions about deploying them; and the volume of campaign resources at the disposal of a nonincumbent candidate has a great deal to do with how well he or she does at the polls.

Other things being equal, the strongest congressional candidates are those for whom politics is a career. They have the most powerful motive and the greatest opportunity to master the craft of electoral politics. They are most likely to have experience in running campaigns and in holding elective office. They have the incentive and opportunity to cultivate other politically active and influential people and to put them under some obligation.

Ambitious career politicians also have the greatest incentive to follow a rational strategy for moving up the informal, but quite real, hierarchy of elective offices in the American political system. An experienced politician will have acquired valuable political assets—most typically, a lower elective office—that increase the probability of moving to a higher office. But these assets are at risk and may be lost if the attempt to advance fails. Thus the potentially strongest congressional aspirants will also make the most considered and cautious judgments about when to try for a congressional seat.[34]

Incumbency is central to their strategic calculations. Politically knowledgeable people are fully aware of the advantages of incumbency and of the long odds normally faced by challengers, and they adjust their behavior accordingly. Hence, for example, typically more than half the candidates for open House seats have previously held an elective office, while such experienced candidates comprise less than a quarter of the candidates challenging incumbents. Within this larger pattern, experienced challengers are more likely to run against incumbents who had closer contests in the last election. Table 3-4 presents the evidence for these points and shows the close association

TABLE 3–4   THE PROBABILITY OF VICTORY AND THE QUALITY OF NONINCUMBENT CANDIDATES FOR THE U.S. HOUSE OF REPRESENTATIVES, 1946–1998

TYPE OF RACE	NUMBER OF CASES	WINNERS (%)	FORMER OFFICEHOLDERS (%)
Open Seats			
No general election opponent	86	100.0	69.8
Held by candidate's party	1,064	72.9	67.7
Held by neither party	234	50.0	52.5
Held by opposite party	1,064	27.1	38.6
Total	2,448	50.0	53.6
Challengers to Incumbents			
Incumbent's vote in last election (%)			
50.0–54.9	1,810	19.6	44.8
55.0–59.9	1,732	8.4	28.5
60.0–64.9	1,649	4.4	19.0
65.0–69.9	1,429	2.1	14.0
70.0 or more	2,160	0.5	8.7
unopposed	1,621	1.0	4.9
Total	10,401	6.0	20.1

Source: Compiled by author.

between the prospects for victory and the presence of experienced House candidates.[35]

The career strategies of potential congressional candidates are complemented and reinforced by those of individuals and groups that control campaign resources. The most important of these resources is money, although other forms of assistance can also be valuable. People and groups contribute to congressional campaigns for reasons ranging from selfless idealism to pure venality. Regardless of the purpose, however, most contribute more readily to nonincumbent candidates in campaigns that are expected to be close.[36] So do political parties. (The situation regarding incumbents is somewhat different and will be discussed later.) Resources are limited, and most contributors deploy them where they have the greatest chance of affecting the outcome; donors naturally try to avoid wasting money on hopeless candidates. Figure 3-7 displays the consequences of this tendency. Candidates for open seats typically have substantially more money to spend than those challenging incumbents, and more money is available to challengers who face incumbents who

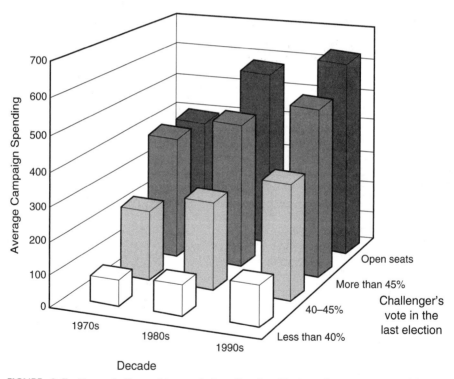

FIGURE 3–7. Electoral Competition and Spending by Nonincumbent House Candidates, 1972-1998 (in thousands of dollars, adjusted for inflation—1998 = 1.00)
Sources: Compiled from data supplied by Common Cause, *1972 Congressional Campaign Finances*, 10 vols, (Washington, DC, 1974) and *1974 Congressional Campaign Finances*, 3 vols. (Washington, DC, 1976), and the Federal Election Commission (1978-1998).

had smaller margins of victory in the previous election (the simplest measure of electoral vulnerability). Notice also that as funds available to nonincumbent candidates have increased over these three decades, they have also become increasingly concentrated in marginal districts and open seats; challengers to nonmarginal incumbents have become relatively weaker by this standard.

Expectations about the likelihood of electoral success, then, influence the decisions of potential candidates and campaign contributors. The better the electoral odds, the more likely the race is to attract a strong challenger, and the more money will be contributed to his or her campaign. Furthermore, strong candidates themselves attract campaign money, and the availability of campaign money attracts strong candidates. A system of mutually reinforcing decisions and expectations thus links nonincumbent candidates and contributors with each other and with perceived electoral prospects. In contests involving incumbents, prospects are governed by an additional consideration: the availability of issues—personal, local, and national—that the candidate and campaign might use effectively to undermine the support the incumbent has enjoyed in past elections.

The strategies pursued by prospective congressional candidates and their prospective backers matter a great deal in a candidate-centered election process, because the quality and experience of challengers, and the campaign resources made available to them, have a powerful effect on election results. I present a variety of evidence for this conclusion in the following pages. For now, the relevant point is that variations in the quality and resources of challengers offer an alternative explanation of increased vote margins enjoyed by incumbents since the 1960s.

Gary Cox and Jonathan Katz, for example, parse the House incumbency advantage into "direct," "scare-off," and "quality" effects. Direct effects are those derived from the expansion of resources and district activities we have already discussed. Scare-off effects contribute to the incumbency advantage when strong challenges are successfully discouraged. Quality effects measure the difference that candidate experience makes. (All incumbents are, by assumption, high-quality candidates; variation is supplied by nonincumbents, many of whom have never before held an elective office). Cox and Katz conclude that the most important source of growth in the incumbency advantage was an increase in the electoral effect of quality differences. The value of incumbency grew, not because of greater resources or more effective deterrence of quality challengers, but because the difference in electoral performance between experienced and inexperienced candidates grew. They attribute this change to the weakening of party ties and the consequent growth of candidate-centered electoral politics.[37]

David Brady, Brian Gaines, and Douglas Rivers's analysis, using somewhat different methods, reaches a similar conclusion. Moreover, they find that the effect of the challenger's quality on the incumbent's vote has grown by about the same amount in Senate and House elections. Senators did not become more secure, however, because unlike House districts, states became more competitive—that is, more evenly balanced in a partisan sense—over the same time span, offsetting the growing incumbency advantage.[38] This research suggests that the incumbency advantage depends not so much on what incumbents do, but on what potential opponents do, and that it has grown because the impact of the opposition's level of mobilization has grown.

MONEY IN CONGRESSIONAL ELECTIONS

Mobilization requires money. Congressional aspirants are wise, indeed, to worry about the availability of money for the campaign. How well nonincumbent candidates do on election day is directly related to how much campaign money they raise and spend. The precise relationship between campaign spending and election results is difficult to pin down, however, because most candidates and contributors act strategically. Potential donors try to avoid wasting their money on hopeless causes. The better a candidate's prospects, the more contributors of all kinds are willing to invest in the campaign. The connection for nonincumbents between spending and votes is therefore at least potentially reciprocal: money may help win votes, but the expectation that a candidate can win votes also brings in money. To the degree that (expected) votes influence spending, ordinary measures will exaggerate the effects of spending on votes.

Spending by incumbents is also reciprocally related to the vote, but in a rather different way: the higher the incumbent's expected vote, the *less* money flows into the campaign. This is not because secure incumbents have trouble raising money; quite the contrary. Many interest groups contribute to campaigns not so much to influence the outcome as to gain influence with, or at least access to, people who are likely to be in a position to help or hurt them. They waste no money on sure losers but have no qualms about giving money to sure winners, even when it is not really needed. Whether or not incumbents tap this source of funds depends on whether they think they need the money (or might some time in the foreseeable future).

Most members of Congress do not particularly enjoy asking for money, and many avoid doing so if they do not see a pressing need for it (given the strength of the opposition they are facing). If they feel threatened, though, incumbents have sources that are not nearly so readily available to challengers. In addition to groups seeking access, party committees and ideological interest groups rally to support threatened incumbents of the preferred party or ideology on the ground that it is easier to hold on to a seat than to take one from the opposition. Incumbents, then, can generally raise as much campaign money as they think they need. Again, the anticipated vote affects spending. But for incumbents, the relationship is negative: the larger their expected vote, the less they raise and spend. To the degree that (expected) votes influence spending, ordinary measures will underestimate the effects of incumbent spending on votes.

To measure the effect of campaign spending on votes or victories, then, it is necessary to subtract the reciprocal effect of (expected) votes or victories on spending. Although theoretically feasible, this turns out to be extremely difficult in practice, and after more than twenty years of research, the appropriate solution remains elusive. We simply do not know the extent to which analyses that ignore the problem overestimate the effects of challenger spending or underestimate the effects of incumbent spending—if at all.

The Connection between Money and Success

Nonetheless, certain things are clear. First, congressional challengers rarely win if they do not spend a substantial amount of money, and the more they spend, the more likely they are to win. Figures 3-8 and 3-9 leave no doubt on this point. Figure 3-8 displays the percentage of winning challengers in House elections from 1972 through 1998 at ascending levels of campaign spending (adjusted for inflation, 1998 = 1.00). It also displays the proportion of challengers at each level of spending. The odds against challengers who spent less than $100,000 were long indeed; only one of 2,675 was successful. A majority (58 percent) of all House challengers fell into this category. Chances were only slightly better for challengers who spent between $100,000 and $200,000; they and the first group include 70 percent of all challengers. Prospects improve sharply as spending exceeds $200,000. The most extravagant challengers (spending $800,000 or more) won about one-third of their races.

Of course, not all election years are alike. Some elections feature national political tides—driven by recessions, scandals, presidential politics, and the like—that strongly favor one party's candidates. Conditions in other years seem

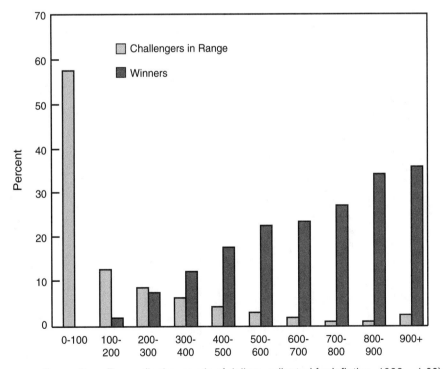

Expenditure Range (in thousands of dollars, adjusted for inflation, 1998 = 1.00)

FIGURE 3–8. Challengers' Expenditures and Victories in House Elections, 1972–1998
Source: Compiled by author.

nearly neutral between parties. Intuitively, a House challenger's chances of winning should vary with the strength and direction of national partisan tides. Figure 3-9 shows that challengers favored by national forces—Democrats in 1974, 1982, and 1996; Republicans in 1980, 1984, and 1994—win more frequently at every level of campaign spending. Those spending more than $400,000 win more than one-third of their contests; anything over $200,000 is enough to make a race of it. In addition, challengers are able to spend more money in good election years; for example, 22 percent spent more than $400,000 in the good years, compared with 13 percent in neutral and bad years. This is further evidence of strategic behavior on the part of contributors.

In the absence of strong partisan tides, challengers have a much harder time winning and need to spend more than $500,000 to get beyond a one-in-ten chance of winning. Against contrary partisan tides, challengers raise the least amount of money and find it difficult to win no matter what they spend.

What do these data tell us about the cost of a minimally competitive challenge? Obviously, it varies from district to district and from state to state, depending on the structure and cost of mass media advertising, the vigor of local parties and other politically active organizations, and local campaign styles. It

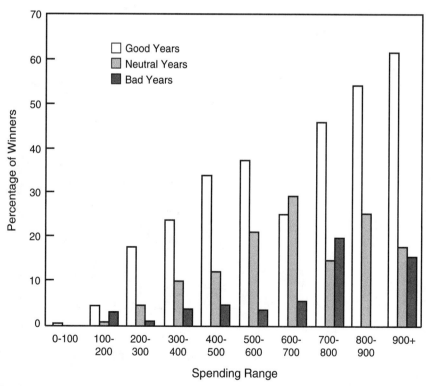

FIGURE 3-9. Winning House Challengers, by Level of Campaign Spending, 1972-1998
Source: Compiled by author.

also varies with national partisan tides, and it has certainly grown over time (even when inflation is taken into account). Still, if we set an arbitrary but reasonable standard for a competitive campaign as one giving the challenger at least a 25 percent chance of winning, $400,000 (in 1998 dollars) is a plausible estimate for the threshold for the entire period. Only 15 percent of all House challengers crossed this threshold; a large majority spent far too little to make a contest of it. If analysis is confined to the most recent elections, the minimum price tag for a competitive House campaign under average conditions today is probably closer to $600,000; every one of the twenty-seven challengers who defeated incumbents in 1996 and 1998 spent more than this amount.

Defeating a House incumbent is clearly expensive (and a serious Senate campaign can cost more than ten times as much in a large state such as California, New York, or Texas); relatively few challengers have been able to raise enough funds to be serious threats. Those who do acquire sufficient resources can make incumbents feel anything but safe. For incumbents, spending a great deal of money on the campaign is a sign of weakness rather than strength. In fact, the more money they spend on the campaign, the worse they do on election day. That is, the relationship between the incumbent's level of spending and share of votes or likelihood of victory is negative. Spending money does not cost them votes, to be sure; rather, incumbents raise and spend more money the more strongly they feel themselves challenged. The more their opponent spends, the more they spend. But challengers evidently get more bang for the buck; therefore, the more spent by both the challenger and the incumbent, the greater the challenger's share of the vote and the more likely the challenger is to win the election.[39]

Table 3-5 displays these relationships, much simplified. It lists the percentage of winning challengers at different combinations of incumbent and challenger spending in the seven most recent elections. The column average shows that the more challengers spent, the more likely they were to win. Only one of the 1,648 (0.1 percent) who spent less than $200,000 won, while a third of those spending more than $800,000 replaced the incumbent. The row average shows that the more incumbents spent, the more likely they were to lose. None in the lowest category of spenders failed to win reelection; 13 percent in the highest category did so. At any given level of incumbent spending, challengers do better the more they spend; at any given level of challenger spending, the incumbent's spending makes little apparent difference in the outcome. The variation across every row (except the first) is statistically significant at $p < .001$; the variation down every column is insignificant ($p > .10$).

More elaborate multivariate models that analyze votes or victories as a function of campaign spending and other variables (national tides, district partisanship, and so forth) tell exactly the same story.[40] The pattern appears in Senate elections as well.[41] Unfortunately, the problem of reciprocal causation renders all such results suspect. Because challengers raise more money the better they are expected to do, this kind of analysis exaggerates the effects of their campaign spending. Because incumbents raise *less* money the better they are expected to do (remember, their spending is reactive), the analysis underestimates the effects of their spending. What we do not know is by how much.

TABLE 3–5   CAMPAIGN SPENDING AND CHALLENGER
VICTORIES, 1986–1998 (IN PERCENTAGES)

	CHALLENGER'S SPENDING[a]					
	<200	200–400	400–600	600–800	>800	Row Average
INCUMBENT'S SPENDING[a]						
<200	0.0	0.0	0.0	0.0	0.0	0.0
	(182)	(2)	(2)	(1)	(0)	(187)
200–400	0.0	3.1	0.0	0.0	0.0	0.2
	(522)	(32)	(6)	(4)	(1)	(565)
400–600	0.0	4.2	12.1	40.0	50.0	2.0
	(448)	(72)	(33)	(5)	(4)	(562)
600–800	0.0	6.6	12.7	36.4	25.0	6.2
	(282)	(121)	(71)	(33)	(12)	(519)
>800	0.8	8.5	14.5	17.4	39.3	13.9
	(123)	(82)	(76)	(92)	(66)	(439)
Column Average	0.1	6.1	12.7	22.2	37.3	4.6
	(1557)	(309)	(188)	(135)	(83)	(2372)

[a]In thousands of dollars, adjusted for inflation (1998 = 1.00); the number of cases is in parentheses.

Scholars have estimated a variety of models designed to take reciprocal causation into account, but the findings vary widely. At one extreme, results simply reinforce the original findings; at the other, they suggest marginal returns on spending are as high for incumbents as for challengers.[42] Most often however, they suggest that the marginal returns on spending are indeed greater for challengers than for incumbents, but to a lesser degree than the original findings would indicate. And at least two studies have found that the returns on spending by first-term incumbents are about as large as the returns on spending by their opponents and much larger than the returns on spending by more senior members.[43]

Despite the uncertainties that remain, several things are abundantly clear. Challengers (and candidates for open seats who face well-financed opponents) rarely win without spending a great deal of money. Even rarer is the losing incumbent who might plausibly blame defeat on a shortage of funds.[44] Moreover, there are solid reasons why challengers should get a larger return on their spending than do incumbents. However, there are also good reasons for believing that, under some circumstances, the incumbent's spending should affect the outcome as well.

Why Campaign Money Is More Important to Challengers

Campaign spending is subject to diminishing returns; the more dollars spent, the less gained by each additional dollar. Congressional incumbents usually exploit their official resources for reaching constituents so thoroughly that the additional increment of information about their virtues put forth during the campaign adds comparatively little to what is already known and felt about them. As we shall see in Chapter 5, the extent to which voters know and like incumbents is unrelated to how much is spent on the campaign. The situation is quite different for nonincumbents. Most are largely unknown before the campaign, and the extent to which they penetrate the awareness of voters—which is crucial to winning votes—is directly related to how extensively they campaign. The money spent on nonincumbents' campaigns buys the attention and recognition that incumbents already enjoy at the outset of the campaign.

If this is true, we would expect spending by both candidates to affect the outcomes of contests for open seats, as indeed it does. Table 3-6 displays the relationships in their most elementary form. Democrats do better the more they spend, Republicans do better the more they spend. Democrats thrive in the combinations appearing in the upper right-hand section of the matrix (winning 81 percent of the time), Republicans thrive in the lower left-hand section (winning 86 percent of the time). Along the diagonal, results are split (Democrats win 54 percent overall). Multivariate analyses recapitulate these results.[45]

In general, then, spending should matter more to nonincumbent candidates because they have yet to get their message out, and getting a message out costs money. It may also matter to incumbents if they have to get out a *new* message. That is, when an incumbent is in trouble for some reason—personal, such as involvement in the House bank scandal in 1992, or political, as with Democrats facing the Republican tide in 1994—and needs to counter with a new pitch, campaign money is essential. It comes down to this: regardless of their potential, if challengers cannot raise lots of money, they can forget about winning. If incumbents are strongly challenged, raising and spending lots of money may

TABLE 3–6 CAMPAIGN SPENDING AND DEMOCRATIC VICTORIES IN OPEN SEATS, 1986–1998 (IN PERCENTAGES)

	DEMOCRAT'S SPENDING[a]				
Average	<200	200–400	400–600	>600	Row
REPUBLICAN'S SPENDING[a]					
<200	66.7	100.0	95.4	100.0	95.3
	(6)	(14)	(22)	(22)	(64)
200–400	33.3	66.7	53.3	63.6	56.3
	(3)	(3)	(15)	(11)	(32)
400–600	0.0	22.2	40.0	68.7	43.8
	(8)	(18)	(15)	(32)	(73)
>600	0.0	0.0	28.5	45.1	30.2
	(20)	(19)	(28)	(82)	(149)
Column Average	13.5	40.4	55.4	59.8	49.0
	(37)	(54)	(80)	(147)	(318)

[a]In thousands of dollars, adjusted for inflation (1998 = 1.00); the number of cases is in parentheses.

not help them much, though there is no reason to think it hurts. Even if the marginal return on spending by incumbents is very small, spending a great deal of money is probably a rational strategy because even a small number of votes may make the difference between winning and losing.

Plainly, though, spending huge sums of money does not ensure reelection. What matters much more is the amount spent by the challenger (and, related to it, how qualified and skillful he or she is). This means that *the incumbent's most effective electoral strategy is to discourage serious opposition*. The most effective way to do this is to avoid showing signs of electoral vulnerability. Even the most implacable political enemies will not mobilize their full range of resources against an incumbent if they see no prospect of success. Maintaining an active presence in the district helps to discourage the opposition.[46] So does working to maintain the electoral coalition that put the member into office in the first place. Since elections are the most pertinent source of information on a member's electoral strength, it is particularly important to avoid slippage at the polls. An unexpectedly weak showing in one election inspires even stronger opposition in the next. As one incumbent put it, "It is important for me to keep the young state representatives and city councilmen away. If they have the feeling that I'm invincible, they won't try. That reputation is very intangible. [But] your vote margin is part of it."[47]

It is also shrewd strategy for incumbents to diminish the intensity of opposition in the district. No one can please everyone, and nothing is to be gained by alienating one's supporters. But occasional friendly gestures to potentially hostile political interests may be sufficient to dampen their enthusiasm for organizing an all-out campaign against the member. From an incumbent's perspective, then, elections are not merely discrete hurdles to be cleared at regular two-year intervals. They are, as Richard F. Fenno, Jr.'s unique research has shown, a series of connected events that form part of a "career in the district," which parallels the career in Washington.[48] Winning is always crucial, of course, but winning in a way that minimizes future opposition is just as desirable in the long run.

THE CAREER IN THE DISTRICT

Other important insights into congressional election processes emerge from thinking in terms of congressional careers rather than single elections. Fenno discovered that House members' careers in the district passed through identifiable stages. In the first, *expansionist phase*, members devote a great deal of time and energy to building up their base of regular supporters. Beginning with a core of solid backers, they work to reach additional individuals and groups in the district that they hope to incorporate into their electoral coalition. The expansionist phase begins before the first election and continues for at least a few more. The capacity of first-term members to increase their electoral margins, even in the face of strongly contrary electoral tides, is a sign of this effort and its efficacy.

At some point, after a few elections, members typically enter into a *protectionist phase*, during which they work to maintain the support they have built up over the years, but no longer attempt to add to it. By this time they have often discouraged serious opposition by a show of growing electoral strength, and they have been in Washington long enough to have acquired some influence and responsibility. Working the district becomes a less attractive alternative to making policy and exercising legislative skills. It is at this stage that members risk "losing touch with the district," to use the politicians' cliche. If they do, they become vulnerable at the polls. But their vulnerability may not become apparent at all until it is tested.

This pattern of congressional career development governs the efficacy of strategies pursued by nonincumbents seeking congressional seats. The best opportunity arises when the incumbent dies or retires, and it is not uncommon to find ambitious young politicians biding their time until a seat becomes open, after which a lively scramble ensues among them for the nomination and election.[49] First-term members also attract unusually vigorous opposition; their challengers are twice as likely to have held elective public office and spend, on average, nearly twice as much money as challengers to more senior incumbents. The strategic assumption is that newly elected members do not have as firm a hold on their districts as they will later develop, so it is better to go after them now than later.[50] Politicians who use electoral margins as evidence of electoral vulnerability will focus on these new incumbents because so many of them initially win office in close elections. Although for a time during the 1970s first-term incumbents were not really any easier to defeat, their greater vulnerability has since returned.

Incumbents who survive the first bid for reelection should be most vulnerable in the protectionist stage of their careers. Electoral support is not won once and for all. It requires continual renewal and reinforcement, all the more now that party loyalties are weaker and the incumbent's personal performance is more central to voters' decisions. Members who work merely to maintain their base of support may actually let it slip, especially if they enjoy a few elections with feeble opposition that disguises any weakening of their hold on the district. A challenger who, through luck or cleverness, puts together a serious campaign against a member whose hold on the district has imperceptibly atrophied may surprise everyone, including the incumbent and challenger.

One example is Duncan Hunter, who defeated Democratic incumbent Lionel Van Deerlin in the 1980 contest for the 42nd District of California. Van Deerlin had not been seriously challenged in years; he was unaware of his own electoral weakness and of the progress his challenger was making until it was too late to do anything about it. Hunter had decided to run only at the last minute and then on the theory that, although he was likely to lose, he would be in a stronger position to take the seat in 1982, especially if, as many anticipated, Van Deerlin retired. Hunter's hesitation did not prevent a vigorous and well-financed campaign, and he wound up with 53 percent of the vote, compared with the 24 percent won by the token Republican challenger in 1978—a shift of 29 percentage points between the two elections.

Van Deerlin was only the most surprised of a number of senior House Democrats in 1980. Republican challengers defeated fourteen incumbents who had served at least five terms, eight who had served at least nine terms. Similar unpleasant surprises awaited some senior incumbents in 1990; eight who had served five or more terms were defeated, and many more had unexpectedly close calls when their vote declined sharply from their showing in 1988. The 1992 and 1994 elections also proved disastrous for some entrenched members, in the first instance largely because of the House Bank scandal (of which more in Chapter 6), in the second, because of the powerful Republican tide. Among the victims (all Democrats) in 1994 were Tom Foley of Washington, Speaker of the House (fifteen terms); Jack Brooks of Texas, chairman of the Judiciary Committee (twenty-one terms); Neal Smith of Iowa, Appropriations subcommittee chairman (eighteen terms); and Dan Glickman of Kansas, chairman of the Intelligence Committee (nine terms).

The 1992 and 1994 elections offer a powerful illustration of how fickle contemporary district electorates can be. A member's personal relationship with constituents can keep the district safely in his or her hands, but only through a continuing high level of personal attention, and only if potent new issues detrimental to the incumbent do not intrude. Mayhew noted that, to say "Congressman Smith is unbeatable" means only that he "is unbeatable as long as he continues to do the things he is doing."[51] After the 1994 election, we should add, and only as long as what he is doing is what voters care about when deciding how to vote. A wide reelection margin is maintained only through unrelenting entrepreneurial effort; let there be a letup or a slipup that attracts and is exploited by a formidable opponent wielding a potent issue, and it can evaporate quickly. The decline of partisanship among voters permits individual representatives to establish personal ties to their districts, but only as long as they are willing to invest the time and energy required to maintain them. Even then, there is no guarantee that personal ties will prevail in the face of troublesome new issues. If they refuse to pay this price, or if troublesome new issues do emerge, they may be even more vulnerable to challengers than they were in the days when they could count on a larger core of party regulars for a reliable base of support.

MOTIVATING CHALLENGERS

Most members are willing to pay the price, at least for a time; retirement or defeat awaits those who refuse.[52] Since most incumbents do work hard to remain in office and are therefore extremely difficult to defeat, it is not absurd to ask why, under most circumstances, anyone challenges them at all. Part of the answer is that a fair proportion of incumbents are not challenged. In 1998, ninety-four House incumbents had no major-party opponent in the general election, and almost all of these were spared primary opposition as well. But most are challenged, even those who appear to be unbeatable. Why?

One reason suggested by studies of congressional challengers is naivete. As David Leuthold notes in his study of San Francisco area congressional campaigns, "Inexperienced candidates often did not realize that they had no chance of winning."[53] Most challengers recognize that the odds are against them, of course, but their hopes may be buoyed by the inherent uncertainties of electoral politics and a large dose of self deception. Writing from personal experience—he is a political scientist who ran for Congress but did not get past the primary—Sandy Maisel points out that "politicians tend to have an in-credible ability to delude themselves" about their electoral prospects.[54]

Maisel's report of his own and other congressional primaries in 1978 pro-vides several additional insights into the question. Many congressional candi-dates had planned for years to run for Congress—some day. The only question was when; and when circumstances seem only a little bit more favorable than usual, their thinking was, "If not now, when?" Or, more desperately, "Now or never."[55]

Candidates can delude themselves all the more easily when they lack the re-sources to discover just how difficult their task is; impoverished candidates cannot afford a top-quality poll to gauge their status with the electorate. They most often rely instead on their own political intuition and, to a lesser degree, on the opinions of local political leaders.[56] Both are inclined to tell them what they want to hear, so it is not difficult to see why they might overestimate their chances.

Other scholars, though, discern rationality rather than naivete when the in-experienced challenge entrenched incumbents. Jeffrey Banks and D. Roderick Kiewiet argue that inexperienced challengers choose to run when their prospect of defeating the incumbent appears dim because this nonetheless maximizes their probability of getting elected to Congress. Because the long odds deter ambitious career politicians, political neophytes are much more likely to win the nomination than they would be if conditions were more promising (had, for example, the incumbent retired). Their much greater chance of winning the nomination more than offsets the smaller chance of knocking off the incumbent in the general election. The odds may be very long, but still the best an inexperienced amateur can envision.[57]

At least a few such candidates are rewarded with unanticipated success, and that no doubt encourages others to take the plunge. In 1988, for instance, Ronald Machtley, a political novice, was nominated unopposed (the expected nominee, a former state party chair, inexplicably failed to meet the filing dead-line) to face Democratic Representative Fernand J. St Germain, the powerful chairman of the Committee on Banking, Finance, and Urban Affairs. He was able to exploit St Germain's ethical problems to achieve "the most improbable triumph in recent Rhode Island history."[58] In 1990, first-time candidates man-aged to defeat Douglas Walgren of Pennsylvania and Robert Kastenmeier of Wisconsin though there was little prior indication that these veteran House in-cumbents were vulnerable.

Moreover, elections such as 1992 and 1994 show that boldness is sometimes rewarded across the board. Challengers who had put themselves in position to exploit the House Bank scandal or popular disgust with Clinton and gridlock ended up with a great shot at the brass ring. No doubt many of the Republican newcomers elected in 1994 were surprised to find themselves in the House, let alone in the majority. Their experience will serve as a seductive object lesson for prospective challengers for years to come.

Even candidates who are certain they will not win find motives for running. The most common reason given is to provide some opposition, to make sure the party is represented on the ballot, "to demonstrate that the party had a spark of life in the district."[59] Party leaders may run themselves when they are unable to find anyone else willing to face a drubbing.[60] Some run to build for their own or the party's future, as did many southern Republicans in the 1950s and early 1960s. Others run to promote strongly held ideological beliefs. Opponents of abortion and other religious conservatives have swelled the ranks of Republican challengers in recent years; in 1992, several of them used the legal requirement that TV stations run campaign ads uncensored to broadcast anti-abortion messages featuring graphic footage of aborted fetuses.[61] Still others evidently run in order to advertise themselves in their professions; this reason is not often volunteered, and with the profession of politics in such low repute, it may no longer be so common. But for much of the postwar period, a remarkable proportion of young attorneys, insurance agents, and real estate brokers turned up as challengers in districts where they had little hope of winning. Finally, some apparently find the process of running itself reward enough.[62]

Challengers who are naive, inexperienced, self-deceiving, or running without hope of winning do not make particularly formidable opponents. Incumbents blessed with such opposition win reelection easily. Still, every so often one is rudely surprised, for uncertainty is an inevitable component of congressional election politics. In important respects, electoral uncertainty has actually increased in recent years. Congressional incumbents have no monopoly on entrepreneurial electoral politics. They now face institutional players—political action committees, national party campaign committees, professional campaign outfits, independent spenders, polling and direct mail firms—equally adept at exploiting current technologies and electoral habits. How this has affected campaign politics is a subject for the next chapter.

ENDNOTES

1. This is evident when we regress the percentage of incumbents seeking reelection who were successful against the election year (1950 = 1, 1952 = 2, ... 1998 = 25). The estimated equation is:

   Percentage of Successful Incumbents = 90.9 + .13 (Elected Year)

   $$(1.5) \quad (.09)$$

   Adusted R^2 = .04.

   The standard errors are in parentheses. The coefficient on the temporal variable (election year) has a t-ratio of 1.45 and so is statistically indistinguishable from zero at conventional levels of statistical significance.

2. John R. Alford and David W. Brady, "Personal and Partisan Advantage in U.S. Congressional Elections, 1846-1990," in *Congress Reconsidered*, 5th ed., eds. Lawrence C. Dodd and Bruce I. Oppenheimer (Washington, DC: Congressional Quarterly Press, 1993), pp. 146-147.

3. Albert D. Cover and David R. Mayhew, "Congressional Dynamics and the Decline of Competitive Congressional Elections," in *Congress Reconsidered*, 2nd ed., eds. Lawrence C. Dodd and Bruce I. Oppenheimer (Washington, DC: Congressional Quarterly Press, 1981), p. 70; see also Robert S. Erikson, "Malapportionment, Gerrymandering, and Party Fortunes in Congressional Elections," *American Political Science Review* 66 (1972): 1240.

4. David W. Brady, Brian Gaines, and Douglas Rivers, "The Incumbency Advantage in the House and Senate: A Comparative Institutional Analysis" (Manuscript, Stanford University, 1994).
5. Andrew Gelman and Gary King, "Measuring Incumbency without Bias," *American Journal of Political Science* 34 (1990): 1142-1164; Michael Krashinsky and William J. Milne, "The Effects of Incumbency in U.S. Congressional Elections, 1950-1988," *Legislative Studies Quarterly* 18 (1993): 321-344; Brady, Gaines, and Rivers, "Incumbency Advantage."
6. Gelman and King compute the incumbency advantage by regressing the Democrat's share of the two-party vote on the Democrat's vote in the previous election, the party holding the seat, and incumbency (which takes a value of 1 if the Democratic candidate is an incumbent, -1 if the Republican is an incumbent, 0 if the seat is open). The coefficient on the incumbency variable estimates the value (in percentage of votes) of incumbency for each election year.
7. Brady, Gaines, and Rivers, "Incumbency Advantage," Table 3.
8. David R. Mayhew, "Congressional Elections: The Case of the Vanishing Marginals," *Polity* 6 (1974):295-317.
9. To calculate the swing ratio, simply divide the change in the percentage of seats a party wins by the change in the percentage of votes it wins; for example, if one party's share of seats rises from 45 percent to 55 percent when its share of the vote rises from 47 percent to 52 percent, the swing ratio is 2.0 ($(55 - 45)/(52 - 47) = 2.0$); see Erikson, "Malapportionment," pp. 1240-1241; Edward R. Tufte, "The Relationship between Seats and Votes in Two-Party Systems," *American Political Science Review* 67 (1973):540-554; Mayhew, "Vanishing Marginals," pp. 312-314; Cover and Mayhew, "Congressional Dynamics," p. 78; Morris P. Fiorina, "The Case of the Vanishing Marginals: The Bureaucracy Did It," *American Political Science Review* 71 (1977):177.
10. John A. Ferejohn and Randall Calvert, "Presidential Coattails in Historical Perspective," *American Journal of Political Science* 28 (1984):131; Gary C. Jacobson, "The Marginals Never Vanished: Incumbency and Competition in Elections to the U.S. House of Representatives, 1952-1982," *American Journal of Political Science* 31 (1987):126-141.
11. Thomas E. Mann, *Unsafe at Any Margin: Interpreting Congressional Elections* (Washington, DC: American Enterprise Institute for Public Policy Research, 1977), p. 90.
12. The increase in volatility remains when effects of changes in the sophomore surge and retirement slump are removed; see Gary C. Jacobson, *The Electoral Origins of Divided Government: Competition in U.S. House Elections, 1946-1988* (Boulder, Colorado: Westview Press, 1990), pp. 17-18.
13. Ibid., pp. 82-93.
14. *Washington Post*, May 24, 1989, B3:4.
15. David R. Mayhew, *Congress: The Electoral Connection* (New Haven: Yale University Press, 1974), pp. 81-82.
16. Ibid., pp. 99-100.

17. Glenn R. Parker and Roger H. Davidson, "Why Do Americans Love Their Congressmen So Much More Than Their Congress?" *Legislative Studies Quarterly* 4 (1979):53-61.
18. Roger H. Davidson and Walter J. Oleszek, *Congress and Its Members*, 6th ed. (Washington, DC: Congressional Quarterly Press, 1998), p. 145.
19. "GOP's House-Cleaning Sweep Changes Rules, Cuts Groups," *Congressional Quarterly Weekly Report* 52 (December 10, 1994):3487.
20. Ibid.
21. Mayhew, *Congress*, p. 311.
22. John A. Ferejohn, "On the Decline of Competition in Congressional Elections," *American Political Science Review* 71 (1977):174.
23. Norman J. Ornstein, Thomas E. Mann, and Michael J. Malbin, *Vital Statistics on Congress 1997-1998* (Washington, DC: Congressional Quarterly Press, 1998), Tables 5-3 and 5-4.
24. Fiorina, *Congress*, p. 180.
25. Glenn R. Parker and Suzanne L. Parker, "The Correlates and Effects of Attention to District by U.S. House Members," *Legislative Studies Quarterly* 10 (1985):239.
26. Paul Feldman and James Jondrow, "Congressional Elections and Local Federal Spending," *American Journal of Political Science* 28 (1984):152; Patrick Sellers, "Fiscal Consistency and Federal District Spending in Congressional Elections" (Paper delivered at the Annual Meeting of the Midwest Political Science Association, Chicago 14-16, 1994); R. Michael Alvarez and Jason L. Saving, "Deficits, Democrats, and Distributive Benefits: Congressional Elections and the Pork Barrel in the 1980s," *Political Research Quarterly* 50 (December 1997):809-831; Kenneth N. Bickers and Robert M. Stein, "The Electoral Dynamics of the Federal Pork Barrel," *American Journal of Political Science* 40 (November 1996):1300-1326.
27. See John R. Johannes and John C. McAdams, "The Congressional Incumbency Effect: Is It Casework, Policy Compatibility, or Something Else?"; Morris P. Fiorina, "Some Problems in Studying the Effects of Resource Allocation in Congressional Elections"; Diana Evans Yiannakis, "The Grateful Electorate: Casework and Congressional Elections"; and John C. McAdams and John R. Johannes, "Does Casework Matter? A Reply to Professor Fiorina," all in *American Journal of Political Science* 25 (1981):512-604; Lynda W. Powell, "Constituency Service and Electoral Margin in Congress" (Paper delivered at the Annual Meeting of the American Political Science Association, Denver, September 2-5, 1982); John R. Johannes and John McAdams, "The Effect of Congressional Casework on Elections" (Paper delivered at the Annual Meeting of the American Political Science Association, New Orleans, August 29–September 1, 1985); Albert C. Cover and Bruce S. Brumberg, "Baby Books and Ballots: The Impact of Congressional Mail on Constituent Opinion," *American Political Science Review* 76 (1982):347-359; John R. Johannes, *To Serve the People: Congress and Constituency Service* (Lincoln: University of Nebraska Press, 1984); Morris P. Fiorina and Douglas Rivers, "Constituency Service, Reputation, and the Incumbency Advantage," in *Members of Congress at Home and in Washington*, eds. Morris P. Fiorina and David Rohde (Ann Arbor: University of

Michigan Press, 1989); George Serra and Albert D. Cover, "The Electoral Consequences of Perquisite Use: The Casework Case," *Legislative Studies Quarterly* 17 (1992):233-246; George Serra, "What's in It for Me? The Impact of Congressional Casework on Incumbent Evaluation," *American Politics Quarterly* 22 (1994):403-420; David W. Romero, "The Case of the Missing Reciprocal Influence: Incumbent Reputation and the Vote," *Journal of Politics* 58 (November 1996):1198-1207.

28. Fiorina, *Congress*, 94-97; Fiorina, "Resource Allocation in Congressional Elections," pp. 545-550; Bickers and Stein, "Federal Pork Barrel."

29. Morris P. Fiorina, "The Incumbency Factor," *Public Opinion* (September/October, 1978):42-44.

30. Jacobson, *Divided Government*, p. 15-19 and 56-57.

31. Parker and Parker, "Attention to District by U.S. House Members," p. 229; see also Glenn R. Parker, *Homeward Bound: Explaining Changes in Congressional Behavior* (Pittsburgh: University of Pittsburg Press, 1986).

32. Charles M. Tidmarch, "The Second Time Around: Freshman Democratic House Members' 1976 Reelection Experiences" (Paper delivered at the Annual Meeting of the American Political Science Association, Washington, DC, September 1-4, 1977), p. 27.

33. "Freshmen: New Powerful Voice," *Congressional Quarterly Weekly Report* 53 (October 28, 1995), p. 3251.

34. Gary C. Jacobson and Samuel Kernell, *Strategy and Choice in Congressional Elections*, 2d ed. (New Haven: Yale University Press, 1983), Chapter 3; Bruce W. Robeck, "State Legislator Candidates for the U.S. House: Prospects for Success," *Legislative Studies Quarterly* 7 (1982):511-512; Thomas A. Kazee, "Ambition and Candidacy: Running as a Strategic Calculation," in *Who Runs for Congress? Ambition, Context, and Candidate Emergence,* ed. Thomas A. Kazee (Washington, DC: Congressional Quarterly Press, 1994), pp. 171-177; L. Sandy Maisel and Walter P. Stone, "Determinants of Candidate Emergence in U.S. House Elections: An Exploratory Study," *Legislative Studies Quarterly* 22 (February 1997):79-96.

35. For additional evidence of strategic behavior among political challengers, see Jon R. Bond, Cary Covington, and Richard Fleisher, "Explaining Challenger Quality in Congressional Elections," *Journal of Politics* 47 (1985):523; William T. Bianco, "Strategic Decisions on Candidacy in U.S. Congressional Districts," *Legislative Studies Quarterly* 9 (1984):360; Gary C. Jacobson, "Strategic Politicians and the Dynamics of U.S. House Elections, 1946-1986," *American Political Science Review* 83 (1989):773-793; David Lublin, "Quality, Not Quantity: Strategic Politicians in U.S. Senate Elections," *Journal of Politics* 56 (1994):228-241. Candidates who have held elective office are not the only high-quality challengers, to be sure; some "ambitious amateurs" are equally effective and equally strategic in their behavior. See David T. Canon, *Actors, Athletes, and Astronauts: Political Amateurs in the United States Congress* (Chicago: University of Chicago Press, 1990). Decisions to contest open House seats are also strategic; see Jon R. Bond, Richard Fleisher, and Jeffrey C. Talbert, "Partisan Differences in Candidate Quality in Open Seat House Races, 1976-1994," *Political Research Quarterly* 50 (1997):281-299.

36. Gary C. Jacobson, *Money in Congressional Elections* (New Haven: Yale University Press, 1980), p. 72-101.

37. Gary W. Cox and Jonathan Katz, "Why Did the Incumbency Advantage in U.S. House Elections Grow?" *Journal of Politics* 40 (1996):478-497.

38. Brady, Gaines, and Rivers, "Incumbency Advantage," p. 14.

39. Jacobson, *Money in Congressional Elections*, p. 136-145; Gary C. Jacobson, "Money and Votes Reconsidered: Congressional Elections, 1972-1982," *Public Choice* 47 (1985):16-40; Gary C. Jacobson, "Enough Is Too Much: Money and Competition in House Elections, 1972-1984," in *Elections in America*, ed. Kay L. Schlozman (Boston: Allen and Unwin, 1987), pp. 173-195; Gary C. Jacobson, "The Effects of Campaigning in House Elections: New Evidence for Old Arguments," *American Journal of Political Science* 34 (1990):334-362. For the contrary argument that incumbent spending has powerful effects, see Donald P. Green and Jonathan S. Krasno, "Salvation for the Spendthrift Incumbent: Reestimating the Effects of Campaign Spending in House Elections," *American Journal of Political Science* 32 (1988):884-907, and Donald P. Green and Jonathan S. Krasno, "Rebuttal to Jacobson's 'New Evidence for Old Arguments,'" *American Journal of Political Science* 34 (1990):363-372.

40. Jacobson, *Money in Congressional Elections*, pp. 136-146; Alan I. Abramowitz, "Incumbency, Campaign Spending, and the Decline of Competition in U.S. House Elections," *Journal of Politics* 53 (1991):34-56; Stephen Ansolabehere and Alan Gerber, "The Mismeasure of Campaign Spending: Evidence from the 1990 U.S. House Elections," *Journal of Politics* 56(1994):1106-1118. Ansolabehere and Gerber show that the result holds if only money spent directly on campaign communications is measured as spending, although the coefficient on communications spending is naturally larger than the coefficient on total spending in their model.

41. Alan I. Abramowitz, "Explaining Senate Election Outcomes," *American Political Science Review* 82 (1988):385-403; Jacobson, *Money in Congressional Elections*, pp. 152-155.

42. Ibid.; Green and Krasno, "Effects of Campaign Spending"; Stephen Ansolabehere and James M. Snyder, Jr., "Money, Elections, and Candidate Quality" (MIT, typescript); Stephen Levitt, "Using Repeat Challengers to Estimate the Effects of Campaign Spending on Election Outcomes in the U.S. House," *Journal of Political Economy* 102 (1994):777-798.

43. Robert S. Erikson and Thomas Palfrey, "Campaign Spending and Incumbency: An Alternative Simultaneous Equation Approach," *Journal of Politics* 60 (1998):355-373; Robert K. Goidel and Donald A. Gross, "A Systems Approach to Campaign Finance in U.S. House Elections," *American Politics Quarterly* 22 (1994):125-153; Christopher Kenny and Michael McBurnett, "An Individual Level Multiequation Model of Expenditure Effects in Contested House Elections," *American Political Science Review* 88 (1994):669-707; Larry Bartels, "Instrumental and 'Quasi-instrumental' Variables, " *American Journal of Political Science* 35 (1991):777-800.

44. Losing House incumbents 1992-1998 spent an average of more than $1 million; 89 percent spent more than $600,000; 74 percent outspent their victorious challenger.

45. Jacobson, "Money and Votes Reconsidered," pp. 28-30.

46. Or so politicians think. One empirical study found that district attention, variously measured, had no discernible effect on the quality of the challenger or the money spent against the incumbent; see Bond, Covington, and Fleisher, "Challenger Quality in Congressional Elections," p. 523. But this study is subject to the same doubts raised about negative finds in other studies of the effects of district attention, discussed earlier.
47. Quoted in Richard F. Fenno, Jr., *Home Style: House Members in Their Districts* (Boston: Little Brown and Company, 1977), p. 13.
48. Ibid., Chapter 6.
49. See Robeck, "State Legislator Candidates," p. 511; Harvey L. Schantz, "Contested and Uncontested Primaries for the U.S. House," *Legislative Studies Quarterly* 5 (1980):550; and David T. Canon, "Contesting Primaries in Congressional Elections: 1972-1988" (Paper delivered at the Annual Meeting of the American Political Science Association, Atlanta, August 31-September 3, 1989), p. 14.
50. For example, here is Martin Franks, then executive director of the Democratic Congressional Campaign Committee, on why first-termers head the Democrats' target list: "The best chance of getting them is now. Every day they are here they become harder to unseat." Quoted in David Kaplan, "Freshmen Find It Easier to Run as Incumbents," *Congressional Quarterly Weekly Report* 43 (November 2, 1985), p. 2225.
51. Mayhew, *Congress*, p. 37.
52. See, for example, the story of how Fred Eckert, a first-term incumbent Republican, managed to lose a Republican district in upstate New York; Linda L. Fowler and Robert D. McClure, *Political Ambition: Who Decides to Run for Congress?* (New Haven: Yale University Press, 1989).
53. David A. Leuthold, *Electioneering in a Democracy: Campaigns for Congress* (New York: John Wiley, 1968), p. 22.
54. L. Sandy Maisel, *From Obscurity to Oblivion: Running in the Congressional Primary* (Knoxville: University of Tennessee Press, 1982), p. 23.
55. Ibid., p. 17.
56. Ibid., Table 2.2; see also Fowler and McClure, *Political Ambition*, p. 68.
57. Jeffrey S. Banks and D. Roderick Kiewiet, "Explaining Patterns of Candidate Competition in Congressional Elections," *American Journal of Political Science* 33 (1989):997-1015. For a contrary view, see David C. Canon, "Sacrificial Lambs or Strategic Politicians? Political Amateurs in U.S. House Elections," *American Journal of Political Science* 37 (1993):1119-1141.
58. "Rhode Island—1st District," *Congressional Quarterly Weekly Report* 46 (December 31, 1988), p. 3618.
59. Robert J. Huckshorn and Robert C. Spencer, *the Politics of Defeat* (Amherst: University of Massachusetts Press, 1971), p. 75.
60. See John F. Bibby, "The Case of the Young Old Pro: The Sixth District of Wisconsin," in *The Making of Congressmen: Seven Campaigns of 1974*, ed. Alan L. Clem (North Scituate, Massachusetts: Duxbury Press, 1976), p. 216, for an example.
61. "Campaign Crusaders Air Graphic Anti-Abortion Ads," *Congressional Quarterly Weekly Report* 50 (September 26, 1992):2970-2971.
62. Canon, *Actors, Athletes, and Astronauts*, pp. 38-39.

CHAPTER FOUR

Congressional Campaigns

I t should be apparent by now that much of the action in congressional election politics takes place outside the formal campaigns and election periods.
This in no way implies that campaigns are inconsequential. The bottom line
is that votes must be sought, and the most concentrated work to win them
takes place through the campaign. The formal campaign is, of course, crucial
to those candidates, including most nonincumbents, who have not been able
to match the more-or-less incessant campaigning now typical of congressional
incumbents.

Congressional election campaigns are decidedly candidate centered. They
are best understood as ventures undertaken by individual political entrepreneurs in a decentralized political marketplace. This does not mean that centralized national organizations—in particular, party committees and political action committees (PACs)—are unimportant. Quite the contrary; they have
become major players by learning to operate effectively in the candidate-
centered electoral system. Credit belongs to parties and PACs, along with independent professional campaign consultants, for the continuing stream of innovations in campaign technology and strategy that have transformed
congressional campaigning in recent years. They also, consequently, share responsibility for higher costs, harsher rhetoric, greater uncertainty, and the effects these things have had on how members of Congress do their job.

Election campaigns have a simple dominant goal: to win at least a plurality of
the votes cast and thus the election. Little else is simple about them, however.
Campaigns confront candidates with difficult problems of analysis and execu-
tion, which, even in the best of circumstances, are mastered only imperfectly.

The analytical work required for an effective congressional campaign is suggested by the variety of campaign contexts set forth in Chapter 2. States and
districts are not homogeneous lumps; voters do not form an undifferentiated
mass. They are divided by boundaries of community, class, race, politics, moral
values, and geography. Candidates (and those who help them put campaigns
together) need to recognize these boundaries and to understand their implications for building winning coalitions. Often, those without political experience
do not, and this in itself guarantees failure.[1]

The basic questions are straightforward: Which constituents are likely to become solid supporters? Who might be persuaded? Which groups are best written off as hopeless? How can potential supporters be reached? How can they
be induced to show up at the polls on election day? What kinds of appeals are
likely to attract their support? All of these questions must be answered twice,
and in different ways, if there is a primary contest. They cannot be addressed at

all without some cognitive handle on the constituency: Campaigners are perforce theorists.

Successful campaigners recognize this, at least implicitly. Members of the House develop highly differentiated images of their constituencies. Their behavior is guided by a coherent diagnosis of district components and forces. Knowledge is grounded in experience; they learn at least as much about their constituents from campaigning and from visiting the district between elections as their constituents learn about them. This kind of learning takes time, and its necessity is another reason for viewing House elections from a time perspective longer than a campaign period or a two-year term.[2] It is also one source of the incumbency advantage and helps to explain why politically experienced nonincumbents make superior House candidates.

The analytic tasks facing Senate candidates are, in most states, substantially more formidable than those facing House candidates. Senate candidates normally deal with larger and more diverse constituencies scattered over much wider areas. Incumbents as well as challengers usually suffer far more uncertainty about how to combine constituent groups into winning coalitions. Few have the opportunity to know their states as intimately as House candidates may know their districts.

In earlier times, candidates could sometimes get a feel for unfamiliar neighborhoods and communities from local party activists who were a part of them. Now they are more likely to rely on professional research—if, of course, they can afford it. Commercial vendors offer detailed voter lists, complete with information on family income, demographics, voting history, addresses, and phone numbers. Professionally conducted polls probe the opinions and attitudes of district residents. Focus groups—small groups of ordinary citizens brought together to mull over candidates and issues under the guidance and observation of experienced researchers—provide a sense of what lies behind the polling results. Intelligence gathering, like every other aspect of campaigning, can now be farmed out to specialists if a campaign has enough money to hire them.[3]

The deepest understanding of the political texture of a state or district will not, by itself, win elections. Effective campaigns require a strategy for gathering at least a plurality of votes and the means to carry out that strategy. The central problem is communication. As the next chapter will show, what voters know about candidates has a strong effect on how they decide to vote. Voters who have no information about a candidate are much less likely to vote for him or her than those who do. The content of the information is equally consequential, to be sure, but no matter how impressive the candidate or persuasive the message, it will not help if potential voters remain unaware of them.

Two resources are necessary to communicate with voters: money and organization. They may be combined in different ways, but overcoming serious opposition requires adequate supplies of both. Money is crucial because it buys access to the media of communication: radio, television, newspapers, direct mail, pamphlets, videos, billboards, bumper stickers, bullhorns, websites, and so on. Organization is necessary to design and execute campaign strategy, to raise money, to schedule the candidate's use of personal time devoted to culti-vating voters and contributors, and to help get out the vote on election day.

CAMPAIGN MONEY

Raising money is, by consensus, the most unpleasant part of a campaign. Many candidates find it demeaning to ask people for money and are uncomfortable with the implications of accepting.[4] Most do it, however, because they cannot get elected without it. The trick, neophyte campaigners are advised, is to "learn how to beg, and do it in a way that leaves you with some dignity."[5]

Congressional campaign finances are regulated by the Federal Election Cam-paign Act (FECA) and its amendments, enforced by the Federal Election Com-mission. The law requires full disclosure of the sources of campaign contribu-tions and also restricts the amount of money that parties, groups, and individuals may give to congressional candidates.[6] The FECA was originally in-tended to limit campaign costs and to reduce the influence of monied interests in electoral politics. The opposite has occurred, partly because the Supreme Court declared limits on campaign spending to be an unconstitutional violation of the First Amendment,[7] partly because the act itself, by establishing a clear legal framework for campaign finance activities, has invited parties and PACs to flourish.[8] Aside from its other effects, the FECA has at least given us reasonably accurate information on the flow of funds through congressional campaigns.

Aggregate figures on the amounts and sources of money contributed to House and Senate campaigns from 1972 through 1998 are presented in Table 4-1. Average campaign receipts have grown steadily, though the growth rate is considerably less impressive than these nominal dollar figures would suggest when inflation is taken into account. In real dollars, contributions to House candidates have grown an average of 8 percent, those to Senate candidates, 9 percent, from election year to election year over this period.

The greatest share of campaign money is contributed by private individuals; Senate candidates are especially dependent on individual donations. PACs are the second-most important source of campaign funds. Their share grew rather steadily until the early 1990s, peaking at 44 percent for House candidates (1990) and 25 percent for Senate candidates (1992) before falling back in the three most recent elections to, respectively, about 35 percent and 19 percent. This category includes the various committees organized by unions, corpora-tions, trade and professional associations, ideological and issue-oriented groups of many kinds, and political leaders.

Political Action Committees

There is a simple explanation for the growth and then modest decline in the fi-nancial importance of PACs. As campaign costs increased and the real value of the dollar declined (losing more than half of its value between 1974 and 1986), candidates, constrained by the FECA's fixed contribution limits, naturally put more effort into soliciting funds from sources that may legally contribute up to

TABLE 4–1 SOURCES OF CAMPAIGN CONTRIBUTIONS TO HOUSE AND SENATE CANDIDATES, 1972–1998

	AVERAGE CONTRIBUTIONS	PERCENTAGE OF CONTRIBUTIONS FROM:				
		Individuals	Parties	PACs	Candidates[a]	Unknown
House						
1972	$ 51,752[b]	60[c]	27	14	—	9
1974	$ 61,084	73	4	17	6	—
1976	$ 79,421	59	8	23	9	—
1978	$ 111,232	61	5	25	9	—
1980	$ 148,268	67[c]	4	29	—	—
1982	$ 222,260	63[c]	6	31	—	—
1984	$ 240,722	51	3	39	6	—
1986	$ 280,260	52	2	39	7	—
1988	$ 282,949	49	2	43	6	—
1990	$ 291,246	48	1	44	7	—
1992	$ 358,925	50	1	39	10	—
1994	$ 414,812	54	1	37	8	—
1996	$ 510,997	55	1	34	7	3
1998	$ 544,349	53	1	36	6	4
Senate						
1972	$ 353,933[b]	67	14	12	0.4	8
1974	$ 455,515	76	6	11	1	6
1976	$ 624,094	69	4	15	12	—
1978	$ 951,390	70	6	13	8	—
1980	$1,079,346	78[c]	2	21	—	—
1982	$1,771,167	81[c]	1	18	—	—
1984	$2,273,635	68	1	20	11	—
1986	$2,721,793	69	1	25	6	—
1988	$2,649,492	68	1	26	6	—
1990	$2,166,031	70	1	24	5	—
1992	$2,638,964	68	1	25	6	—
1994	$3,659,650	61	1	17	22	—
1996	$3,274,940	63	1	19	13	4
1998	$3,530,099	62	1	19	12	6

[a]Includes candidates' loans unrepaid at time of filing.
[b]Some contributions before April 7, 1972, may have gone unrecorded.
[c]Includes candidates' contributions to their own campaigns.

Sources: Compiled by author from data supplied by Common Cause (1972 and 1974) and the Federal Election Commission (1976–1994).

$10,000—the PACs—and less into soliciting private individuals, who may contribute only one-fifth as much. As Figures 4–1 and 4–2 indicate, the number of PACs available for solicitation also grew dramatically during the first decade under the FECA, as did the amount of money at their disposal. This growth flattened out in the mid-1980s while campaigns continued to raise larger sums, eventually reducing the PACs' share of the total.

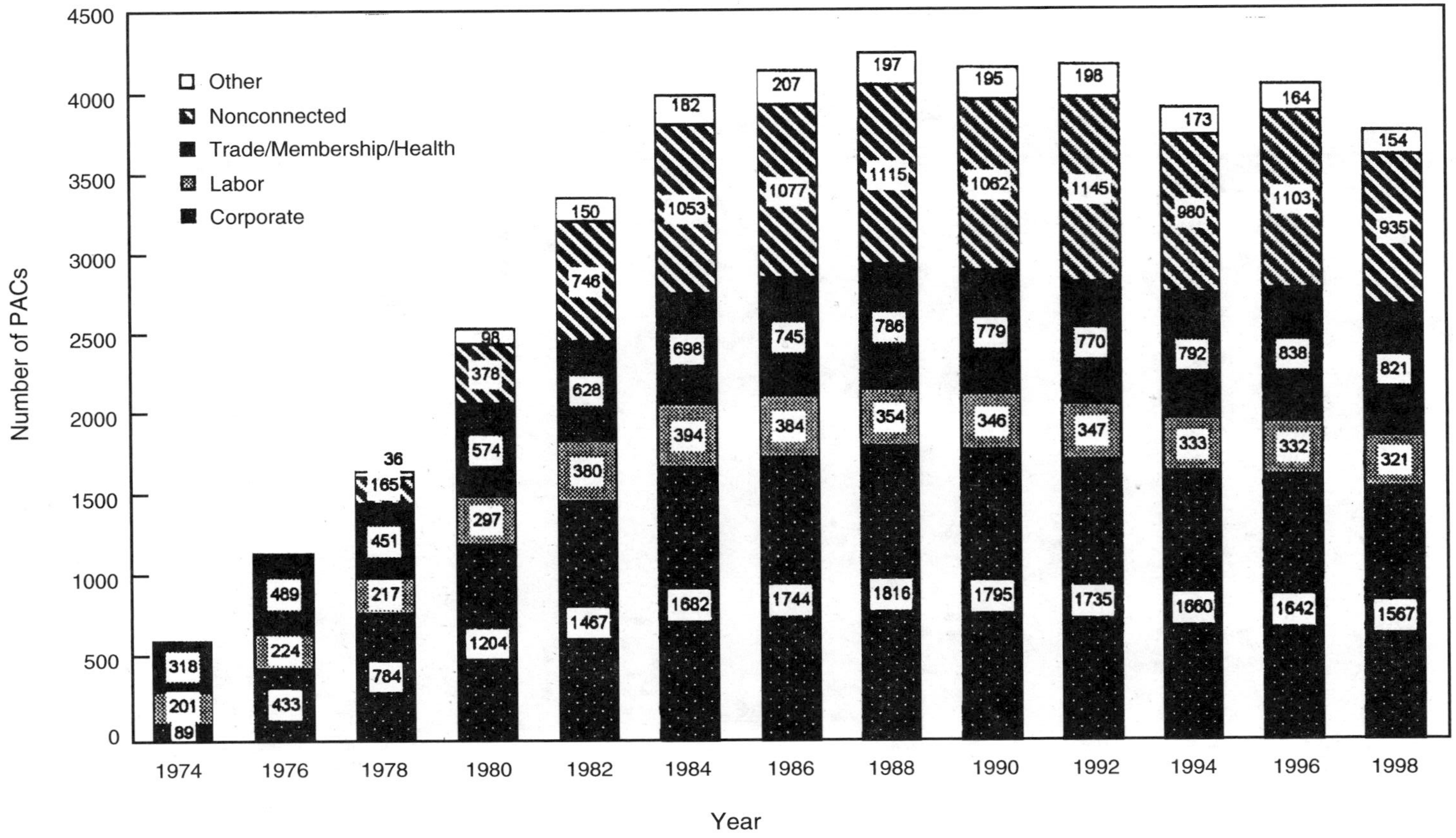

FIGURE 4-1. Political Action Committees, 1974–1998
Source: Federal Election Commission.

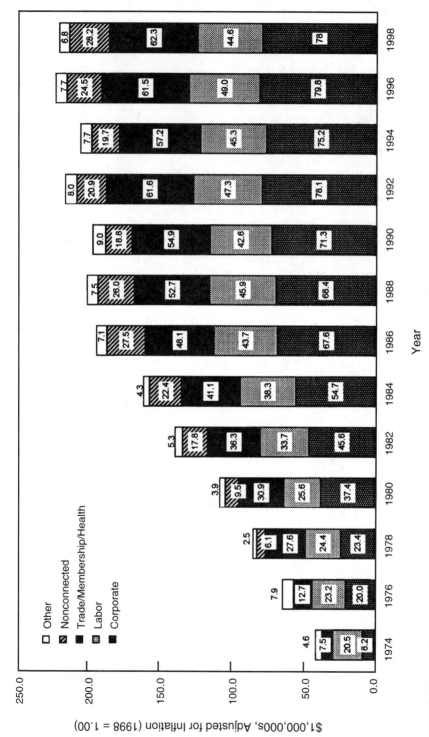

FIGURE 4–2. Contributions by Political Action Committees, 1974–1998
Source: Federal Election Commission.

Business-oriented PACs have grown the most in both numbers and total contributions to congressional candidates under the FECA. The number of corporate PACs rose from 89 to 1,816 between 1974 and 1988 before falling off to 1,567 in 1998, and corporate PAC contributions have multiplied more than eightfold in real (inflation-adjusted) dollars since 1974. Corporate PAC contributions surpassed those of labor PACs in 1980, and because business associations predominate in the trade/membership/health category, labor's importance relative to business as a source of campaign funds has declined.

This development initially promised headaches for Democrats. Organized labor has traditionally been the Democrats' principal source of PAC funds, and only labor PACs have shown much inclination to supply the venture capital so important to the party's nonincumbent candidates. The overwhelming preference of labor PACs for Democratic candidates is documented in Figures 4-3a-b. Initially, the growing financial strength of corporate and trade association PACs was expected to benefit Republicans, and according to the data in Figures 4-4a-b and 4-5a-b, this expectation was borne out in 1978 and 1980. Republican challengers in both House and Senate contests were treated generously (compared to other election years) by business-oriented PACs in these elections.

After 1980, however, business PACs became far more even-handed—49 percent of corporate, and 54 percent of trade association PAC dollars went to Democrats in 1994, for example—but only because so many of them pursued a dual strategy. They were generous to incumbents of either party who were in positions to help or hurt their interests and likely to remain there. As long as Democrats controlled Congress, business-oriented PACs sought to keep doors open and to avoid antagonizing Democratic members who looked unbeatable. Hence their generosity to incumbent Democrats and stinginess with Republican challengers. They were, however, also willing to support promising nonincumbent Republicans—insofar as they could find any—as part of a long-term strategy aimed at electing a more Republican, hence more ideologically congenial, Congress. Nonincumbent Democrats were given very short shrift.

Because PACs contribute strategically, the pattern of PAC contributions displayed in these figures varies with electoral expectations. Business-oriented PACs give more to nonincumbent Republicans when Republican prospects look bright, particularly in Senate elections (note 1980 and 1994), and more to Republican incumbents when the opportunities for taking seats from Democrats look dim and Republican incumbents face strong Democratic challenges, as in 1982 or, for Senate elections, 1984 and 1986.[9]

Labor does the same thing from the opposite side, investing relatively more in Democratic challenges when conditions favor Democrats (for example, 1982, 1986 and 1996), relatively less when they do not. Because it matters a great deal how much challengers raise and spend, strategic contributions by PACs and other donors reinforce national partisan trends, with important consequences (discussed at length in Chapter 6). Both business and labor PACs tend to give lavishly to candidates for open seats of their preferred party; the absence of an incumbent makes for a more competitive election and the best opportunity to take a seat from the other party.

Several notable trends appear in these data. Note first the sharp decline in proportion of corporate and trade association PAC money given to nonincum-

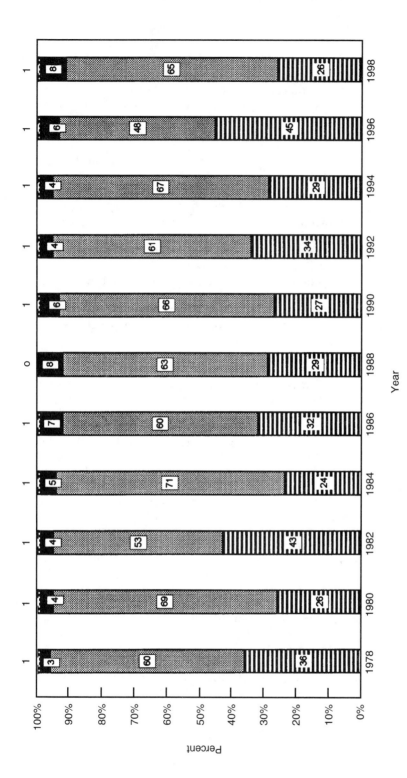

FIGURE 4–3A. The Distribution of Labor PAC Contributions to House Candidates, 1978–1998

Source: Federal Election Commission data.

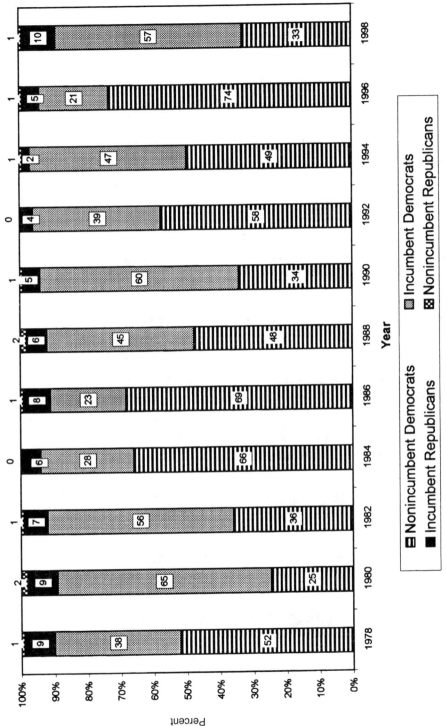

FIGURE 4–3B. The Distribution of Labor PAC Contributions to Senate Candidates, 1978–1998
Source: Federal Election Commission.

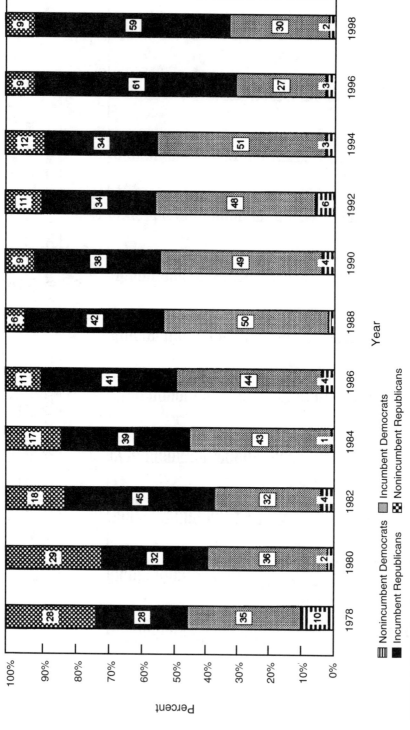

FIGURE 4-4A. The Distribution of Corporate PAC Contributions to House Candidates, 1978–1998
Source: Federal Election Commission.

66

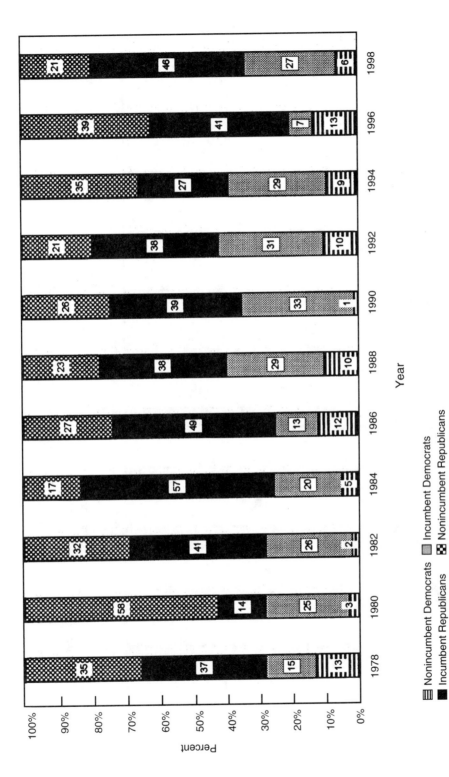

FIGURE 4-4B. The Distribution of Corporate PAC Contributions to Senate Candidates, 1978–1998
Source: Federal Election Commission.

Legend:
- Nonincumbent Democrats
- Incumbent Democrats
- Incumbent Republicans
- Nonincumbent Republicans

Year

Percent

67

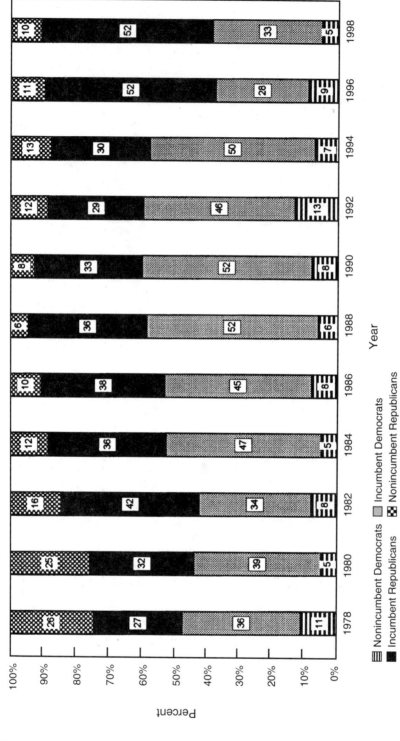

FIGURE 4-5A. The Distribution of Trade/Membership/Health PAC Contributions to House Candidates, 1978–1998
Source: Federal Election Commission.

Legend: Nonincumbent Democrats · Incumbent Democrats · Incumbent Republicans · Nonincumbent Republicans

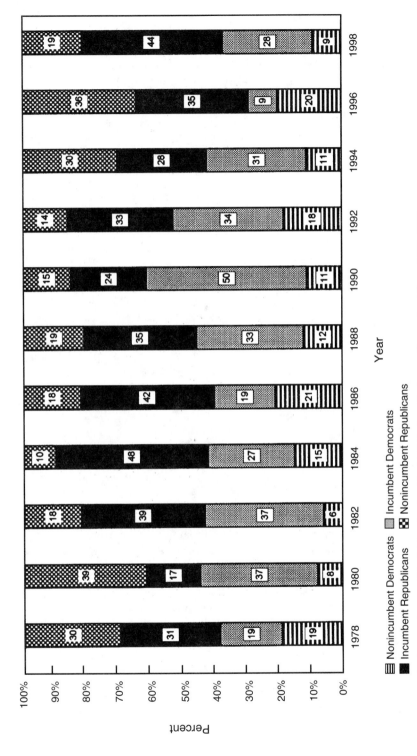

FIGURE 4–5B. The Distribution of Trade/Membership/Health PAC Contributions to Senate Candidates, 1978–1998
Source: Federal Election Commission.

bent Republican House candidates (from more than 25 percent in 1978 and 1980 to a paltry 6 percent in 1988) and the parallel rise in money given to Democratic incumbents (from 35 percent to more than 50 percent) through the 1980s. These patterns reflect several realities. First, Republican challengers were, as a group, unusually unpromising in the 1986–1990 period.[10] Second, and related, Republican challengers lacked telling issues. (Both of these phenomena are discussed in Chapter 6.) Finally, Democratic officials pursued business PAC funds vigorously, with pointed reminders as to which party would, in all likelihood, control Congress after the election.[11] Indeed, Democrats were so successful at raising PAC money, at least for their incumbents, that by the late 1980s, Republican leaders, who had initially celebrated PACs as a healthy expression of pluralist democracy, wanted to ban them outright.[12]

The 1994 election changed all that. Even before election day, the Republican surge caught the eye of PAC officials, who began opening their coffers to competitive nonincumbents. Some were no doubt responding to prospective Speaker Newt Gingrich's October threat that those who did not join the Republican cause could expect "the two coldest years in Washington" after the election.[13] After the election, pragmatic business PACs scrambled to atone for years of supporting incumbent Democrats by helping newly elected Republicans to retire their campaign debts and prepare for 1996. Willing to make a marriage of convenience with Democrats as long as Democrats were running the show, they were now free to pursue a love match with the ideologically more compatible Republicans. And Republicans no longer talked of banning PACs.[14] Without their majority status and committee power to attract PAC contributions from business interests, the balance of PAC campaign resources shifted against the Democrats.

The shift is clearly evident in Figures 4-4a-b and 4-5a-b, most strikingly in the data for House elections. In the period 1988–1994, corporate PACs gave an average of 53 percent of their money to Democrats, 49 percent to Democratic incumbents. For the two elections following the Republican takeover of Congress, the respective figures were 31 percent and 29 percent. A nearly identical shift occurs in the pattern of trade association PAC donations. Of course, some of the change reflects the increase in the relative number of Republican incumbents; but a more detailed analysis taking this and other relevant factors into account found that loss of majority status cost Democrat incumbents an average of roughly $36,000 in corporate and trade association PAC contributions, a reduction of about 19 percent in money from these sources.[15]

PAC contributions to Senate candidates are also influenced by majority status, although contribution patterns are a good deal more variable across elections years, reflecting variations in the incidence of competitive campaigns and in the set of states holding Senate elections. Over the years covered by Figures 4-4b and 4-5b, Democrats running for reelection to the Senate got an average of 47 percent of corporate and 42 percent of trade association PAC contributions when Democrats controlled the Senate, compared with 32 percent and 28 percent, respectively, when they did not. Again, a more detailed analysis indicates that, all else being equal, Senate majority status is worth an average of about $51,000 in corporate and trade association PAC contributions.[16]

The "nonconnected" category is made up largely of PACs with clear ideological or issue agendas, many of which therefore care more about influencing the makeup of Congress than about having access to officeholders. They thus comprise the only set with any inclination to be more generous to nonincumbents than to incumbents. The notable shift, displayed in Figures 4-6a-b, over time among nonconnected PACs from a strongly pro-Republican to a pro-Democratic bias reflects a change in the composition of this category. These groups raise most of their money through direct mail appeals, which are most effective when they invoke threats that make people fearful or angry enough to send a check, which is easier to do in opposition than in power. Conservative PACs thus flourished in the late 1970s, when all bad things could be blamed on Jimmy Carter, Tip O'Neill, and Teddy Kennedy. Later, liberal PACs found gold in the Reagan administration, which, along with policies that threatened liberal values, offered such serviceable villains as James Watt (a Secretary of the Interior openly hostile to the environmental movement) and Edwin Meese (an uncompromisingly conservative Attorney General). Conservative ideological PACs began to revive once Bill Clinton became available as bogeyman, and in 1994 nonincumbent Republicans running for the House got more money than Democrats from nonconnected PACs for the first time since 1984. Even these groups show a substantial shift favoring Republican candidates since their party took over majority status in 1994.

Party Money

Judging by the evidence presented in Table 4-1, the political parties are an unimportant and diminishing source of campaign money. They now account for only a tiny share of direct contributions received by House and Senate candidates. However, these data vastly understate the amount of help, financial and otherwise, congressional candidates receive from party sources.

Direct party contributions are limited to $5,000 per candidate per election for House candidates. This means that any party committee can give, at most, $10,000 to a candidate in an election year ($15,000 if there is a primary runoff). Both the national committees and the congressional campaign committees of each party can contribute this amount, so direct national party contributions can amount to $20,000 in House campaigns, perhaps 5 percent of what it costs to run a minimally serious campaign. The maximum allowable contribution to Senate candidates from all national party sources is even smaller: $17,500. Parties cannot be a major source of *direct* campaign contributions because the FECA will not allow it.

The FECA contains a special provision allowing party committees to spend money *on behalf of* congressional candidates, however. This coordinated spending, as it is called, is also limited, but the limits are higher and, unlike contribution limits, rise with inflation. The original limit of $10,000 set in 1974 for House campaigns had, by 1998, grown to $32,550. The ceiling on coordinated party spending for Senate candidates varies with the state's population; in 1998 it ranged from $65,100 in the five least populous states to $1,517,937 in California. The Senate limit applies to House candidates in states with a single

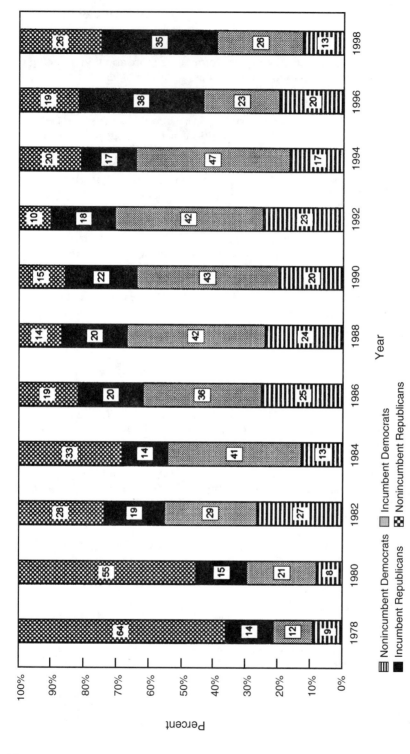

FIGURE 4–6A. The Distribution of Nonconnected PAC Contributions to House Candidates, 1978–1998
Source: Federal Election Commission.

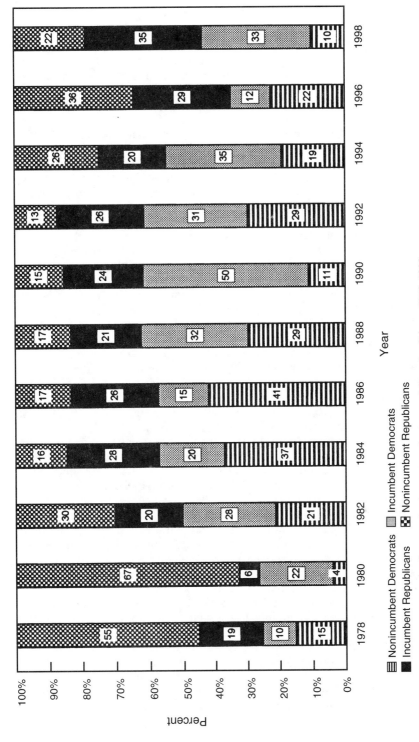

FIGURE 4-6B. The Distribution of Nonconnected PAC Contributions to Senate Candidates, 1978–1998
Source: Federal Election Commission.

House seat.[17] State party committees are permitted to spend the same amount as national party committees on coordinated campaign spending but rarely have the money to do so. The parties have solved this problem by making the national party committee the state party's agent for raising and spending the money. In practice, this ploy doubles the amount the national party may spend on its candidates.

National party committees may thus play an important part in financing congressional campaigns. In 1998, for example, national party sources could give as much as $95,100 worth of assistance to a House candidate (direct donations of $5,000 in both the primary and general elections from the party's national committee, the congressional campaign committee, and the state party committee, plus twice $32,550 in coordinated expenditures). For Senate candidates, the total varied from $147,700 to $3,053,374, depending on the state's voting-age population. Although these are significant sums, they still amount to only about 20 percent of what it costs to mount a competitive campaign.

Of course, national party committees can spend money for candidates only after they have raised it. Following the FECA's enactment, Republican committees quickly outstripped their Democratic counterparts in raising funds. Between 1976 and 1984, total receipts for the National Republican Congressional Committee (NRCC) and National Republican Senatorial Committee (NRSC) grew from $14 million to $140 million. Over the same period, total receipts of the Democratic Congressional Campaign Committee (DCCC) and Democratic Senatorial Campaign Committee (DSCC) increased only from $195,000 to $19 million. Subsequently, Democratic fundraising continued to grow at a leisurely pace, and Republican fundraising fell off, so the discrepancy has shrunk. Democratic Senate and House committees raised about $60 million in 1998, compared with the Republicans' $126 million.

Republican superiority in fundraising initially gave the party's congressional candidates a considerable advantage in party resources, but the Democrats closed some of the gap in the 1990s (see Figures 4-7 and 4-8). Both parties now raise enough money to support their competitive candidates to the legal limit. In the hotly contested elections of 1994, for example, party committees spent more than $300,000 each for fourteen Republican and fourteen Democratic Senate candidates and more than $50,000 each for 140 Republican and 103 Democratic House candidates. Ironically, Republicans could not turn their early party financial advantage into an electoral advantage; and when the Democrats finally matched the Republicans in party support for congressional candidates, they lost control of Congress.

Coordinated party expenditures can be made for almost any campaign activity. The only condition is that the party as well as the candidate have some control over how the money is spent. The "Hill" committees, as they are called, typically foot the bill for conducting polls, producing campaign ads, and buying media time—major expenses in areas where technical expertise is essential. In 1992, for example, the NRCC conducted polls for 117 Republican House candidates and produced 188 TV ads for 45, including 22 nonincumbents. The DCCC itself produced no ads for Democratic candidates, but 240 used the party's media center to create their own. Party committees compile

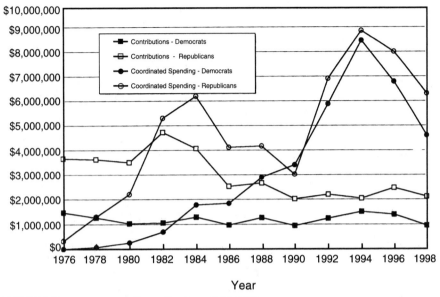

FIGURE 4–7. Party Money in House Elections, 1976-1998
Source: Federal Election Commission.

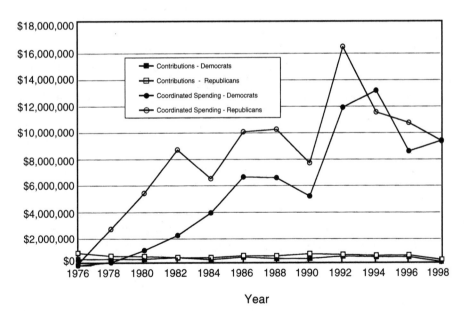

FIGURE 4–8. Party Money in Senate Elections, 1976-1998
Source: Federal Election Commission.

lists of voters for targeting, develop and hone campaign issues, and conduct "opposition research"—combing the public (and sometimes private) records of the other party's candidates to find weak points to attack. Both parties' committees also scrutinize the records of their own incumbents to detect points of vulnerability that might require special defenses.[18]

Coordinated spending does not begin to exhaust the services now performed by the Hill committees. They run programs to train candidates and campaign managers in all aspects of campaigning: fundraising, personnel management, legal compliance, advertising, press relations, and so on. Prior to the 1996 elections, for example, the Republican National Committee (RNC) held training seminars in forty-one states involving 6,000 Republican candidates and activists, the NRCC conducted three four-day candidate schools, and the NRSC offered seminars on fundraising and campaign techniques attended by representatives of twenty-two Senate campaigns. The Democratic National Committee (DNC) organized training sessions for 3,000 campaign operatives, and the DCCC and DSCC conducted training seminars for nonincumbent candidates and their campaign staffs.[19] Party committees also offer strategic advice before and during campaigns. Especially on the House side, the Hill committees have become trade schools of modern electoral politics.

The Hill committees have also assumed a central role in helping candidates raise money from PACs and other contributors. In addition to advising on fundraising techniques and targets, they serve as matchmakers between potential contributors and promising but needy candidates. PACs use party cues in making strategic investment choices, so making their party's "watch" list of competitive races has become crucial to the prospects of nonincumbent candidates. The Hill committees also arrange to have powerful, safe incumbents use their fundraising prowess to help nonincumbents and freshmen; according to one report, Speaker Newt Gingrich got more than 150 Republican incumbents with safe seats to raise $50,000 each for colleagues at risk and promising nonincumbent Republicans in 1996.[20] Hill committee staff also help candidates find suitable managers, consultants, pollsters, media specialists, direct-mail outfits, and other campaign professionals.

Expanded national party involvement in campaigns has not, however, shifted the focus of electoral politics away from individual candidates and back to parties. Rather, most of the parties' activities are explicitly designed to produce candidates who are more competitive in the candidate-centered system as it currently operates. Republicans in particular set a high priority on recruiting and training candidates, because their "farm team"—candidates holding the lower elective offices that serve as stepping-stones to Congress—was, at least prior to the 1990s, much thinner than the Democrat's. During the 1980s, national-level Republican committees even invested in state legislative races, mainly to elect more Republicans to the bodies that draw congressional district lines, but also to expand their pool of seasoned candidates. (State legislatures are the single most important source of future members of Congress; half the present members of the House have served in them.) Gingrich, while serving as Minority Leader, formed a political action committee to recruit, train, and finance candidates for state legislatures; Republicans whose initial forays into state politics were sponsored by Newt Gingrich's GOPAC swelled the ranks of the majority that elected him Speaker in 1995.[21]

The explosion of national party activity—financial and otherwise—in congressional election politics represents a sharp departure from past congressional campaign practices. Formerly, parties were most active in congressional campaigns at the state and local levels. The declining vigor of these party units and their separation from congressional campaigns helped foster the system of personal, independent campaigning now typical of congressional candidates. Parties at the national level focused on presidential elections, making only the most limited forays into other federal elections.

Recent Republican initiatives and Democratic efforts to match them have altered this pattern radically. From the beginning, national party activities clearly had the potential to reduce diversity and independence in the conduct of campaigns; the mere existence of a centralized source of advice on campaign management, strategy, and tactics imposes some uniformity on campaigns. Yet party officials are more concerned with winning elections than with restructuring electoral politics and so adapt their activities to current political habits. Not until the 1990s did the political environment offer campaign themes that resonated across numerous districts and states, and not until 1994 did these themes have a strong partisan thrust. But once conditions were right, the Republicans' national party infrastructure helped individual candidates to take full advantage of their extraordinary opportunity. I tell the story of 1994 in greater detail in Chapter 6.

Self-Financing by Candidates

Aside from individuals, PACs, and parties, candidates can also obtain campaign money from their own pockets. The Supreme Court's decision in *Buckley v. Valeo* overturned limits on how much of their own money candidates may spend to get elected, which gives no small advantage to wealthy candidates. They can finance as lavish a campaign as the family fortune allows without the aggravation fundraising entails, while their opponents must spend time hustling limited donations from a large number of individuals and groups. Peter Fitzgerald, for example, spent $11.7 million of his own money in defeating incumbent Carol Moseley-Braun in a 1998 race for one of Illinois' Senate seats. The inflation-adjusted record for a successful personal investment is held, appropriately enough, by Senator Jay Rockefeller, who loaned his 1984 Senate campaign $10.3 million (the equivalent of $16.2 million in 1998 dollars). Tapping the family fortune does not guarantee victory, to be sure; in 1994, Michael Huffington spent an astonishing $28.4 million from his own pocket in a failed attempt to take a California Senate seat from Dianne Feinstein. Two years earlier, Huffington had spent a record $5.4 million to win a House seat.

Most wealthy candidates make personal loans rather than gifts to the campaign, because if they win they can then raise funds from people and PACs now anxious to be their friends to pay off at least part of the debt (although a few, like Herb Kohl of Wisconsin, have refused PAC money). When they lose, the debt usually becomes their gift to the campaign. And they lose far more often than they win. In elections from 1990 through 1998, only five each of the top twenty self-financers in both House and Senate contests were successful (and two of the Senate victors were incumbents). On average, candidates contributing substantial sums to their own campaigns do only slightly better than candidates financed by others.[22] Even (nonincumbent) candidates who are not wealthy normally must be prepared to invest some of their own money—about $20,000 is typical of a serious contender[23]—to pay start-up costs and to demonstrate commitment, with little hope of recouping any of it if they lose.

Fundraising Tactics

The most important aspect of fundraising is convincing potential donors that their money will not be wasted. Donors must be persuaded that the candidate has a plausible chance of winning and would be more attentive to their values and interests than would the opponent. Incumbents are, of course, in the best position to be persuasive. For nonincumbents, techniques of persuasion range from polls and old election returns to a smooth tongue backed by a lively imagination, from recitation of a political record to solemn promises. PACs and other contributors, understandably wary of such salesmanship, often take cues from each other and, more importantly, from party campaign committees in deciding who is worth an investment.

With or without party matchmaking, large contributions must usually be solicited face-to-face by the candidate or a prominent, high-status fundraiser. Smaller contributions are sought at meetings, rallies, dinners, or through direct mail appeals sent to individuals at home. This last method can be expensive; in 1992, Congressman Robert Dornan of California spent $1,151,338 to raise $1,407,922; $967,650 of the total went to direct-mail solicitation.[24] The growing popularity of direct-mail fundraising has become the source of some concern, since direct-mail pleas are most successful when they play on strong emotions such as anger, fear, or frustration, to convince people to support the candidate. Extremist candidates—Dornan, a flamboyant conservative firebrand, again serves as an example—are thus best able to exploit this method.[25]

However the money is acquired, timing is crucial. It is as important to have money available when it is needed as it is to have it in the first place. In general, money available early in the campaign is put to much better use than money received later. Early money is seed money for the entire campaign effort; it is needed to organize, plan, and raise more money. This circumstance adds to the advantage of personal wealth and also enhances the importance of national party and other organizations that are willing to make contributions and provide help early in the campaign. Emily's List, a PAC devoted to electing pro-choice women to Congress, takes its name from an acronym extolling this approach: "Early Money Is Like Yeast (it makes the dough rise)." Emily's List is also the premiere exponent of "bundling"; rather than contribute money directly to candidates, the PAC directs the individual contributions of its members to designated candidates. That way, it can provide help exceeding the $5,000 PAC contribution limit. In 1992, for example, Emily's List contributed only $365,318 directly to its chosen candidates but channeled another $6.2 million to them via bundling.[26]

CAMPAIGN ORGANIZATIONS

Campaigns require organization. Raising funds, handling the legal formalities, gathering intelligence, designing and executing advertising strategies, holding events, and identifying supporters and getting them to the polls on election day, are complex and demanding tasks that have to be carried out in a brief and inflexible time frame. It takes experience and savvy to do any one of them well. It is neither easy nor cheap to build a good campaign organization.

Many incumbents keep at least an embryonic campaign organization permanently in place, often as personal staff. Other candidates must normally build organizations from scratch, one reason seed money is so important. There was a time when, in many places, vigorous party organizations operated on a permanent basis and worked for entire party tickets. This is rarely the case now. Even when parties were robust, congressional candidates were not centers of attention, for local parties were interested primarily in patronage, and members of Congress controlled little of that. Now that local party organizations have lost much of their value as campaign allies, congressional candidates are even more on their own when it comes to mounting a campaign

For candidates who can afford it, the easiest way of acquiring a campaign organization is to buy one. Professional campaign specialists have taken over many of the functions formerly performed by local parties and have pioneered a variety of new electoral techniques adapted to an age of television and computers. It is possible for a candidate to hire a single outfit that will handle the entire campaign. More commonly, candidates engage a team of specialists—campaign managers, accountants, media consultants, pollsters, fundraisers, researchers, and the like. Professional services do not come cheap. Incumbents can afford them; often challengers cannot and must soldier on without much professional assistance. In 1992, for example, virtually every incumbent had a paid campaign manager, while 35 percent of challengers' House campaigns were managed by volunteers.[27] Senate challengers, with larger campaigns and bigger budgets, are much more likely to make use of professional campaign services. Hiring experienced professionals is now one sign of a serious campaign, and candidates who cannot afford to do so are unlikely to attract much attention from PACs or party committees.[28]

Short of buying one complete, the only way most nonincumbent congressional candidates can have an adequate campaign organization is to assemble one themselves (though promising candidates can expect some help from national party officials). Close political friends, the "personal constituency" that Fenno noticed all his congressmen had acquired, form the core. Other components are added as they are available. Some Democrats, for example, receive organizational help from labor unions. Fragments of local parties can sometimes be used. Inner-city African-American candidates may work through neighborhood churches. Republican candidates espousing "family values" are helped by Christian fundamentalist congregations and other conservative organizations. Single-issue groups, such as environmentalists, opponents of gun control, or those on opposite sides of the abortion issue, provide organizational help to supporters of their cause. Almost any existing group with political interests can be absorbed into a campaign organization. In some Florida districts, condominium activists form a cadre of "articulate people with organizational literacy, an interest in issues, a knack for politics, and plenty of time on their hands" who can be recruited into congressional campaigns.[29] The kind of organization a candidate assembles depends on what kinds of groups are available, which ones he or she can appeal to, and the candidate's range of contacts, resources, and level of political skill.

The campaign organizations of poorly funded House challengers tend to be personal, ephemeral, and dependent on volunteers. Because they are emphemeral and rely on people giving their time and energy without pay, a great deal of effort goes into internal organizational maintenance. Xandra Kayden observed that "most of the campaign staff devotes most of its time to creating and maintaining the campaign organization."[30] Such campaign organizations cannot be hierarchical because sanctions are so few. They cannot "learn" from their mistakes because they exist for such a short time and go out of business at the very time the real effectiveness of their work is measured—on election day. It is not surprising that so few are successful.

CAMPAIGN STRATEGIES

In a broad sense, everyone knows what campaigns are supposed to do: find and expand the pool of eligible voters favoring the candidate, and get them to the polls on election day. Just how to do it is another matter. As one political veteran told John Kingdon, "I don't know very much about elections. I've been in a lot of them."[31] In fact, the central motif of almost every discussion of campaign strategy is uncertainty.

What is the most efficient way to reach voters? No one knows for sure. The most frequently expressed sentiment is that "half the money spent on campaigns is wasted. The trouble is, we don't know which half."[32] The effects of uncertainty about what works and what does not pervade campaign decision making. Successful candidates are inclined to do what they did in the past; they must have done something right, even if they cannot be sure what; a degree of superstition is understandable. Other candidates also follow tradition. Kayden concludes that, "basically, campaigns produce literature because campaigns have always produced literature."[33] The same may be said of yard signs, bumper stickers, and campaign buttons. They appear in every election year, not so much because they have ever been shown to be effective, but because everyone expects them and their absence would be noticed, if only by the campaign's activists (hence they may be part of organizational maintenance).

On the other hand, uncertainty also invites innovation. Challengers, underdogs, and former losers have an incentive to try new tactics, if only to get desperately needed attention from the news media. For example, Lawton Chiles won a surprise victory in the 1970 Florida Senate election by walking the length of the state, talking and listening to people along the way. Other candidates quickly imitated him. While it was still fresh, the tactic generated abundant free publicity and far more attention than Chiles and the other candidates could afford to buy. Similarly, Tom Harkin, challenging the Republican incumbent for Iowa's 5th District in 1972, made news by working for a day at a time in a variety of blue-collar jobs, ostensibly to get close to the common experience. Others soon picked up the idea.

Whatever seems to work is imitated by others,[34] so the novelty and therefore effectiveness of such tactics fade. But there is always something new. In 1980, Kenneth Snider, Democratic challenger in Indiana's 8th District, dropped in on voters with the helicopter he had purchased especially for the campaign; the news media loved it.[35] Snider lost the election, but won a respectable 45 percent of the vote. Two years later Republican Dan Burton, campaigning in his 1948 fire engine, was more successful; he now represents Indiana's 6th District.[36]

Other modes of transportation have not been overlooked. Challenger Gene Freund undertook what might be called the "Tour d'Iowa," pedaling his bicycle 800 miles through twenty-seven counties of Iowa's 5th District in 1988.[37] In 1986, another challenger had been desperate enough for publicity to bicycle 340 miles across the Nevada desert along the shoulder of Interstate 80 in August.[38] Neither of these cyclers crossed the finish line first, but David Minge's 500-mile bike tour through forty-seven towns in nine days helped him win Minnesota's 2nd District in 1992. Minge repeated the tactic in 1994, narrowly holding off a challenger who, among other things, campaigned from a train; since then, Minge has continued to pedal his way to widening electoral margins.[39]

Sometimes a vehicle can even embody the campaign's central theme. In 1994, Greg Ganske campaigned for Iowa's 4th District in the "Nealmobile," a DeSoto made in 1958, the year the incumbent, Neal Smith, was first elected to the House. A sign on the roof asked: "WHY is it still running?"[40] In a year when "career politician" was a nasty epithet, Ganske drove the Nealmobile right into the House. Candidates also travel in battered pickup trucks, old station wagons, and other humble vehicles to show that they are just plain folks, not out-of-touch Washington insiders.

Campaign Media

Two groups of activities are common to all full-scale campaigns. One is mass media advertising, which absorbs about 45 percent of a typical campaign budget.[41] The candidate's name and perhaps a short message are presented to voters via some combination of television, radio, newspaper advertisements, billboards, and mass mailings. The choice of media is partly strategic and partly dictated by cost and available resources. About a third of House campaigns, for example, do not use paid television.[42] In large metropolitan areas it is inefficient and too expensive for candidates without extraordinarily ample funds. Candidates must pay for the audience they reach; at the extreme (the greater New York City media market), constituents may comprise less than 5 percent of the audience. The more efficiently television markets fit a district, the more likely House candidates are to use television advertising.[43]

Still, House candidates with enough money buy television time even if it is very wasteful, for it may be the only way to reach many potential voters. In 1984, for example, Andrew J. Stein, an unsuccessful Democratic challenger running in Manhattan's "Silk Stocking" district, spent more than $869,000 on media, most of which went for television. The feeling that television advertising is essential regardless of price is one important force driving up the cost of campaigning. Radio advertising is also "wasteful" in large media markets, but the costs are much lower, and radio audiences sort themselves out demographically for targeting, so campaigns often use radio where TV is beyond their means.

Senate campaigns are usually able to use television much more efficiently because constituencies are entire states, though cost and efficiency still vary considerably across states.[44] The use of television helps candidates who are not already well known (i.e., challengers) and can be added to the list of factors that make Senate campaigns so much more competitive, on the average, than House campaigns.

With enough money on both sides, a television campaign can take on the character of an ongoing debate, where "one day's set of TV ads for one candidate [is] followed soon after by his opponent's set of counterads, and the process repeated several times in an intricate series of tactical moves."[45] There is no apparent limit to how much television advertising voters will tolerate. Senator Jesse Helms's 1984 reelection campaign in North Carolina was on the air almost continuously for the eighteen months preceding the election; 150 different ads were produced for the campaign. His opponent, James Hunt, also saturated the airwaves, though for a shorter period.[46] Helms won, spending a record $16.5 million to Hunt's $9.5 million in what was up to then the most expensive Senate contest ever held.

Well-funded House campaigns in districts with inefficient television coverage often rely heavily on direct mail, which can pinpoint the district's voters. The 1984 campaign between Representative Jerry Patterson and Bob Dornan for a district located in Orange County, California, was conducted largely through the mails. Each inundated voters with some twenty mailings. Both sent tens of thousands of potholders—a common campaign gimmick in California— to district households.[47] Dornan's successful challenge cost more than $1 million; Patterson spent about $700,000. In 1992, Steve Horn, running for another district in the Los Angeles media market, spent 57 percent of his $458,310 campaign budget on direct-mail advertising; he spent $350 on broadcasting.[48] The growing sophistication of both data processing and lists segmenting the voting population have greatly increased the efficiency with which direct-mail appeals can be targeted to specific audiences.[49] Improved data bases and much cheaper technology have also led to increased use of the telephone to get out campaign messages and mobilize voters. "A telephone call, as unwelcome as it may be, cuts through . . . apathy and cynicism by forcing voters to listen to a political message," or so its practitioners claim.[50]

Technological innovation hasn't ignored television. Now that most American families own VCRs, candidates can get around the high cost of broadcasting by distributing their ads directly on videocassettes. Anne Eshoo, campaigning in California's 12th District in 1988, distributed 110,000 copies of a

knockout video, complete with cute graphics attacking "sacred cows," hip music, and a Milan-style desk with an Apple computer, in which she made an extended pitch and said that while places like Iowa or Nebraska or Orange County could make do with an ordinary congressman, Silicon Valley should have someone special.[51]

Eshoo lost that election but won the seat in 1992. Some candidates now mail out videos to accompany fundraising letters; this raises the cost but also gets more attention from recipients.

Finally, candidates have recently discovered the Internet. A survey of 270 campaigns for federal, state, and local office during the 1998 election found 63 percent with websites and another 21 percent planning to create them. Several statewide campaigns bought banner ads on newspapers' websites, including Barbara Boxer's successful campaign for reelection to the Senate in California. Clicking on Boxer's banner ad transported browsers to her Internet campaign site, where they could read about her and her policy positions, sign up to volunteer for her campaign, or order buttons and bumper stickers.[52]

Regardless of which combination of media is chosen, a fundamental goal is to get the candidate's name before the public. Though little else is certain about the effects of mass communications, it is well established that mass media coverage is positively related to public awareness of people, products, messages, and events. As we shall see in the next chapter, the more nonincumbent candidates spend on a campaign, the more voters are likely to know who they are. Getting voters' attention is only one hurdle, of course, but clearing it is essential.

Personal Campaigning

The second basic type of campaign activity centers around the candidate's personal contact with potential voters. Most politicians have faith in the personal touch; if they can just talk to people and get them to listen, they can win their support. There is some evidence for this notion. Larry Pressler, who represented South Dakota in Congress from 1974 to 1996, won his first House election with a campaign that consisted largely of meeting people one-on-one. "I tried to shake 500 hard hands a day," Pressler has said. "That is where you really take their hand and look at them and talk to them a bit. I succeeded in doing that seven days a week. I put in a lot of twelve-hour days, starting at a quarter to six in the morning at some plant in Sioux Falls or Madison."[53] Pressler estimates that he shook 300 to 500 hands in about eighty days. "You would not believe the physical and mental effort this requires." Shaking one hand per minute, a candidate would have to work for more than eight hours without stop to reach 500 people.[54]

The difficulty with this approach is that even House districts now contain more than 600,000 people, and states can be much more populous. It is simply impossible to meet more than a small fraction of the electorate during a single campaign. But candidates often agree with Pressler that it is worth trying, especially challengers whose only advantage may be the time they can devote to one-on-one campaigning. Some go door-to-door, "shoe-leathering" the neighborhoods; in 1990, first-time candidate Rick Santorum rang 25,000 doorbells in his upset victory over the incumbent in Pennsylvania's 18th District;[55] four years later, Santorum won election to the Senate.

Many candidates greet the early shift at the factory gate, shaking hands, passing out leaflets, showing workers they care enough to get up as early as the workers must. Most will accept any opportunity to speak to a group, and it is not uncommon for candidates to show up wherever people congregate in sufficient numbers: shopping malls, community picnics, parades, sporting events, and the like. As Santorum proved, energetic grassroots campaigns of this sort are occasionally successful even in this high-tech era,[56] and because they offer about the only hope to unknown candidates not blessed with great personal wealth, they remain common.

Many of the candidate's activities are designed to reach voters beyond those in the immediate audience by attracting the attention of the news media. Indeed, campaigns work so hard to get "free" media exposure that campaign professionals commonly refer to it as "earned" media.[57] The main reason for walking the length of the state or pedaling across the district is that it makes news. Campaign events are designed not so much for the immediate audience as for the larger audience watching television or reading the newspaper at home. The temptation to resort to gimmickry is not always resisted. Ronald Machtley began his successful campaign to replace Fernand St Germain accompanied by a "250-pound hog named Lester H. Pork ('Les Pork') to symbolize his opposition to St Germain's big spending policies."[58] Mark Sanford donned camouflage hunting clothes to declare "a war on career politicians" in his successful bid for South Carolina's 1st District in 1994.[59] Paid campaign ads may also be used to gain media exposure; one consultant recommends using "shock mailers" to provoke opponents into outraged responses, which then give the charges much wider publicity when the news media report the squabble.[60] A more gentle tactic was used in Russ Feingold's successful challenge to Wisconsin Senator Bob Kasten in 1992: humorous ads, including one featuring a mock personal endorsement by Elvis, that delighted the media. Kasten eventually countered with his own Elvis spot attacking Fiengold on the issues.[61]

The candidate's time is a scarce resource, so an important function of the campaign organization is to arrange for it to be used effectively. An exhausting day of travel and meetings that results in few contacts with voters or little money raised is a campaign manager's nightmare. Time wasted cannot be retrieved. But candidates and their aides cannot tailor the social and political world to suit their needs; they have to be ready to exploit opportunities for meeting people and making news as they arise.

CAMPAIGN MESSAGES

Along with letting voters know who the candidate is, the campaign is designed to persuade them to vote for him or her. Uncertainty dominates here as well. There is no magic formula for appealing to voters; what works in one district or election year may not work in another. Nonetheless, according to campaign professionals, to be effective, every campaign needs to develop and project *some* consistent campaign theme. The theme explains why the candidate should be elected and why the opponent should not. It attempts to frame the choice—to establish what the election is *about*—in a way that underlines the candidate's strengths and plays down the candidate's weaknesses. The goal is not to change people's political attitudes, but rather to define the choice so that a vote for the candidate is consistent with them.[62] The available themes and approaches are often rather different for incumbents, challengers, and candidates for open seats, so it is best to consider these categories separately.

Challengers' Campaigns

Challengers certainly hope to convince people of their own virtues—at minimum, that they are qualified for the office—but they are not likely to get far without directly undermining support for the incumbent. The trick is to find some vulnerable point to attack, and challengers are happy to exploit whatever is available. There are inevitably at least a few members beset with scandal—moral or ethical lapses, felony convictions, signs of senility or alcoholism—that offer obvious targets, although a surprising number of incumbents with such liabilities manage to win reelection.[63] In 1992, the House Bank scandal provided ammunition to challengers of the more than 200 incumbents seeking reelection who had written unfunded checks (see Chapter 6 for details). Individual political failings—excessive junketing, lack of attention to the district or to legislative duties—also invite attack. The defeat of incumbent Walter Huddleston in Kentucky's 1984 Senate race is widely attributed to a television ad, featuring a pack of bloodhounds searching for him in places far from Washington, DC, that underlined the charge that Huddleston had neglected his duties. Congressional travel became a common target in the 1990s, as challengers used it to symbolize insulation of "career politicians" from the lives of ordinary people.

Challengers also routinely try to show that incumbents are out of touch with district sentiments by attacking specific roll-call votes, the ideological or partisan pattern of votes, or a combination of the two. They also try to hang unpopular policies or politicians around their necks. Although cases are known in which a single wrong vote led to defeat, it is by no means easy to nail members with their voting records. Members are aware that they may be called to answer for any vote and on controversial issues take pains to cast an "explainable"[64] vote. That is, any vote likely to offend important groups in the member's electoral coalition or in the district at large will be cast only if it can be supported by a plausible explanation, one that does not make the member look bad if it is questioned.

Normally, a few "wrong" votes do not seriously weaken an incumbent, though a string of them lends plausibility to the charge that a member is mismatched with the constituency and ought to be replaced. On occasion, however, challengers have been able to turn one or two key votes into potent symbols of the incumbent's divided loyalties. House Democrats running for reelection in 1994 did significantly worse if they had supported Clinton's 1993 budget (containing "the biggest tax increase in history"), the North American Free Trade Agreement Implementation Bill, or the Omnibus Anti-Crime Bill (opposed by the gun lobby for its ban on assault weapons and depicted by Republicans as "larded with pork"). The more loyal they were to president and party on these votes, the more electoral damage they suffered; the more Republican the district's voting patterns in presidential elections, the more severe the damage.

General ideological or partisan attacks have been a mainstay of challengers' campaigns for decades. Incumbents are criticized for being too liberal or too conservative for the constituency or for their guilt by association with unpopular parties, causes, or leaders. This approach lost some of its punch in the

1960s and 1970s, as members strove to avoid ideological categorization or personal responsibility for party decisions when it would hurt them politically back home. By soliciting support as individuals rather than as representatives of a party or cause, they sought to undermine the force of such charges.

As electoral politics took on a more ideological cast in the 1980s, incumbents—particularly Democrats—found it more difficult to sidestep attacks of this sort. The initial sign of change was the defeat of nine Senate Democratic incumbents, five of them veteran liberals, in 1980. Newly emerged party committees, PACs, and single-issue organizations led the charge with harsh, negative campaigns featuring highly emotional issues, such as abortion and the Panama Canal treaties.[65] Most prominent was the National Conservative Political Action Committee (NCPAC), which began merciless personal attacks on six targeted Senate Democrats more than a year before the election, long before it was known who their opponents would be. The campaigns, run independently of any candidate or party, were aimed solely at discrediting the incumbents, softening them up for whomever turned out to be the challenger.

Four of the six were defeated, and NCPAC claimed full credit. But all of them were in serious trouble with or without NCPAC, and other groups, notably the NRSC and anti-abortion groups, which were also very active in these campaigns, claimed a major share of the credit for the results. NCPAC targeted another group of Democratic Senators in 1982, but by then it had itself become the issue. Its chairman, Terry Dolan, had conceded, in a moment of candor, one advantage of independent campaigning: "A group like ours could lie through its teeth and the candidate it helps stays clean."[66] Targeted Democrats responded by reminding voters of Dolan's admission and working, with some success, to make NCPAC's activities, rather than its charges, the main issue.[67]

Going Negative

Although NCPAC soon faded, its legacy was evident in the growing popularity among campaign professionals of "going negative." Until the 1980s, harsh personal attacks on an opponent were considered a sign of desperation, ineffective and likely to backfire. Challengers on the ropes sometimes resorted to them; incumbents ignored the attacks on the theory that reacting would only bring them unwarranted attention. They were most common in campaigns of "sure losers."[68] No longer. Campaign consultants have become convinced that negative advertising works. One Democratic consultant put it this way: "People say they hate negative campaigning. But it works. They hate it and remember it at the same time. The problem with positive is that you have to run it again and again to make it stick. With negative, the poll numbers will move in three or four days."[69] *Campaigns & Elections*, which bills itself as "The Magazine for Political Professionals," devoted several articles in its July 1995 issue to helpful hints on "going negative"; example: "Attack Mail: The Silent Killer."[70] Campaign professionals distinguish between accurate *comparative* ads that highlight differences between the candidates (fair) and strictly personal attacks of questionable accuracy or relevance (unfair), though voters may not always appreciate the distinction. The best experimental research suggests that negative ads do inform the public but also discourage people from voting.[71]

The logic, if not the civility, of attacking opponents is compelling in a system of candidate-centered electoral politics. If members of Congress win and hold office by eliciting trust and regard as individuals, then the way to undermine their support is to destroy their constituents' trust and regard. Even national issues unfavorable to the incumbent's party—bad economic news, scandals, failed policies, an unpopular president—need to be personalized to be used effectively to weaken an incumbent. When national issues are scarce, as in the late 1980s, character assaults are about the only tactic readily available.[72]

National issues helpful to challengers did become available in the early 1990s, and they were quick to exploit them. Intense public dissatisfaction with Congress's performance offered a potent theme to those challengers who could demonize the incumbent as a career politician guilty by association with the government's failings. Demonizing *individual* incumbents, as opposed to the class of officeholders, is not easy, however. For years, members of Congress managed to avoid the fallout from the public's routine dissatisfaction with Congress's institutional performance. Rather than defend the place, they would join in the criticism: "Members of Congress run *for* Congress by running *against* Congress."[73] They defended their own personal performances vigorously but the collective actions of Congress not at all.

The effectiveness of this strategy began to break down in 1990, when voters reacted to an unpopular October budget deal that cut programs and raised taxes by reducing their support for incumbents of both parties.[74] It was further undermined in 1992, when the House Bank scandal allowed challengers to connect members personally, through their record of bad checks, with congressional malfeasance.[75] And it failed almost completely for Democrats in 1994, when Republicans succeeded in turning hostility to government into hostility to Democrats by depicting them as adherents of an intolerable status quo, exemplified by their unpopular president's "big government" solution to the health care system's shortcomings (see Chapter 6).

In the search for campaign issues, then, challengers are necessarily opportunists. It is a matter of finding and exploiting the incumbent's mistakes— neglect of the district, personal lapses, "bad" votes—or discovering a way to saddle the incumbent with personal responsibility for government's shortcomings. A challenger cannot hope to win without reordering the campaign agenda. Incumbents thrive on campaigns that center around personal performance, experience, and services. Few members are vulnerable if they can persuade voters that this is what the contest is about; as we shall see in Chapter 5, even losing incumbents get high marks on these dimensions. Challengers succeed only when they can frame issues in a way that makes these dimensions less relevant and other considerations more salient.

From this perspective, the burgeoning role of party committees and other institutional participants in congressional election politics takes on added importance. National campaign committees have helped their challengers by polling between elections to probe for soft spots in incumbents' support, tracking their votes to store up ammunition for the next election, attacking them between elections with negative advertising, and quickly spreading the word about successful innovations in strategy and tactics. Dozens of groups now rate roll-call votes, target incumbents opposing their views, advise favored challengers on tactics, and mobilize campaign volunteers—in addition, of course, to providing campaign money. All of these things add to the uncertainty and worry of incumbents; aware of the resources available to be mobilized against them, most act as if they were anything but safe.

Incumbents' Campaigns

Incumbents pursue reelection throughout their term in office, so their campaign strategies are visible in all their dealings with constituents. Naturally, they try to avoid mistakes that would give opponents campaign issues, but in an uncertain and complicated political world, this is not always possible. They therefore work to maintain the kind of relationship with constituents that will allow them to survive a damaging vote or contrary political tide. Fenno's insightful account of how House members do this, in fact, describes effective campaigning by any congressional candidate, incumbent or challenger.

Fenno traveled extensively with eighteen House members as they made the rounds of their districts. He found that each member projected a personal *home style* that defined his relationship to the groups he relied on for political support. Home styles varied according to the character of the district and the personality of the individual member, but in one way or another, all members basically sought to inspire *trust* among their constituents.[76] They did this by emphasizing their personal qualifications, including moral character, by identifying with their constituents ("I am one of you," they implied, "so you can trust me to make the right decisions—those you would make under the same circumstances"), and by working to develop bonds of empathy with groups and individuals they met.

For most of the members Fenno watched, issues, policy, and partisanship were not prominent objects of discussion with constituents and were not used to elicit support. Even members who did display an issue-oriented home style used issues primarily to cement ties of trust; *how* they addressed the issue rather than the issue itself was what mattered. Members used issues to show themselves to be the kind of people constituents would want in Washington.

Along with trust, members emphasized their *accessibility*. Constituents were reminded continually that lines of communication were open, that they had access to the member whenever they needed it. The payoffs are clear. A member who is trusted, accessible, and thought to be "one of us" will have much less trouble defending him- or herself against personal attacks. His or her explanations for controversial votes will be heard more sympathetically; institutional or partisan failures, even notorious ethical lapses, may go unpunished.

This kind of relationship cannot be developed overnight, nor can it be maintained without continual reinforcement. Its importance is the reason why, as one congressman put it, "it's a personal franchise you hold, not a political franchise."[77] Nonincumbents may aspire to it, but they have little chance to achieve it in the brief period of a single election campaign. Those who have held other elective offices in the district or who are already familiar to district voters for other reasons—a previous campaign, family name, celebrity status as athletes, entertainers, or newscasters—have a head start.

In addition to keeping district connections in good repair, incumbents have now begun to deal with the growing threat of harsh personal and political attacks and well-financed challenges by campaigning preemptively. Incumbents have always raised and spent money reactively, in proportion to what their challengers raise and spend against them. They now spend increasing amounts of money preemptively in order to inoculate voters against anticipated attacks.

Both patterns are evident when incumbents' expenditures are regressed on challengers' expenditures in House elections from 1972 through 1998; the results are reported in Table 4-2 For comparison, the dollar figures have been adjusted for inflation (1998=1.00). Look first at the intercept, which indicates how much, on average, an incumbent would spend if the challenger spent nothing at all. It has increased dramatically, from $127,800 to $558,600 (in 1998 dollars) between 1972 and 1998; House incumbents have been raising and spending increasing sums of money regardless of the kind of challenge they face. Second, the regression coefficients (slopes) tend to increase over these years (1998 is an exception), indicating that incumbents now tend to match a larger proportion of the dollars spent by their challengers.

The same campaign professionals who promote negative campaigns recommend a preemptive strategy to cope with them. "Inoculation and preemption are what win campaigns," according to one Republican consultant. Said another, "If you know what your negatives are and you know where you are vulnerable, you can preempt it."[78] Hence, for example, Republican Senator James Abdnor of South Dakota, expecting to be challenged by the state's governor for

TABLE 4–2 INCUMBENTS' EXPENDITURES AS A FUNCTION OF CHALLENGERS' EXPENDITURES IN HOUSE ELECTIONS, 1972–1998

YEAR	NUMBER OF CASES	INTERCEPT		REGRESSION COEFFICIENT: CHALLENGER'S EXPENDITURES		R^2
1972	319	127.8	(8.6)	.56	(.04)	.34
1974	322	126.5	(8.4)	.63	(.04)	.41
1976	329	162.7	(9.3)	.55	(.04)	.36
1978	309	211.8	(11.3)	.49	(.04)	.38
1980	339	205.1	(16.7)	.74	(.05)	.41
1982	315	309.0	(16.0)	.58	(.05)	.34
1984	341	346.7	(15.6)	.63	(.04)	.39
1986	319	412.8	(23.7)	.73	(.07)	.27
1988	328	427.6	(20.2)	.79	(.06)	.32
1990	405	417.0	(15.5)	.74	(.07)	.24
1992	312	523.9	(25.4)	.82	(.08)	.23
1994	336	484.3	(24.3)	.64	(.06)	.24
1996	360	471.7	(24.4)	.88	(.05)	.45
1998	308	558.6	(22.1)	.46	(.04)	.30

Note: Expenditures are in $1,000s, adjusted for inflation (1998=1.00); standard errors are in parentheses; all coefficient are significant beyond $p<.001$; a few senior party leaders are excluded because most of their spending went to support other candidates rather than to counteract their own challengers.

renomination on grounds of ineffectiveness, began broadcasting ads in November 1985 that had prominent Republican senators bearing witness to his effectiveness. Another Republican thought to be in trouble for 1986, Senator Paula Hawkins of Florida, also began airing commercials in 1985. A year before the election she had already spent $750,000 on media advertising alone.[79] Both these attempts at preemption failed, however; evidently, the candidates' real weaknesses could not be masked by rhetoric. More successful was Democratic Senator Patrick Leahy, who ran an ad warning his Vermont constituents, "Oh boy, it's going to get knee deep around here. Dick Snelling has hired some famous dirty tricksters to foul the airwaves with a big bucks, political smear campaign . . . Do we really have to go through this in quiet, sensible, beautiful Vermont?"[80]

Although incumbents, at least in the House, engage more or less continuously in activities aimed at assuring reelection—including, now, preemptive campaigning—their real campaigns start when it becomes clear who the challenger will be in the primary or general election or both. Different challengers present different problems and inspire different campaign strategies. Inept, obscure, or underfinanced opponents can be dealt with by routine maintenance of ties with groups in the electoral coalition, and otherwise ignored. Senator Daniel Inouye, for example, had little reason to mention his 1998 opponent, one Crystal Young who spent no money on the campaign but got some publicity when she "alleged that actress Shirley McLaine implanted electromagnetic needles in her."[81]

Ignoring the opposition is a standard tactic of incumbents who feel relatively secure: Why give an unknown opponent free publicity? More serious opponents compel more vigorous campaigns, with the strategy adapted to the relative strengths and weaknesses of both candidates. Incumbents also adjust to opponents' campaign tactics once their effectiveness has been demonstrated. For example, counterattack or, better yet, preemptive assault on the challenger's character and credibility has replaced the older practice of ignoring personal attacks. Incumbents also adapt their strategies to national political conditions; many Democrats who were happy to link themselves with their party and Bill Clinton in 1992 sought to declare their independence in 1994.

Common to most incumbents' campaigns is an emphasis on the value of experience and seniority (for the capacity it gives members to serve the district more effectively) and reminders of the things that the member has done over the years for constituents. When the insider image these accomplishments evoked became a potential liability in the early 1990s, some switched to emphasizing their status as outsiders opposed to the status quo by advocating term limits, balanced budgets amendments, and the end to congressional perks. This was a favorite (and uniformly successful) tack taken by Republican incumbents in 1994. In special circumstances, special ploys may be necessary. Senator Milton Young, running for reelection to the Senate from North Dakota in 1974 at the age of 76, countered suggestions that he was getting too old by running a TV spot showing him splitting a block of wood with a karate chop.[82]

Despite the knowledge members acquire of their constituencies, uncertainty plagues incumbents as well as nonincumbents. Each election may present a new challenge and a new set of electoral variables. Since incumbents are not sure which of their actions got them elected previously, they cannot be sure what combination of campaign activities will serve them in altered circumstances. Although in a normal election year most members are reelected easily (at least in the House), most of them have had close calls at one time or another, and all have vivid memories of seemingly entrenched colleagues who suffered sudden massive vote losses and unexpected defeats.

Because of uncertainty, members tend to exaggerate electoral threats and overreact to them. They are inspired by worst-case scenarios—what would they have to do to win if everything went wrong?—rather than objective probabilities. Hence, we find members who conduct full-scale campaigns even though the opposition is nowhere to be seen. The desire to win decisively enough to discourage future opposition also leads many incumbents to campaign a good deal harder than would seem objectively necessary. The sense of uncertainty and risk felt by incumbents has grown in recent years, along with the money, professional talent, and technology potentially available to their opponents. The specter of fickle electorates, combined with active organizations ready to mobilize extensive campaign resources against them should they show signs of vulnerability, undermines whatever confidence comfortable reelection margins might otherwise inspire. The electoral shakeups of the early 1990s are a reminder that they are wise to take nothing for granted.

Candidates for Open Seats

Candidates for open seats face somewhat different electoral situations, because none of the contestants is an incumbent or challenger with the accompanying advantages or disadvantages. They are much more likely to face difficult primary contests, because the opportunity offered to ambitious politicians by an open seat attracts more and better-qualified candidates. Indeed, the primary is often a more difficult hurdle than the general election.[83]

Both candidates are likely to have some experience in elective office and, therefore, some familiarity with at least a part of the constituency and some useful relationships with electorally important segments of it (recall Table 3-4). Both are likely to have adequate campaign resources because contests for open seats are notoriously competitive; the best chance by far to take a seat from the opposing party occurs when no incumbent is involved. As a consequence, candidates for open seats are typically better known and better liked than challengers—but not as well as incumbents.[84] No particular pattern of campaign strategy is typical of candidates for open seats other than a highly variable mixture of the approaches used by incumbents and challengers that coincides with their electoral position between the two.

Because candidates competing for open seats are normally much more closely balanced in skills and resources than are challengers and incumbents, the outcome is more strongly influenced by partisan trends, both local and national. Without the pull of incumbency, votes are cast more consistently along party lines, so election results reflect state or district partisanship more consistently. Presidential coattails (discussed more fully in Chapter 6) are stronger; that is, voters are more likely to cast congressional votes consistent with their presidential vote, so the fates of candidates for open seats are tied more closely to the top of the ticket in presidential election years.[85] Open seats also register partisan tides more strongly; in years with big swings, such as 1974 (pro-Democratic), 1980 and 1994 (pro-Republican), a disproportionate share of the winning party' gains come from open seats.[86]

SENATE CAMPAIGNS

As we observed in Chapter 3, Senate elections are, on average, considerably more competitive than House elections. Senate incumbents win less consistently and by narrower margins than do House incumbents. Nearly every state is potentially winnable by either party; thirty-nine states have chosen senators from both parties in elections since 1984, and all but one of the remaining states—Hawaii—have elected governors of the party opposite their senators' during this time. Greater partisan balance by itself makes Senate elections more competitive, but it also creates a strategic electoral environment that enhances competition in several ways.

First, Senate incumbents are usually faced with more formidable opponents.[87] About two-thirds of Senate challengers in recent elections had previously held elective office. Among the successful first-time candidates have been two former astronauts (John Glenn and Harrison Schmitt), a former basketball star (Bill Bradley), a lawyer-turned-actor (Fred Thompson), and several prominent millionaire businessmen.

Formidable challengers attract campaign resources. Senate campaigns in general attract proportionately greater contributions because the donations are, in a sense, more cost-effective, especially in smaller states.[88] Senate contests are usually closer, so campaign resources are more likely to affect the outcome. Parties and groups with particular policy agendas are aware that, when it comes to passing legislation, one senator is worth 4.35 representatives. A party has to defeat far fewer incumbents to take over the Senate than to take over the House. It makes strategic sense for campaign contributors to focus on the Senate, and that is what they have done. The campaign finance laws also make it easier for national party organizations to participate extensively in Senate contests and, to an increasing degree, they do. Thus Senate challengers are much more likely to enjoy adequately funded campaigns.

Senate challengers can also use their campaign resources more effectively. Most Senate constituencies have the size and structure to make television advertising cost-efficient. Resources are usually sufficient to justify using campaign professionals and the technical paraphernalia of modern campaigns: computers, polls, direct-mail advertising and solicitation, and so forth. The news media are much more interested in Senate campaigns, so much more free attention and publicity is bestowed on Senate candidates than on their House counterparts.[89] It is little wonder that Senate challengers and other nonincumbents are much better known by voters than are House challengers.[90]

Furthermore, Senate incumbents find it much more difficult to develop and maintain the kind of personal relationships with constituents that Fenno observed among House incumbents. The reason is obvious. Senate districts—states—are, with six exceptions, more populous than congressional districts, often very much so. The opportunities for personal contacts with constituents and attention to individual problems are proportionately fewer. It also follows that the larger the state, the more difficult it is for a senator to cultivate firm ties to constituents. The larger Senate staffs cannot make up the difference.[91]

Senators' activities in Washington are also more conspicuous. Action in the Senate is more visible; the Senate has fewer members, and they are given more attention by the news media.[92] Senators are thus more likely to be associated with controversial and divisive issues.[93] Senators do not have the pressure of a two-year election cycle to keep them attuned to the folks back home. Electoral coalitions may fall into disrepair, and a careless senator may discover that he or she must begin almost from scratch when reelection time rolls around.

Lavishly funded and professionally run Senate campaigns have been the proving ground for the latest innovations in campaign tactics and techniques. One recent development is interactive campaigning, in which the campaign themes and messages of each candidate are rapidly altered in response to what the opposition is saying and, more importantly, to what their tracking polls tell them about the effectiveness of both campaigns. Polling technology is the key. In the words of a Democratic consultant, "It's relatively simple and not very expensive now to sample public opinion. In the last month of a campaign, both sides will poll nightly, test how that day's media and campaigning has played, and trace the results."[94] Instead of planning and executing a single strategy over the course of an entire campaign, strategic flexibility is now the watchword. Observed another consultant, "When candidates come in here now, their first questions to me are: Can you respond quickly? Can you attack quickly? Can you do a fast turnaround?"[95] With enough money, turnaround can be fast indeed. In California's 1994 Senate campaign, Dianne Feinstein saw her campaign ads answered within 24 hours by new commercials produced and distributed statewide by Michael Huffington's lavishly funded campaign team.[96]

"VOTER EDUCATION" AND "ISSUE ADVOCACY" CAMPAIGNS

Candidates have never enjoyed exclusive control over congressional campaigns; generic party advertising and independent campaigns conducted by PACs have been part of the process since the adoption of the FECA. But their part has been minor. Independent spending has never accounted for more than 3 percent of total campaign spending and in most elections has been closer to 1 percent. Generic party advertising promoting the whole national ticket has waxed and waned in fashion but has usually been quite modest. In the 1990s, however, interest groups and parties developed a new avenue for large-scale involvement in electoral politics beyond the control of the candidates. The Court's *Buckley* decision construed the FECA "to apply only to expenditures for communications that in express terms advocate the election or defeat of a clearly identified candidate for federal office." Subsequent decisions have confirmed that the First Amendment protects the right to conduct unrestricted so-called "voter education" or "issue advocacy" campaigns, even if clearly intended to influence voters (by, for example, tendentious comparisons of candidates' issue positions), as long as such terms as "vote for," "elect," "vote against," "defeat," or "reject," are not used.[97]

Such prominent organizations as the Christian Coalition, AFL-CIO, Sierra Club, Americans for Limited Terms, as well as more shadowy groups, such as Americans for Job Security (the First Amendment also protects the anonymity of contributors to advocacy campaigns), have begun to invest heavily in "voter education" and "issue advocacy" in recent campaigns. Given a green light by the courts, the parties have also jumped in; the DSCC spent an estimated $8 million, and the RNC and NRSC, an estimated $37 million on issue ads in 1998. Most notable was the $10 million Republican effort in the final weeks of the campaign attacking Clinton for his involvement with Monica Lewinsky: "Should we reward Bill Clinton? Should we make the Democrats more powerful?" asked one of the ads.[98]

Precise spending figures for these campaigns are often unavailable because they do not come under Federal Election Commission (FEC) jurisdiction, but one research group concluded that interest groups and parties spent between $260 million and $330 million on them during the 1998 election cycle, up from the $135–150 million spent in 1996, which included a presidential contest (by comparison, independent spending by PACs explicitly endorsing or opposing candidates and so reported to the FEC amounted to only about $9 million in 1998).[99] "Voter education" campaigns can be effective; the $25–35 million spent by the AFL-CIO against sixty-four Republican incumbents in 1996 deprived targeted freshmen of their sophomore surges and, arguably, cost as many as seven of them their seats.[100] Proposals to close (or widen) this gap in the network of campaign finance regulation are currently before Congress, state legislatures, and courts, so it is uncertain how rapidly this mode of campaigning will grow. But it could easily become a major component of congressional election politics, especially if regulatory reform were to close off other avenues for investing in electoral politics.

CONCLUDING OBSERVATIONS

Congressional practices are undergoing a period of rapid change, as the effects of organizational, technical, and financial innovations appear in more and more contests. Several consequences are worth noting. First, as already suggested, members of Congress face substantially greater electoral uncertainty. They face more volatile electorates and less predictable and potentially more threatening opposition; abundant, centrally disposed resources are available to be mobilized against them quickly on any sign of vulnerability. New techniques and tactics may hold unpleasant surprises, and strategies for coping with them are still unsure. Sharpened sensitivity to the electoral implications of their activities in office is a natural result, and this, as we shall see in Chapters 7 and 8, has an important effect on how Congress works as an institution.

But it is also important to emphasize that the large majority of incumbents in the House, and many Senate incumbents, escape serious competition altogether and so win by quite comfortable margins. Indeed, the impressive new technology for probing electorates, along with the growing cost of competitive campaigns, has evidently led to a sharp bifurcation of effort. Electoral resources (including high-quality candidates) are increasingly concentrated in a small subset of House districts and in selected Senate races, making life more difficult for those incumbents who appear sufficiently vulnerable to invite an all-out challenge. But those who avoid becoming targets face increasingly feeble opposition, because promising challengers have little incentive to incur the growing cost in money, time, privacy, and family life of conducting a serious challenge unless prospects for victory are very good indeed.

ENDNOTES

1. See Linda L. Fowler, "Candidate Perceptions of Electoral Coalitions: Limits and Possibilities" (Paper delivered at the Conference on Congressional Elections, Rice University and the University of Houston, Houston, January 10-12, 1980).
2. Richard F. Fenno, Jr., *Home Style: House Members in Their Districts* (Boston: Little, Brown, 1978), pp. 171-172.
3. See any edition of *Campaigns & Elections* for the ads of vendors of these and all other campaign services.
4. Gary C. Jacobson, *Money in Congressional Elections* (New Haven: Yale University Press, 1980), pp. 170-171.
5. Diane Granat, "Parties' Schools for Politicians Grooming Troops for Election," *Congressional Quarterly Weekly Report* 42 (May 5, 1984), p. 1036.
6. Individuals may give no more than $1,000 per candidate per campaign (the primary and general election campaigns are each considered separate campaigns) up to a total of $20,000 in an election year; nonparty political action committees may give no more than $5,000 per candidate per campaign; party contribution limits are discussed later in this chapter.
7. *Buckley v. Valeo* (96 S. Ct. 612).
8. Gary C. Jacobson, "Parties and PACs in Congressional Elections," in *Congress Reconsidered*, 4th ed., eds. Lawrence C. Dodd and Bruce I. Oppenheimer (Washington, DC: Congressional Quarterly Press, 1988), pp. 117-121. For a balanced and thoroughgoing account of all aspects of campaign finance, see Frank J. Sorauf, *Money in American Elections* (Glenview, Illinois: Scott, Foresman, 1988).
9. Theodore J. Eismeier and Philip H. Pollack III, *Business, Money, and the Rise of Corporate PACs in American Elections* (New York: Quantum Books, 1988), pp. 79-94.
10. Gary C. Jacobson, *The Electoral Origins of Divided Government: Competition in U.S. House Elections, 1946-1988* (Boulder, Colorado: Westview Press, 1990):62-64.
11. For a fascinating account of how Tony Coelho, chairman of the Democratic Congressional Campaign Committee, persuaded business PACs to support Democratic candidates, see Brooks Jackson, *Honest Graft: Big Money and the American Political Process*, updated ed. (Washington, DC: Farragut Publishing Company, 1990).

12. Chuck Alston and Glen Craney, "Bush Campaign-Reform Takes Aim at Incumbents," *Congressional Quarterly Weekly Report* 47 (July 1, 1989): 1648-1659.

13. "Momentum Helps GOP Collect Record Amount from PACs," *Congressional Quarterly Weekly Report* 52 (December 3, 1994):3457.

14. "To the '94 Victors Go the Fundraising Spoils," *Congressional Quarterly Weekly Report* 53 (April 15, 1995):1055-1059.

15. Gary W. Cox and Eric Magar, "How Much Is Majority Status in the U.S. Congress Worth?" *American Political Science Review* 93 (June 1999): 302-303.

16. Ibid., pp. 304-306.

17. Federal Election Commission, "FEC Announces 1998 Party Spending Limits," news release, March 6, 1998.

18. Paul Herrnson, *Congressional Elections: Campaigning at Home and in Washington* (Washington, DC: Congressional Quarterly Press, 1995), pp. 88-92.

19. Ibid., p. 86.

20. Ibid., p. 93.

21. John F. Persinos, "The GOP Farm Team," *Campaigns and Elections*, March 1995, p. 20.

22. Jennifer Steen, "Self-Financing Candidates in American Elections," dissertation website, http://socrates.berkeley.edu/~jsteen/facts.htm, November 4, 1999.

23. Clyde Wilcox, "I Owe It All to Me: Candidates' Investments in Their Own Campaigns," *American Politics Quarterly* 16 (1988):278.

24. Dwight Morris and Murielle E. Gamache, *Handbook of Campaign Spending: Money in the 1992 Congressional Elections* (Washington, DC: Congressional Quarterly Press, 1994), p. 29.

25. Xandra Kayden, "The Nationalizing of the Party System," in *Parties, Interest Groups, and Campaign Finance Laws*, ed. Michael J. Malbin (Washington, DC: American Enterprise Institute for Public Policy Research, 1980), p. 266.

26. Ilka M. Knepper, "Emily's List: Verdraengen Political Action Committees Amerikanische Parteien?" Master's thesis, Zentrum fuer Europa- und Nordamerikastudien, Fachbereich Politikwissenschaft, Georg-August-Universitaet Goettigen, 1994, p. 92; Herbert E. Alexander and Anthony Corrado, *Financing the 1992 Election* (Armonk, New York: M.E. Sharpe, 1995), p. 212.

27. Herrnson, *Congressional Elections*, p. 64.

28. Paul S. Herrnson, "Do Parties Make a Difference? The Role of Party Organizations in Congressional Elections," *Journal of Politics* 48 (1986): 612-613.

29. Michael Barone and Grant Ujifusa, *The Almanac of American Politics 1990* (Washington, DC: National Journal, 1989), p. 279.

30. Xandra Kayden, *Campaign Organization* (Lexington, Massachusetts: D.C. Health, 1978), p. 61.

31. John W. Kingdon, *Candidates for Office: Beliefs and Strategies* (New York: Random House, 1968), p. 87.

32. One of Fenno's congressmen raised it to 75 percent; see Fenno, *Home Style*, p. 17.

33. Kayden, *Campaign Organization*, p. 120.

34. Majorie Randon Hershey, *Running for Office: The Political Education of Campaigners* (Chatham, New Jersey: Chatham House, 1984), pp. 69-79.

35. "The Outlook: Senate, House, and Governors," *Congressional Quarterly Weekly Report* 38 (October 11, 1980):3014, 3017.

36. Alan Ehrenhalt, "House Freshmen: Campaign Traditionalists," *Congressional Quarterly Weekly Report* 41 (January 8, 1983):30.

37. Jonathan Roos, "Freund Hopes to Grab Coattails," *Des Moines Register*, August 23, 1988, A2.

38. "Outlook: Nevada," *Congressional Quarterly Weekly Report* 44 (October 11, 1986):2453.

39. Michael Barone and Grant Ujifusa, *The Almanac of American Politics 1994* (Washington, DC: National Journal, 1993), p. 691; "Minnesota," *Congressional Quarterly Weekly Report* 52 (October 22, 1994): 3032.

40. "Challenger Hits Iowa's Smith with Incumbency, Earmarks," *Congressional Quarterly Weekly Report* 52 (September 10, 1994):2533.

41. Morris and Gamache, *Handbook of Campaign Spending*, Tables 1-5 and 1-6.

42. Herrnson, *Congressional Elections*, p. 183.

43. Edie N. Goldenberg and Michael W. Traugott, *Compaigning for Congress* (Washington, DC: Congressional Quarterly Press, 1984), p. 120; Stephen Ansolabehere, Alan Gerber, and James M. Snyder, Jr., "Television Costs and Greater Congressional Campaign Spending: Cause and Effect or Coincidence?" manuscript, August 1999.

44. Charles Stewart III and Mark Reynolds, "Television Markets and Senate Elections," *Legislative Studies Quarterly* 15 (1990):495-523.

45. Alan Ehrenhalt, "Technology, Strategy Bring New Campaign Era," *Congressional Quarterly Weekly Report* 43 (December 7, 1985): 2559.

46. Ibid., p. 2563.

47. Steven Pressman, "From Television to Potholders, Consultants Leave Their Mark on 1984 Congressional Races," *Congressional Quarterly Weekly Report* 42 (December 22, 1984):3154.

48. Morris and Gramache, *Handbook of Campaign Spending*, p. 200.

49. "We've Got Mail," *Campaign & Elections*, June 1999; p. 22.

50. John Jameson, Chris Glaze, and Gary Teal, "Effective Phone Contact Programs and the Importance of Good Data," *Campaigns & Elections*, July, 1999, pp. 64-71.

51. Barone and Ujifusa, *Almanac of American Politics 1990*, p. 111.

52. Karen Foerstel, "Home Pages as Hustings: Candidates Work the Web," *Congressional Quarterly Weekly Report*, 56 (September 5, 1998): 2321-2324.

53. Alan L. Clem, "The Case of the Upstart Republican," in *The Making of Congressmen: Seven Campaigns of 1974*, ed. Alan L. Clem (North Scituate, Massachusetts: Duxbury Press, 1976), p. 140.

54. Ibid.

55. Barone and Unifusa, *Almanac of American Politics 1994*, p. 1119.

98   THE POLITICS OF CONGRESSIONAL ELECTIONS

56. Ehrenhalt, "House Freshmen," pp. 37, 41.
57. Craig Varoga, "Lone Star Upset," *Campaigns & Elections*, March 1995, p. 35.
58. Barone and Ujifusa, *Almanac of American Politics 1990*, p. 1087.
59. "South Carolina," *Congressional Quarterly Weekly Report* 52 (October 22, 1994):3050.
60. Eva Pusateri, "Shock Mailers That Jolt Your Audience," *Campaigns & Elections*, May 1995, p. 41.
61. Barone and Ujifusa, *Almanac of American Politics 2000*, (Washington, DC: National Journal, 1999) p. 1446.
62. Joel Bradshaw, "Who Will Vote for You and Why: Designing Campaign Strategy and Theme," (Paper presented at the Conference on Campaign Management, The American University, Washington, DC, December 10-11, 1992).
63. For example, Robert Leggett won reelection to the 4th District of California in 1976, even after having been a principal subject of the "Koreagate" investigation and having it known publicly that he had fathered two children by an aide, had been supporting two households for years, and had even forged his wife's name to the deed for the second house. For a more general analysis of the electoral effects of corruption charges, see John G. Peters and Susan Welch, "The Effects of Charges of Corruption on Voting Behavior in Congressional Elections," *American Political Science Review* 74 (1980):697-708; Susan Welch and John R. Hibbing, "The Effects of Charges of Corruption on Voting Behavior in Congressional Elections, 1982-1990," *Journal of Politics* 59 (1997):26-39; and Stephen C. Roberds, "Incumbent Scandals in U.S. House Elections" (Paper delivered at the Annual Meeting of the Midwest Political Science Association, Chicago, April 15-17, 1999).
64. John Kingdon, *Congressmen's Voting Decisions* (New York: Harper and Row, 1973), pp. 46-53.
65. Hershey, *Running for Office*, Chapters 6 and 7.
66. *Dollar Politics*, 3rd ed. (Washington, DC: Congressional Quarterly Press, 1982), p. 88; originally quoted in the *Washington Post*, August 10, 1980.
67. Rhodes Cook, "Senate Elections: A Dull Affair Compared to 1980's Upheaval," *Congressional Quarterly Weekly Report* 40 (November 6, 1982):2792.
68. Goldenberg and Traugott, *Campaigning for Congress*, p. 123.
69. Ehrenhalt, "New Campaign Era," p. 2561.
70. Richard Schlackman and Jamie "Buster" Douglas, "Attack Mail: The Silent Killer," *Campaigns & Elections*, July 1995, p. 25.
71. Stephen Ansolabehere, Shanto Iyengar, Adam Simon, and Nicholas Valentino, "Does Attack Advertising Demobilize the Electorate?" *American Political Science Review* 88 (1994): 829-838.
72. Paul Taylor, "Accentuating the Negative," *Washington Post* national weekly edition, October 20, 1986, p. 6.
73. Fenno, *Home Style*, p. 168; emphasis is Fenno's.
74. Gary C. Jacobson, "Deficit Cutting Politics and Congressional Elections," *Political Science Quarterly* 108 (1993):390-396.

75. Gary C. Jacobson and Michael A. Dimock, "Checking Out: The Effects of Bank Overdrafts on the 1992 House Elections," *American Journal of Political Science* 38 (1994):601-624; see also Chapter 6.

76. Fenno, *Home Style*, p. 55.

77. Ibid., p. 114.

78. Ehrenhalt, "New Campaign Era," p. 2563.

79. Ibid., pp. 2563-2564.

80. Taylor, "Accentuating the Negative," p. 6.

81. Barone and Ujifusa, *Almanac of American Politics 2000*, p. 497.

82. Michael Barone, Grant Ujifusa, and Douglas Matthews, *The Almanac of American Politics 1980* (New York: E.P. Dutton, 1979), p. 669.

83. Harvey Schantz, "Contested and Uncontested Primaries for the U.S. House," *Legislative Studies Quarterly* 5 (1980):550; Jeffrey S. Banks and D. Roderick Kiewiet, "Explaining Patterns of Candidate Competition in Congressional Elections," *American Journal of Political Science* 33 (1989):997-1015.

84. The evidence is in the next chapter.

85. Jeffrey Mondak, "Presidential Coattails in Open Seats: The District-Level Impact of Heuristic Processing," *American Politics Quarterly* 21 (1993): 307-319; Gregory H. Flemming, "Presidential Coattails in Open Seat Elections," *Legislative Studies Quarterly* 20 (1995):197-211.

86. See Ronald Keith Gaddie, "Congressional Seat Swings: Revisiting Exposure in House Elections," *Political Research Quarterly* 50 (1997): 699-710.

87. Peverill Squire, "Challenger Quality and Voting Behavior in U.S. Senate Elections," *Legislative Studies Quarterly* 17 (1992):247-264; David Lublin, "Quality, Not Quantity: Strategic Politicians in U.S. Senate Elections," *Journal of Politics* 56 (1994):228-241.

88. David Magleby, "More Bang for the Buck: Campaign Spending in Small-State U.S. Senate Elections" (Paper delivered at the Annual Meeting of the Western Political Science Association, Salt Lake City, March 30-April 1, 1989).

89. Kim Fridken Kahn, "Senate Elections and the News: Examining Campaign Coverage," *Legislative Studies Quarterly* 16 (1991):349-374.

90. John R. Alford and John R. Hibbing, "The Disparate Electoral Security of House and Senate Incumbents" (Paper delivered at the Annual Meeting of the American Political Science Association, Atlanta, August 31-September 3, 1989), pp. 17-19; see also Table 5-3.

91. Gary C. Jacobson and Raymond E. Wolfinger, "Information and Voting in California Senate Elections," *Legislative Studies Quarterly* 14 (1989):518-519; John R. Hibbing and John R. Alford, "Constituency Population and Representation in the United States Senate," *Legislative Studies Quarterly* 15 (1990):581-598; Bruce I. Oppenheimer and Frances Sandstrum, "The Effect of State Population on Senate Elections" (Paper delivered at the Annual Meeting of the Midwest Political Science Association, Chicago, April 6-8, 1995). However, one careful study found little difference in the level of regard voters have for senators compared to representatives and little disadvantage for senators from large states com-

pared to senators from small states. See Jonathan Krasno, *Challengers, Competition, and Reelection: Comparing Senate and House Elections* (New Haven, Connecticut: Yale University Press, 1994), Chapter 3.

92. Timothy Cook, "House Members as Newsmakers: The Effects of Televising Congress," *Legislative Studies Quarterly* 9 (1986):211.

93. Barbara Sinclair, "Washington Behavior and Home-State Reputation: The Impact of National Prominence on Senators' Visibility and Likability," *Legislative Studies Quarterly* 15 (1990):486–490.

94. Ehrenhalt, "New Campaign Era," p. 2560.

95. Ibid.

96. *Los Angeles Times*, September 12, 1994, p. 1.

97. Jonathan D. Salant, "GOP Bumps Up Against Court Precedent in Trying to Block AFL-CIO," *Congressional Quarterly Weekly Report* 54 (April 13, 1996):996–997.

98. Karen Foerstel, "Parties, Interest Groups Pour Money into Issue Ads," *Congressional Quarterly Weekly Report* 56 (October 31, 1998):2948–2949.

99. Ibid., p. 2948.

100. Gary C. Jacobson, "The Effect of the AFL-CIO's 'Voter Education' Campaign on the 1996 House Elections," *Journal of Politics* 61 (1999): 185–194.

CHAPTER FIVE

Congressional Voters

Virtually every issue raised in the previous two chapters was examined from the perspective of some implicit notions about how congressional voters operate. Discussions of the sources of the incumbency advantage, the importance of campaign money, and House–Senate electoral differences, to mention a few examples, were all grounded in particular assumptions about voting behavior in congressional elections. So, too, are the campaign and career strategies of congressional candidates. Their activities are guided by beliefs about what sways voters and, at the same time, help to define what voters' decisions are supposed to be about. An adequate understanding of voting behavior in congressional elections is important to congressional scholars and politicians alike.

Neither group has reason to be fully satisfied; voters continue to surprise both scholars and candidates on election day. Studies over the past two decades have produced a great deal of fresh information about congressional voters, however, and we know much more about them than we did just a few years back. This chapter examines voting behavior in congressional elections and how it relates to the other phenomena of congressional election politics. It begins with a discussion of voter turnout, then turns to the fundamental question of how voters come to prefer one candidate to the other.

TURNOUT IN CONGRESSIONAL ELECTIONS

Voting requires not only a choice among candidates, but also a decision to vote in the first place. A majority of adult Americans do not, in fact, vote in congressional elections. This has long been true of midterm elections and has recently become the case in presidential election years as well (see Figure 5-1). Obviously, participation in congressional elections is strongly influenced by whether or not there is a presidential contest to attract voters to the polls; turnout drops by an average of 13 percentage points when there is not. Even in presidential election years, House voting is about 4 percentage points lower than presidential voting. After reaching a high point in the early 1960s, turnout in both midterm and presidential election years has trended downward, although in 1992, turnout in House elections exceeded 50 percent for the first time in twenty years. In 1994 and 1998, turnout reached 36 percent, up from its all time modern midterm low of 33 percent in 1990.

These data raise a number of questions; not all of them have satisfactory answers. The most salient question—why the long-term decline in turnout—has been the subject of intensive investigation, but political scientists have yet to

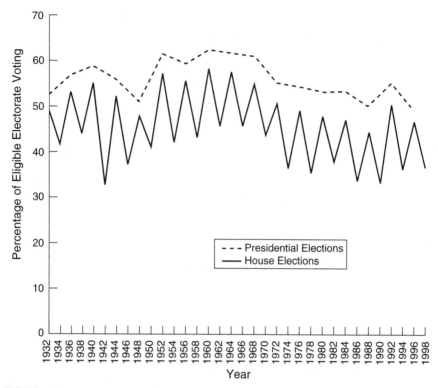

FIGURE 5–1. Voter Turnout in Presidential and Midterm Election Years, 1932-1998
Sources: Norman J. Ornstein, Thomas E. Mann, and Michael J. Malbin, *Vital Statistics on Congress 1997-1998* (Washington, DC: Congressional Quaterly Press, 1998), Table 2-1. Data for 1998 are from the Center for the Study of the American Electorate, news release, November 5, 1998.

agree on a definitive answer.[1] The mystery is all the deeper because the single demographic factor most strongly linked to participation—level of education—has been increasing in the population at the same time voting has been dropping. The most thorough examination of the question to date, undertaken by Steven Rosenstone and John Mark Hansen, places most of the blame on a decline in grassroots efforts by parties and other organization (unions, social movements) to get voters to the polls.[2] A full review of the question would take us too far afield; it is enough for our purposes to recognize that members of Congress are elected by an unimpressive proportion of eligible voters. In midterm elections, little more than a third of the adult population shows up at the polls.

Who Votes?

The low level of voting in congressional elections raises a second question: Who votes and who does not? The question is important because politicians wanting to get elected to Congress or to remain there will be most responsive to the concerns of people they expect to vote. If voters and nonvoters have noticeably different needs or preferences, the former are likely to be served, the latter slighted.

The question of who votes and who does not has been studied most thoroughly by Raymond Wolfinger and Steven Rosenstone. They report that turnout is affected most strongly by education; the more years of formal education one has, the more likely one is to vote. Voting also increases with income and occupational status, but these are themselves strongly related to education and have only a modest influence on turnout once education is taken into account.[3] Voting also increases with age, and some occupational groups—notably farmers and government workers—show distinctly higher levels of participation than their other demographic characteristics would lead us to expect. Other things equal, turnout is about 6 percentage points lower among people living in the South, a residue of the era when one-party rule was fortified by formal and informal practices that kept poor whites as well as blacks from the polls.[4]

Wolfinger and Rosenstone's demonstration that turnout varies most strongly with education comes as no surprise, since every other study of American voting behavior has found this to be the case. The accepted explanation is that education imparts knowledge about politics and increases one's capacity to deal with complex and abstract matters like those found in the political world.[5] People with the requisite cognitive skills and political knowledge find the cost of processing and acting on political information lower and the satisfactions greater. Politics is less threatening and more interesting. Similarly, learning outside of formal education can facilitate participation. People whose occupations put them in close touch with politics or whose livelihoods depend on governmental policy—government workers and farmers—vote more consistently, as do people who simply have longer experience as adults.

Curiously, the connection between education and voting participation does not hold in most other Western-style democracies. Western Europeans of lower education and occupational status vote at least as consistently as the rest of the population. The reason, according to Walter Dean Burnham, is that the strong European parties of the left provide the necessary political information and stimuli to their chosen clientele. The sharply lower turnout at the lower end of the American socioeconomic scale can thus be interpreted as another consequence of comparatively weak parties interested mainly in electoral politics and patronage.[6]

Better educated, wealthier, higher-status, and older people are clearly overrepresented in the electorate. When their preferences and concerns were substantially different from those of nonvoters, governmental policy will be biased in their favor. Wolfinger and Rosenstone, citing survey data from the 1970s, argued that the views of voters were not very different from those of the population as a whole, so differential participation did not impart any special bias.[7] In the 1980s and 1990s, however, policy issues that divided people according to economic status became more prominent, and the underrepresented groups suffered. Cuts in government spending to reduce federal budget deficits hit welfare recipients far harder than senior citizens or business corporations.

Another question posed by the turnout data is whether congressional electorates differ between presidential and midterm election years. Do the millions of citizens who only vote for congressional candidates because they happen to be on the same ballot with presidential candidates change the electoral environment in politically consequential ways? One prominent study, based on surveys of voters taken in the 1950s, concluded that they did. The electorate in presidential years was found to be composed of a larger proportion of voters weakly attached to either political party and subject to greater influence by political phenomena peculiar to the specific election, notably their feelings about the presidential candidates. At the midterm, with such voters making up a much smaller proportion of the electorate, partisanship prevailed. This resulted in a pattern of "surge and decline," in which the winning presidential candidate's party picked up congressional seats (the surge), many of which were subsequently lost at the next midterm election when the pull of the presidential candidate was no longer operating. The theory of surge and decline explained why, in every midterm election between 1934 and 1998, the president's party lost seats in the House.[8]

Aggregate shifts in congressional seats and votes from one election to the next will be examined at length in the next chapter. At this point, suffice it to say that the view of electorates underlying this theory has not been supported by subsequent evidence. More recent research suggests that midterm voters are no more or less partisan than those voting in presidential years and that the two electorates are demographically alike.[9] The addition or subtraction of voters drawn out by a presidential contest does not seem to produce significantly different electorates.[10]

These observations about turnout refer to the electorate as a whole, but congressional candidates are, of course, much more concerned about the particular electorates in their states and districts. As noted in Chapter 2, turnout is by no means the same across constituencies; it varies enormously. One obvious source of variation is the demographic makeup of the district: average level of education, income, occupational status, age distribution, and so on. These factors are, at least in the short run, fairly constant in any individual state or district; but turnout also varies in the same constituency from election to election (quite apart from the presidential year–midterm difference), and these variations are, for our purposes, the most interesting.

The generally low level of voting in congressional elections means that a large measure of the fundamental electoral currency—votes—lies untapped. This affects campaign strategy in several ways. Even incumbents who have been winning by healthy margins recognize that many citizens did not vote for them (even if they did not vote against them) and that they could be in for trouble if an opponent who can mobilize the abstainers comes along. This is not an idle worry. Generally, the higher the turnout, the closer the election; the lower the turnout, the more easily the incumbent is reelected.[11] Successful challengers evidently draw to the polls many people who normally do not bother to vote. The wisdom of defusing the opposition and discouraging strong challenges is again apparent. Experienced campaigners know that getting one's supporters to the polls is as important as winning their support in the first place; well-organized campaigns typically devote a major share of their work to getting out the vote. One important source of the Republicans' triumph in 1994 was their more effective mobilization of supporters. Superior mobilization also contributed to the Democrats' pickup of House seats in the 1998 elections—notable because the president's party almost always loses seats at the midterm.

The effort to get out the vote presupposes that there is a vote to be gotten out, that people brought to the polls will indeed support the candidate. After all, what finally matters is what voters do in the voting booth. And this raises a question of fundamental interest to politicians and political scientists alike. What determines how people vote for congressional candidates? What moves voters to support one candidate rather than the other? The entire structure of congressional election politics hinges on the way voters reach this decision.

PARTISANSHIP IN CONGRESSIONAL ELECTIONS

The first modern survey studies of congressional elections identified partisanship as the single most important influence on individuals' voting decisions, and it has remained so despite a detectable decline in party influence from the 1960s through the 1970s, since partially reversed. The pioneering survey studies of voting behavior in both presidential and congressional elections conducted in the 1950s found that a large majority of voters thought of themselves as Democrats or Republicans and voted accordingly. Particular candidates or issues might, on occasion, persuade a person to vote for someone of the other party, but the defection was likely to be temporary and did not dissolve the partisan attachment.[12]

Alternative Interpretations of Party Identification

The leading interpretation of these findings was that voters who were willing to label themselves Democrats or Republicans identified with the party in the same way they might identify with a region or an ethnic or religious group: "I'm a Texan, a Baptist, and a Democrat." The psychological attachment to a party was rooted in powerful personal experiences (best exemplified by the millions who became Democrats during the Depression) or was learned, along with similar attachments, from the family. In either case, identification with a party was thought to establish an enduring orientation toward the political world. The result, in aggregate, was a stable pattern of partisanship across the entire electorate. Thus, from the New Deal onward, the Democrats enjoyed consistent national majorities. Individual states or congressional districts were, in many cases, "safe" for candidates of one party or the other.

This did not mean that the same party won every election, of course. Some voters did not think of themselves as belonging to a party, and even those who did would defect if their reactions to particular candidates, issues, or recent events ran contrary to their party identification strongly enough. But once these short-term forces were no longer present, the long-term influence of party identification would reassert itself and they would return to their partisan moorings. For most citizens, only quite powerful and unusual experiences could inspire permanent shifts of party allegiance.

This interpretation of party identification has been undermined from at least two directions since it was developed. First, the electoral influence of partisanship diminished steadily throughout the 1960s and 1970s. Fewer voters were willing to consider themselves partisans, and the party attachments of those who did were likely to be weaker. The percentage of people declaring themselves to be strong partisans fell from 36 in 1952 to 23 in 1978; the percentage declaring themselves to be weak or strong partisans fell from 75 to 60 over the same period. Even those who still admitted to partisan attachments were a good deal more likely to defect to candidates of the other party than they had been earlier.[13]

Although no definitive explanation for the period of decline in electoral partisanship has been developed, it is no doubt related to political events of the 1960s and 1970s. Each party brought disaster upon itself by nominating a presidential candidate preferred only by its more extreme ideologues, the Republicans with Goldwater in 1964, the Democrats with McGovern in 1972. In 1968, the Vietnam War and the civil rights issue split the Democrats badly and fostered the strongest third-party showing since 1924. Republicans suffered in turn as the Watergate revelations forced their disgraced president from office. Jimmy Carter's inept handling of the economy and troubles with Iran laid the Democrats low in 1980. More generally, the political alliances formed in the battle over the New Deal were fractured along multiple lines as new problems and issues—most notably social issues concerning abortion, crime, and sexuality—forced their way onto the political agenda.

Voters responded to these political phenomena as they were expected to respond to short-term forces, defecting when their party preferences were contradicted strongly enough. As defections become more widespread and partisanship, in general, continued to decline, an interpretation of party identification that, among other things, more easily accommodated change gained plausibility. The alternative interpretation emphasizes the practical rather than psychological aspects of party identification. It has been presented most fully by Morris P. Fiorina, who argues that people attach themselves to a party because they have found, through past experience, that its candidates are more likely than those of the other party to produce the kinds of results they prefer.

Since it costs time and energy to determine the full range of information on all candidates who run for office, voters quite reasonably use the shorthand cue of party to simplify the voting decision. Past experience is a more useful criterion than future promises or expectations because it is more certain. Party cues are recognized as imperfect, to be sure, and people who are persuaded that a candidate of the other party would deal more effectively with their concerns vote for him or her. More importantly, if cumulative experience suggests that candidates of the preferred party are no longer predictably superior in this respect, the party preference naturally decays.[14] Party ties are subject to modification, depending on the answer to the proverbial voters' question, "What have you done for me lately?"[15]

The virtue of this alternative interpretation is that it can account for both the observed short-run stability and long-run lability of party identification evident in individuals and the electorate. For example, it offers a plausible explanation for the evidence of a significant shift in party identification away from the Democrats and toward the Republicans during the 1980s. According to National Election Studies data, the 52–33 advantage in percentage share of party identifiers held by Democrats in 1980 had, by 1994, shrunk to 47–42.[16] The biggest change took place in the South, where the proportion of voters identifying themselves as Republicans grew from less than 32 percent in 1980 to 48 percent in 1998.[17] Moreover, self-described Republicans turned out to vote in higher proportions than did Democrats in 1994, so that for the first time in the forty-two-year history of the National Elections Studies, Republicans enjoyed a lead in party identification among voters, 48–46.

The Republicans' gains in party identification were not fully sustained, however. The Democrats' advantage expanded to 52–38 in 1996 and to 53–37 in 1998, as House Republicans' missteps on the budget in 1995 and the unpopular attempt to impeach and convict Bill Clinton in 1998 cost their party public support (see Chapter 6). Still, the Democrats' lead is narrower than it was before the Reagan administration, and because Republican identifiers tend to turn out at higher levels and to vote more loyally for their party, the national partisan division remains closely balanced.[18] These swings show that party identification can change in response to political experiences far less earthshaking than the Great Depression; and partisanship appears to be rather more sensitive to short-term influences than the psychological model would predict.[19]

Partisanship and Voting

The issue of which interpretation makes more empirical sense (or which combination of the two views—they are by no means irreconcilable) will not be settled here. What matters most for our purposes is that, however party identification is interpreted, it remains an important influence on congressional voters, but an influence that varies in strength over time. Figures 5-2 and 5-3 dis-

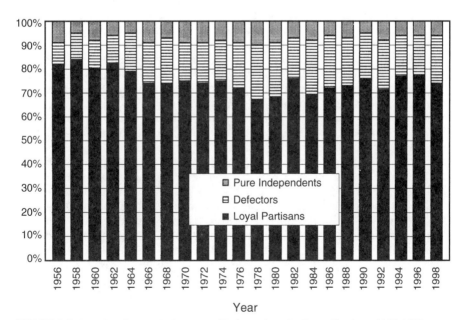

FIGURE 5–2. Party-Line Voters, Defectors, and Independents in House Elections, 1956–1998
Source: American National Election Studies.

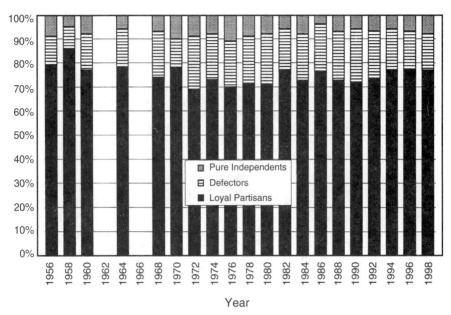

FIGURE 5–3. Party-Line Voters, Defectors, and Independents in Senate Elections, 1956–1998
Source: American National Election Studies.

play the trends in partisan voting in House and Senate elections since 1956. Notice that, despite the common perception that voters have become increasingly
detached from parties, the share of the electorate composed of voters who
label themselves as pure independents, leaning toward neither party, has not
grown. What did grow for a time was the proportion of voters who vote contrary to their expressed party affiliation. By the end of the 1970s, defections in
House elections were typically twice as common as they were in the 1950s.
Since the 1970s, party loyalty has recovered, although not to its earlier levels.
In the 1990s, about 75 percent of House voters have been loyal partisans, about
19 percent, partisan defectors. The trends for Senate electorates have been similar, with a visible increase in party loyalty between the 1970s and 1990s.

The decline of party loyalty had important consequences for House elections,
because, as Figures 5-4 and 5-5 show us, the growth in defections was entirely
at the expense of challengers. The crucial evidence is from the 1956-1976 surveys; from 1978 onward, the vote question has been asked in a way that exaggerates the reported vote for incumbents (typically by about 8 percentage
points). The actual rate of defections to incumbents has thus been lower—and
has almost certainly fallen further since the mid-1970s—than the figure suggests.[20] Voters sharing the incumbent's party are as loyal now as they ever were.
Voters of the challenger's party have become much less faithful (even discounting for exaggeration), generally defecting at very high rates from 1972 through
1992 elections. Only beginning in 1994 do we see a sustained reduction in de-

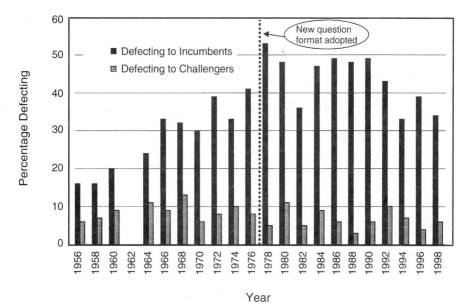

FIGURE 5–4. Partisan Voters Defecting to Incumbents and Challengers in House Elections, 1958-1998
Source: American National Election Studies.

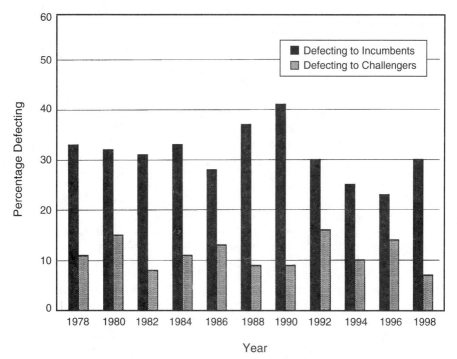

FIGURE 5–5. Partisan Voters Defecting to Incumbents and Challengers in Senate Elections, 1978-1998
Source: American National Election Studies.

fections to incumbents. Defections also clearly favor Senate incumbents, but by a considerably narrower and, in the 1990s, decreasing margin.

The trends in Figure 5-4 and 5-5 display, at the level of individual voters, the change in the vote advantage of House incumbents that was evident in the aggregate figures discussed in Chapter 3. They also reiterate the familiar House–Senate differences in this regard. But they do not explain either phenomenon. As Albert Cover has pointed out, there is no logical reason why weaker party loyalty could not produce defections balanced between incumbents and challengers or even favoring the latter.[21] After all, voters are about as likely to desert their party in Senate elections as in House elections, but the defections are considerably less likely to favor incumbents. Other factors must be involved.

INFORMATION AND VOTING

One other factor is information. At the most basic level, people hesitate to vote for candidates they know nothing at all about. Among the most consistent findings produced by studies of congressional voters over the past generation is that simple knowledge of who the candidates are is strongly connected to voting behavior. Prior to the 1978 election study, knowledge of the candidates was measured by whether or not voters remembered their names when asked by an interviewer. Very few partisans defect if they remember the name of their own party's candidate but not that of the opponent; more than half usually defect if they remember only the name of the other party's candidate; defection rates of voters who know both or neither fall in between. The pattern holds for Senate as well as House candidates.[22]

This suggested one important reason why incumbents do so well in House elections: voters are much more likely to remember their names. In surveys taken during the 1980–1998 period, for example, from 42 to 54 percent (average, 46 percent) could recall the incumbent's name, but only 10 to 26 percent (average, 17 percent) that of the challenger. If only one of the two candidates is remembered, it is the incumbent 95 percent of the time. But understanding the effects of differential knowledge of the candidate's names does not clear up all the basic questions.

First, it does not explain the growth in partisan defections to incumbents. Beyond question, incumbents are comparatively much better known, through both past successful campaigns and vigorous exploitation of the abundant resources for advertising themselves that come with the office. But as campaign spending and official resources have grown, their familiarity among voters has not; indeed, it has declined, as Figure 5-6 illustrates.[23] Voters' familiarity with House challengers declined even more, but the difference was not enough to contribute much to the rising value of incumbency. Second, voters favor incumbents even when they cannot recall either candidate's name, so there must be more to the choice than simple name familiarity.[24] Voters are, in fact, often willing to offer opinions about candidates—incumbents and challengers alike—even without remembering their names.[25]

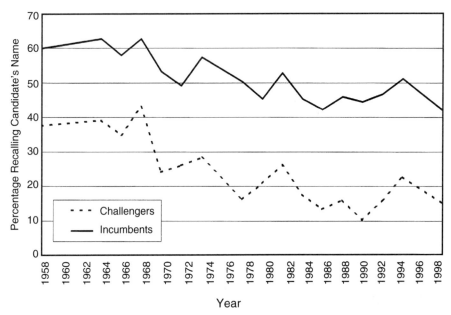

FIGURE 5–6. Name Recall of House Challengers and Incumbents, 1958–1998 (Voters Only)
Source: American National Election Studies; comparable data are not available for 1960, 1962, 1976 and 1996.

Recall and Recognition of Candidates

Such discoveries forced scholars to reconsider what is meant by "knowing" the candidates. Thomas Mann was first to show that many voters who could not recall a candidate's name could recognize the name from a list, information always available in the voting booth.[26] Beginning in 1978, the National Election Studies have thus included questions testing the voter's ability both to recall and to recognize each candidate's name. The studies have also included a battery of questions designed to find out what else voters know about the candidates, what sort of contact they have had with them, and what they think of them on a variety of dimensions. The data collected since 1978 allow a much more thorough examination of voting behavior in congressional elections than was possible previously and are the center of attention in the rest of this chapter. Unfortunately, however, these newer data cannot cast much light on what changes have occurred in patterns of congressional voting, since comparable data from earlier elections do not exist.[27]

The more recent studies of congressional voters leave no doubt that voters recognize candidates' names much more readily than they recall them.[28] Table 5–1 shows that voters are twice as likely to recognize as to recall House candidates in any incumbency category. The same is true for Senate candidates, except in the case of incumbents and candidates for open seats, whose names are already recalled by more than half the voters. These figures also leave no doubt

TABLE 5–1   INCUMBENCY STATUS AND VOTERS' FAMILIARITY WITH CONGRESSIONAL CANDIDATES, 1980–1998 (IN PERCENTAGES)

YEAR	INCUMBENTS Recalled Name	INCUMBENTS Recognized Name[a]	CHALLENGERS Recalled Name	CHALLENGERS Recognized Name[a]	OPEN SEATS Recalled Name	OPEN SEATS Recognized Name[a]
House Elections						
1980	46	92	21	54	32	82
1982	54	94	26	62	29	77
1984	45	91	18	54	32	80
1986	42	91	13	46	43	84
1988	46	93	16	53	33	71
1990	45	93	10	37	26	78
1992	43	87	15	56	23	79
1994	51	93	22	57	36	82
1998[b]	42	91	15	45	52	83
Mean:	46	92	17	52	34	80
Senate Elections						
1980	61	99	40	81	47	89
1982	61	97	37	78	73	95
1986[c]	61	97	41	77	61	94
1988	51	96	30	74	73	97
1990	57	98	31	69	31	86
1992	55	96	33	82	59	93
1994[d]	—	98	—	84	—	92
1998[bd]	—	96	—	71	—	77
Mean:	58	97	35	77	57	90

[a]Includes only respondents who reported voting and who could recognize and rate the candidates on the feeling thermometer or, if they could not rate the candidates, could recall the candidates' names.
[b]Comparable data are not available for 1996.
[c]Data are not available for 1984 Senate candidates.
[d]Recall question not asked.
Sources: American National Election Studies.

that the House incumbent's advantage in recall is matched by an advantage in recognition. More than 90 percent of voters recognizes the incumbent's name. The shift in focus from name recall to recognition nicely resolves the apparent anomaly of voters favoring incumbents without knowing who they are. Many more voters also recognize the challenger than recall his name, but these voters still amount to little more than half the electorate. Candidates for open seats are better known than challengers but not so well known as incumbents; indeed, the data will show that they fall between incumbents and challengers on almost every measure. This is exactly what we would expect, knowing the kinds of candidates and campaigns typical of open seat contests.

Senate candidates are better known than their House counterparts in each category, and Senate incumbents are clearly better known than their challengers (though the more populous the state, the lower the proportion who can recall the senator's name[29]). But the gap is smaller than it is for House candidates. Again, this is the kind of pattern we would anticipate, owing to the distinctive circumstances of Senate electoral politics outlined in the previous chapter.

Familiarity is supposed to matter, of course, because of its connection to the vote; Table 5-2 displays the connection for some recent elections.[30] In both House and Senate elections, the more familiar voters are with a candidate, the more likely they are to vote for him or her, with the effect also depending, symmetrically, on the degree of familiarity with the other candidate. Defections are concentrated in the upper right-hand corner of each table; party loyalty predominates in the lower left-hand corner. Only about 5 percent of House voters and 13 percent of Senate voters defected to candidates who were less familiar than their own; more than half of both Senate and House voters defected to candidates who were more familiar. Independent voters, omitted from this table, voted for the better-known candidate 86 percent of the time in the House races, 82 percent of the time in the Senate contests.

Why is familiarity of so much benefit to congressional candidates? The answer proposed by Donald Stokes and Warren Miller, that, "in the main, to be perceived at all is to be perceived favorably," has not found much support in later work.[31] It does not work so simply. Since 1978, surveys have asked respondents what they liked and disliked about House candidates; the same questions were asked about Senate candidates in the 1988–1992 Senate Election Studies. As the figures in Table 5-3 indicate, the more familiar voters are with candidates, the more likely they are to find things they both like and dis-

TABLE 5–2 FAMILIARITY WITH CANDIDATES AND VOTING BEHAVIOR IN CONGRESSIONAL ELECTIONS (PERCENTAGE OF VOTERS DEFECTING)

	FAMILIARITY WITH OWN PARTY'S CANDIDATE		
	Recalled Name	Recognized Name[a]	Neither
House Elections (1998)			
Familiarity with other party's candidate:			
Recalled name	12	33	66
Recognized name[a]	6	31	68
Neither	0	2	15
Senate Elections (1988–1992)			
Familiarity with other party's candidate:			
Recalled name	20	49	75
Recognized name[a]	9	30	63
Neither	8	7	25

[a]Recognized name and could rate candidate on the thermometer scale but could not recall candidate's name.
Sources: American National Election Study, 1998, and Senate Election Studies, 1988, 1990, and 1992.

TABLE 5-3 INCUMBENCY STATUS AND VOTERS' LIKES AND DISLIKES OF HOUSE AND SENATE CANDIDATES (IN PERCENTAGES)

YEAR	RECALLED NAME		RECOGNIZED NAME[a]		NEITHER		MARGINAL TOTALS	
	Like Something	Dislike Something	Like Something	Dislike Something	Like Something	Dislike Something	Like Something	Dislike Something
House 1978–1998								
Incumbents	71	32	49	15	12	7	56	22
Challengers	43	35	28	16	2	2	16	13
Open Seats	60	37	33	21	6	3	38	23
Senate 1988–1992								
Incumbents	67	43	50	22	17	3	59	34
Challengers	52	49	26	26	4	3	31	29
Open Seats	56	48	36	27	4	3	43	35

[a]Includes only respondents who reported voting and who could recognize and rate the candidate on the feeling thermometer or, if they could not rate the candidates, could recall the candidate's name.

Sources: American National Election Studies, 1978–1998, and Senate Election Studies, 1988, 1990, 1992.

like about them. Familiarity by no means breeds only favorable responses. More important, the benefits of incumbency obviously extend well beyond greater familiarity. Incumbents are better liked—by a wide margin—as well as better known than challengers. At any level of familiarity, voters are more inclined to mention something they like about the incumbent than about the challenger; negative responses are rather evenly divided, so the net benefit is clearly to the incumbent. Voters tend to favor Senate as well as House incumbents on this dimension, though the difference is smaller; Senate candidates tend to attract a higher proportion of negative responses, reflecting the greater average intensity of these contests.

Another survey question allows further comparison of voters' feelings about House and Senate candidates. Respondents are asked to rate candidates they recognized on a "thermometer" scale of 0 to 100 degrees, with 0 as the most unfavorable, 100 as the most favorable, and 50 as neutral. The mean temperatures for House and Senate candidates in different incumbency categories are shown in Figures 5-7 and 5-8.

House and Senate challengers are, on average, rated about the same (the important difference lying in the proportion of voters who could rate them at all), as are candidates for open seats. But House incumbents are more warmly regarded than Senate incumbents, and so the average gap between House incumbents and their challengers (13.8 degrees) is larger than that between Senate incumbents and their challengers (8.9 degrees). Notice that the House incumbents' advantage has shrunk in recent elections, averaging 10.1 degrees in 1992–1998 compared to 16.0 degrees in the earlier years covered.

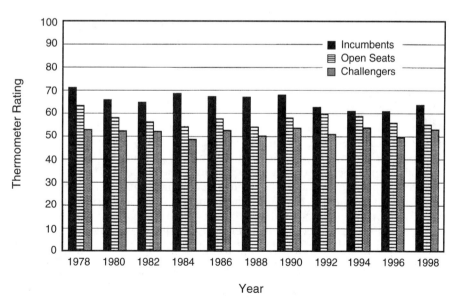

FIGURE 5–7. Voters' Ratings of House Candidates on the 100-Point Thermometer Scale, 1978–1998
Source: American National Election Studies.

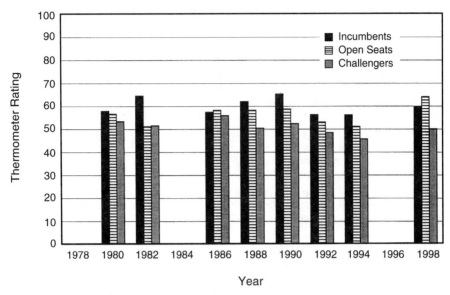

FIGURE 5–8. Voters' Ratings of Senate Candidates on the 100-Point Thermometer Scale, 1978–1998
Source: American National Election Studies.

The Senate figures tend to mirror aggregate election results. Recall from Table 3-1 that more than a quarter of Senate incumbents lost general elections in 1980 and 1986, two years in which the Senate incumbents' advantage in thermometer ratings is much narrower than usual. Indeed, Democratic challengers in 1986 were, on average, rated higher (60.6 degrees) than their incumbent Republican opponents (57.7 degrees), an indication of unusual weakness among the Republican Senate class of 1980 (the Democrats retook control of the Senate in 1986).

Contacting Voters

Why are House incumbents so much better known and liked than their opponents? Why are Senate challengers more familiar to voters than House challengers? One obvious explanation is based on the frequency with which messages about members of the various categories reach voters. The percentages of voters reporting contact with House and Senate candidates are listed in Table 5-4. The table lists entries for two separate House election years so that we may compare the frequencies of contacts reported in a year with unusually obscure and underfinanced challengers (1990) with those reported in a year with a relatively high proportion of well-financed and successful challenges (1994). Voters are twice as likely to report contact of every kind with incumbents than with challengers in House races. Almost every voter was reached in some way by the incumbent, while even in a year with unusually vigorous challenges barely half the voters report contact of any kind with the challenger.

TABLE 5–4   VOTERS' CONTACTS WITH HOUSE AND SENATE CANDIDATES (IN PERCENTAGES)

TYPE OF CONTACT	INCUMBENT 1990	INCUMBENT 1994	CHALLENGER 1990	CHALLENGER 1994	OPEN SEAT 1990	OPEN SEAT 1994
House Candidates						
Any	92	90	29	52	81	80
Met Personally	20	15	2	4	10	7
Saw at Meeting	19	14	3	3	10	7
Talked to Staff	13	14	2	5	4	7
Received Mail	70	63	12	25	48	49
Read about in Newspaper	67	65	20	34	59	55
Heard on Radio	30	33	7	18	20	27
Saw on TV	51	61	16	34	58	57
Family or Friend had Contact	38	32	7	9	21	16
Senate Candidates (1988–1992)						
Any	99		85		96	
Met Personally	25		9		10	
Saw at Meeting	26		9		11	
Talked to Staff	21		7		12	
Received Mail	83		51		66	
Read about in Newspaper	93		75		85	
Heard on Radio	60		45		55	
Saw on TV	94		75		85	

Sources: American National Election Studies, 1990 and 1994, and Senate Election Studies, 1988–1992.

Still, the two election years look quite different for challengers, with much higher levels of contact reported in 1994.

Senate incumbents have a substantially smaller advantage over their challengers in frequency of reported contacts. The differences between House and Senate challengers are sharpest in the area of mass media publicity. Notice especially the difference in the proportion of voters reached through television. Richard Fenno's observations of senators and Senate candidates led him to conclude that a major difference between House and Senate elections is the much greater importance of the mass media in the latter. The news media are much more interested in Senate candidates because they are much more interested in senators.[32] As noted in the previous chapter, Senate campaigns are also wealthier and can use paid television more extensively and more efficiently than can House campaigns. The consequences are evident in the survey data; both factors enhance the Senate challenger's ability to catch the attention of voters, an essential ingredient of electoral success.

Although it is no surprise that senators and Senate candidates reach a larger proportion of voters through the mass media, it is certainly a surprise that more voters report meeting them personally and talking to their staffs than report equivalent contacts with their counterparts in the House. We would expect that the much larger constituencies represented by senators would make personal contacts less common. Part of the reason these data show the opposite pattern is that the Senate Election Study has equal size samples from every state, so voters from smaller states are overrepresented. But even adjusting for state size, House members and candidates evidently have no advantage in personal contacts. Only in the very largest states—those with voting age populations in excess of five million—do voters report significantly fewer personal contacts with Senate candidates.

The main House–Senate difference, then, is in mass media contacts. For Senate incumbents, the news media's greater interest is a mixed blessing. Senators are accorded more attention but are also subject to higher expectations. A House member running for the Senate explained it to Fenno this way:

> People don't treat me differently. They don't see any difference between the two jobs. Maybe they think it's a higher office, but that doesn't make any difference. But the media hold me to a much higher standard than they did as a House member. They expect me to know more details. Am I treated differently running for the Senate? By the people, no; by the media, yes.[34]

House incumbents normally do not attract much attention from the news media. This means that, except during campaigns, they produce and disseminate much of the information about themselves that reaches the public. To a large extent, they control their own press; no wonder it is good press, and no wonder voters tend to think highly of them.[35] In most cases, only a vigorous campaign by the challenger spreads information critical of their performance, with effects that are analyzed later in this chapter.

Table 5-4 also reinforces the vital point that not all nonincumbent candidates are alike. Voters report more contact of all sorts with candidates for open seats than with challengers. The figures for open-seat candidates are sometimes closer to those for incumbents than to those for challengers. House incumbents hold a wide advantage over challengers in these categories, but not simply because they are incumbents and their opponents are not. Their opponents are, rather, much weaker candidates than they might be—or than appear when no incumbent is running. This is a natural consequence of the strategies followed by potential House candidates and their potential supporters as discussed in Chapter 3.

Incumbents benefit from their superior ability to reach voters, because the more different ways voters come into contact with a candidate, the more likely they are to remember the candidate and to like (but also dislike) something about him or her. To see this, we will examine the results of some probit equations estimating the effects of contacts on voter awareness and evaluations of House candidates. Probit analysis is a standard procedure for estimating the effects of independent variables on a categorical dependent variable—that is, one that takes only a small number of discrete values. Here, all of our dependent variables happen to be dichotomous; that is, they take only two values. For example, a voter either recalls the candidate's name or does not; the voter either likes something about the candidate or does not.

Probit analysis allows us to estimate how changes in the independent variables affect the probability of one outcome as opposed to the other. The procedure is analogous to regression analysis, with the important differences being that the estimated probability is constrained to take a value between 0.0 and 1.0 (and so always makes sense as a "probability"), and that the relationships are nonlinear: the effect of any independent variable depends interactively on the current levels of the other independent variables.[36] This makes it difficult to interpret the coefficients directly, so the results are also displayed in tables that show the estimated probabilities at various settings of the independent variables. All this will be clearer with our specific examples. The variables used in this and subsequent analyses here and in the next chapter are listed in Table 5-5.

The connection between various kinds of contact (combined into four basic modes[37]) and voters' knowledge and evaluations of the candidates is shown in Tables 5-6 and 5-7.[38] Table 5-6 lists the probit coefficients (with their standard errors) estimating the effects of each mode of contact on the likelihood that a voter would recall, recognize, and like or dislike something about a House challenger or incumbent in 1988. Although weakly intercorrelated, each of these modes of contact is independently related to the probability that voters know and like or dislike something about both types of candidates. All but a

TABLE 5–5   DEFINITIONS OF PROBIT EQUATION VARIABLES

Respondent's House vote	1 if Democratic, 0 if Repbulican
Recall candidate/Recognize candidate	1 if respondent recalled (recognized) candidate, 0 otherwise
Type of Contact:	
Personal	1 if respondent has met candidate, attended a meeting where candidate spoke, or had contact with staff, 0 otherwise
Mail	1 if respondent received anything in the mail about the candidate, 0 if not
Mass media	1 if respondent learned about candidate by reading newspapers, listening to the radio, or watching television, 0 otherwise
Indirect	1 if respondent's family or friends had any contact with the candidate, 0 if not
Party identification	1 if strong, weak, or independent Democrat, 0 if independent-independent, -1 if strong, weak, or independent Republican
Democrat is incumbent	1 if Democrat is incumbent, 0 otherwise
Republican is incumbent	1 if Republican is incumbent, 0 otherwise
Familiarity with Democrat/Familiarity with Republican	1 if respondent recalls candidate's name, .5 if name is recognized but not recalled, 0 if name is not recognized or recalled
Likes something about candidate/ Dislikes something about candidate	For each variable, 1 if respondent mentions anything liked (or disliked) about the candidate, 0 otherwise
Clinton vote	1 if for Bill Clinton, 0 if for Ross Perot, -1 if for Bob Dole

TABLE 5–6   PROBIT EQUATIONS ESTIMATING THE EFFECTS OF CONTACTS ON VOTERS' KNOWLEDGE AND EVALUATIONS OF HOUSE CANDIDATES, 1994

INDEPENDENT VARIABLE	DEPENDENT VARIABLE:							
	Recall		Recognize		Like Something		Dislike Something	
Challengers								
Intercept	−1.53	(.10)	−.51	(.07)	−1.90	(.13)	−1.83	(.12)
Personal	42	(.21)	.90	(.40)	.76	(.21)	−.09	(.23)
Mail	.25	(.14)	30	(.16)	.39	(.15)	.27	(.15)
Mass Media	1.03	(.13)	1.30	(.12)	1.04	(.16)	.92	(.16)
Indirect	.47	(.20)	1.34	(.41)	.81	(.21)	.38	(.22)
Incumbents								
Intercept	−.82	(.13)	.58	(.14)	−.70	(.13)	−1.17	(.14)
Personal	.24	(.13)	.60	(.40)	.70	(.13)	.11	(.13)
Mail	.55	(.11)	.72	(.19)	.44	(.11)	.28	(.11)
Mass Media	.44	(.14)	.66	(.18)	.27	(.13)	.47	(.15)
Indirect	.26	(.12)	.68	(.35)	.40	(.12)	.00	(.12)

Note: Standard errors are in parentheses; any coefficient larger than twice its standard error is statistically significant at $p < .05$.

TABLE 5.7   THE EFFECTS OF CONTACTS ON VOTERS' KNOWLEDGE AND EVALUATIONS OF HOUSE CANDIDATES, 1994

TYPE OF CONTACT	PROBABILITY OF VOTER'S RESPONSE TO CANDIDATE			
	Recall	Recognize	Like Something	Dislike Something
Challengers				
None	.17	.37	.13	.14
Personal	.25	.60	.24	.13
Mail	.22	.45	.18	.17
Mass Media	.38	.69	.30	.29
Indirect	.26	.70	.25	.13
Any two[a]	.30-.49	.66-.89	.32-.49	.16-.36
Any three[a]	.40-.59	.88-.95	.52-.67	.22-.43
All four	.60	.96	.75	.41
Incumbents				
None	.30	.64	.33	.24
Personal	.36	.63	.50	.26
Mail	.43	.79	.44	.29
Mass Media	.40	.78	.39	.33
Indirect	.36	.78	.42	.24
Any two[a]	.42-.54	.86-.88	.49-.61	.26-.40
Any three[a]	.53-.60	.93-.93	.60-.70	.31-.42
All four	.65	.96	.75	.42

[a]Range of values listed because the probability depends on pair or trio chosen.
   Source: Probit equations in Table 5–6.

handful of the coefficients are larger than twice their standard errors and so achieve at least a .05 level of statistical significance.

A comparison of the coefficients suggests that, in general, mass media contact has the strongest effect on these probabilities for challengers. This is confirmed by Table 5-7, which interprets the probit equations for various combinations of the independent variables. The table lists the probability of each response, depending on the modes of contact individually and in combination. Note that respondents are twice as likely to recognize, recall, and evaluate challengers if they report contact with them through the mass media. For incumbents, each type of contact has about the same size effect. Notice the significant effect for both incumbents and challengers of indirect contact ("word-of-mouth" contact through experiences of family or friends), confirming politicians' faith in the ripple effects of their work to reach voters.

The effects of different modes of contact are cumulative. The more contacts voters have had with a House candidate, the more likely they are to know and like or dislike something about the candidate. Voters who were reached through all four modes are far more likely to be aware of candidates and to offer evaluative comments about them than voters not reached at all, and among such voters, the incumbent's advantage in recognition and affect disappears. Note also that the probability of both liking and disliking something about a candidate increases with contact, but that the increase is greater for positive comments. The net effect of successful attempts to reach voters is clearly helpful to candidates.

The Effects of Campaign Spending

The impact of contacts on familiarity and evaluations—and the importance of these to the vote choice—helps to explain why campaign money is so important to challengers. The connection between a House challenger's level of campaign spending and the probability that a voter will report having had contact with the candidate (through each of the basic modes, or any of them) is shown in Table 5-8. The likelihood of every kind of contact increases with expenditures, though at a decreasing rate. For example, as spending goes from $30,000 to $300,000, the probability of any contact at all increases from .42 to .66, the likelihood of contact through mass media goes from .39 to .61, and the probabilities of personal contact, contact via the mails, and indirect contact through family and friends all increase as well.

Notice, however, that the incumbent retains a lead in every measure of contact but personal, even if the challenger spends $500,000. This is not merely a consequence of the incumbent's usual financial advantage; the incumbent's level of spending has only a modest and often statistically insignificant effect on these variables. Rather, it is a consequence of past campaigns and the district-oriented activities engaged in by House members whether or not an election is imminent.

For challengers, greater spending produces greater familiarity among voters as well; a high-spending campaign can cut the incumbent's lead in voter recall and recognition by more than half.[39] The data in Table 5-8 help to explain why campaign money is crucial to challengers and other nonincumbent House candidates. Without it, they cannot reach voters, remain obscure, and

TABLE 5–8   CAMPAIGN EXPENDITURES AND VOTERS' CONTACTS AND FAMILIARITY WITH CHALLENGERS, 1994

CAMPAIGN EXPENDITURES	TYPE OF CONTACT					Recall Name	Recognize Name
	Any	Personal	Mail	Mass Media	Indirect		
$ 10,000	.32	.13	.20	.29	.12	.18	.36
$ 30,000	.42	.16	.26	.39	.16	.24	.47
$ 50,000	.48	.18	.29	.44	.18	.27	.52
$ 80,000	.52	.19	.32	.48	.19	.30	.57
$100,000	.55	.20	.34	.50	.20	.32	.59
$150,000	.59	.21	.37	.54	.22	.35	.63
$200,000	.62	.22	.39	.57	.24	.37	.65
$250,000	.64	.23	.40	.59	.25	.39	.67
$300,000	.66	.24	.42	.61	.26	.40	.69
$400,000	.68	.25	.44	.64	.27	.42	.71
$500,000	.70	.26	.46	.66	.28	.44	.73
Incumbents[a]:	.90	.27	.63	.81	.32	.51	.94

Note: Table entries are probabilities derived from probit estimates. The intercepts, the probit coefficients on campaign expenditures (natural log of expenditures), and standard errors from the probit equations are:

TYPE OF CONTACT	INTERCEPT	COEFFICIENT	STANDARD ERROR
Any	−4.58	.41	.03
Personal	−3.78	.21	.05
Mail	−4.25	.31	.04
Mass Media	−4.47	.39	.03
Indirect	−4.47	.27	.05
Recall	−4.48	.32	.04
Recognize	−4.21	.40	.03

[a]Mean for all incumbents; voters' contacts with incumbents vary little or not at all with the incumbent's campaign expenditures.

so are swamped by the opposition. Similar data for incumbents shows that they receive comparatively little benefit from campaign expenditures; the campaign adds little to the prominence and affection they have gained prior to the campaign by cultivating the district and using the many perquisites of office.

The same situation holds among Senate candidates, although the analysis is more complicated because state populations vary so widely.[40] Controlling for the voting age population of the state, the probability of a respondent's recalling a 1988–1992 Senate challenger rises from .18 to .75 as the challenger's per voter spending rises from its lowest to its highest observed level; the probability of respondent's recognizing the challenger rises from .34 to .94. For incumbent Senate candidates, the equivalent increases are much smaller: from .53 to .61 and from .91 to .94, respectively. Again, campaign spending has a bigger payoff to challengers than to incumbents; if they spend enough, Senate challengers become as well known as incumbents.

MODELS OF VOTING BEHAVIOR

How well voters know and like the candidates matters, finally, because familiarity and evaluations are directly related to the vote. The series of probit equations reported in Table 5-9, based on analysis of data from recent House and Senate elections, suggest how these relationships work. More importantly, they make a fundamental point about the electoral effects of incumbency.

The first equation treats the vote choice as a function of party identification and incumbency status. Not surprisingly, these variables have a strong impact on the vote. Estimates of the size of the impact appear in Table 5-10, which in-

TABLE 5–9   PROBIT MODELS OF THE VOTING DECISION IN RECENT HOUSE AND SENATE ELECTIONS

	HOUSE			SENATE
	1994	1996	1998	1988–1992
Equation 1				
Intercept	−.26[a] (.12)	.31 (.18)	−.11 (.18)	.00 (.05)
Party identification	.97 (.06)	1.05 (.06)	.86 (.07)	.69 (.02)
Democrat is incumbent	.70 (.14)	.27 (.20)	.78 (.21)	.56 (.06)
Republican is incumbent	−.45 (.16)	−1.17 (.19)	−.61 (.20)	−.51 (.07)
Equation 2				
Intercept	.05 (.17)	.41 (.21)	−.55 (.24)	−.10 (.08)
Party identification	.93 (.06)	1.04 (.06)	.86 (.07)	.69 (.03)
Democrat is incumbent	.35 (.15)	.07 (.20)	.63 (.23)	.41 (.07)
Republican is incumbent	−.18 (.17)	−1.02 (.20)	−.15 (.21)	−.37 (.08)
Familiarity with Democrat	1.03 (.20)	.83 (.18)	1.54 (.21)	.95 (.08)
Familiarity with Republican	−1.39 (.19)	−.95 (.19)	−.93 (.25)	−.79 (.09)
Equation 3				
Intercept	.26 (.20)	.51 (.26)	−.60 (.26)	−.12 (.10)
Party identification	.87 (.08)	.95 (.08)	.73 (.08)	.59 (.03)
Democrat is incumbent	.17 (.19)	.03 (.26)	.64 (.27)	.31 (.08)
Republican is incumbent	−.32 (.21)	−1.04 (.25)	−.07 (.24)	−.39 (.08)
Familiarity with Democrat	.48 (.26)	.38 (.23)	1.30 (.24)	.79 (.11)
Familiarity with Republican	−1.08 (.25)	−.64 (.24)	−.82 (.30)	−.57 (.11)
Likes something about Democrat	1.72 (.20)	1.53 (.17)	1.14 (.19)	1.09 (.06)
Dislikes something about Democrat	−1.36 (.20)	−1.25 (.19)	−1.00 (.23)	−.82 (.07)
Likes something about Republican	−1.52 (.20)	−1.20 (.16)	−.59 (.18)	−1.15 (.06)
Dislikes something about Republican	.89 (.21)	1.09 (.19)	.51 (.19)	.86 (.07)

[a]Standard errors are in parentheses.
Note: Dependent variable is vote for Democrat; a coefficient that is at least twice its standard error is statistically significant at $p<.05$.
Source: American National Election Studies, 1994, 1996, 1998, and Senate Election Studies, 1988, 1990, 1992.

TABLE 5–10   PROBIT ESTIMATES OF THE EFFECTS OF PARTY IDENTIFICATION, INCUMBENCY, AND CANDIDATE FAMILIARITY AND AFFECT IN CONGRESSIONAL ELECTIONS

	HOUSE ELECTIONS			SENATE ELECTIONS
	1994	1996	1998	1988–1992
Equation 1				
Party Identification	.43	.47	.40	.33
Incumbency	.28	.35	.33	.26
Equation 2				
Party Identification	.43	.47	.40	.33
Incumbency	.13	.27	.19	.19
Familiarity	.54	.42	.55	.41
Equation 3				
Party Identification	.41	.44	.34	.29
Incumbency	.12	.26	.17	.17
Familiarity	.37	.25	.48	.33
Likes/dislikes	.88	.85	.65	.75

Note: Entries are the difference in the probability of voting for the Democrat between the most pro-Democratic and the most pro-Republican settings on the indicated variables, with the other variables in the equation set at their mean values. For example, in Equation 2 for the Senate elections, a respondent who recalled the Democrat but did not even recognize the Republican would, other things equal, have a probability of voting for the Democrat .41 higher than would one who recalled the Republican but did not recognize the Democrat.
   Source: Estimated from the equations in Table 5–9.

terprets the equations in Table 5–9 by showing how much the probability of voting for the Democrat varies between the most pro-Democratic and pro-Republican setting on the independent variable of interest, with the values of the other variables set at their means. For example, the first equation indicates that in 1998, the probability of voting for the Democrat in a House race was .40 higher when the respondent identified with the Democratic rather than the Republican party. Incumbency has a large effect as well in these elections, the probability of voting for the Democrat being, for example, .33 higher if the Democrat rather than the Republican were the incumbent in 1998. In the other election years, party identification has a somewhat larger effect on the vote, although incumbency remains a potent factor as well.

The second equation in Table 5–9 adds a composite familiarity variable for each candidate to the set of explanatory variables. The effect of partisanship is unchanged, but the impact of incumbency shrinks; the probit coefficients are smaller and three of the six are statistically insignificant. The entries in Table 5–10 indicate that the difference made by incumbency status (when familiarity and party identification are set at their mean values) now ranges between .13 and .27, depending on the year and office. Familiarity has a large effect, far larger than that of incumbency; it would seem that a substantial portion of the incumbency advantage derives from the greater familiarity incumbents enjoy—

the conventional hypothesis. But the third equation suggests further that the incumbency variables are, in part, surrogates for voters' evaluations of the candidates.

Each of the four evaluative variables derived from the likes/dislikes questions has a strong impact on the vote. Cumulatively, these evaluations make an enormous difference; a respondent who likes something about the Democrat and dislikes something about the Republican (without also liking something about the Republican and disliking something about the Democrat) has a probability ranging from .65 to .88 higher of voting for the Democrat than a respondent who takes the opposite position on all four variables. That is, voters who have only good things to say about one candidate and bad things to say about the other are almost certain to vote for the favored candidate, regardless of party identification or incumbency status. Clearly, some of this effect may be rationalization; respondents, when prodded, will come up with reasons for their vote preference. Even discounting for rationalization, however, the impact of candidate evaluations measured in this way is still very impressive.

Two points are clear from this analysis. The first is that voters are not strongly attracted by incumbency per se, nor does the incumbency advantage arise merely from greater renown. Of greater proximate importance are the very favorable public images most House members acquire and the relatively negative images—if any—projected by their opponents.[41] The second is that there is little difference in the patterns for House and Senate elections. In particular, the effect of incumbency is no smaller in Senate than in House elections, confirming the point that the greater vulnerability of Senate incumbents derives not from the behavior of voters but from the context of the elections (a more even partisan balance, more talented and better-funded challengers).

EVALUATING INCUMBENTS

Voters respond positively to House and Senate incumbents for a variety of reasons. Survey respondents since 1978 have been asked a number of general and specific questions about the incumbent's performance in serving the state or district and as a legislator in Washington. Table 5-11 presents data on some of the responses from recent House and Senate election surveys. The left-hand columns in the table list the percentage of voters who were able to offer a response to each question. For example, 20 percent had asked the House incumbent for assistance or information, received some reply, and therefore were able to indicate their level of satisfaction with it (item 3). The distribution of responses on this question shows that 56 percent of those who could respond on this question were very satisfied, and the right-hand column in the table indicates that 90 percent of those who were very satisfied with the incumbent's response voted for him. Dissatisfied voters were much less likely to vote for the incumbent. Notice the *absence* of a House–Senate difference on this and all of the other questions. Again, voters respond to senators and representatives in the same way.

It is apparent from the left-hand columns that a large majority of voters could evaluate incumbents' general job performance and diligence at keeping in

TABLE 5–11   EVALUATIONS OF THE INCUMBENT'S PERFORMANCE AND THE VOTE IN HOUSE AND SENATE ELECTIONS (IN PERCENTAGES)

CRITERION	RESPONDING House	Senate		RESPONSE House	Senate	VOTE FOR INCUMBENT House	Senate
General Job Performance	91	90	Approve	85	80	88	86
			Disapprove	15	20	12	8
District Services							
1. How good a job of keeping in touch with people	95	94	Very good	33	29	88	87
			Fairly good	46	53	80	72
			Fairly poor	12	11	41	40
			Very poor	9	7	24	21
2. Expectations about incumbent's helpfulness in solving voters' problems	91	93	Very helpful	29	35	95	90
			Somewhat helpful	53	47	67	70
			Not very helpful	14	5	29	24
			It depends	4	3	58	54
3. Level of satisfaction with response to voter-initiated contact	20	19	Very satisfied	56	55	90	90
			Somewhat satisfied	35	30	63	70
			Not very satisfied	8	9	18	40
			Not at all satisfied	11	7	13	26
4. Level of firend's satisfaction with response to voter-initiated contact	19	23	Very satisfied	57	53	88	88
			Somewhat satisfied	32	34	62	75
			Not very satisfied	5	8	57	37
			Not at all satisfied	6	5	13	14
5. Could voter recall anything special incumbent did for the district	27	32	Yes	27	32	77	78
			No	73	68	63	64
6. General agreement or disagreement with incumbent's votes	46	56	Agreed	55	50	96	92
			Agreed, disagreed about equally	36	34	79	64
			Disagreed	9	16	16	11
7. Agreed or disagreed with vote on a particular bill	18	—	Agreed	71	—	93	—
			Disagreed	29	—	43	—
8. Which candidate would do a better job on most important problem	26	—	Incumbent	72	—	97	—
			Challenger	28	—	11	—

Sources: The Senate data are from the pooled 1988–1992 Senate Election Studies; the House data are from the 1998 American National Election Study for general job performance and question 1, from the 1994 Study for questions 3, 4 and 5, from the 1990 Study for questions 2, 7, and 8, and from the 1988 Study for question 6. In every case, I include the most recent responses available for the particular question.

touch and could offer an opinion on whether or not they would be likely to help with a problem if asked to do so. Forty-six percent were able to determine whether or not they generally agreed with the way the House incumbent voted, 56 percent, with the way the Senator voted. Fewer—from 18 to 32 percent—were able to respond in terms of more specific personal and district services, and voting and policy items. But most voters could respond in terms of at least one of them. That is, a majority of voters were able to evaluate incumbents in other than broad, general terms.

Reactions to incumbents, both general and specific, are largely favorable. Four-fifths of the voters offering a response approved of the incumbents' performance in both offices. Despite a modest decline in the level of approval enjoyed by House incumbents in recent years (from 92 percent in 1988 to a low of 81 percent in 1994, before rising to 83 percent in 1996 and 85 percent in 1998), they still attract far more approval than does the body in which they serve. More than 80 percent think that the incumbent would be helpful or very helpful if they brought him a problem. Satisfaction with the incumbents' response to voter requests runs very high indeed; most were "very satisfied," as were friends who made similar requests. Far more voters generally agreed with the incumbent's votes than disagreed with them, though most agreed with some and disagreed with others. In 1998, 72 percent thought the incumbent would do a better job dealing with what they considered to be the most important problem facing the nation, though this figure was well below the 93 percent who thought so in 1988.

The significance of these positive responses is apparent from their association with the vote. On every question, the more positive the reaction to the incumbent, the more likely the respondent is to vote for him. The pattern is very similar for both House and Senate candidates. Naturally, respondents' assessments of incumbents on these dimensions are overlapping and interrelated, but they have a cumulative effect as well. If the positive and negative responses are summed up, the greater the number of positive responses, the more frequently the respondent reports voting for the incumbent; the greater the number of negative responses, the more inclined respondents are to vote for the challenger.

The payoffs reaped by members of both houses from attention to constituents and emphasis on their personal character and performance are also evident in voters' responses to open-ended survey questions about what they like and dislike about candidates. These responses also reveal an important shift over time in the way voters typically respond to these questions. As many as five responses are coded for each question. Their distribution by type for House incumbents, challengers, and candidates for open seats in five selected elections from 1978 to 1998 are shown in Table 5-12.

Issues pertaining to job performance, experience, and district and individual services are mentioned most frequently as qualities voters liked about incumbents. Such issues are mentioned much more rarely for nonincumbents, which is not much of a surprise. A plurality of positive comments about candidates of all kinds have to do with personal characteristics, which frequently seem, at least on the surface, empty of political content. This is probably an illusion; experimental research has shown that voters form affective evaluations of candidates based on campaign information, then often forget the information but remember the affective evaluation. When later asked why they like or dislike a candidate, they give some reasons that rationalize their feeling, but they are not necessarily the reasons that led to the feelings in the first place.[42]

TABLE 5–12   VOTERS' MENTIONS OF THINGS THEY LIKED AND
DISLIKED ABOUT HOUSE CANDIDATES, SELECTED
YEARS, 1978–1998 (IN PERCENTAGES)

	YEAR						CHANGE
	1978	1984	1988	1994	1996	1998	1978–1998
Things Liked about Incumbents							
Personal	39	40	31	28	31	37	−2
Performance/experience	19	16	12	17	18	14	−5
District service/attention	25	22	26	22	17	15	−10
Party	1	3	3	4	7	5	4
Ideology/policy	12	12	19	23	22	24	12
Group associations	5	7	9	5	5	4	−1
Number of respondents	749	969	846	694	905	394	—
Number of mentions	859	1106	925	875	1160	537	—
Mentions per respondent	1.15	1.14	1.09	1.26	1.28	1.36	.21
Things Disliked about Incumbents							
Personal	40	41	32	28	23	27	−13
Performance/experience	15	7	6	17	10	8	−7
District service/attention	9	7	13	5	8	1	−9
Party	7	10	11	12	17	14	7
Ideology/policy	22	29	35	35	38	43	21
Group associations	6	5	4	3	3	6	0
Number of respondents	749	969	846	694	905	394	—
Number of mentions	190	243	171	332	412	211	—
Mentions per respondent	.25	.25	.20	.48	.46	.53	.28
Things Liked about Challengers							
Personal	58	57	45	35	36	40	−18
Performance/experience	6	6	4	7	10	15	9
District service/attention	3	5	7	3	5	5	2
Party	4	5	8	13	13	12	8
Ideology/policy	27	21	26	38	34	25	−2
Group associations	3	5	10	3	3	4	1
Number of respondents	749	969	846	694	905	394	—
Number of mentions	139	298	189	254	360	179	—
Mentions per respondent	.19	.31	.22	.39	.40	.45	.16
Things Disliked about Challengers							
Personal	44	38	53	20	22	23	−21
Performance/experience	7	7	3	11	12	12	5
District service/attention	0	11	1	1	5	3	3
Party	7	11	21	23	25	39	32
Ideology/policy	42	32	23	42	33	18	−24
Group associations	1	4	0	3	3	6	5
Number of respondents	749	969	846	964	905	394	—
Number of mentions	122	188	78	143	307	102	—
Mentions per respondent	.16	.19	.09	.22	.34	.26	.10

	YEAR						CHANGE
	1978	1984	1988	1994	1996	1998	1978–1998
Things Liked about Candidates for Open Seats							
Personal	55	55	57	35	36	44	−11
Performance/experience	8	9	15	14	8	6	−2
District service/attention	6	4	1	4	6	1	−5
Party	4	11	12	10	13	15	11
Ideology/policy	18	16	14	34	31	32	14
Group associations	9	6	1	3	6	1	−8
Number of respondents[a]	232	228	152	308	172	128	—
Number of mentions	143	172	86	221	112	118	—
Mentions per respondent	.61	.75	.56	.72	.65	.92	.31
Things Disliked about Candidates for Open Seats							
Personal	42	34	41	20	17	23	−19
Performance/experience	12	3	5	14	4	6	−6
District service/attention	3	0	2	3	2	0	−3
Party	5	9	34	29	39	28	23
Ideology/policy	35	45	15	32	39	40	5
Group associations	3	6	3	2	0	4	1
Number of respondents[a]	232	228	152	308	172	128	—
Number of mentions	60	67	59	113	52	53	—
Mentions per respondent	.26	.29	.39	.37	.30	.41	.15

[a]Number of respondents is doubled for the Open Seat category, because they comment on two candidates.
Note: Some columns do not sum to 100 because of rounding.
 Source: American National Election Studies.

The reasons voters do give for liking or disliking candidates depend on what is on their minds at the time they are asked, and that, in turn, is determined by whatever campaign messages have caught their attention.[43] Campaigns frame the decision differently in different years. Notice that since 1978, the proportion of both positive and negative comments about candidates' personal characteristics have fallen, while the proportion of comments concerning party, ideology, and policy have grown. These trends, summed across all three types of House candidates, are displayed in Figure 5-9. Clearly, the content of electoral politics, at least as it is refracted through the minds of voters, has become less personal, and more explicitly political, since the 1970s. Although personal criteria continue to predominate among positive comments, political criteria now predominate among negative comments. In 1978, 83 percent of positive comments concerned the candidate's personal characteristics, experience, service, or performance, only 12 percent concerned party, policy, or ideology. In 1998, the respective figures were 66 percent and 29 percent. Similarly, the percentage distribution of negative comments between these categories changed from 29–64 to 57–36 over this period. Notice also that party, ideology, and policy are invariably more commonly mentioned as things disliked than as things liked about candidates.

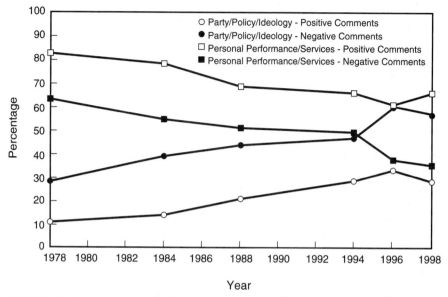

FIGURE 5–9. Criteria for Evaluating House Candidates, Selected Years, 1978–1998
Source: American National Election Studies.

These changes in the frame have worked to the detriment of incumbents. House members thrive when voters focus on their personal virtues and services to the district and its inhabitants. They become more vulnerable when the focus is on their party, ideology, or policy stances, for these repel as well as attract voters. Notice that the incidence of negative comments about House incumbents has been much higher in the 1990s (negative mentions per respondent are twice as frequent as in earlier elections). The ratio of likes to dislikes for incumbents is also much smaller in the 1990s (an average of 2.6:1, compared with more than 4.5:1 for each of the earlier election years). The changes first registered in the 1994 election were not, then, merely an artifact of the strong anti (Democratic) incumbent sentiments prevailing that year, for they were sustained through the next two elections.

The distribution of evaluative comments about Senate candidates, displayed in Table 5–13, is not very different from the distribution of comments about House candidates during the same period. The incidence of personal comments is about the same; references to performance and experience are more common for senators, references to services and attention less common. References to party, ideology, and policy are also distributed similarly. In general, it appears that the patterns for House candidates have become more like the patterns for Senate candidates in recent elections. Once again, voters do not think much differently about House and Senate candidates. They do, however, have more thoughts about them; the number of comments per respondent is generally larger for Senate candidates, particularly nonincumbents.

TABLE 5–13   VOTERS' MENTIONS OF THINGS THEY LIKED AND DISLIKED ABOUT SENATE CANDIDATES, 1988–1992 (IN PERCENTAGES)

	INCUMBENTS	CHALLENGERS	CANDIDATES FOR OPEN SEATS
Things Liked about Candidates			
Personal	31	42	33
Performance/experience	26	13	17
District service/attention	15	4	8
Party	4	10	8
Ideology/policy	19	27	29
Group associations	5	3	3
Number of respondents	3142	3142	1298
Number of mentions	3573	1700	1047
Mentions per respondent	1.14	.54	.81
Things Disliked about Candidates			
Personal	34	29	28
Performance/experience	10	11	11
District service/attention	8	3	2
Party	13	27	23
Ideology/policy	29	29	34
Group associations	5	2	4
Number of respondents	3142	3142	1298
Number of mentions	1652	1435	699
Mentions per respondent	.53	.46	.54

Note: Some columns do not sum to 100 because of rounding.
Source: American National Election Study: Pooled Senate Election Study, 1988, 1990, 1992.

Although there has been measurable decline from the remarkably high levels of regard for incumbents found in the late 1970s, survey evidence continues to confirm that all of the actions members of Congress are purported to undertake in pursuit of reelection still pay off in some way. Individual voters respond, for example, to the advertising (familiarity, contacts), credit-claiming (personal and district services), and position-taking (general and specific agreement with members' votes and issue stances) that David Mayhew identifies as the characteristic means by which incumbents pursue reelection.[44] On the other hand, the home styles developed by the House members whom Fenno observed no longer seem quite so effective as they once did. Fenno found that, in the 1970s, members typically worked to project images devoid of partisan or even programmatic content, presenting themselves instead as trustworthy, hardworking people who deserve support for their experience, services, and personal qualities more than for their political beliefs or goals.[45] Partisan, policy, and ideological considerations have clearly become more prominent since Fenno did his research, and the strategy he described conspicuously failed a number of House Democrats in 1994.

Finally, it is also apparent that the electoral strategy of discouraging the opposition before the campaign begins is effective and often effectively pursued. Despite an upsurge in competition in the early 1990s, most incumbent House members continue to face obscure, politically inexperienced opponents whose resources fall far short of what it takes to mount a serious campaign. It is obvious from the survey data how this would ease the incumbent's task of retaining voters' support. House incumbents appear to be doubly advantaged compared with their Senate counterparts. They are more highly regarded (compare the thermometer ratings in Figures 5-7 and 5-8) and more likely to face obscure opponents (compare the figures on familiarity in Table 5-1). These are not separate phenomena. Not only do popular incumbents discourage serious opposition, but in the absence of vigorous opposition, information that might erode the incumbent's popularity seldom reaches voters.

WINNING CHALLENGERS

The connection between the vigor of the challenge and the popularity of the incumbent is evident when we observe how voters respond when incumbents are seriously challenged. The most serious challenges are, by definition, the successful ones. Voters' responses to the survey questions about both challengers and incumbents in districts where the challenger won are sharply different from those in districts where incumbents won. This is evident from the data in Table 5-14, which lists responses to selected questions about winning and losing challengers and incumbents in the 1994 House elections and 1988-1992 Senate elections.

Winning challengers are much better known by voters. Half the electorate can recall their names and nearly all can recognize them and rate them on the thermometer scale. Incumbents are also better known in these races—a full-scale campaign generates more information all around—but their advantage over the challenger in familiarity practically disappears. So does their advantage in voter evaluations. Not only are winning challengers better known, they are also rated significantly higher on the thermometer scale. The incumbents they have defeated are rated significantly lower, leaving the challenger with a clear advantage.

The same is true of the incidence of voters' liking or disliking something about the candidates. The data indicate that successful challengers do two things: They make voters aware of their own virtues, and they make voters aware of the incumbent's shortcomings. The frequency of both positive and negative comments is significantly higher for winning challengers, but the jump in positive comments is much greater. For losing incumbents, the frequency of positive comments is significantly lower, while the incidence of negative comments is significantly higher. Again, winning challengers enjoy a clear advantage on this dimension. Finally, we observe a sharply lower job approval rating for losing compared to winning incumbents of both houses of Congress.

When I examined the equivalent data from earlier elections for the previous editions of this book, I found that losing incumbents had *not* been rated lower than winning incumbents on most of these evaluative dimensions. Voters were

TABLE 5–14   VOTERS' RESPONSES TO WINNING AND LOSING CHALLENGERS AND INCUMBENTS (IN PERCENTAGES)

	1994 CHALLENGER (HOUSE)		1988–1992 CHALLENGER (SENATE)	
	Won (N=92)	Lost (N=609)	Won (N=303)	Lost (N=2106)
Familiarity with Candidates				
Recalled challenger's name	55[a]	18	51[a]	30
Recognized challenger's name	97[a]	52	98[a]	82
Neither	3[a]	48	2[a]	18
Recalled incumbent's name	63[a]	49	59	55
Recognized incumbent's name	98	93	99	99
Neither	2	7	1	1
Contact with Challenger				
Any	90[a]	46	97[a]	84
Met personally	7	3	10	9
Received mail from challenger	54[a]	21	58	50
Read about challenger	64[a]	30	86[a]	74
Saw challenger on TV	80[a]	27	91[a]	73
Family or friends had contact with challenger	25[a]	7	—	—
Evaluations of Candidates				
Challenger's thermometer rating[b]	61[a]	52	57[a]	48
Incumbent's thermometer rating[b]	45[a]	63	51[a]	65
Likes something about challenger	49[a]	14	53[a]	29
Dislikes something about challenger	24[a]	11	38[a]	29
Likes something about incumbent	38[a]	56	45[a]	61
Dislikes something about incumbent	47[a]	26	45[a]	32

[a]Difference in responses to winning and losing challengers is significant at $p<.05$.
[b]Measured in degrees, not percentages.
Sources: 1994 American National Election Study and American National Election Study: Pooled Senate Election Study, 1988, 1990, and 1992.

just as inclined to like something about the losers as about the winners; they were also just as likely to approve of the incumbents' general job performance, to think that the incumbents would be of assistance if asked, and to remember something specific the incumbents had done for the district.[46]

In the past, incumbents did not lose by failing to elicit support on grounds of general performance and services to constituents. They lost when challengers were able to project a positive image of their own and to persuade voters that incumbents had liabilities that outweighed their usual assets. In the 1990s, however, voters in districts that have rejected incumbents have been far more critical of the incumbent's performance on all these dimensions—another indication that their circumstances have changed for the worse.

As we would expect, voters are much more likely to report contacts with winning challengers than with losing challengers, though the differences are considerably larger for House than for Senate challengers. The most important differences for House challengers show up in contacts through the mass media: mail, newspapers, and television. In fact, winning challengers are encountered as often as incumbents via these media; compare the figures in Table 5–4. The differences that tend to remain between incumbents and winning challengers are in the modes of contact associated with holding office over a period of years: personal and staff contacts and, of course, the mail.

It is no mystery why winning challengers reached so many voters and were so much more familiar to them. They ran much better financed campaigns than did the losers. The winning House challengers in the districts covered by the survey spent more than $600,000 on average, compared to less than $140,000 for the losing challengers. The winning Senate challengers also spent significantly more money on the campaign than the losers.

In general, voters react to winning House challengers very much as they do to candidates for open seats and to most Senate challengers.[47] Competitive challengers also make it possible for more voters to make ideological and policy distinctions between House candidates, again producing contests that are more like Senate elections, in which policy issues and ideology usually play a larger role.[48] This is further evidence that differences between House and Senate elections, and among the varieties of House contests, must be attributed primarily to varying characteristics of House and Senate challengers and their campaigns. To say this is to reiterate that differences among candidacies, rather than differences in patterns of voting behavior, are what distinguish House from Senate elections.[49]

ISSUES IN CONGRESSIONAL ELECTIONS

A broader implication of this argument is that congressional voters behave the way they do because politicians behave the way they do. We have seen, for example, how well voters' reactions to House incumbents fit the strategies they follow to win reelection. One explanation is that members of Congress simply understand what appeals to voters and act accordingly. However, the deviant cases (that is, challenger victories) and senatorial elections suggest that the matter is not so simple. Voters react differently, depending on the style and content (not to mention volume) of appeals that candidates make to them. Political strategies are based on assumptions about how individual voters operate; but voting behavior is constrained by the electoral context created by strategic decisions.

It is a classic case of mutual causation. As Fiorina has pointed out, converging patterns of electoral strategy and electoral behavior typical of congressional elections in the 1960s and 1970s conspired to crowd national issues out of electoral politics.[50] But this trend was not immutable. As challengers (Republicans in 1980, Democrats in 1982, Republicans in 1994, Democrats in 1996) found that they could win votes by linking the incumbent to national policy failures and unpopular leaders, national issues reentered the electoral equation—at least in those contests where active, well-funded challengers worked to inject them into the campaign.[51] Even in the 1970s, when issues seemed to have little measurable impact on individual voting once other variables were taken into account, congressional elections had a profound impact on national policy, partly because the results were interpreted by politicians to reflect voters' preferences on policy matters. They could point to solid evidence that, in aggregate, congressional election results are highly sensitive to national issues and conditions and therefore justify such interpretations. A resolution to this curious paradox, along with an examination of how national issues enter congressional election politics, is pursued in the next chapter.

ENDNOTES

1. Eric R.A.N. Smith and Michael Dolny, "The Mystery of Declining Turnout in American National Elections" (Paper delivered at the Annual Meeting of the Western Political Science Association, Salt Lake City, March 30–April 1, 1989).
2. Steven J. Rosenstone and John Mark Hansen, *Mobilization, Participation, and Democracy in America* (New York: MacMillan, 1993), p. 215.
3. Raymond E. Wolfinger and Steven J. Rosenstone, *Who Votes?* (New Haven: Yale University Press, 1980), pp. 24–26.
4. Ibid., p. 94.
5. Ibid., p. 18.
6. Walter Dean Burnham, "Shifting Patterns of Congressional Voting Participation" in *The Current Crisis in American Politics*, ed. Walter Dean Burnham (New York: Oxford University Press, 1982), pp. 166–203; see also Rosenstone and Hansen, *Mobilization, Participation, and Democracy*, pp. 211–248.
7. Wolfinger and Rosenstone, *Who Votes?*, pp. 104–114; see also Stephen D. Shaffer, "Policy Differences between Voters and Non-Voters in American Elections," *Western Political Quarterly* 35 (1982):496–510.
8. Angus Campbell, "Surge and Decline: A Study of Electoral Change," in *Elections and the Political Order*, Angus Campbell et al. (New York: John Wiley, 1966), pp. 40–62.
9. Except that midterm electorates are somewhat older. See Raymond E. Wolfinger, Steven J. Rosenstone, and Richard A. McIntosh, "Presidential and Congressional Voters Compared," *American Politics Quarterly* 9 (1981):245–255; see also Albert D. Cover, "Surge and Decline Revisited" (Paper delivered at the Annual Meeting of the American Political Science Association, Chicago, September 1–4, 1983), pp. 15–17, and James E. Campbell, *The Presidential Pulse of Congressional Elections* (Lexington, Kentucky: University of Kentucky Press, 1993), pp. 44–62.
10. This does not mean that presidential elections do not affect congressional elections in other ways, of course; that issue is taken up in Chapter 6.
11. Gregory A. Caldeira, Samuel C. Patterson, and Gregory A. Markko, "The Mobilization of Voters in Congressional Elections," *Journal of Politics* 47 (1985):490–509; Franklin D. Gilliam, Jr., "Influences on Voter Turnout for U.S. House Elections in Non-Presidential Years," *Legislative Studies Quar-*

terly 10 (1985):339-352; Robert A. Jackson, "A Reassessment of Voter Mobilization," *Political Research Quarterly* 49 (1996):331-349. The anticipation of a close election itself increases turnout; see Stephen P. Nicholson and Ross A. Miller, "Prior Beliefs and Voter Turnout in the 1986 and 1988 Congressional Elections," *Political Research Quarterly* 50 (1997):199-213.

12. See Angus Campbell, Philip E. Converse, Warren E. Miller, and Donald E. Stokes, *The American Voter* (New York: John Wiley, 1960), Chapter 6.

13. Warren E. Miller and Santa A. Traugott, *American National Election Studies Data Sourcebook 1952-1986* (Cambridge: Harvard University Press, 1989), p. 81; see also Figure 5-2, below.

14. Morris P. Fiorina, *Retrospective Voting in American National Elections* (New Haven: Yale University Press, 1981).

15. Samuel L. Popkin, John W. Gorman, Charles Philips, and Jeffrey A. Smith, "Comment: What Have You Done for Me Lately? Toward an Investment Theory of Voting," *American Political Science Review* 70 (1976):779-805.

16. This figure includes independents who lean toward one party or the other as partisans; excluding leaners, the Democratic advantage falls from 41-23 to 35-31 from 1980 to 1994.

17. This change was the extension of a long-term trend that has seen the Republicans grow from less than 20 percent of the southern electorate in the 1950s to parity with the Democrats in the 1990s; see Gary C. Jacobson, "Party Polarization in National Politics: The Electoral Connection," in *Polarized Politics: Congress and the President in a Partisan Era*, ed. Jon R. Bond and Richard Fleisher (Washington, DC: Congressional Quarterly Press, 2000), p. 16.

18. Alan I. Abramowitz, "The End of the Democratic Era? 1994 and the Future of Congressional Election Research," *Political Research Quarterly* 48 (1995):873-889.

19. The sensitivity of aggregate distribution of party identification to political conditions is shown clearly in Michael B. MacKuen, Robert S. Erikson, and James A. Stimson, "Macropartisanship," *American Political Science Review* 83 (1989):1125-1142.

20. Robert B. Eubank, "Incumbent Effects on Individual Level Voting Behavior in Congressional Elections: A Decade of Exaggeration," *Journal of Politics* 47 (1985):964-966; Gary C. Jacobson and Douglas Rivers, "Explaining the Overreport of Votes for Incumbents in National Election Studies" (Paper delivered at the Annual Meeting of the Western Political Science Association, Pasadena, California, March 18-20, 1993); Janet Box-Steffensmeier, Gary C. Jacobson, and J. Tobin Grant, "Question Wording and the House Vote Choice: Some Experimental Evidence," Public Opinion Quarterly, forthcoming.

21. Albert D. Cover, "One Good Term Deserves Another: The Advantage of Incumbency in Congressional Elections," *American Journal of Political Science* 21 (1977):532.

22. Gary C. Jacobson, *Money in Congressional Elections* (New Haven: Yale University Press, 1980), p. 16.

23. The reasons for this decline remain obscure; see Gary C. Jacobson, "The Declining Salience of U.S. House Candidates, 1958-1994" (Paper presented

at the Annual Meeting of the American Political Science Association, Boston, September 3-6, 1998).

24. John A. Ferejohn, "On the Decline of Competition in Congressional Elections," *American Political Science Review* 71 (1977):171; Candice J. Nelson, "The Effects of Incumbency on Voting in Congressional Elections, 1964-1974," *Political Science Quarterly* 93 (1978/79):665-678.

25. Jacobson, *Money*, pp. 19-20; also Alan I. Abramowitz, "Name Familiarity, Reputation, and the Incumbency Effect in a Congressional Election," *Western Political Quarterly* 28 (1975):668-684.

26. Thomas E. Mann, *Unsafe at Any Margin: Interpreting Congressional Elections* (Washington, DC: American Enterprise Institute for Public Policy Research, 1978), pp. 30-34.

27. For consideration of the difficulties of making comparisons over time using available data, see Morris P. Fiorina, "Congressmen and Their Constituents: 1958 and 1978," in *The United States Congress*, ed. Dennis Hale (New York: Transaction Books, 1983).

28. The *feeling thermometer* is used to test whether the respondent recognized a candidate's name. Respondents are asked to indicate their degree of warmth or coolness toward a number of individuals on a scale of 0 to 100. If they do not recognize a name listed, they are to say so and proceed to the next without offering a "temperature."

29. John R. Alford and John R. Hibbing, "The Disparate Electoral Security of House and Senate Incumbents" (Paper delivered at the Annual Meeting of the American Political Science Association, Atlanta, August 31-September 3, 1989), p. 14.

30. The results are typical of every election for which we have data; see the earlier editions of this book.

31. Donald E. Stokes and Warren E. Miller, "Party Government and the Saliency of Congress," *Elections and the Political Order*, p. 205. Contrary findings are reproted by Abramowitz, "Name Familiarity," pp. 673-683, and Jacobson, *Money*, p. 16.

32. Richard R. Fenno, Jr., *The United States Senate: A Bicameral Perspective* (Washington, DC: American Enterprise Institute for Public Policy Research, 1983), p. 11.

33. Jonathan S. Krasno, *Challengers, Competition, and Reelection: Comparing Senate and House Elections* (New Haven: Yale University Press, 1994), p. 47.

34. Fenno, *Senate*, pp. 18-19; the Senate Election Study confirms this candidate's view that voters have very similar expectations of senators and representatives; see Krasno, *Challengers, Competition, and Reelection*, pp. 17-35.

35. Alan I. Abramowitz, "A Comparison of Voting for U.S. Senator and Representative in 1978," *American Political Science Review* 74 (1980):639.

36. For a comparison of probit and ordinary least-squares regression, see John Aldrich and Charles Cnudde, "Probing the Bounds of Conventional Wisdom: A Comparison of Regression, Probit, and Discriminant Analysis," *American Journal of Political Science* 19 (1975):571-608.

37. Personal contact is defined as having met the candidate, attended a meeting at which he spoke, or having had contact with the candidate's staff;

mail contact is having received something in the mail from the candidate; mass media contact is having learned about the candidate by reading newspapers and magazines, listening to the radio, or watching television; indirect contact is reporting that a family member or acquaintance has had some kind of contact with the candidate.

38. Data are from the 1994 NES Study because it is the most recent survey containing the contact questions; comparable analysis of earlier surveys containing these questions produces very similar results; see the second and third editions of this book.

39. For additional evidence on this point, see Gary C. Jacobson, "Enough Is Too Much: Money and Competition in House Elections, 1972-1984," in *Elections in America*, ed. Kay L. Schlozman (Boston: Allyn & Unwin, 1987), pp. 192-195; Jacobson, "The Effects of Campaign Spending in Congressional Elections," *American Political Science Review* 72 (1978): 480-485.

40. Campaign spending rises with a state's population, but at a diminishing rate, so that the more populous the state, the lower the per-voter expenditures.

41. Abramowitz, "Voting for U.S. Senator and Representative," p. 636; Thomas E. Mann and Raymond E. Wolfinger, "Candidates and Parties in Congressional Elections," *American Political Science Review* 74 (1980):622-629; Barbara Hinckley, "House Re-Elections and Senate Defeats: The Role of the Challenger," *British Journal of Political Science* 10 (1980):441-460.

42. Milton Lodge and Marco R. Steenbergen, with Shawn Brau, "The Responsive Voter: Campaign Information and the Dynamics of Candidate Evaluation," *American Political Science Review* 89 (1995):309-336.

43. John Zaller and Stanley Feldman, "A Theory of Survey Response," *American Journal of Political Science* 36 (1992):586-589.

44. David R. Mayhew, *Congress: The Electoral Connection* (New Haven: Yale University Press, 1974), pp. 49-68.

45. Richard F. Fenno, Jr., *Home Style: House Members in Their Districts* (Boston: Little, Brown, 1978), Chapters 3 and 4.

46. See the first edition of this book, pp. 117-118.

47. See Tables 5-1, 5-2, and 5-3.

48. Alan I. Abramowitz, "Choices and Echoes in the 1978 U.S. Senate Elections: A Research Note," *American Journal of Political Science* 25 (February, 1981):112-118; Gerald C. Wright, Jr., and Michael Berkman, "Candidates and Policy in U.S. Senate Elections," *American Political Science Review* 80 (1986):567-588; Gary C. Jacobson, "Reagan, Reaganomics, and Strategic Politics in 1982: A Test of Alternative Theories of Midterm Congressional Elections" (Paper delivered at the Annual Meeting of the American Political Science Association, Chicago, September 1-4, 1983), pp. 19-22.

49. Barbara Hinckley, "House Re-Elections and Senate Defeats: The Role of the Challenger," *American Political Science Review* 74 (1980):458-469; Alford and Hibbing, "Electoral Security," pp. 18-23; Peverill Squire, "Challengers in Senate Elections," *Legislative Studies Quarterly* 14 (1989):544; Krasno, *Challengers, Competition, and Reelection*, pp. 154-170; Paul

Gronke, *Settings, Institutions, Campaigns, and the Vote* (Ann Arbor: University of Michigan Press, forthcoming).

50. Morris P. Fiorina, *Congress: Keystone of the Washington Establishment*, 2nd ed. (New Haven: Yale University Press, 1989), Part I.

51. See Gary C. Jacobson and Samuel Kernell, "National Forces in the 1986 U.S. House Elections," *Legislative Studies Quarterly* 15 (1990):72–85.

CHAPTER SIX

National Politics and Congressional Elections

I n 1995, the first Republican-controlled Congress elected in more than 40 years began a sustained effort to dismantle programs and overturn policies that had accumulated under decades of Democratic rule. Their targets included welfare programs for poor families, regulations protecting the environment and consumers, and Medicare spending. Spending cuts were justified by the goal of balancing a federal budget that had been running large deficits since the early 1980s. At the same time, Republican leaders pushed for large tax cuts skewed toward upper-income families. This combination of policies would redistribute income from poorer to wealthier citizens, extending a trend initiated in 1981 under the Reagan administration. Many of the programs scheduled for elimination had first seen the light of day in the explosion of social welfare legislation that followed the 1964 elections. Others had been enacted in the 1930s as part of the New Deal, which was the last time such a radical shift in national policy had been attempted.

Each of these major changes in the direction of national policy was the product of the preceding congressional election. The New Deal, the Great Society, and the Republicans' conservative counterattack on the welfare state were all made possible by a major shift of congressional seats from one party to the other. The New Deal happened because the 1932 elections gave Franklin D. Roosevelt large and cooperative majorities in Congress, with reinforcements in 1934 and 1936. Lyndon Johnson's War on Poverty went into high gear when Democrats increased their share of House seats from 59 to 68 percent in 1964; it was stopped cold when Democratic representation dropped back to 57 percent following the 1966 elections. The Reagan administration's early victories on tax and welfare spending reduction were possible because the 1980 election had given Republicans control of the Senate for the first time since 1952 and thirty-three additional House seats, raising their share in that body from 36 to 44 percent; their much broader assault on welfare and regulatory programs had to wait, however, until 1994, when they won majorities in both houses.

Congressional elections are collective as well as individual events. When the wins and losses in all the separate contests are added up, the sums determine which party controls the House and Senate and with what size majority. The aggregate outcome also gives everyone in national politics at least a speculative sense of what is on the public's mind. The raw numbers and their interpretation establish the opportunities and constraints that guide the direction of national policy for at least the next two years and often a good deal longer.[1] The

141

electoral politics of Congress may center largely on individual candidates and campaigns, but the collective results of congressional elections are what shape the course of national politics.

This is true not only in a specific and practical sense—the Republican gains in 1994 leading directly to a reduced federal role in helping poor people, for example—but also more fundamentally. The possibility of responsible representative government in the United States depends on the capacity of congressional elections to influence the course of public policy. This, in turn, is contingent on aggregate election results reflecting, in a meaningful way, the basic concerns of the public. How well they do this—how the millions of individual voting decisions in hundreds of distinctly individual contests combine to produce intelligible election results—is the subject of this chapter.

POLITICAL INTERPRETATIONS OF CONGRESSIONAL ELECTIONS

Before the tools of survey research came into common use, politicians and political analysts had little problem interpreting aggregate congressional election results. It was widely believed that economic conditions (prosperity or recession, unemployment, or price levels) and presidential politics (the popular standing of presidents or presidential candidates—influenced to be sure, by economic conditions, but also by triumphs or blunders overseas, scandals, and other national issues) shaped the electoral prospects of congressional candidates. Thus it was possible to look at a set of figures like those in Table 6-1 and, with a little knowledge of contemporary events, make sense of them.

Republicans triumphed in 1946 because of economic dislocation and inflation brought on by postwar demobilization; Democrats made a comeback in 1948 behind Truman's spirited campaign in defense of the New Deal and because of economic problems—strikes, rising prices—that could be blamed on the Republican Congress. Public dissatisfaction with the second Truman administration was clearly expressed in the 1950 and 1952 elections. A major recession took its toll on Republicans in 1958. The Goldwater debacle lengthened Johnson's coattails in 1964, the Republicans coming back in 1966 as discontent with Johnson's policies spread.

Republican congressional candidates were punished in 1974 for Nixon's Watergate sins and a recessionary economy. Inflation, Iran, and incompetence at the top of the ticket spelled disaster for Democrats in 1980, but they rebounded in 1982 on the strength of a recession that produced the highest unemployment levels since the Great Depression. In elections from 1984 through 1988, voters registered relative satisfaction with the status quo in congressional as well as presidential elections; when they became disgusted with both parties in 1990, the administration's party naturally suffered more. With the end of divided government in 1992, popular discontent was focused fully on the Democrats as the party in power, so the Republican swept to a historic victory in 1994. Republican overreaching on the budget and Bill Clinton's impeachment reduced their House majorities in 1996 and 1998. Plainly, it is no great chal-

TABLE 6–1   NET PARTY SHIFT IN HOUSE AND SENATE SEATS, 1946–1998[a]

YEAR	HOUSE	SENATE	PRESIDENT'S PARTY[b]
1946	56 R	13 R	D
1948	75 D	9 D	D
1950	28 R	5 R	D
1952	22 R	1 R	R
1954	19 D	2 D	R
1956	2 D	1 D	R
1958	49 D	15 D	R
1960	22 R	2 R	D
1962	1 R	3 D	D
1964	37 D	1 D	D
1966	47 R	4 R	D
1968	5 R	6 R	R
1970	12 D	2 R	R
1972	12 R	2 D	R
1974	49 D	4 D	R
1976	1 D	0	D
1978	15 R	3 R	D
1980	33 R	12 R	R
1982	26 D	1 R	R
1984	14 R	2 D	R
1986	5 D	8 D	R
1988	2 D	0	R
1990	8 D	1 D	R
1992	10 R	0	D
1994	52 R	8 R	D
1996	9 D	2 R	D
1998	6 D	0	D

[a]D indicates Democrats, R indicates Republicans.
[b]Denotes party of winning candidate in presidential election years.
   Sources: Norman J. Ornstein, Thomas E. Mann, and Michael J. Malbin, *Vital Statistics on Congress 1997–1998* (Washington, DC: Congressional Quarterly, 1998), Table 2–3; data for 1998 compiled by author.

lenge to interpret congressional elections as national events controlled by national political conditions, and most political professionals do so routinely.

Models of Aggregate Congressional Election Results

Social scientists have examined the impact of national forces on congressional elections rather more systematically without upsetting the conventional wisdom. Numerous studies have investigated the effects of national economic conditions, variously measured, on the national division of the two-party vote for representative.[2] Although the variety of approaches taken to the question (different economic indices, time periods, and control variables) has engendered important disagreements, most specifications produce the expected systematic relationship between the state of the economy and aggregate congressional election outcomes: The better the economy is performing, the better the congressional candidates of the president's party do on election day.

Edward Tufte took this work a step further by adding a measure of the popular standing of the president to the analysis. Tufte began with the familiar fact of political life that the president's party nearly always loses seats in midterm elections; the figures in Table 6-1 attest to it. The president's party lost House seats in every postwar midterm until 1998, dropping an average of twenty-six. And most of the time, the party of the winning presidential candidate picks up House seats in a presidential election year (the postwar average is thirteen). The theory of surge and decline, outlined in the previous chapter, was an attempt to explain these phenomena as part of a single system. Investigations of individual voting behavior produced little support for the theory. The theory also failed to explain the size of the midterm loss of the president's party, which has varied from one to fifty-six House seats in postwar elections.

Tufte showed that the division of the congressional vote in midterm elections was strongly and systematically related to simple measures of the economy (change in real income per capita over the election year) and presidential approval (percent approving the president's performance in office in the Gallup Poll closest to election day). He also applied his model to presidential election years, using relative candidate evaluations in place of presidential approval ratings.[3]

The regression equation reported in Table 6-2 is an updated variant of Tufte's model. The dependent variable is the change in the percentage of House seats held by the president's party before and after the election. I include a control for the party's "exposure"—the share of seats it holds above or below its average over the previous eight elections—because the more seats a party holds, the more of its seats are vulnerable to the opposition.[4] The exposure figure has been adjusted to incorporate the sharp and sustained swing favoring the Republicans that followed the redistricting for the 1990s.[5] National conditions are represented by the change in real income per capita in the year

TABLE 6–2   THE EFFECTS OF NATIONAL CONDITIONS ON U.S. HOUSE ELECTIONS, 1946–1998

VARIABLE	COEFFICIENT	STANDARD ERROR
Intercept	−18.68	3.49
Exposure	−.78	.12
Change in real income per capita (%)	1.32	.32
Presidential approval (%)	.27	.07
Adjusted R^2	.71	
Durbin-Watson Statistic	2.24	
Number of Cases	27	

Note: The dependent variable is the percentage of seats gained or lost by the president's party; see the text for a description of the variables; all coefficients are statistically significant at $p<.01$, two-tailed test.

preceding the election and the president's level of popular approval in the last Gallup Poll taken prior to the election.

The equation explains 71 percent of the variance in the share of House seats a party wins or loses, and all of the other variables work as expected. According to the coefficients, the difference between the highest and lowest values of presidential approval (74 percent and 32 percent) translates into a difference of forty-nine House seats, as does, coincidentally, the difference between the highest and lowest values of income change (6.0 percent and −2.6 percent). Of course, the equation also leaves 29 percent of the variance unexplained, a fact of considerable importance when we turn our attention to specific election years later in this chapter.

The results of this and other analyses leave little doubt that economic conditions and presidential performance ratings affect aggregate House election results. Both also have a significant impact on aggregate Senate election results, although there is, not surprisingly, more unexplained variance on the Senate side.[6] Furthermore, congressional electorates behave rationally; the party of the administration is held responsible for the performance of its president and of the economy. Tufte recognized that "many different models of the underlying electorate are consistent with electoral outcomes that are collectively rational,"[7] but less cautious scholars have interpreted collective rationality to be a demonstration of equivalent individual rationality. The problem with this interpretation is that it finds only modest support in survey studies of individual voters.

The strong connection between aggregate economic variables and aggregate election results naturally inspired scholars to investigate the effects of economic conditions on individual voting behavior. At least four different kinds of economic variables might influence the vote choice: personal financial experiences and expectations, perceptions of general economic conditions, evaluations of the government's economic performance, and party images on economic policies.[8]

Most aggregate-level studies are based on the assumption that personal financial well-being is the primary criterion used by voters: "Rational voters are concerned with their real income and wealth."[9] The aggregate economic variables (change in real per capita income, percent unemployed) were chosen because they represent direct economic effects on individual citizens. Survey studies have turned up very little evidence that personal finances directly influence individual congressional voters, however. The occasional effects that do appear in some election years are generally indirect and much too weak to account for the robust relationships that Tufte and others have found between national measures of economic conditions and election outcomes.

Survey research does produce some evidence suggesting that economic conditions may influence the vote in one or more of the other ways. But the reported effects are almost always modest and explain little additional variance in the vote once other variables (of the kind examined in the previous chapter) are taken into account. The behavior of individual voters does not conform to any straightforward model of economic rationality.[10]

Survey findings about the electoral effects of voter evaluations of presidents are somewhat more consistent with the aggregate evidence. Samuel Kernell found that, in midterm elections from 1946 through 1966, approval or disapproval of the president's performance was correlated with congressional preferences (with party identification controlled) and that disapproval had a greater effect than approval.[11] Other evidence from elections in the 1960s also showed voter evaluation of presidents to influence congressional voting.[12] More recent studies have reported conflicting findings. Evaluations of Ford (in 1974) and Carter (in 1978) made little difference, but assessments of Reagan (in 1982 and 1986), Bush (1990), and Clinton (1994) had a substantial influence on the House vote.[13]

A related and more remarkable discovery is that reactions to Watergate did not appear to have a very large impact on individual voting decisions, despite the heavy losses suffered by Republicans in 1974. Several studies found Watergate's effects to be indirect and unimpressively small,[14] although more sophisticated methods of analysis have uncovered a significant link between voters' reactions to Ford's pardon of Nixon and the congressional vote choice.[15]

Various attempts have been made to account for the often feeble connection between the economic and presidential popularity variables and individual congressional voting without abandoning the original premise of individual economic rationality; none has been fully convincing.[16] Fiorina has made the strongest empirical case, arguing that personal economic experiences "affect more general economic performance judgments, both types of judgments feed into evaluations of presidential performance, and more general judgments, at least, contribute to modifications of party identification," which is known to be strongly related to the vote.[17] Even granting this complex process, the effects are a good deal weaker than the strong aggregate relationships would predict.

PRESIDENTIAL COATTAILS

The impact of voters' feelings about the presidential candidates is puzzling in a different way. Customarily, this has been discussed in terms of *coattail effects*. The term reflects the notion that successful candidates at the top of the ticket—in national elections, the winning presidential candidate—pull some of their party's candidates into office along with them, riding, as it were, on their coattails. Just how this works is a matter of considerable debate. Perhaps the presidential choice has a direct influence on the congressional choice; people prefer to vote for candidates sharing their presidential favorite's party affiliation. Or perhaps both choices are influenced by the same set of considerations—for example, disgust with the failures of the current administration or delight with a party platform to which both candidates are committed—and so move in the same direction. It is even conceivable that, on occasion, support for the head of the ticket spills over from support for candidates for lower offices.

Regardless of the mechanisms operating, if a large number of fellow partisans are swept into office along with the president, political interpretation usually favors the traditional view embodied in the term itself. A presidential winner whose success is not shared by other candidates of his party is presumed to have no coattails.

The question of whether or not the president has strong coattails is of more than academic interest. Sheer numbers matter; administrations get more of what they want from Congress the more seats their party holds in the House and Senate. Roosevelt's New Deal, Johnson's Great Society, and Reagan's budget victories all depended on large shifts in party seats. George Bush, in contrast, had no choice but to compromise with a strongly Democratic Congress from the beginning of his presidency, and Bill Clinton was left in a similar position when his party failed to regain their congressional majorities in 1996. Aside from sheer numbers, members of Congress who believe that they were elected with the help of the president are more likely to cooperate with him, if not from simple gratitude, then from a sense of shared fate: They will prosper politically as the administration prospers. Those convinced that they were elected on their own, or despite the top of the ticket, have less reason to cooperate.

Finally, a partisan sweep that extends to Congress also sends a potent message to the incumbents who survived (and to other Washington politicians). If the electorate seems to have spoken clearly and decisively, political wisdom dictates that its message be heeded, at least for a while.[18] The resistance of recalcitrant senior Democrats to the Kennedy–Johnson programs collapsed for a time after the 1964 election. Republican gains in 1980 transformed more than a few congressional Democrats into born-again tax- and budget-cutters. The 1988 congressional election returns, in contrast, left Democrats under little pressure to follow Bush's lead, and the 1992 elections, in which the Democrats lost a net ten House seats, were scarcely a ringing endorsement of Bill Clinton's plans.

How such considerations affect congressional politics is discussed more thoroughly in the next chapter. The political significance of coattail effects (or, more precisely, the perception of them) is mentioned here because most of the aggregate evidence available indicates that coattails became increasingly attenuated between the 1950s and the 1980s. Both *cross-sectional* (relating the presidential and congressional vote at the district level) and *time-series* (relating the national presidential and congressional vote over a series of election years) studies show a diminishing connection between presidential and congressional voting over this period.[19] Evidence from 1992 and especially 1996, however, indicates that the linkage has tightened once again, at least temporarily.

One perspective on the link between presidential and congressional elections is provided by the data in Table 6-3, which lists the number and percentage of House districts that delivered split verdicts—majorities for the presidential candidate of one party, the House candidate of the other—in presidential election years from 1920 through 1996. The change after 1952 is striking. The proportion of split results is naturally larger in years with presidential landslides—it reached peaks of 44 and 45 percent, respectively, in 1972 and 1984—but from the 1960s through the 1980s, it exceeded 30 percent even in years with comparatively close presidential contests. The 1992 and 1996 elections are clear exceptions, however, with fewer divided districts than in any elections since 1952. Clinton may have not had lengthier coattails than Reagan or Bush (see Table 6-1), but partisan consistency was clearly on the rise in the 1990s.

TABLE 6-3 DISTRICTS WITH SPLIT RESULTS IN PRESIDENTIAL AND HOUSE ELECTIONS, 1920-1996

| | DISTRICTS WITH SPLIT RESULTS[a] | | |
YEAR	Districts	Number	Percentage[b]
1920	344	11	3.2
1924	356	42	11.8
1928	359	68	18.9
1932	355	50	14.1
1936	361	51	14.1
1940	362	53	14.6
1944	367	41	11.2
1948	422	90	21.3
1952	435	84	19.3
1956	435	130	29.9
1960	437	114	26.1
1964	435	145	33.3
1968	435	139	32.0
1972	435	192	44.1
1976	435	124	28.5
1980	435	143	32.8
1984	435	196	45.0
1988	435	148	34.0
1992	435	103	23.7
1996	435	110	25.5

[a]Congressional districts carried by a presidential candidate of one party and a House candidate of the other.
[b]Prior to 1952 complete data on every congressional district are not available.
Source: Norman J. Ornstein, Thomas E. Mann, and Michael J. Malbin, *Vital Statistics on Congress 1997-1998* (Washington, DC: Congressional Quarterly, 1997), Table 2-16.

Further evidence is presented in Figures 6-1 and 6-2, which show changes in the simple correlation between the district level House and presidential vote, and the incidence of ticket splitting reported in the NES surveys, from 1952 through 1996. The correlation between the House and presidential vote, which stood at .86 in 1952, declined to as low as .52 in 1972, before rebounding to .83 in 1996. This is not merely a consequence of realignment in the South, where conservative voters now vote Republican at the congressional level as they have been at the presidential level since Barry Goldwater's candidacy in 1964, for the same trends appear if the analysis is confined to nonsouthern districts.[20] The incidence of major party ticket splitting—voting for a Democrat for one office, a Republican for the other—shows the same pattern inverted, with a sharp rise in ticket splitting from the 1950s to the 1970s, followed by a decline culminating in 1996 to the lowest levels in three decades.[21]

Because the extent to which presidential and congressional election results coincide has such profound implications for national politics, it is worth considering some of the individual-level evidence in more detail. It suggests that even

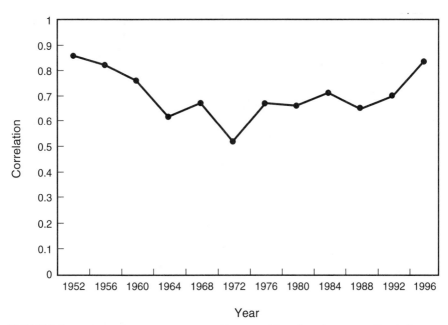

FIGURE 6–1 Correlations between District-Level House and Presidential Voting, 1952-1996
Source: Compiled by author.

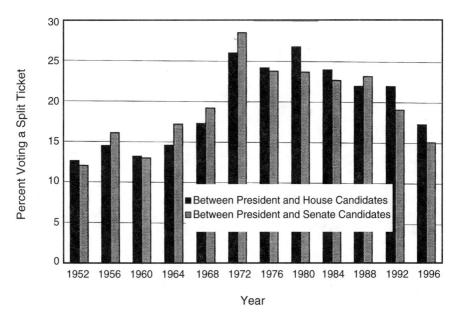

FIGURE 6–2 Ticket Splitting in National Elections, 1952-1996
Source: American National Election Studies, 1952-1996.

in elections with a high incidence of split results and split-ticket voting, presidential coattails continue to exert a pull. Still, coattail contributions to congressional victories for the president's party have been erratic and usually modest in recent elections. Understanding why this is so will tell us something important about how national political forces influence congressional elections.

A simple test for the presence of coattail effects of some kind can be made by adding a variable representing the presidential vote to the full probit model (Equation 3) presented in Table 5-9. The results, reported and interpreted in Table 6-4, indicate that the presidential vote choice had a large and statistically significant impact on the probability that a voter would vote for the Democratic House candidate, even with party identification and the candidate-oriented variables controlled. The first column lists a range of hypothetical probabilities of voting for the Democrat (assumed to be based on the party and candidate variables) unaffected by the presidential vote. The second column shows how these probabilities change if the voter voted for Dole, the third, for Perot, and the fourth, for Clinton. For example, a voter who otherwise (on the basis of the other variables) had a .5 probability of voting for the Democrat would have a .7 probability of doing so if he voted for Clinton, but only a .3 probability if he voted for Dole.

TABLE 6–4   COATTAIL EFFECTS (PROBIT ESTIMATES)

PROBABILITY OF VOTING FOR REPUBLICAN HOUSE CANDIDATE							
	VOTED FOR			DIFFERENCE IN PROBABILITY			
INITIAL PROBABILITY	Dole	Perot	Clinton	1996	1992	1988	1984
.10	.04	.12	.21	.17	.09	.09	.10
.25	.12	.29	.44	.32	.18	.19	.19
.40	.22	.44	.61	.39	.23	.24	.24
.50	.30	.54	.70	.40	.24	.25	.25
.60	.39	.64	.78	.39	.23	.24	.24
.75	.56	.78	.88	.32	.18	.19	.19
.90	.79	.91	.96	.17	.09	.09	.10

PROBIT EQUATION (1996)	COEFFICIENT	STANDARD ERROR
Intercept	.16	.29
Party Identification	.48	.10
Democrat Is Incumbent	.36	.29
Republican Is Incumbent	−1.07	.27
Familiarity with Democrat	.28	.25
Familiarity with Republican	−.49	.26
Likes Something about Democrat	1.60	.19
Dislikes Something about Democrat	−1.34	.22
Likes Something about Republican	−1.15	.18
Dislikes Something about Republican	1.07	.20
Presidential Vote (Clinton vs. Dole)	.87	.12
Voted for Perot	.18	.25
Percent correctly predicted (Null=52.4)	92.6	

Source: American National Election Study, 1996.

The difference in the probability of voting Democratic contingent on the choice between Dole and Clinton is listed in the fifth column. It is characteristic of probit coefficients that their effects are largest in the middle range of probabilities. The final three columns provide the same estimates for the equivalent equations from 1984, 1988, and 1992.[22] The estimate effects are virtually identical across the first three elections, but they are noticeably larger in 1996, again confirming the stronger association between House and presidential voting that year.

Yet another way to check for coattail effects is to observe the consequences of partisan defection in the presidential campaign on the congressional vote. The pattern for the 1952 through 1996 elections is shown in Figures 6-3 and 6-4. Clearly, party identifiers who voted for the other party's presidential candidate were a good deal more likely to vote for its House or Senate candidate as well in every election year. On average, more than 50 percent of the presidential defectors also defected in both House and Senate elections, compared with only about 13 percent of the presidential loyalists.

The aggregate effects of presidential coattails depend on how defection rates differ between the two parties' identifiers. For example, about 80 percent of the defectors in 1980, and 85 percent in 1984, were Democrats voting for Reagan, so this pattern must have helped Republican congressional candidates. A simple calculation shows that, had presidential defections been divided equally while other things remained the same, the reported vote for House Republicans would have been 3 percentage points lower in 1980 and 5 percentage points lower in 1984; the Republican vote for senator would have been 2

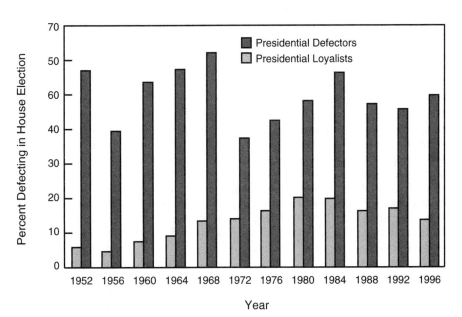

FIGURE 6–3 Partisan Defections to House Candidates, by Presidential Loyalty, 1952–1996
Source: American National Election Studies.

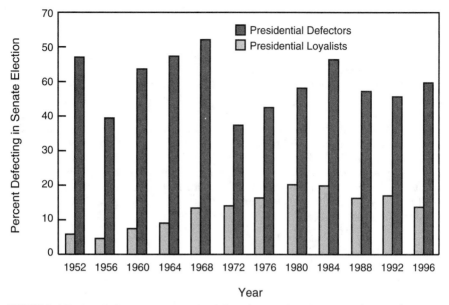

FIGURE 6–4 Partisan Defections to Senate Candidates, by Presidential Loyalty, 1952–1996
Source: American National Election Studies.

points lower in 1980, 4 points lower in 1984. Presidential defections were more evenly balanced in 1988—about 60 percent were Democrats voting for Bush—so the net effect is smaller, adding about 1 percentage point to the Republican vote in both House and Senate contests. In 1992, defections were so evenly balanced that neither party enjoyed any net benefit, but in 1996 the balance finally favored Democrats, adding about 2.6 percentage points to their total House and Senate totals.

Plainly, nontrivial coattail effects have been discernible in recent elections. The effects were evidently stronger in 1984 than in the other years under examination, a curious result, because the aggregate results imply that Reagan's coattails were considerably shorter in 1984 than they had been in 1980. In 1980, Republicans picked up thirty House and twelve Senate seats; in 1984, they picked up only fourteen House seats while losing two Senate seats. Despite Reagan's huge landslide and a sharp increase in the proportion of voters calling themselves Republicans, Republicans held ten fewer House seats after 1984 than they did after 1980. Similarly, Clinton's victory in 1996 brought the Democrats only meager gains in the House and they actually lost Senate seats (see Table 6-1).

The elections of 1984 and 1996 are not the first for which aggregate and survey evidence of coattail effects conflict. In 1972, Richard Nixon won more than 60 percent of the vote, yet Republicans gained only twelve House seats and lost two Senate seats. Nonetheless, coattail effects were detectable at the level of individual voters. Just as in 1980, 1984, 1988, and 1992, voters in 1972 who defected to the other party's presidential candidate were significantly more likely to defect to the other party's House candidates as well.[23] Almost 90 percent of the defectors were Democrats voting for Nixon; again, it is possible to calculate that, had defections been divided evenly and the other patterns remained stable, the Republican House vote would have been 5 percentage points lower.

Here, then, is evidence of a connection at the level of individual voters that is not apparent at the aggregate level, whereas for national economic conditions and midterm presidential popularity, strong aggregate relationships tend to atrophy at the individual level. The solution to both of these puzzles lies in understanding the interactions between national conditions and the career and campaign strategies of individual congressional candidates.

NATIONAL CONDITIONS AND STRATEGIC POLITICS

It is entirely possible for national conditions, personalities, and issues to affect congressional election results without directly impinging on individual voters at all. Samuel Kernell and I have presented the full explanation of how this can be so elsewhere—in *Strategy and Choice in Congressional Elections*[24]—so I will merely summarize it here.

A great deal of evidence, some of which was presented in Chapter 5, indicates that, in present-day congressional elections, the vote decision is strongly influenced by the voters' knowledge and evaluations of the particular pair of candidates running in the district or state. National issues such as the state of the economy or the performance of the president may influence some voters some of the time—for example, voters who think that one candidate will do a better job dealing with the most important national problem almost invariably vote for that candidate—but for many voters the congressional choice is determined by evaluations of candidates as individuals, often with little reference to national policies or personalities. Even in 1994, when national issues did shape voters' decisions to an unusual extent, the choice offered locally between a pair of candidates remained crucial, and, as in all recent elections, the relative political talents and campaign resources of congressional challengers were decisive in framing that choice.

Variations in the attractiveness of challengers and the vigor of their campaigns are by no means random. The decisions to run for Congress and to contribute to campaigns are subject to strategic calculation. As I pointed out in Chapter 3, the strongest potential candidates—those already holding a place on the political career ladder—also have the greatest incentive for careful strategic behavior, for they have the most to lose if a bid for a higher office fails. Their plans are invariably conditioned by a reading of the odds on winning. People who contribute to campaigns also take full account of the candidate's electoral chances. Some clear evidence of strategic behavior on the part of candidates and contributors was presented in Tables 3-9 and 3-10. More experienced candidates run more lavishly financed campaigns when the incumbent seems vulnerable or when no incumbent is running.

Another important consideration is whether it promises to be a good or bad year for the party. And that, it is widely believed, depends on national economic and political conditions. A booming economy and a popular president (or presidential candidate) are assumed to favor the party in power; economic problems and other national failings that are blamed on the administration are costly to its congressional candidates. *Exactly those things that politicians and political scientists who look at aggregate data believe influence congressional voters also guide the strategic decisions of potential candidates and contributors.*

This means that when the partisan outlook is gloomy, shrewd and ambitious politicians figure that the normally long odds against defeating an incumbent are even worse than usual and wait for a better day. People who supply campaign resources to the party's candidates also decline to waste them trying to defeat incumbents they dislike and instead deploy them to defend their own favorite incumbents who may be in more trouble than usual.

Politicians of the other party, sensing that electoral tides are moving in their direction, view the chances of winning as better than usual, so more and better candidates compete for the nomination to challenge incumbents.[25] One thing that encourages them to make the race is easier access to campaign funds; contributors are also more willing to invest in challenges because political conditions seem favorable. Because the marginal effects of campaign spending are so much greater for challengers than for incumbents, the contrasting offensive and defensive contribution strategies do not simply cancel one another out; rather, they add to the vote totals of the party favored by national political conditions.

Thus when conditions appear to favor one party over the other, the favored party fields an unusually large proportion of formidable challengers with well-funded campaigns, while the other party fields underfinanced amateurs willing to run without serious hope of winning. In addition, incumbents of the disadvantaged party are marginally more likely to retire when facing the prospect of a tougher-than-usual campaign; the struggle for one more term may not be worth the effort.[26] This, too, means that the disadvantaged party will have relatively fewer strong candidates.

The choice between pairs of candidates across states and districts in an election year thus varies systematically with the strategic decisions of potential candidates and associated activists. These decisions are systematically informed by perceptions of national political and economic conditions. Voters need only respond to the choice between candidates and campaigns at the local level to reflect, in their aggregate behavior, national political forces. It is not necessary for individual-level analogs of national forces—the voter's personal economic experiences and feelings about the president or presidential candidates—to influence the vote directly in order to affect the aggregate results. Some voters are no doubt moved by such considerations—the favored party's candidates certainly strive to show how national conditions affect voters' lives—but pervasive individual rationality of this sort is not essential for the process to work. The intervening strategic decisions of congressional elites provide a mechanism sufficient to explain how national forces can come to be expressed in congressional election outcomes.

The logic of this explanation is straightforward enough; there is also considerable evidence for it. Politicians routinely sniff the political winds early in the election year; speculation about what will happen in the fall is a common feature of political news in January and February. Predictions are explicitly based on economic conditions and the public standing of the administration. Other information, from polls and special elections, for example, is also sifted for clues. Signs and portents are readily available, widely discussed, and taken seriously.[27]

They are also usually heeded. In 1974, for example, Watergate, recession, and the low standing of Nixon in the polls made it very difficult for Republicans to recruit good candidates at all levels. Republicans expected it to be a bad year, and candidates and activists refused to extend themselves in a losing cause.[28] Democrats saw it as a golden opportunity, and an unusually large proportion of experienced candidates challenged Republican incumbents.[29] Their strategic decisions contributed to the Democrats' best year in the past three decades.

Campaign contributors also respond to election year expectations. Some indication of this is found in the data in Table 6-5, which lists House campaign expenditures in constant (1998=1.00) dollars, according to party and incumbency status, for elections from 1972 through 1998. Partisan differences in expenditures (which depend, of course, on contributions) are relatively smaller in years when national conditions do not seem to establish a clear favorite. The patterns for 1974 and 1994 show what happens when strong national tides are expected. In 1974, Democratic challengers typically spent more than 2.8 times as much as Republican challengers; they even outspent Democratic incumbents. Republican incumbents, on the defensive, spent 74 percent more than Democratic incumbents and four times as much, on average, as Republican challengers. In 1994 it was the Republicans' turn to go on the offensive and the Democrats' to try to save endangered incumbents. Republican challengers outspent Democratic challengers by 60 percent; Democratic incumbents outspent Republican incumbents by 32 percent, spending four times as much as Democratic challengers. The patterns could hardly be clearer. Campaign contributions—and hence expenditures—were sharply responsive to perceived political trends in 1974 and 1994.

Not all election years follow this pattern so decisively. For example, all the signs for 1982 pointed to a very good year for Democrats, yet Democratic challengers were not especially well funded and were actually outspent by Republican challengers. The pattern of expenditures for 1984 seems to reflect a good Republican year, and so it was; yet, as we have seen, Republican House gains were rather limited, especially compared with 1980. The 1986 election found Republicans on the defensive—no surprise, given the sorry historical record for the administration's party in its second midterm election (see Table 6-1)— but Democratic gains were very modest. The surprise is that the pattern of campaign spending indicates a defensive Republican strategy in 1988 as well. Both parties' challengers were snubbed in 1990. Overall, though, the relationship between the relative levels of spending by the two parties' challengers (measured by the ratio of Republican to Democratic challenger spending) and the size of the partisan seat swing across these elections remains quite high ($r=.80$).

TABLE 6–5   AVERAGE CAMPAIGN EXPENDITURES BY HOUSE CANDIDATES, 1972–1998, BY PARTY AND INCUMBENCY STATUS (IN THOUSANDS OF 1998 DOLLARS)

YEAR	PARTY	INCUMBENTS	CHALLENGERS	OPEN SEATS
1972	Democrats	189	117	385
	Republicans	204	127	346
1974	Democrats	153	196	341
	Republicans	267	68	266
1976	Democrats	230	133	407
	Republicans	269	159	274
1978	Democrats	276	177	522
	Republicans	389	180	472
1980	Democrats	331	148	375
	Republicans	380	226	432
1982	Democrats	409	196	431
	Republicans	447	212	461
1984	Democrats	488	158	551
	Republicans	449	229	584
1986	Democrats	528	219	608
	Republicans	584	168	671
1988	Democrats	535	204	680
	Republicans	587	134	739
1990	Democrats	503	122	648
	Republicans	496	111	572
1992	Democrats	686	154	539
	Republicans	603	196	440
1994	Democrats	669	168	613
	Republicans	506	268	662
1996	Democrats	605	314	674
	Republicans	773	219	668
1998	Democrats	574	266	729
	Republicans	701	256	781

Note: Data are from candidates with major party opposition only.

Source: Compiled by author from data supplied by Common Cause (1972 and 1974) and the Federal Election Commission (1976–1998).

Campaign finance data do not exist for elections prior to 1972, so there is no way to know whether campaign contributions reflected strategic advantages and disadvantages in earlier election years. It is possible, however, to show that variations in the relative quality of each party's candidates are strongly related to national conditions and aggregate election results in the way necessary for the explanation to be valid. The regression equations in Table 6-6 demonstrate that the relative aggregate quality of each party's challengers reflects, among other things, national conditions.

For this analysis, the quality of a party's challengers is measured as the percentage of them who have held elective office. The independent variables are

TABLE 6–6 DETERMINANTS OF THE PERCENTAGE OF
EXPERIENCED HOUSE CHALLENGERS, 1946–1998

VARIABLE	DEMOCRATS (EQUATION 1)		REPUBLICANS (EQUATION 2)		DEMOCRATS-REPUBLICANS (EQUATION 3)	
Intercept	59.80^a	(12.77)	-5.70	(10.72)	65.50^a	(12.52)
Party of administration	-32.87^a	(9.48)	6.23	(7.96)	-39.10^a	(9.30)
Seats won by Democrats last election (%)	$-.29$	(.19)	$.32^a$	(.16)	$-.61^a$	(.18)
Change in real income per capita (2nd quarter)	1.24^a	(.48)	.08	(.41)	1.16^a	(.47)
Presidential approval (2nd quarter)	$.27^a$	(.10)	$-.05$	(.08)	$.32^a$	(.09)
1992 or later	-10.37^a	(3.46)	2.72	2.91	-13.08^a	(3.39)
Adjusted R^2	.48		.01		.60	
Number of cases	27		27		27	

Note: The dependent variable in Equations 1 and 2 is the percent of challengers of the designated party who have held elective office; for Equation 3, it is the difference between the two; the independent variables are described in the text; standard errors in parentheses.
[a]Statistically significant at $p<.05$, one-tailed test.

presidential approval and real income change, plus the current partisan division of House seats (to take the opportunities created by "exposure" into account). Because the administration's party (not just the Democratic party) is supposed to be rewarded or punished for the administration's performance, presidential approval and income change are multiplied by -1 when a Republican is in the White House, and a fourth variable, the party of the administration, is included as a control. National conditions are measured in the second quarter (April–June) of the election year because this is the period during which most *final* decisions about candidacy must be made.[30] I have also included a variable controlling for the effects of the sustained shift in favor of Republicans in the 1990s, which has reduced the proportion of strong Democratic challengers.[31]

The coefficients from Equation 1 indicate that both economic conditions and the level of public approval of the president have a large and significant impact on the quality of Democratic challengers. Neither one matters to Republicans, who are sensitive only to the opportunities offered by the current level of Democratic strength in the House (Equation 2). However, a composite variable measuring the relative quality of challengers is affected significantly by all of these variables. This is the key variable, because relative quality is what matters for aggregate results on election day. The evidence is presented in Table 6-7. The dependent variable here is the change in the percentage of House seats won by the Democrats from the prior to the current election. As before, I control for the Democrats' exposure and for the party of the administration. The other variables are measured as in Table 6-6 except that real income change is the average for the election year and presidential approval is taken from the last Gallup Poll before the election.

TABLE 6-7   NATIONAL FORCES, STRATEGIC POLITICIANS, AND INTERELECTION SEAT SWINGS IN HOUSE ELECTIONS, 1946–1998

VARIABLE	(EQUATION 1)		(EQUATION 2)		(EQUATION 3)	
Intercept	68.83	(9.31)	52.65^a	(10.59)	19.98	(7.66)
Party of administration	-38.14^a	(7.77)	-28.81	(7.63)		
Seats won by Democrats last election (%)	$-.83^a$	(.12)	$-.62^a$	(.12)	$-.38^a$	(.13)
Change in real income per capita (2nd quarter)	$.82^a$	(.35)	.46	(33)		
Presidential approval (2nd quarter)	$.30^a$	(.08)	$.24^a$	(.07)		
Quality of Democratic challengers			$.24^a$	(.11)	$.53^a$	(.10)
Quality of Republican challengers			$-.45^a$	(.15)	$-.70^a$	(.17)
1992 or later	-9.77^a	(2.42)	-6.06^a	(2.51)		
Adjusted R^2	.75		.82		.71	
Number of cases	27		27		27	

Note: The dependent variable is the change in the percentage of seats won by the Democrats from the previous election; standard errors are in parentheses.
[a]Statistically significant at $p<.05$, one-tailed test.

The first equation in Table 6-7 presents another variant of the standard referendum model discussed earlier. As usual, both presidential approval and economic performance have a significant impact on party fortunes. The second equation adds the aggregate quality variable for each party's challenger; both of these variables have a strong, statistically significant impact on the House seat swing; Democrats gain more seats the better their challengers and lose more seats the better the Republican challengers. Note in particular that the quality of Republican challengers is, if anything, more strongly related to election results than the quality of Democratic challengers, even though high-quality Republican challengers appear to be less strategic in their behavior than high-quality Democratic challengers. Note also that the effect of real income change is reduced by nearly half (compared to Equation 1) and ceases to be statistically significant; presidential approval continues to have a significant influence, though it is reduced somewhat.

A model that includes the quality variables but not income change or presidential approval (Equation 3) explains nearly as much (71 percent) as the model that does the opposite (Equation 1, 75 percent). That is, fully 71 percent of the variance in postwar House seat shifts can be explained by just three variables: the quality of each party's challengers and exposure. The coefficients from Equation 2 indicate that, controlling for other factors, a one percentage point difference in quality of Democratic candidates is worth about one House seat; the range between its highest and lowest values (32) covers thirty-three seats. A one percentage point difference in the quality of Republican challengers is worth about two House seats; the range between its highest and lowest values (16) covers thirty-one seats.

In general, then, the political strategies of congressional elites are responsive to national forces and help to translate them into aggregate election results.[32] Complete evidence—on candidates, campaign finances, and voting behavior—is available only as far back as the early 1970s, and the data on experienced challengers extends back only to 1946. It is very likely that in earlier electoral periods, national forces influenced voters more directly. It would be difficult to argue, for instance, that many congressional voters in 1932, 1934, or 1936 were not responding directly to their economic experiences during the Great Depression or to their feelings about Franklin D. Roosevelt. Individual congressional candidates were important only insofar as they were committed to a position for or against the New Deal. Elections such as these were, of course, the source of the conventional wisdom about the effects of national forces on the fates of congressional candidates. Shrewd politicians would be well advised to adjust their career strategies to take advantage of favorable national tides and to avoid contrary currents.

The strong postwar trend toward a more candidate-centered style of electoral politics would reduce the electoral importance of national forces while enhancing that of individual candidates and campaigns. In more candidate-centered electoral politics, the resources and talents of challengers would have a larger impact on district-level results. Elite strategies would thus make a greater independent contribution to a party's electoral performance.

If, over the years, individual candidates and campaigns became comparatively more important and national forces less so, politicians would not necessarily abandon their traditional strategies. They would, rather, continue to respond strategically to national trends because, increasingly as a consequence of their own strategic choices (and those of other congressional activists), their expectations about election outcomes continued to be realized. At the extreme, their expectations could come to be based on false assumptions, their prophecies wholly self-fulfilling. National economic and political conditions might affect congressional elections only because congressional elites expect them to do so.

There is no reason to think that this point has been reached. Electoral prophecies are, at present, self-reinforcing, but not exclusively self-fulfilling. The quality of challengers has, however, become a more important part of the equation, and the effects of national conditions depend increasingly on what candidates do with national issues at the local level.[33] Consequently, the electorate's ability to exercise democratic control by acting as, in V.O. Key's phrase, a "rational god of vengeance and reward,"[34] has become more contingent and variable, depending to an increasing degree on elite decisions that are only partially determined by the economy and other systematic national forces.

Campaign Themes

At the district level, in addition to shaping alternatives by influencing strategic decisions to run or contribute money, national conditions affect the success or failure of candidacies by defining the campaign themes available to candidates in different situations. They shape the substantive content of campaigns and thus determine the form in which national issues are presented to, and therefore influence, individual voters. The connections between national issues and individual voting decisions are forged by the rhetoric of campaigns and so vary as do the campaigns. Variation occurs both across districts in a single election year and across election years. Variation across election years helps to explain why survey findings about the determinants of the vote are so often inconsistent from one election to the next.[35] Variation across districts helps to explain why there is such a wide divergence among district-level interelection vote swings (recall Table 3-2).

Remember from the discussion of voting behavior in Chapter 5 that to succeed, challengers must accomplish two basic tasks: building support for themselves and undermining that of their incumbent opponents. The first is insufficient without the second. Adverse conditions (for the incumbent) contribute to the first task by encouraging better-qualified challengers to run and by increasing the campaign resources available to them when they do. They contribute to the second task by giving challengers a campaign theme has some prospect of undermining the incumbent's support.

Incumbents are, as a class, remarkably adept at taking credit for the good things that government does while avoiding responsibility for its failures. Under neutral or favorable conditions, a member who cultivates his or her district diligently and avoids personal scandal makes an extremely difficult target. But if people are sufficiently unhappy with an administration, if the economic situation is sufficiently dire, it may become a good deal more difficult to avoid guilt by association—if there is an energetic challenger continually reminding voters of the connection. This is crucial. A vigorous campaign is still essential to defeat incumbents no matter how bad the political conditions for them personally or for their party.

Thus national conditions continue to create problems or opportunities for congressional candidates; but how they are handled or exploited makes more difference now than in the past, and this varies among candidates, between parties, and across election years. When a party does not field enough challengers with the resources and skills to take full advantage of the opportunities created by national conditions, partisan swings are dampened; when it does, partisan swings are enhanced. Similarly, incumbents often survive individual political or personal shortcomings if they avoid challengers capable of exploiting them. These are among the clearest lessons of recent electoral history, to which we now turn.

HOUSE ELECTIONS, 1980–1998

1980

In 1980, as Ronald Reagan was defeating incumbent President Jimmy Carter, the Republicans picked up thirty-four House seats (as well as twelve Senate seats to win a majority in that body). It would be tempting to conclude, as many commentators did, that Democratic congressional candidates were punished wholesale for the failings of the Carter administration, sharing the blame for an unprecedented combination of high inflation and high unemployment and American hostages held for more than a year by Iran's revolutionary government. But punishment was anything but wholesale. Otherwise, how could 77 of the 186 Democratic House incumbents have improved on their 1978 vote?

A more detailed look at the results shows that Republican advances were strongly contingent on their ability to mount strong challenges. The most striking evidence concerns campaign spending; 42 percent (24 of 57) of Republican challengers who spent more than $300,000 (in 1998 dollars) won, while only 2 percent (3 of 154) who spent less than this amount were successful, and in two of the four cases, the Democrat had been involved in the Abscam bribery scandal. Marginal Democrats (those who had won in 1978 with less than 60 percent of the vote) attracted better financed opponents (with 55 percent spending more than $300,000, compared to 16 percent for opponents of nonmarginal Democrats), but well-financed challengers did better against nonmarginal Democrats (winning twelve of twenty contests) than against marginal Democrats (winning eleven of thirty-four contests).

Obviously, not every strong Republican challenge succeeded in 1980. The point is that almost every winning challenge involved a formidable individual campaign that might easily have been effective even without Reagan's victory or Carter's problems. At the very least, successful challengers had positioned themselves to take full advantage of whatever help the national campaigns and other national forces might bestow, and this was a necessary condition of their success. Because potential Republican candidates and contributors anticipated a good year, the party fielded a unusually large class of challengers capable of exploiting the opportunities that arose, so the party enjoyed its best House election year since 1966.

1982

The 1982 elections revealed a potential for elite strategies to counteract rather than reinforce national trends, but they also showed that politicians were still well-advised to take national conditions into account. Had the 1982 elections followed the pattern of previous postwar midterms, the Republicans would have lost between forty and sixty House seats. The economy was in its worst postwar recession, and Reagan's job performance rating in the last preelection Gallup Poll was lower (42 percent approving) than that of any president since Truman in 1946 (and the lowest of Reagan's entire presidency). Under these conditions, Tufte's midterm equation, updated through 1978, predicted Republicans to win 41.2 percent of the vote, a drop of more than 7 percentage points from 1980. Given the relationship between the share of votes and the share of seats won by parties in postwar House elections, the equation implies that the Republicans should have lost about fifty-eight seats.[36] Other referendum models predicted smaller Republican losses, but none came close to predicting that Republicans would lose as few as twenty-six seats, which was the actual result.[37]

At least part of the reason Republicans did so much better than predicted is that neither they nor the Democrats behaved consistently in ways that reinforced the anticipated effects of national forces. Republicans dodged disaster by using their abundant financial and organizational resources (see Chapter 4) to conduct a countercyclical campaign. The national party's active recruitment drive produced a much stronger group of challengers than would have emerged spontaneously under election-year conditions. Party officials recruited energetically in 1981, when the administration was scoring its major legislative successes and a bright Republican future could be envisioned. They worked successfully to retain most of those who had been recruited, even as conditions turned bleak. It helped that they could promise well-funded campaigns despite the contrary national trends, at least insofar as party money was concerned. Every Republican challenger with any real hope of winning could count on the maximum amount of help the national party could legally offer (more than $50,000 at the time). As a result, Republicans fielded their most experienced group of challengers since 1972.

In response to what the Republicans were doing—and to their shocking losses in 1980—Democrats also departed from expected patterns in what promised to be a good Democratic year. One anticipated reaction did hold. After a slow start, Democrats had no difficulty attracting qualified challengers. The economy's precipitous decline excited the ambitions of a large number of career-minded challengers; 40 percent of the Democratic House challengers had previously held elective office, a proportion exceeded only in 1974 (42 percent) during the twenty-seven postwar elections. First-term Republicans were special targets; 60 percent faced challengers with experience in elective office.

But (as Table 6–5 attests), money did not flow into the campaigns of Democratic challengers in nearly the proportion expected in a good Democratic year.[38] The reason is that Democratic incumbents, stunned by what had happened to some of their eminent colleagues in 1980, and fearful of the resources Republican challengers might mobilize against them for 1982, went on a fundraising binge. "Panic is not too strong a word to describe it," said one Democratic campaign official. "Even people who were traditionally safe went out and really raised money in Washington and around the country in a way that they haven't before."[39]

Most of this panicky fundraising took place in 1981 and the first half of 1982, before the thrust of national conditions was fully evident. By the time Democratic incumbents felt secure enough to relax their fundraising efforts, they had absorbed so much of the available money that many otherwise promising challengers were unable to finance their campaigns adequately.[40] In the end, many incumbent Democrats accumulated much more money than they needed, but the party at that time had no institutional means to redirect any of the surplus into the campaigns of promising challengers. The economy had given the Democrats an extraordinary opportunity, but they were not organized to exploit it. National Democratic committees had little to contribute, and Democratic incumbents who suddenly found themselves home free and flush with cash could not be persuaded to part with it.

Republicans, with greater central control over campaign assets, could react strategically to changing circumstances. When the October 8 announcement that unemployment had reached a postwar high of 10.1 percent threatened disaster for the whole Republican ticket, national party officials responded by rushing assistance to newly endangered candidates. The party spent $2.5 million in the last eighteen days of the campaign on the most doubtful contests. The Republican strategy was finally aimed at minimizing losses; in the end, the party gave up on its challengers and concentrated instead on endangered incumbents and candidates for open seats.[41] The post-election consensus among officials of both parties was that the National Republican Congressional Committee's last minute help kept an additional ten to twenty House seats from going to the Democrats.[42]

Thus Republicans avoided a major disaster in 1982 in part because the national party committees worked to counter the effect of bad times. They also showed that a change in strategic behavior could weaken the connection between national conditions and aggregate election results, confirming that elite strategies help create the connection in the first place.

This is not to argue that national conditions were open to unconstrained manipulation and were therefore, by themselves, unimportant. Quite the contrary. They forced issues onto the electoral agenda and made competing arguments more or less persuasive. Republican campaigns were clearly damaged when unemployment hit double digits a month before election day.[43] It was not so much a problem of losing the votes of the unemployed as of losing ground in the battle to define the economic issues. National conditions contribute real campaign advantages and disadvantages to individual candidates, and hence it is entirely rational for congressional elites to take them into account in their strategic thinking. Still, the fact remains that the electoral impact of national conditions is strongly mediated by the decisions and strategies of congressional elites.

The next three elections were far less exciting, without major partisan swings and with relatively few seats changing party control. Low House turnover during the period inspired an epidemic of hand-wringing about the alleged death of electoral competition. In fact, however, electoral swings were modest in these elections because national conditions and issues were not conducive to partisan change. Divided party control of the federal government— Republican presidents and Democratic congresses—helped to dampen the impact of the issues that did arise. Anticipating little help from the political climate, neither party mounted more than a handful of strong challenges again until the 1990s.

1984

The 1984 elections produced a landslide without coattails in the orthodox sense. Ronald Reagan won 59 percent of the two-party vote and forty-nine of fifty states, but Republicans picked up only fourteen House seats; Republicans were weaker in the House after 1984 than they had been after 1980, when Reagan's margin of victory was considerably narrower. Yet at the level of individual voting behavior, Reagan's coattails were substantial and longer in 1984 than they had been in 1980. How could this be?

Part of the reason Republicans added so few House seats was that too few Republican challengers were positioned to benefit from Reagan's sweep and whatever boost his coattails offered. Campaign professionals in both parties agreed that Republicans "didn't field a good enough crop of candidates to take advantage of the political climate out there."[44] The proportion of Republican challengers with experience in elective office was lower in 1984 than it had been in 1980 or 1982.

Why did ambitious Republican careerists pass up such a golden opportunity? Several circumstances conspired to reduce the number of strong Republican challengers. First, political career strategies are shaped by what happened in the previous election as well as by current national conditions. Politicians, like generals, are inclined to prepare for the last war. Easy reelection in 1978 lulled many House Democrats into a false sense of security in 1980, and a surprising number of ostensibly "safe" Democratic incumbents were defeated. The survivors ran scared in 1982, soaking up so much of the campaign money available to Democrats that their party was unable to exploit fully the deep recession and Reagan's low performance ratings, because many otherwise promising and attractive Democratic challengers remained underfunded. Republican successes in 1980 (and the national party's recruitment work) inspired many attractive Republican challengers to take on Democratic incumbents in 1982; but against recession and fully mobilized Democratic incumbents, their failure was nearly total. Thus "a lingering bad memory of the 1982 elections (persuaded) many Republicans to bypass House campaigns" in 1984.[45] In effect, the Republican had expended some of their most promising talent in the wrong election.

Neither were early signs pointing toward 1984 very encouraging to Republicans. Through 1983, the strength of the economic revival was uncertain and Reagan was running behind potential Democratic presidential contenders more often than not in straw polls.[46] Nor was there any indication of a major party realignment or ideological shift to the right.[47] Not until well into 1984 did it become clear that the economic upturn would continue through election day and that Reagan had forged a wide lead over every Democratic prospect. By then it was too late for potential congressional candidates to decide to run.

The pattern of contributions to Republican House candidates reflected the relatively small number of competitive challengers. Unlike 1980, when they helped to send a number of surprised Democratic incumbents into early retirement, business (PACs) took few chances in 1984. Incumbents and a few "blue chip" challengers were the main beneficiaries of their largess. The high average expenditures of Republican House challengers in 1984 (see Table 6–5) masks a very skewed distribution of funds. Money was concentrated in a few competitive campaigns. Fifteen fortunate Republican challengers were able to raise and spend more than $500,000; eight of them won, and all but two received more than 45 percent of the vote. Most of the rest were ignored by contributors. The reason? "The challengers this year don't measure up," one PAC official explained.[48] On the financial side, then, Republicans were not as well positioned to exploit Reagan's victory in 1984 as they had been in 1980.

Reagan's coattails were also short in 1984 because his national campaign offered little help to Republican challengers trying to persuade voters to abandon Democratic incumbents. In the 1980 campaign, Reagan had proposed major, rather explicit policy changes: tax cuts, budget cuts, sharply increased defense spending, a full-scale assault on inflation. The broader campaign theme of "vote Republican, for a change" was designed to tap the public's deep discontent with the entire drift of American political life, not merely with Jimmy Carter. The substance of the national campaign was readily adapted to the needs of Republican congressional challengers. The logic of "throwing the rascals out" extended downward to other Democrats in federal office.

In 1984, Reagan refused to specify any concrete plans for the second term and instead rested his case for reelection entirely on his administration's past performance. He carefully avoided the trap (set by the Mondale campaign) of disclosing just who would bear the cost of dealing with the nation's central economic problem, the massive federal budget deficit. The president's vague assurances that economic growth would take care of the deficit without additional action by government gave Republican challengers no help in persuading voters that more Republicans were needed in Congress for the president to reach his second-term objectives. Their problem was compounded when Reagan, pursuing an all-embracing personal victory, claimed for his own such Democratic heroes as Roosevelt, Truman, and Kennedy. Why vote against congressional Democrats if your favorite Republican campaigns from the rear platform of Truman's train (as had Reagan)?

Landslides without coattails also occurred in 1956 (Eisenhower won 58 percent of the vote while Republicans were losing two seats in the House, one in the Senate) and 1972 (Nixon received 62 percent of the vote; Republicans gained twelve seats in the House while losing two Senate seats). The parallels with 1984 are striking. All three campaigns took place during a time of rising prosperity and improvements in foreign policy, and voters were asked simply to ratify what had been done in the first term. Continuity, not change, was the theme. The campaigns emphasized how much better things were than they had been four years earlier but were vague about future intentions. Each exploited the aura of the presidency and stressed the personal qualities of the president. This has proven to be a sound strategy for successful presidents, but it does nothing to help congressional challengers of the president's party.

No matter how popular a president, a backward-looking, defensive national campaign that offers voters continuity but few specific changes for the future gives the party's other candidates little rhetorical leverage. If continuity is the goal, why replace the incumbents of either party? If times are good, if peace and prosperity are at hand, incumbents of the other party can hardly be blamed for obstructing progress; indeed, they might plausibly claim a share of the credit for what has gone right. Unless an incumbent representative has stubbornly resisted presidential initiatives that are popular in the district or identifies too strongly with the losing party's locally unpopular presidential candidate, the winning party's national campaign, however successful, will offer its challengers little ammunition to persuade voters to turn incumbents out of office.

Thus, in 1984, Republicans mounted too few vigorous House challenges, and their national campaign themes provided too little leverage to get much mileage out of Reagan's overwhelming victory. Their failure to add more than a handful of House seats, combined with a net loss of two Senate seats, under-mined any claims to a popular mandate for Republican policies that Reagan's personal sweep might have inspired.

1986

The 1986 House elections were, by historical standards, remarkably unevent-ful. Between 1946 and 1982, the president's party lost an average of thirty of its House seats at midterm. The midterm loss during a president's second term av-eraged forty-three seats; the best the president's party did in any of these elec-tions was to lose "only" twenty-eight seats. In 1986, the Republicans lost a net of five seats. A mere six incumbents were defeated, five Republicans and one Democrat, with the Democrats netting one additional open seat. This stasis is all the more notable when set against the 1986 Senate elections, in which De-mocrats defeated seven Republican incumbents, gained eight seats, and took over majority control (I will have more to say about Senate elections later in this chapter).

Why was there so little action in the 1986 House elections? First, national conditions were not conducive to any substantial Democratic gains. The econ-omy was in its fourth year of steady growth; real income per capita increased by 3.1 percent during 1986. President Reagan enjoyed widespread popular support, with 63 percent approving of his job performance at election time; the Iran-Contra affair had not yet become public knowledge. These circum-stances, combined with the fact that Republicans had made only limited gains in 1984 and so had relatively few seats "at risk," protected House Republicans from the customary fate of the president's copartisans at the second midterm. The 1986 result was not at all out of line from what we would expect from the parameters reported in Table 6-2.

Second, neither party mounted many serious challenges. By the measure of experience, both Republicans and Democrats fielded unusually weak cohorts of challengers. Only 10 percent of the Democratic incumbents faced Republi-can challengers who had previously held elective office—the smallest propor-tion in any postwar election up to that time. Republican incumbents were only half as likely to face experienced Democratic challengers as in 1982 (19 per-cent compared to 40 percent). Furthermore, comparatively few challengers en-joyed adequately funded campaigns. On average, 1986 House challengers spent less in real dollars than any class of challengers since 1978.

It is not difficult to understand why neither party's potential challengers saw much promise in 1986. Certainly Republicans would doubt their chances of de-feating Democrats who had survived Reagan's triumphant landslide in 1984, particularly now that he no longer headed their ticket. Ambitious Democrats, aware of the usual second-term midterm pattern, may have had more reason to challenge Republican incumbents. But the growing economy, Reagan's ap-proval rating—21 points higher than it had been in the recession year of 1982—and the dearth of Republican targets as a legacy of 1984 would be dis-couraging. In particular, Republican incumbents who had survived 1982 would scarcely appear vulnerable in 1986. Campaign contributors, responding to the same considerations—as well as to the shortage of attractive candidates—did not find many attractive "investments" among challengers.

With the absence of national trends and the convergent expectations and strategies of politicians and their supporters, it is not so surprising that the 1986 House elections proved uneventful. Ironically, election day found the economy still growing nicely and Reagan's performance receiving widespread popular approval. And survey evidence indicates that approval of Reagan and optimism about the economy translated into votes for Republican House challengers—especially when combined with a well-financed campaign. Republicans might have done considerably better in 1986 had they fielded a group of challengers as talented and well-funded as those who ran in 1982.[49]

1988

The 1988 House elections produced even less change than 1986. Only nine seats switched party control, the fewest in American electoral history; 402 incumbents were returned to office, the most in history; only 7.6 percent of representatives elected to the 101st Congress were newcomers, the lowest proportion ever. Although the average vote for House candidates was 0.7 percentage points more Republican than it had been in 1986, incumbents of both parties actually improved on their 1986 performance. The average Republican incumbent's vote was 2.3 percentage points higher than in 1986; the average Democratic incumbent's vote was 0.2 percentage points higher.

Only 13 percent of House incumbents fell into the marginal category—receiving less than 60 percent of the major-party vote—another record low; the mean vote share of all House incumbents with major party opponents was 68.4 percent, a figure exceeded (barely) only in the 1986 election. Nearly every incumbent who did lose was a casualty of ethical rather than political lapses. The number of open seats switching party control—three—is also the lowest on record.

The proximate reason so few House seats changed hands is the same as it was in 1986: a dearth of qualified candidates, issues, and money to challenge incumbents. *Both* parties fielded their weakest cohort of challengers on record. In 1988, 16.6 percent of the Democratic challengers and 9.4 percent of the Republican challengers had previously held elective office, all-time lows for both parties in any postwar election to that date. The proportion of experienced candidates among all 1988 challengers, 12.4 percent, was more than two standard deviations below the 1946–1986 mean of 21.3 percent. Seventy-nine incumbents had no major party opposition at all, the most since 1958, before Republicans began to contest seats in many parts of the South. Sixty Democratic incumbents were spared Republican challenges in 1988, compared to thirty-eight in 1980. Providers of campaign money responded to unpromising challengers in their customary way, by ignoring them. The average challenger spent less money (in constant dollars) than in any election since 1976.

Experienced politicians and activists from both parties evidently concluded that 1988 was not a propitious year to take on incumbents. Their thinking reflects a political climate once more devoid of clear partisan currents. Neither party had reason to expect a particularly good year. The economy continued to expand steadily, inflation remained relatively low, and unemployment continued to drift downward. But the experience of the October 1987 stock market crash, combined with gloomy speculations stirred by the budget and trade deficits and deeper questions about the position of the United States in the international economy, left serious doubts about both short- and long-run economic prospects. Americans enjoyed prosperity but worried about the economic future.[50]

Republicans could claim credit for presiding over peace as well as prosperity. Successful negotiations with the Soviet Union to rid Europe of short-range nuclear missiles had been followed by a new round of talks aimed at much broader arms reductions; wars in Iran, Afghanistan, and Angola were winding down; democracies had supplanted dictatorships in a number of countries. Still, the administration's successes were counterbalanced by revelations of the secret attempt to sell arms to Iran in exchange for hostages and to use the profits to finance the Contras in Nicaragua. Other trouble spots where the United States was active—El Salvador, the Middle East, the Persian Gulf—also held distinct risks, particularly after President Reagan's competence to manage foreign policy had been called into question.

Reagan's approval rating dropped sharply when the Iran-Contra affair came to light and was slow to recover. The percentage of respondents in the *New York Times*/CBS News Polls approving of his job performance, which had remained in the mid- to high-60s through the first ten months of 1986, suffered a 21-point decline between October and November. It rebounded only modestly thereafter, hovering close to the 50 percent mark throughout 1987 and the first half of 1988.[51] The Iran-Contra revelations brought a premature lame-duck aura to the administration. Despite peace and prosperity, most presidential polls, generic or specific, put the Democrats ahead throughout the first half of 1988.[52]

In sum, nothing in the national political climate suggested that either party's candidates could count on a particularly favorable partisan tide or could expect special help from national issues. Neither, of course, did either party have anything special to fear from national forces. But without exploitable issues or favorable trends, both parties' challengers could expect to have trouble raising money and persuading voters to desert incumbents.

Just as in 1984, the 1988 presidential campaigns contained little to boost congressional candidates of the winner's party. As Reagan's vice president, Bush naturally ran a campaign promoting themes of affirmation and continuity, but as before, these were not themes that could be exploited by Republican challengers to attack Democratic incumbents. It is difficult to make a case for throwing anyone out of Congress with a campaign theme song that croons, "don't worry, be happy."

Beyond this general stance, the tactics adopted by the Bush campaign were singularly unhelpful to Republican congressional candidates. Attacks on Michael Dukakis's patriotism, liberalism, and commitment to law and order did not transfer easily to congressional Democrats. Members representing constituencies where such charges could hurt had long since erected defenses against them. They had their own carefully considered positions on gun control, the death penalty, and other galvanizing social issues. As usual, congressional Democrats did not hesitate to put whatever distance they deemed necessary between themselves and the top of the ticket.

The Bush campaign's positive themes—calling for a "kinder, gentler, nation," including a greater commitment to education, child care, and the environment—were scarcely calculated to give voters reasons for evicting Democrats from Congress. The decision to say nothing explicit about plans for dealing with the budget deficit was probably shrewd electoral politics: Any detailed proposal would have made more enemies than friends. But it also meant that the only standard Republican candidates could rally around was a promise of "no new taxes," which was not particularly effective at a time when majorities favored tax increases to deal with a number of specific problems and were, in any case, rightly skeptical about Bush's ability to keep his promise.[53]

1990

The 1990 elections took place amid deep public discontent with national politics and politicians, but neither party was poised to exploit popular anger, so its electoral effects were modest. The results nonetheless exposed the real vulnerability of many seemingly impregnable incumbents, strongly foreshadowing the upheavals of 1992 and 1994. The national tide ran against incumbents of both parties in 1990, though more strongly against Republicans than Democrats. The average vote for House incumbents was 3.9 percentage points lower than it had been in 1988, reaching its lowest level—64.5 percent—since 1974. For the first time in any post war election, the mean vote for incumbents of *both* parties fell. The mean vote for Republican incumbents fell more (−5.6 points) than the mean vote for Democratic incumbents (−3.1 points), but the trend against Republicans was evident mainly in open seats, where Republicans lost six of the seventeen seats they were defending, while taking none of the twelve held by Democrats. The swing away from incumbents did not, however, result in many seats changing hands. Only fifteen of 406 House incumbents (nine Republicans and six Democrats) met defeat. Democrats netted only eight House seats (nine if Bernard Sanders, a Vermont socialist who runs as an independent but votes like a liberal Democrat, is included).

Turnover was modest despite discernable trends against incumbents and Republicans because most contests had been settled long before the issues driving the trends had emerged. Eighty-four House incumbents had no major-party opponent at all. Those who were opposed were blessed with the weakest group of challengers yet, weaker, even, than the 1988 crop; only 10 percent of both party's incumbents faced challengers who had ever held elective public office. Little money flowed into the coffers of such an unpromising lot; House challengers raised less money (in real terms) in 1990 than in any election since 1974. The average challenger spent 15 percent less (in inflation-adjusted dollars) than in 1988, 33 percent less than 1982, the peak financial year for challengers in the 1980s.[54]

Some postelection analysts claimed that the 1990 election underlined the decisive power of incumbency because so few incumbents were defeated even though the public's disgust with government was at a peak.[55] But measured against the weakness of their opposition, the overall performance of House incumbents was less than impressive. A more formidable set of challengers might have deposed a lot more of them.

What accounts for the extraordinary weakness of both parties' challengers in the 1990 House elections? Part of the explanation lies in the timing of emerging trends. The events that left voters angry with the Congress and the president took place late in the election year. National conditions early in the election year were far less promising to challengers of either party.

Certainly the Democrats' early prospects were uninspiring. George Bush's level of popular support in the January Gallup Poll—80 percent approving his performance—was the highest for any president at the same stage in his presidency, and it remained high through the first half of the year. The economy appeared to be slowing, but the recession that had been anticipated for so long was not yet in evidence, and a "soft landing" after the boom of the mid-1980s seemed possible. Conditions augured a repeat of 1986 rather than 1982. Moreover, Republicans had done so poorly in the 1988 House elections that Democrats suffered a dearth of likely targets.

Not anticipating any help from national politics, few Democratic challengers were in position to exploit the economic downturn, Republican missteps on the deficit reduction package, or Bush's 20-point drop in approval during October. The Democrats' main success came in open seats, which, as usual, attracted experienced, well-financed nonincumbents independently of national expectations.

The same conditions that discouraged Democrats should have encouraged potential Republican challengers, but they faced other daunting realities. One was the president's party's dismal historic record in midterm elections. Another was that Bush's popularity promised them little help; after all, Republican challengers had derived little benefit from Reagan's successes, and Bush's victory in 1988 had not prevented Republican losses in the House.

Timing favored incumbents in yet another way. The prospect of redistricting after 1990 deterred experienced potential challengers of both parties. Why endure the hard work and expense of mounting a full-scale campaign to capture a district that may change drastically, or even disappear, before 1992? Better to wait a couple of years until the new boundaries are in place and the new districts, along with anticipated retirements, produce a bumper crop of open seats. Thus when the public mood turned hostile to officeholders as a class and incumbency itself became a potential liability, relatively few challengers of either party were poised to exploit their windfall, and so while most House incumbents saw their vote drop, often sharply, only a small number were turned out of office.

The unprecedented decline in support for incumbents of both parties, with the larger swing against Republicans, stemmed primarily from the federal government's attempt to come to grips with the budget deficit. The savings-and-loan debacle[56] and widely publicized ethical lapses certainly contributed to the public's increasingly jaundiced view of politicians, but it was brought into sharp focus only by the squabbling over deficit reduction legislation in October. I leave the details of the 1990 budget story for the more general discussion of budget politics in Chapter 7; however, the basic point is that the Republican president and Democratic majorities in Congress, after much haggling, cut a deal to reduce the deficit by a combination of tax increases and programmatic cuts. Both the unedifying process (which included months of unproductive closed-door negotiation, numerous leaks, trial balloons, and false starts—and a brief shutdown of some governmental agencies when a deadline was not met) and the product (an agreement that raised taxes and cut back on some popular social programs) angered large segments of the public.

Anger at the result arose more naturally from a sense of betrayal that was inevitable once both sides got serious about deficits. Deficits were the product of divided government. In the 1980s, Americans elected Republican presidents on the promise of "no new taxes" and Democratic majorities in Congress committed to maintaining or increasing their favorite domestic programs. Responding to their electoral constituencies, Republican administrations accepted large deficits rather than raise taxes to pay for government programs that Democratic congresses refused to cut; and Democratic congresses accepted large deficits rather than reduce government programs when Republican presidents refused to accept tax increases to pay for them.

When leaders on both sides finally became convinced that large, permanent deficits were too destructive economically (and perhaps politically) to be tolerated further, compromise was the only feasible solution. But a compromise meant that both parties would have to betray their core supporters. Bush had to go back on his pledge of "no new taxes" and accept not only various excise tax increases, but higher marginal income tax rates as well; congressional Democrats had to agree to reduce or limit the growth in spending on popular social programs and to accept the regressive excise taxes. Betrayal turned voters against politicians in both parties, but Republicans felt more political heat because Bush's original stance was more sharply etched and more central to his party's appeal.

There is more than a little irony in this turn of events. Republican presidents and Democrats in Congress prospered politically during the 1980s by pandering to their respective constituencies, promising something for nothing, benefits and programs without the taxes to pay for them. When, in 1990, leaders of both parties finally took some hesitant steps toward fiscal responsibility, they felt the political wrath of an indignant public they had left unprepared to face fiscal reality. Luckily for the incumbents of both parties, the action came so late that voters had only limited vehicles (acceptable replacements) for venting their displeasure, and few members lost their seats. They could not, however, count on their luck holding forever.

1992

The cycle of uneventful House elections ended with a bang in 1992. The 1992 elections yielded the largest crop of new representatives in more than forty years, with 110 newcomers joining the House in January 1993. The influx of new members sharply altered the House's demographic makeup. The number of women representatives rose from twenty-eight to forty-seven; of African-Americans, from twenty-five to thirty-eight; of Hispanics, from eleven to seventeen. (I discuss similar dramatic changes in the Senate later.)

Despite all of this turmoil, *partisan* change in Congress was exceedingly modest. Republicans, though losing the presidency, picked up ten seats in the House, leaving the Democrats with a reduced but still comfortable 258-176 majority. The coincidence of a large turnover in membership with a small partisan swing in the House is a historical oddity. In other postwar elections, a large turnover of House seats has been accompanied by a large partisan swing. Uniquely in 1992, a very large turnover coincided with a very small net partisan shift.[57]

The peculiarities of the 1992 congressional election reflect the converging effects of three basic environmental forces—divided government, a stagnant economy, and reapportionment—refracted through such signal events as the Anita Hill-Clarence Thomas dispute, the House banking scandal, and a Democratic presidential victory, and filtered through the strategic choices of political elites. The appropriate metaphor for the course of politics leading up to 1992 is not a tide but a roller coaster. The budget problems that had been so prominent in 1990 were temporarily forgotten after the election as everyone's attention turned to the Gulf War. The dramatic diplomatic and military successes that drove Saddam Hussein's Iraqi forces from Kuwait in early 1991 raised George Bush's performance ratings to unprecedented heights. Congress' public standing also improved markedly, but the war issue threatened political problems for the members—almost all of them Democrats—who had voted against authorizing the president to send soldiers against Iraq. By the war's end, George Bush looked unbeatable for 1992, and Republicans were relishing the prospect of recruiting Gulf War heroes to challenge Democratic doves. The war, Bush's popularity, and the prospect of reapportionment promised a banner Republican year in 1992.

The Republicans' high expectations foundered on the economy. The 1990 midterm elections had coincided with a recession; but so had midterms in five of the previous six postwar Republican administrations. (The Reagan administration in 1986 is the exception). The Republicans' problem was that, although the economy had rebounded strongly from these earlier midterm recessions, only a feeble, fitful recovery followed the 1990 recession. The economy's annual growth rate from the bottom of the recession in the first quarter of 1991 through the third quarter of 1992 was less than 2 percent, not enough to make a dent in the high unemployment figures. The economy's annual growth rate for the entire Bush presidency was less than 1 percent, the lowest for any administration since the Depression.

The economy's continuing weakness steadily sapped the support the president had acquired by bringing the Gulf War to a successful conclusion. Public attention turned from foreign affairs, a venue where Republicans have enjoyed an advantage for years, to domestic economic issues, where the faltering economy played to the Democrats' strength.[58] Still, the economy fed the public's disaffection with Congress as well as with the president; polls showed that ratings of Congress and the president suffered from bad economic news at the same time and to the same degree.[59] Evidently, the public was not disposed to make distinctions when it came to allocating blame, so the weak economy was not an unalloyed Democratic advantage. Ultimately, though, it did help congressional Democrats because it contributed so much to Bill Clinton's victory.

Americans in 1992 had no shortage of reasons for disdaining Congress: bank overdrafts, pay raise subterfuges, ethical lapses, the savings-and-loan debacle. But what gave these issues their potency was something more basic: the government's apparent inability to address a host of economic problems that had driven public confidence in the economy to a seventeen-year low.[60] The difficulty for voters was that twelve years of divided government had made the assignment of blame for economic and other troubles problematic. When one party controls both Congress and the White House, the public has an obvious target for its wrath: the party running the show. Whether or not the ruling party is actually to blame for bad times is beside the point; for better or worse, responsibility comes with power. Divided government invites each party to blame the other, and the public ends up agreeing with, and blaming, both.

The electoral consequences of a sour economy under divided government were complicated by an accident of the calendar, because House seats had to be reapportioned and district boundaries redrawn for 1992 to reflect the population shifts recorded by the 1990 census. Election years that end in "2" typically produce higher turnover in the House than do other years; members whose districts disappear or are changed in politically damaging ways are more likely than usual to retire—and more likely than usual to be defeated if they do not. Still, in recent decades, reapportionment has added, on average, only about ten new members to the House beyond the normal turnover. Two additional circumstances exaggerated the effect of redistricting for 1992. First, the effort to carve out districts in which racial minorities formed a majority of voters wherever feasible, discussed in Chapter 2, led to more radical changes in district boundaries than usual. Second, districts in several of the largest states were redrawn for 1992 by mapmakers who, in contrast to past practices, studiously ignored the interests of incumbents. In previous reapportionment cycles, state legislatures did more of the work and routinely sought to protect the incumbents of one or both parties (depending on whether one or both controlled the state government and thus had any say in the matter). Courts, largely indifferent to the fate of incumbents and parties, did far more to shape districts for the 1990s.

Both the pressure for "minority-majority" districts and court intervention worked, in principle, to the advantage of Republicans. Most black and Hispanic voters favor Democrats, so ethnic gerrymanders concentrate Democratic votes in districts in which they are "wasted" because the party wins by many more votes than it needs—precisely what a partisan Republican gerrymander would accomplish. Courts also drew maps more congenial to Republicans than the predominantly Democratic state legislatures would have devised on their own.

By itself, redistricting would have inspired an unusually large number of House retirements and produced a bumper crop of vulnerable incumbents in 1992. But the effects of redistricting were strongly reinforced by two other circumstances: the public's overwhelming contempt for members of Congress as a class and the House banking scandal, which gave an individual focus to many voters' otherwise diffuse disdain.

Until its abolition in 1992, the House Bank had existed in one form or another since 1830. The paychecks of members who used its services were automatically deposited in their accounts, which they could draw on by writing personal checks. For as long as anyone could remember, the bank gave members free "overdraft protection." That is, the bank honored a check even when a member's account held insufficient funds to cover it. The bank refused to cover the checks of only the most flagrant abusers of this privilege. This indulgence was a political disaster waiting to happen, and, for members of the House, it happened at the worst possible moment. Auditors' reports of hundreds of members writing thousands of overdrafts became public knowledge in 1991. Coming at a time when the public was already primed to think the worst of Congress and Republicans were desperate for any issue that might unlock the Democrats' decades-old grip on the House, damage control proved impossible. Hounded by constituents, the media, the White House, junior House Republicans hungry for an issue, and, finally, innocent members who wanted to be absolved of suspicion, the House leadership could not sidetrack the issue. Members were left with no alternative but to vote to disclose all of the names of the bad check writers and the numbers of overdrafts they had written.

The combination of redistricting, widespread disgust with Congress, and the individual vulnerability of members with significant overdrafts combined to produce a dramatic increase in the overall level of competition for House seats. In sharp contrast to 1990, the public's anger at Congress rose in plenty of time to shape the career decisions of potential candidates in 1992. Among incumbents, individual targets could be identified according to their vulnerability on the overdraft issue by mid-April 1992 at the latest. The troubles of some were known even earlier. The upheavals expected from redistricting, which had justified patience in 1990, dictated boldness in 1992.

There was thus a remarkable jump in the sheer number of people seeking major-party nominations for Congress. The Federal Election Commission received filings from 2,950 candidates, a thousand more than the 1982–1990 average. This surge produced a precipitous drop in the number of seats won without major party opposition in the general election. Only thirty-four seats went uncontested by one of the major parties in 1992, compared to eighty-five such seats in 1990 and an average of seventy-one for the previous decade. Indeed, fewer House seats went uncontested in 1992 than in any other postwar election to that date. Postwar highs in the number of voluntary retirements from the House (sixty-six) and of incumbents defeated in primary elections (nineteen) guaranteed that the number of open seats that were up for grabs in the general election (ninety-one) also set a postwar record; the previous high was sixty-five, the 1946–1990 average, about forty-four.

The quality of challengers in 1992 was also considerably improved over recent elections. In 1992, 22 percent of both parties' challengers had previously held elective office, up from the postwar low of 10 percent for both parties in 1990. Still, this percentage was lower than in other recent election years in which the incumbents of at least one party fared poorly, such as 1974 and 1982. The politically ambitious professionals had a wider selection of opportunities in 1992 because an unusual number of seats lacked an incumbent, and, as always, experienced candidates flocked to compete for open seats.

Heightened competition led to closer contests. The average share of the two-party vote won by incumbents in 1992 (63.6 percent) was the lowest since 1966 and the proportion of marginal incumbents (those who won with less than 60 percent of the two-party vote) was the highest since 1964: 33.4 percent. These figures are all the more impressive because they were recorded after many of the most vulnerable incumbents had already retired from the House or been defeated in primary elections.

Reapportionment and the general disdain for Congress, which was given individual focus by the House banking scandal, share principal responsibility for high turnover. Reapportionment threw a record number of House incumbents into districts with other incumbents; some retired, some moved, and some (a total of nine in the primary and general elections) lost contests to other incumbents in redrawn districts. But the consequences of redistricting were greatly amplified by the publication of each member's record with the House Bank.

Table 6-8 displays the consequences of these disclosures. The likelihood of exit from Congress by every route—retirement, defeat in the primary, and defeat in the general election—increased significantly with the number of bank overdrafts. When the 103rd Congress convened in 1993, more than half the members of the 102nd whose overdrafts had reached triple digits were gone, while 83 percent of those with a completely clean record reassumed their seats. Had members with overdrafts been returned to Congress at the same rate as those without any, the 103rd would have seventy-eight newcomers instead of 110, and turnover would have been about average for a year ending in "2."

The House banking scandal and its consequences were profoundly ironic. Contrary to the view initially spread by the media and accepted by the public, the overdrafts violated no laws and cost the taxpayers no money.[61] Yet the scandal ended many more congressional careers than policy disasters such as

TABLE 6–8   HOUSE BANK OVERDRAFTS AND MEMBERSHIP ATTRITION (IN PERCENTAGES)

FATE OF REPRESENTATIVE	NUMBER OF OVERDRAFTS			
	None	1–99	100–199	200 or more
Retired from politics[a]	8.9	11.9	15.0	33.3
$x^2 = 13.09, p<.005$	(168)[b]	(219)	(20)	(27)
Defeated in primary[c]	2.0	2.2	18.8	27.8
$x^2 = 37.91, p<.001$	(146)	(181)	(15)	(18)
Defeated in general election[d]	2.8	5.6	23.1	15.4
$x^2 = 11.83, p<.01$	(140)	(172)	(13)	(13)
Not in 103rd Congress[e]	17.3	24.7	50.0	59.3
$x^2 = 28.86, p<.001$	(168)	(219)	(20)	(27)

[a]Left the House but did not run for another office.
[b]Number of cases from which percentages were calculated.
[c]Based on members seeking reelection; excludes four pairs of incumbents competing with one another because of redistricting.
[d]Based on members winning renomination; excludes five pairs of incumbents competing with one another because of redistricting.
[e]For any reason.
Note: Ted Weiss (D-NY), who died September 14, 1992, is not included; Walter B. Jones (D-NC), who died September 15, 1992, but had already announced his retirement, is included.
    Source: Gary C. Jacobson and Michael Dimock, "Checking Out: The Effects of Bank Overdrafts on the 1992 House Elections," American Journal of Political Science 38 (1994):606.

the savings-and-loan debacle, which left taxpayers holding the bag for hundreds of billions of dollars, or the quadrupling of the national debt from $1 billion to $4 billion in little more than a decade. Members of Congress routinely escape individual blame for major policy failures because the legislative process diffuses responsibility; the action is so complex, the details of policy so arcane, each individual's responsibility so obscure, that it is impossible to figure out who is culpable and who is not. Everyone with a checking account understands what it means to balance a checkbook, however, and each House member's culpability was precisely measured in the count of unfunded checks.[62]

High turnover always changes the face of Congress in some way; usually the change is partisan and generational. In 1992, the major changes were instead demographic; forty of the 110 newly elected members were ethnic minorities, women, or both. The increase of more than 50 percent in the number of African-Americans and Latinos serving in the House is a direct result of the ethnic gerrymanders carried out at the behest of the courts. The "Year of the Woman," on the other hand, although helped along by redistricting, was primarily an artifact of the Thomas hearings.

The proximate reason for the abrupt increase in the number of women elected to the House and Senate in 1992 was the abrupt increase in the number of politically talented and experienced women who sought and won nominations for congressional seats in competitive states and districts. The surge of experienced, well-financed women candidates was in turn a direct consequence of the widespread outrage that was generated by the October 1991 Senate Judiciary Committee hearings in which Anita Hill accused Supreme Court nominee Clarence Thomas of sexual harassment. The all-male committee's treatment of Hill and her accusations infuriated many women, provoking the startling upsurge in political activity among women that was a unique feature of the 1992 elections.

The Year of the Woman—more precisely, the year of the Democratic woman (twenty of the twenty-three newly elected women were Democrats)—was forged in the primaries. The success rate of women candidates in general elections for the House (44 percent of those running) was not dramatically higher than it had been over the previous two decades (39 percent), but the number of women running, 106, was far above the previous high of sixty-nine in 1990. More important, half the nonincumbent women were running for open seats. In the end, nearly all of the gains made by women in the 1992 House elections were the consequence of Democratic women taking open seats. Democratic women did unusually well in 1992, then, because they won an uncommonly large share of the nominations for seats that their party's candidates would have had a serious chance of winning regardless of gender—seats not defended by an incumbent.

They also did well because they were, by the standard of experience, high-quality candidates. This is evident from Table 6-9, which lists the proportion of nonincumbent candidates (by gender, party, and type of race) who had previously held some elective public office, along with their electoral fates. The Democratic women running for open seats were the most experienced of any subgroup, and their success rate was the highest of any. Observe, however,

TABLE 6–9   EXPERIENCE, SEX, AND SUCCESS OF
NONINCUMBENT HOUSE CANDIDATES, 1992
(IN PERCENTAGES)

	Prior Elective Office		WINNERS			
			Prior Office		No Prior Office	
CHALLENGERS						
Democrats						
Men	24.7	$(93)^a$	8.7	(23)	2.9	(70)
Women	18.5	(27)	40.0	(5)	0.0	(22)
Republicans						
Men	24.3	(181)	13.6	(44)	5.1	(137)
Women	21.4	(14)	0.0	(3)	0.0	(11)
OPEN SEATS						
Democrats						
Men	66.7	(66)	71.4	(42)	38.2	(21)
Women	69.2	(26)	83.2	(18)	50.0	(8)
Republicans						
Men	53.3	(75)	52.5	(40)	28.6	(35)
Women	30.8	(13)	50.0	(4)	11.1	(9)

[a]Number of cases from which percentages were calculated.

Source: Gary C. Jacobson, "Unusual Year, Unusual Election," in *The Elections of 1992*, ed. Michael Nelson (Washington, DC: Congressional Quarterly Press, 1993), p. 171.

that prior elective office is strongly related to electoral success in all categories; winning is far more closely linked to experience than to gender. Women won a lot more House seats in 1992, not because being female was such a great advantage in the general election, but because so many of the high-quality candidates in competitive districts were women.

Although the 1992 elections brought high turnover and sharp changes in the House's demography, they registered little partisan change. The forces that generated turnover did not have a consistent partisan thrust. Conditions that favored Republicans—reapportionment, the House banking scandal (more Democrats than Republicans had written overdrafts), the low repute of a Congress run by Democrats, perhaps the Gulf War—were offset by conditions that favored Democrats—the stagnant economy, George Bush's unpopularity, and Bill Clinton's vigorous and successful presidential campaign.

Ross Perot's remarkable showing in the 1992 presidential election—he won 19 percent of the vote nationally, and as much as 33 percent in his best House district—naturally raises the question of whether his candidacy had any effect on the congressional contests. It did, but not in any way that affected who won or lost. As disdainers of politics as usual, Perot's supporters might be expected to dislike incumbents, so we would expect that the higher Perot's vote in the district, the better a challenger would do. This is what we observe, but only in districts that are not competitive in the first place. In districts where the incumbent received less than 60 percent of the vote, Perot's level of support was not related to the vote; only in districts won by more than 60 percent is the relationship substantively large and statistically significant. In the low information context of a noncompetitive campaign, anti-establishment sentiments spilled over into House voting. But competitive House campaigns evidently framed the choices in their own terms.

1994

The 1992 elections, extraordinary as they were, turned out to be only a prelude to an even greater upheaval in 1994. For the first time in forty-two years, Republicans captured the House of Representatives. The fifty-two seat gain that gave them a 230–204 majority was the largest net partisan swing since 1948. Why did Republicans, after four decades of futility, suddenly win a clear majority of House seats? The short answer is that they won by inverting political patterns that had given Democrats comfortable House majorities despite a generation of Republican superiority in presidential elections. In an earlier edition of this book, I offered this summary explanation for the Republicans' inability to win control of the House:

> Republicans have failed to advance in the House because they have fielded inferior candidates on the wrong side of issues that are important to voters in House elections and because voters find it difficult to assign blame or credit when control of government is divided between the parties.[63]

In 1994, the Republicans won the House by fielding (modestly) superior candidates who were on the right side of the issues that were important to voters in House elections and persuading voters to blame a unified Democratic government for government's failures. They exploited favorable national issues more successfully than any party in decades. But marketable national campaign themes did not by themselves give the Republicans their House majority. To win House seats, Republicans still needed plausible candidates with enough money to get the messages out to district voters. Even in 1994, the effects of national issues, important as they were, depended on how they were injected into local campaigns.

House Democrats had long thrived by adhering to former House Speaker Tip O'Neill's dictum that "all politics are local." All politics were *not* local in 1994. Republicans succeeded in framing the local choice in national terms, making taxes, social discipline, big government, and the Clinton presidency the dominant issues. They did so by exploiting three related waves of public sentiment that crested simultaneously in 1994. The first was public disgust with the politics, politicians, and government in Washington. The second was the widespread feeling that American economic and social life was out of control and heading in the wrong direction. The third was the visceral rejection of Bill Clinton by a crucial set of swing voters, the "Reagan Democrats" and supporters of Ross Perot.

Public contempt for members of Congress as a class had, by 1994, been growing for more than two decades. All of the regular polling questions measuring attitudes toward government found an increasingly angry and distrustful public. Disapproval of Congress's performance reached an all-time high of 79 percent in one 1994 poll, but this was only the latest incremental extension of a long-term trend. Rising distrust and anger had been fed by several streams. One major stream flowed directly from the politics of divided government during the Reagan–Bush years. Divided government encouraged the kind of partisan posturing, haggling, delay, and confusion that voters hate whenever Republican presidents and Democratic Congresses faced major policy decisions. It also guaranteed that voters would wind up feeling betrayed by the inevitable compromises that made agreement possible.

The formal end of divided government in 1992 was supposed to end gridlock. It did not. Many of the Clinton administration's most ambitions plans—notoriously, health care reform—died in an agony of conflict and partisan recrimination. The truth, revealed early in the 103rd Congress when Minority Leader Bob Dole led a successful Republican filibuster against Clinton's economic stimulus package, was that divided government had not ended at all. Divided partisan control of *policy making* persists as long as the minority party holds at least 40 seats in the Senate and can therefore kill any bill it wants to kill.[64]

The illusion of unified government put the onus of failure on the Democrats; the reality of divided government let Senate Republicans make sure that the administration would fail. Clinton was elected on a promise of change. Senate Republicans could prevent change, and they did. It was not difficult, for while everyone may agree that change is desirable, rarely do we find ready consensus on what to change *to*. The health care issue is exhibit A. If voters did not get change with Clinton—or if they did not like the changes he proposed—the alternative was to elect Republicans.

Public anger at a government paralyzed by gridlock was intensified by the widespread sense that the problems the political establishment had failed to address were indeed serious. The benefits of economic growth during the Reagan–Bush years went largely to families in the top income decile. The broad middle class had, by many measures, made little economic progress; incomes (including fringe benefits) of the families in the middle half of the distribution were nearly flat over the two decades between 1973 and 1992.[65] Although the economy grew during the first two years of the Clinton administration, the fruits of growth again went largely to families at the upper end of the economic scale. Hence in the October *Los Angeles Times* Poll, 53 percent of the respondents thought the economy remained in recession. The economic discontent that elected Clinton in 1992 had barely faded by 1994, and this time it helped to elect a Republican Congress.[66]

Economic prosperity, moreover, is not the only measure of the quality of life. The public institutions that serve ordinary people—public schools, police, courts—seemed in the early 1990s to be in trouble. The issues of crime, illegal immigration, and unmarried teenage welfare mothers that dominated the 1994 campaigns in many places were not new, but they gained new urgency as signs that American society was out of control. For millions of Americans, government had delivered neither physical nor economic security, failing conspicuously to reverse what they saw as moral and cultural decline. The large majority that believed the nation was on the wrong rather than the right track (57 percent compared to 37 percent in the exit poll) indicated that the longing for "change" that put Clinton in the White House had not been satisfied. Two thirds of those who thought the nation was on the wrong track voted for the Republican House candidate, compared to only 29 percent of those who thought the nation was on the right track.

Stagnant incomes, declining public services, and the rising fear of crime leave large segments of the population with poorer lives and diminished prospects. It is in this context that the perks and peccadilloes of politicians— scandals involving senior leaders in the House and the Keating Five in the Senate, bank overdrafts, unpaid restaurant bills, post-office shenanigans, and pay-raise subterfuges—were so damaging to members of Congress. The image of representatives as self-serving, easily corrupted, and indifferent to the needs of the average citizen or the good of the nation had pervaded the 1992 elections and helped produce the largest turnover in the House since World War II. Members were unable to shake that image in the 103rd Congress, and with that Democrats were ostensibly in full control of the government, they became the principal targets of popular wrath and disappointment.[67]

The Clinton Problem

Bill Clinton's reputation as a leader was, of course, the chief target and victim of the Republicans' gridlock strategy. But this was not the only problem Clinton posed for congressional Democrats. Although his overall performance ratings were not, comparatively speaking, all that bad, he had thoroughly alienated important groups of swing voters: the so-called "Reagan Democrats" and much of the largely male Perot constituency. The cultural symbolism portrayed by many of the administration's actions was anathema to socially conservative white men, especially in the South. The conspicuous attention to race and gender "diversity" in making appointments called to mind the affirmative action programs they detest. Support for gays in the military and gun control, the role and style of Hilary Rodham Clinton, reminded these swing voters of the cultural liberalism that was at the core of what they did *not* like about the Democratic party. Clinton's reputation with this segment of the electorate was probably worsened by one of his most notable successes: the passage of the North American Free Trade Agreement, which put him at odds with traditional blue-collar Democratic constituents.

The 1994 American National Election Study (NES) revealed that only 37 percent of southerners approved of Clinton's performance, his lowest rating in any region. Among white southern men, Clinton's approval stood at a dismal 28 percent. Moreover, the relationship between presidential approval and the House vote was notably stronger in 1994 than in other recent midterms. About 73 percent of House votes were consistent with presidential ratings (that is, for the Democrat if the respondent approved of Clinton's performance, for the Republican if the respondent disapproved). The comparable figure for 1990 was 60 percent, for 1986, 63 percent, and for 1998, 70 percent; only in 1982 did consistency, at 74 percent, match the 1994 figure.

Clinton's low level of approval was thus more damaging to his copartisans than usual and was concentrated among swing voters. White respondents in the NES survey reported voting 10 percentage points more Republican in 1994 than they had in 1992; support for Republicans among white southerners went up 14 points. In the exit polls, fully 44 percent of the white southern males said that their House vote was a vote against Clinton (20 percent said it was a vote for Clinton; for non-southern males, the comparable figures were 33 percent and 24 percent). Perot supporters, who had split their House votes evenly between the parties in 1992, voted two-to-one Republican in 1994.[68]

Voters in 1994 were angry with government; Democrats were the party of government, not only because they were in charge, but also because their party believes in government. Republican candidates, who like to claim that they do not, offered themselves as vehicles for expressing antigovernment rage by taking up the banner of structural panaceas—term limits, a balanced budget amendment, cuts in congressional staff and perks—that were broadly popular and had special appeal to the alienated voters who had supported Perot. The policy issues that resonated best with voters in 1994—crime, immigration, welfare dependency, taxes, big government—were also Republican issues. Recognizing Clinton's unpopularity, especially in the South and especially among white males, Republican candidates sought to portray their opponents as Clinton clones; many of them used TV ads that had a picture of their opponent's face digitally "morphing" into Clinton's face.

Republicans were thus able to frame the choice in many swing districts as one, not between an accomplished provider of pork and diligent servant of district interests and a challenger whose ability to deliver the goods was at best doubtful, but between a supporter of liberal elitist Bill Clinton, big government, high taxes, and politics as usual, and a challenger opposed to these horribles. The House Democrats' customary strategy of emphasizing the projects, grants, and programs they have brought to the district and the value of their experience and seniority not only failed but was turned against them. The more they reminded people of pork and clout, the more they revealed themselves as insiders, that loathed class of career politicians. With the choice framed this way, the old ploy of running for Congress by running against Congress—joining the chorus of criticism to put oneself apart from, and above, the institution—was rendered threadbare as well. The Democrats were unable to duck individual responsibility for the House's collective shortcomings.

Ironically, the Republicans' "Contract with America," which became so prominent in setting the Republican agenda after the election, had, in itself, little impact on the voters. On September 27, more than 300 Republican House candidates signed a pledge on the steps of the capitol to act swiftly on a grab-bag of proposals for structural and legislative change, including constitutional amendments requiring a balanced budget and imposing term limits on members of Congress, major cuts in income taxes, and reductions in spending on welfare programs for poor families. Although the contract got some attention in the media and was a target of Democratic counterattacks, most voters went to the polls blissfully unaware of its existence. The *New York Times*/CBS News Poll of October 29–November 1 found that 71 percent of respondents had never heard of the contract and another 15 percent said it would make no difference in how they voted. Only 7 percent said it would make them more likely to vote for the Republican House candidate, while 5 percent said it would make them less likely to do so. The most prominent Republican effort to nationalize the campaign thus remained almost invisible to voters. This does not mean that individual parts of the contract were not used effectively by Republican campaigners; on the contrary. But the contract itself had far more impact on Republican candidates (before and after the election) than on voters.

Nationalizing the Vote

Although the contract had little to do with it, Republicans did succeed in nationalizing the elections to a much greater degree than usual in recent elections. In effect, they ran a set of midterm congressional campaigns that mirrored their successful presidential campaigns. As a result, their House victories echoed their presidential successes far more clearly than at any time during the last forty years.

Most of the seats Republicans took from Democrats were in districts that leaned Republican in presidential elections. A serviceable measure of a district's presidential leanings can be computed by taking the average division of its two-party vote between the presidential candidates in 1988 and 1992.[69] The national mean for this measure of district presidential voting habits is 49.9 percent Democratic; its median is 48.3 percent Democratic. As Table 6–10 shows, Republican gains in 1994 were heavily concentrated in districts where the Democrat's vote, averaged over the two elections, fell below 50 percent. For example, thirty-one open seats formerly held by Democrats were at stake. Republicans won all sixteen open Democratic seats in districts where George Bush's share of the two-party vote, averaged together for 1988 and 1992, exceeded 50 percent; they won only six of the fifteen where the Democrat's presidential average exceeded 50 percent. Republican challengers defeated 29 percent (21 of 73) of incumbent Democrats in districts where Bush's average exceeded 50

TABLE 6–10 DISTRICT PARTISANSHIP AND ELECTORAL OUTCOMES IN 1994 HOUSE ELECTIONS (PERCENTAGE OF REPUBLICAN VICTORIES)

	DISTRICT LEANS				
	Republican		Democratic		sig.
Seats held by Democrats					
Incumbents	28.8	$(73)^a$	8.6	(152)	$p<.001$
Open Seats	100.0	(16)	40.0	(15)	$p<.001$
Seats held by Republicans					
Incumbents	100.0	(141)	100.0	(16)	n.s.
Open Seats	100.0	(16)	20.0	(5)	$p<.001$
Total	78.9	(246)	19.1	(188)	$p<.001$

[a]Number of districts from which percentages were calculated.

Note: Republican-leaning districts are defined as those in which the two-party vote for George Bush, averaged across 1988 and 1992, was greater than 50 percent; Democratic-leaning districts are those in which this average fell below 50 percent.

Source: Gary C. Jacobson, "The 1994 House Elections in Perspective," in *Midterm: Elections of 1994 in Perspective*, ed. Philip Klinkner (Boulder, Colorado: Westview Press, 1996).

NATIONAL POLITICS AND CONGRESSIONAL ELECTIONS   183

percent, but only 9 percent (13 of 152) in districts where Bush's average fell short of this mark.

The handful of switches to the Democrats followed the same pattern: Democrats took four of five open Republican seats where the Democrats' average share of the vote exceeded 50 percent; they won none of other sixteen open Republican seats and defeated no Republican incumbents. The net effect of seats changing party hands in 1994 was a closer alignment of district-level presidential and House results than in any election since 1952—all the more remarkable because no presidential candidates were on the 1994 ballot.

Republicans won the House in 1994 because an unusually large number of districts voted locally as they had been voting nationally. The same is true, necessarily, of individual voters. The most notable change was a sharp increase in party loyalty among self-identified Republicans, particularly in districts with Democratic incumbents. The Republican defectors who had, in the past, helped Democrats win Republican-leaning districts deserted in large numbers. Congressional Republicans were thus finally able to cash in on their party's gains in party identifiers registered in polls a full ten years earlier.[70]

The Republican party's successful organizational effort to nationalize the campaign was helped enormously by the new national networks of conservative talk-show hosts and conservative Christian activists. Conservatives in general and evangelical Christians in particular turned out at notably higher rates than other voters and comprised a significantly larger proportion of the electorate than in 1992.[71] Republican leaders did an outstanding job of organizing and mobilizing the groups in their coalition and of coaching their candidates in the art of using the party's themes effectively against Democrats.

Although the key to the Republican victory in 1994 lay in nationalizing the House elections, this does not mean that candidate-centered, locally focused electoral politics was superceded. The 1994 elections were not "nationalized" in the sense that electoral forces operated consistently across districts. Although the mean district vote swing to Republicans was, by recent historical standards, quite large (5.9 percentage points, the largest since 1974), it was only slightly more uniform than the recent norm,[72] and the electoral value of incumbency was only slightly less impressive than usual (recall Figure 3-3). Lucky for the Democrats that it was not; the pattern of results displayed in Table 6-10 suggests that, without the incumbency advantage, the Democratic minority in the 104th Congress would have been considerably smaller.

Moreover, strategic behavior both reflected and magnified election year trends. Democrats behaved as if they expected it to be a bad year for their party and helped to make it so. Strategic Democratic retirements clearly hurt their party's overall performance. Although about the same proportion of House Democrats and Republicans retired (11 percent), most of the Republicans left to run for higher office (13 of 20, 65 percent), while most of the departing Democrats (20 of 27, 71 percent) did not. Among retirees who did not leave to pursue another office, age is the only variable with any predictive power for Republicans, while age, previous vote margin, and district presidential partisanship all contributed significantly to Democratic retirements; the closer the margin in 1992 and the more Republican the district in presidential voting, the more likely a Democrat was to retire. In simple percentages, 18 percent of the Democrats in districts that leaned Republican in presidential elections retired, compared with only 7 percent of the Democrats in districts that leaned Democratic in presidential elections. The retirements of the former group proved disastrous for the party; as Table 6-10 indicated, Republicans took every one of the sixteen seats thereby exposed. Another sign of the Democrats' strategic response to expectations was the unusual distribution of uncontested seats. For the first time in the entire postwar era, Democrats conceded more seats to Republicans (35) than Republicans conceded to Democrats (17) in the general election.

The quality of challengers also reflected rational career strategies, though as usual, potential Democratic challengers were much more sensitive to election year expectations than were Republicans. Democrats have long enjoyed a stronger "farm system" supplying experienced House candidates because they hold more of the lower-level offices that form the typical stepping stones to Congress (particularly in state legislatures). Normally, therefore, Democrats have a substantial advantage in experienced challengers. On average over the previous twenty-four post-war congressional elections, 26 percent of the Republican incumbents, but only 16 percent of Democratic incumbents, faced challengers who had previously held elective public office. Prior to 1994, Republicans fielded the more experienced crop of challengers only twice: in 1966, when they picked up forty-seven seats, and 1992, when they picked up ten seats while losing the White House. They did so again in 1994, but mainly because so few experienced Democrats were willing to take the field; only 14 percent of Republican incumbents faced experienced Democratic challengers, the second lowest proportion in any postwar election.

The Republicans' proportion of experienced challengers (16 percent) was merely average for them, but then many of their most highly touted challengers were unapologetic amateurs running as antigovernment outsiders. Despite all of the rhetoric condemning "career politicians," however, experienced Republican challengers greatly outperformed the novices, picking up significantly more votes and victories. Experienced Republican challengers won 43 percent (15 of 35) of the races they entered, compared with 11 percent (19 of 173) of inexperienced Republican challengers. Naturally, experienced challengers were more common in districts with Republican presidential leanings. But even controlling for local partisanship and other relevant variables, experienced challengers did significantly better on election day.[73]

One reason experienced Republican challengers did better than the amateurs is that, as always, they raised and spent much more money. The distribution of campaign funds in 1994 followed the expected pattern in a year when campaign activists expect a strong partisan tide (see Table 6-5). Republican challengers were significantly better funded than Democratic challengers. Not only was their average spending higher, but more of them were financed beyond the threshold usually required for a competitive campaign (31 percent spent in excess of $300,000). Experienced Republican challengers were especially well funded, spending an average of $454,966 compared to $201,307 for the other Republican challengers. Democrats, on the defensive, channeled relatively more money to incumbents; Republican incumbents had far less to worry about and could get away with lower spending. As usual, both parties generously funded their candidates for open seats who were remotely competitive regardless of national trends.

The strategic allocation of Republican campaign funds was also strongly influenced by local conditions. Republican challengers raised and spent more money in districts that leaned Republican in presidential elections, particularly in districts where Democratic incumbents had made themselves vulnerable by supporting their party and president on key roll-call votes. Thus Democratic loyalists in Republican-leaning districts were the principal targets of the most lavishly-funded Republican challenges. Not surprisingly, the data show that they were most likely to lose the election as well.[74]

Multivariate analysis indicates that not only did support for the party's (and administration's) positions hurt Democrats indirectly by stimulating better-funded opposition, it hurt them directly as well. That is, House Democrats did not suffer across the board in 1994 for the alleged sins of their party and president; their difficulties were proportional to their support for the administration on the most visible issues before the 103rd Congress. Put another way, the Republicans' national campaign themes were evidently effective to the degree that individual Democrats were vulnerable to the charge of supporting the administration on controversial issues. National campaign themes were more effective in districts with a stronger inclination toward Republicans in presidential elections and where Bill Clinton was especially unpopular—the South.[75]

In sum, although all politics were not local in 1994, the electoral effect of national issues varied across districts and regions, depending on incumbency, the quality of candidates, the level of campaign spending, the partisan makeup of the district, and the behavior of the incumbent. Wielding potent campaign themes drawn from national issues, Republicans needed only reasonably attractive and well financed candidates to take seats from Democrats in districts that leaned Republican in presidential elections. Democratic retirements from such districts created a host of open-seat opportunities that well-funded Republican candidates exploited to the hilt. Against incumbent Democrats, Republicans did best where they fielded experienced, well-financed challengers against Democrats whose votes tied them to the Clinton administration in districts where the president (and his party more generally) were relatively unpopular— where, in other words, the local campaign could give their national themes the most extensive publicity, and the local context gave these themes their greatest resonance. Poorly funded Republican challengers were largely unsuccessful even in districts where the Democrat should have been vulnerable.[76] The central issues in the 1994 House elections may have been national, but how they played out still depended strongly on local circumstances.

After the upheavals of 1992 and 1994, the next two congressional elections appear positively mundane. Voters in both elections endorsed the status quo, retaining Republican majorities in both Houses of Congress. Yet in both cases, although for different reasons, the status quo they endorsed was anything but ordinary.

1996

Despite Bill Clinton's easy reelection, Republican candidates did remarkably well in the 1996 House races. They lost only eight House seats on election day; moreover, because five Democratic opportunists had switched to the Republican side of the aisle after the 1994 election and Republicans enjoyed a net gain in special elections that were held during the 104th Congress, the party ended up with only three fewer House seats in 1996 than it had won in 1994. That a Democrat could win the White House by eight million votes without winning control of Congress would have been unthinkable only a few years earlier; every one of the twenty-six successful Democratic presidential candidates from Thomas Jefferson in 1800 through Bill Clinton in 1992 had brought Democratic majorities into the House with them. Yet by the time it happened, few informed political observers were surprised, a sign of how profoundly the balance of partisan competition shifted in the 1990s.

Why were Democratic candidates for Congress unable to cash in on Clinton's victory? After all, Clinton's own reelection prospects had been dramatically enhanced by his victory in a showdown with the Republican Congress over the budget in 1995. When Republicans had tried to force Clinton to accept their package of tax and spending cuts by threatening to shut down the government, he had held firm. The Republicans' rhetoric (Speaker Newt Gingrich had told the Public Securities Association, "I don't care what the price is. I don't care if we have no executive offices, no bonds for 60 days"[77]) helped Clinton to paint them as extremists, and the Republican Congress took most of the blame for the two government shutdowns that occurred when Clinton vetoed the Republicans' budget and government's spending authority lapsed in late 1995. The public took Clinton's side in the dispute by decisive margins, and public ratings of Congress and Gingrich turned sharply downward. At the same time, Clinton's approval ratings rose, and he assumed a permanent lead over Bob Dole in the presidential horse race polls; by the time Congress relented and let the government go back to work in January 1996, the presidential election was effectively decided.[78]

But if the House Republicans' mistakes reelected Clinton, why did they not also cost the Republicans control of Congress? The answer lies in changes in the structure of electoral competition for congressional seats that were both manifested and magnified by the 1994 elections and in the electoral politics of divided government during good times.

I have already noted one important structural change: the post-1990 redistricting that produced a more favorable set of districts for Republicans. But a second, related improvement in the Republicans' competitive position emerged from the 1994 election itself. Most of the seats the party added in 1994 were seats a Republican should have held in the first place. We can calculate from the data in Table 6–10 that of the fifty-six districts newly taken by Republicans in 1994, thirty-seven (66 percent) had voted Republican, on average, in the two preceding elections. Democrats took back only four of these thirty-seven seats (11 percent), compared to six of the other nineteen (32 percent). Moreover, because Democrats still outnumbered Republicans in districts favoring the other party's presidential candidates (48 to 38), going into 1996, the Democrats still held the larger share of vulnerable seats. In 1996 they lost seven of those seats, while Republicans were losing twelve of theirs.

The Democrats' problems were compounded by another legacy of 1994: the loss of majority control. Predictably, the unaccustomed insults of minority status prompted a voluntary exodus of Democrats from the House, giving Republicans a shot at open seats in Republican-leaning districts. A higher number and proportion of Democrats than Republicans voluntarily left the House in 1996, and, as in 1994, a disproportionate share of the departing Democrats abandoned seats that had been voting Republican at the presidential level, particularly in the South; of twelve such seats in 1996, the Democrats lost six. Revealingly, twenty-three of the twenty-eight retiring House Democrats announced their departures before the end of 1995, while a majority of Republican retirees (11 of 21) announced theirs in 1996. Strategic retirements inspired by the Republicans' seeming ascendancy during most of 1995 made it harder for Democrats to exploit the shift in public opinion away from the Republican Congress after the budget showdown.

In addition, as we saw in Chapter 4, the Republican takeover of Congress transformed the campaign money market. Democrats no longer had the majority status and committee control to attract campaign contributions from business-oriented PACs, which after 1994 were freer to follow the Republican hearts as well as their pocketbooks in allocating donations. Not only did such PACs have less reason to contribute to incumbent Democrats, they also had less reason to worry about contributing *against* incumbent Democrats, whose ability to retaliate against interests that funded their opponents had diminished sharply.

Finally, the shock of 1994, the prospective imbalance of campaign funds, and the expectation that they were likely to be in the minority evidently made it more difficult for the Democrats to recruit high-quality candidates to take on incumbent Republicans. As always, experienced challengers were far more successful than the rest. Democratic challengers who had previously held elective public office won 26 percent (12 of 47) of the contests they entered, compared to only 4 percent (6 of 158) of the amateurs. The Democrats' problem was that only 22 percent of their challengers were experienced, a figure below their postwar average of 26 percent and not at all typical of a good Democratic year. The Democrats needed to pick up at least nineteen seats to retake the House in 1996. In each of the five postwar elections in which they have added nineteen or more seats to their total, at least 31 percent of the challengers had served in elective office; the average for these elections (1948, 1958, 1964, 1974, and 1982) is 36 percent. If history is any guide, the Democrats did not have a sufficient number of high-quality challengers to retake the House in 1996.

The Campaigns

Strategic career decisions taken by prospective Democratic congressional candidates, along with the other structural shifts in the balance of competition for seats, clearly made it harder for the Democrats to exploit Clinton's victory. But it would have been difficult to exploit in any case. The anticongressional Republican stance so helpful to Clinton was not as helpful to Democrats for several reasons. First, many potentially vulnerable House Republicans did what Democrats had routinely done to hold on to seats against contrary national tides during their forty-two years of control: run as independent champions of local district interests. Had they stuck together throughout the 104th Congress as they had in the early months on the Contract with America, the 1996 elections might have become a referendum on their collective performance as a party. In the end, however, the Republicans' brief flirtation with responsible party government (see Chapter 8) succumbed to the desire of individual members to win reelection and of the party as a whole to keep its majority. After the budget debacle, Republicans with moderate constituencies bolted the party on such issues as repeal of the assault weapons ban, weakening endangered species protection, and raising the minimum wage.[79] The Contract with America, so prominent in 1994 and 1995, was conspicuous by its absence from most of the Republican incumbents' 1996 campaigns.

Second, Clinton's reelection strategy was unhelpful to congressional Democrats. The closest historical precedent for the Republican triumph of 1994 was 1946, the last time the Republicans won control of Congress at the midterm with a Democrat in the White House. Democrats hoped, and Republicans feared, that the precedent for 1996 would be 1948, when Harry Truman's political resurrection swept the Democrats back into control of Congress. Unfortunately for the Democrats, the historical model for 1996 was not 1948, but 1984, when Ronald Reagan rode to easy reelection on a tide of good economic news while his party was picking up only fourteen seats in the House and losing three in the Senate.

Both Reagan and Clinton ran upbeat campaigns extolling a strong economy and popular policy successes. Both drew on extraordinary political skills to extend their personal appeal beyond their party's normal electoral base. Both won easy reelection. But neither of their campaigns offered much leverage to their congressional challengers. If times are good and the president deserves another term, why replace incumbents of the majority party in Congress, who can plausibly claim a share of the credit for peace, prosperity, and progress? Recall that the other status-quo elections held under divided government— Dwight D. Eisenhower's reelection and Richard Nixons' reelection in 1972— offer confirming examples. As Table 6-11 shows, every postwar president reelected to a second full term had remarkably short coattails. All four saw their party lose seats in the Senate, and their largest pickup in the House was Reagan's paltry fourteen seats in 1984.

Third, the difficulty for Democratic challengers was amplified by the very strategy that revived Clinton's presidency. By accepting so many of the Republicans' goals—agreeing to balance the budget by 2002, declaring that "the era

TABLE 6–11 CONGRESSIONAL RESULTS WHEN PRESIDENTS ARE ELECTED TO A SECOND FULL TERM

YEAR	PRESIDENT	VOTE	HOUSE	SENATE
1956	Eisenhower (R)	57.7%	2 D	1 D
1972	Nixon (R)	61.8%	12 R	2 D
1984	Reagan (R)	59.2%	14 R	2 D
1996	Clinton (D)	54.5%	8 D	2 R

Note: "D" refers to Democrats, "R" to Republicans; the vote percentage is calculated from the major party vote.

of big government is over," signing a bill to end welfare entitlements that had been part of the social safety net since the New Deal, opposing gay marriages, and supporting prayer in school—Clinton took command of the political center. But by campaigning on a record indistinguishable from that of a moderate Republican, he gave voters little reason to elect more Democrats to Congress.

Clinton helped congressional Republicans in other ways as well. His firm opposition to unpopular budget cuts, assaults on environmental regulation and the Department of Education, and kindred Republican proposals in 1995 forced Republicans to rein in their most extreme impulses and alerted them to the political danger lurking in revolutionary rhetoric and radical policy changes. His maneuvering toward consensus on the budget decisions and on issues such as welfare reform, minimum wage, and health insurance portability gave them a chance to look responsible and effective.

Moreover, the administration's aura of scandal and widespread doubts about Clinton's personal character offered voters an additional reason to keep Republicans in a position to keep an eye on him. Indeed there is some evidence that the revelations late in the campaign of foreign contributions to the Democratic National Committee moved many late-deciding voters into the Republican column, reducing Clinton's margin of victory and thereby impeding the Democrats' effort to retake the House.[80] In addition, despite the implied affront to Dole, Republican leaders did not hesitate to make the near certainty of Clinton's reelection an argument for voting Republican for Congress. A majority of voters did so, and Republicans kept control of Congress.

1998

From one perspective, the results of the 1998 House elections were stunning. For only the second time since the Civil War, the president's party increased its strength in the House at midterm.[81] Democrats gained five seats, leaving the Republicans with a narrow 223–211 majority.[82] Shocked and angered by their losses, House Republicans drove Speaker Newt Gingrich, architect of their historic 1994 victory, to resign.

From another perspective, however, there is little remarkable about what happened in 1998. The national conditions that normally shape midterm elections had their usual effects. The voters, for good and familiar reasons, delivered a ringing endorsement of the political status quo. What makes the election nonetheless remarkable is, of course, that despite the president's involvement in a scandal that transfixed Washington throughout 1998 and led to his impeachment in the House and trial and acquittal in the Senate, the status quo that voters endorsed clearly included Bill Clinton in the White House.

That voters did opt for the status quo in 1998 is beyond question. Only six House incumbents met defeat, and only seventeen House seats switched party control; the first number ties and the second sets the record for least change in any midterm. Both Democratic and Republican incumbents enjoyed an average vote gain of 2.8 percentage points over 1996. The 395 members returned to office in 1998 are the most for any midterm House election ever. The contrast between the first and second midterm elections of the Clinton presidency could scarcely be starker.

The triumph of the status quo in 1998 is fully consistent with national conditions. House Democrats went into the 1998 elections with only two more seats than they had held after their 1994 disaster, so their exposure was minimal. The economy was booming, with both inflation and unemployment at thirty-year lows. Moreover the federal budget was in surplus for the first time in nearly thirty years, and violent crime and welfare dependency were dramatically lower than just a few years earlier. Consistent with these highly favorable trends, Bill Clinton's job approval rating stood at 66 percent in the final Gallup Poll taken before the election, the highest for any president in any midterm preelection poll since Gallup began asking the question more than fifty years ago.[83] Plugging the appropriate values for 1998 into the equation in Table 6-2 generates the prediction that the Democrats would pick up nine seats, so their actual gain of six accurately reflected the fundamentals prevailing in 1998.

These fundamentals scarcely posed a threat to incumbent Republicans, however. Clinton and his fellow Democrats could not claim exclusive credit for good times, because Republicans controlled the Congress. As always, divided government divides credit or blame for the government's performance as well. Thus as Clinton's approval ratings reached new heights, so did ratings of the Republican Congress; in early 1998, approval of Congress reached 57 percent, the highest level recorded in the twenty-five years the question has been asked. Incumbents of both parties benefited; in October, 58 percent of Gallup's respondents thought that most members of Congress deserved reelection, compared to 29 percent in 1992, 39 percent in 1994, and 55 percent in 1996.[84] With conditions so favorable to the political status quo, neither party stood to make much in the way of gains.

The 1998 election results, then, are about what we would expect if no one had ever heard of Monica Lewinsky. But this, of course, raises the central puzzles posed by the 1998 elections: Why did transgressions that led special prosecutor Kenneth Starr to recommend and the House to impeach Clinton fail to bring down the president's job approval and, with it, congressional Democrats? How is it that a scandal that obsessed the Washington community throughout the election year could have so little apparent impact on the results? What, if any, impact did the scandal actually have?

The Scandal and the Campaigns

News stories reporting Clinton's sexual relationship with Lewinsky, and charges that he had committed perjury and obstruction of justice to cover it up, surfaced just before the president's annual State of the Union address in January 1998. Clinton flatly and publicly denied all charges. The scandal's buzz helped boost the audience for the speech, which was watched by an estimated fifty-three million Americans. In it, Clinton resolutely ignored his personal problems, reminding people instead of the happy trends we have already noted, along with other blessings flowing from peace and prosperity during his watch. The public clearly got the message Clinton was trying to convey, and Clinton's approval ratings jumped to the highest levels of his presidency, surpassing 70 percent in some polls.

The public's reaction to the State of the Union address ended speculation that the Lewinsky affair would lead to Clinton's quick exit, but the scandal still complicated strategic election year calculations. The customary forecasting cues available in early 1998 offered little hope for challengers of either party. Public satisfaction with the economy, the president, the Congress, and the United States in general was extraordinarily high.[85] Unless these assessments deteriorated sharply before election day, it would be very difficult to persuade voters to opt for change of any kind. But the Lewinsky scandal obviously did contain the potential for a dramatic deterioration in the public's rating of the president, leaving the predictive value of his current standing in serious doubt.

The scandal flared up just in time to discourage potential Democratic challengers not already daunted by the dismal track record of challengers representing the president's party at midterm. Mere mention of "impeachment" evoked memories of Watergate's devastating effect on the Republicans in 1974. Moreover, Clinton was far and away the Democrats' best fundraiser; if the scandal impaired his financial touch, Democratic candidates' fundraising problems would be compounded.[86]

The same considerations that spooked Democrats should have heartened Republicans. Yet potential Republican challengers faced the same uncertainty about how Clinton's self-inflicted travails would play out. Perhaps the public would finally turn against the president, taking their disaffection out on congressional Democrats. Yet nothing in the initial public reaction to the story promised a swelling Republican tide. Indeed, rather the opposite; and Clinton's astonishing capacity to bounce back was a matter of public record. With relatively few Democratic targets vulnerable on their own, and with the public seemingly delighted with the status quo, potential Republican challengers had ample reason to question their own prospects.

As a consequence of these considerations, neither party recruited a cohort of challengers likely to take more than a handful of seats from the other side. Nearly a quarter of House incumbents enjoyed a completely free ride; fifty-five Republicans and thirty-nine Democrats were unopposed in the general election, numbers dramatically higher than those of the three most recent elections. Among those spared major party opposition were ten Republicans and eight Democrats who had won less than 55 percent of the vote in 1996 or who represented districts won by the other party's presidential candidate that year. That so many such likely targets failed to draw even token challenges is strong evidence of widespread strategic capitulation by both sides in 1998.

The challengers who did show up were not a very formidable group. Only 18.5 percent of Republican incumbents faced Democrats with prior elective office experience, well below the 26 percent or so expected from either the postwar average or national conditions prevalent early in the election year. Democrats were apparently more skittish about their chances than the economy or Clinton's standing early in the election year would lead us to expect, suggesting that the scandal's shadow did indeed take a toll. This is probably the only way in which the Lewinsky affair actually hurt congressional Democrats in 1998.

The proportion of Democratic incumbents facing experienced Republican challengers was similar, 18.0 percent, and stood slightly above the postwar average (16.4 percent) or the proportion projected from national conditions (14.5 percent). The scandal may have made Republicans a bit more optimistic than usual, but the data may also merely reflect the larger pool of experienced politicians created by Republican gains in state and local elections in the 1990s. On the whole, though, neither party fielded a large enough class of formidable challengers either to signal or to justify optimism about changing the status quo.

The public's initial reaction to the Lewinsky scandal established a pattern that persisted through the rest of the election year. People's opinions on Clinton's performance as president diverged sharply from opinions on his culpability in the affair. From the very first, more people than not believed Clinton had had an affair with Lewinsky and had lied about it under oath. As the year wore on, the proportion of skeptics grew, and views of Clinton's personal character and honesty became increasingly negative.[87]

These beliefs did not, however, lessen approval of Clinton's policies or job performance or lead to widespread demands for his departure. Instead, the public soured on Kenneth Starr and his investigation. By March, moderate Republicans had begun to worry that Starr's unpopularity might rub off on them and that anything short of an open and shut case for impeachment would be politically disastrous.[88] In April, with public support for Clinton undiminished, Newt Gingrich joined other conservative Republican leaders in a full-scale offensive, attacking Clinton for "the most systematic, deliberate obstruction of justice, coverup, and effort to avoid the truth we have ever seen in American history."[89] The attacks were designed to mollify the party's socially conservative core supporters and to persuade the broader public that the scandal was about perjury and obstruction of justice, not sex. While perhaps achieving the first goal, Gingrich failed conspicuously to achieve the second.

Republicans believed they had at last struck political gold when, on August 17, Clinton testified on videotape for a grand jury and then publicly confessed to having had a relationship with Lewinsky that was "not appropriate" and lying about it to the American people. Republican candidates immediately began calling for Clinton to resign and linking their opponents to the White House. "Our intention is to brand every single Democrat in the state with the scarlet 'C,'" said the executive director of the South Carolina Republican Party. "Bill Clinton . . . has re-energized our base . . . We will gratuitously use Clinton's face on all our literature."[90]

Congressional Democrats, feeling betrayed, publicly vented their disappointment, disgust, and embarrassment, and several called on Clinton to resign. When Starr's report, recommending impeachment for perjury and obstruction of justice and containing excruciatingly detailed descriptions of Clinton's sexual dalliance with Lewinsky, was delivered with great fanfare to the House of Representatives, 138 Democrats joined the Republicans in voting to release its full text to the public. The report was posted on the Internet on September 11; ten days later, Clinton's videotaped grand jury testimony was also made public.

To the frustration of Republicans and wary relief of Democrats, the Starr report and video testimony left public opinion on Clinton and impeachment almost unchanged. His job approval ratings remained high and in some polls even improved. The proportion of Americans wanting him out, either by impeachment or resignation, rose briefly before the contents of the report and videotape were fully exposed, then began to recede, falling back below 30 percent as election day approached. At no point did less than a solid majority want Clinton to remain in office.

Why did the Lewinsky scandal fail to undermine Clinton's support? Survey data support several complementary explanations. First, the scandal could not disillusion people who had no illusions to begin with. His August confession and the subsequent impeachment hearings merely confirmed what most people already believed and thus had already factored into their assessments of Clinton. He retained popular support, not because people thought him an innocent victim of his enemies' machinations or that his behavior was excusable, but despite the common belief that he was guilty as charged and was mostly to blame for his troubles.[91]

Second, while most Americans condemned Clinton's behavior and character, most also liked what had been happening with the things that directly affected their own lives—jobs, inflation, incomes, crime rates—during his presidency. As we have seen, the public had good reason to be satisfied with national economic and social trends during the Clinton administration and to want them to continue. The positive trends continued through the election year and beyond, clearly to Clinton's benefit. At the time Clinton's trial was about to begin in the Senate, more than 60 percent of the public approved of his performance on the budget, crime, and foreign policy, and more than 80 percent approved of his performance on the economy.[92]

Third, people who liked Clinton's policies but disapproved of his behavior had a convenient way to avoid cognitive dissonance: they could adopt the view that the scandal was about sex and that the president's sex life was a private, not public, matter. In polls taken during 1998, nearly two thirds of the public consistently took this position. And finally, Clinton was fortunate in his enemies. Over the course of the scandal, the public came to disdain Clinton's antagonists—Starr, Republican congressional leaders, the news media—even more than they did him.[93]

But most important, and basic to all of these other explanations, is that the public's response to the scandal was starkly partisan. This was particularly true of people identifying themselves as Democrats; Clinton retained his support largely because ordinary people in his own party refused to turn against him. In polls taken during September and October, self-identified Democrats divided on average about 85-15 against impeachment or resignation, while Republican identifiers favored both by about 60-40.[94] The partisans who turned out to vote in 1998 were even more polarized. Among Democratic voters surveyed by NES, 92 percent approved of Clinton's performance, 90 percent opposed his resignation, and 93 percent opposed his impeachment. Among Republican voters, only 40 percent approved of Clinton's performance, 70 percent wanted him to resign, and 63 percent wanted him impeached if he didn't resign. If nothing else, the public's reaction to the events of 1998 stands as eloquent testimony to the continuing power of party identification to shape Americans' responses to politics. (I discuss how the voters' partisan response shaped impeachment politics in Chapter 8.)

With Clinton's public support holding steady, the House Republicans' decision on October 8 to hold impeachment hearings was not popular, and Congress's approval ratings, while remaining high by historical comparison, began to slide. Instead of a winning issue, congressional Republicans found themselves in a serious political bind. Their core constituency of social conservatives demanded impeachment and would be unforgiving of anything less, while the broader public was overwhelmingly opposed to removing the president

The public's reaction to the events of August and September made it increasingly unlikely that the Clinton-Lewinsky scandal would, by itself, swing elections to Republican congressional candidates. With so much of the electorate sick of hearing about it, just bringing the matter up risked a backlash, and so candidates on both sides tended to ignore it. Mindful of the polls, most Republican candidates carefully avoided suggesting that the election should be a referendum on impeachment. Yet this left them with little else to say, for having staked victory on Clinton's troubles, they were unprepared to wage campaigns on issues that voters were saying they did care about. And those issues—notably education, health maintenance organization (HMO) reform, and protecting Social Security—were the kind on which voters think Democrats do a better job anyway. The public's distinction between Clinton the president and Clinton the person freed Democrats to campaign on Clinton's policy agenda without defending his character or behavior. A few Democratic challengers even turned the impeachment issue to their advantage. In one notable instance in New Jersey, Democratic challenger Rush Holt upset incumbent Michael Pappas in a campaign that featured TV ads showing Pappas literally singing the praises of Kenneth Starr on the floor of the House.[95]

Although most of the public seemed unmoved by the scandal, Republicans still hoped that it would help them by mobilizing their Clinton-hating core supporters while discouraging disaffected Democrats from voting. The party's $10 million media blitz during the last week of the campaign sought to exploit the scandal to these ends. But in the end, it was Republicans disaffected because they opposed impeachment who were more likely to stay home.[96]

In the end, then, the election was not a referendum on impeachment—to the great good fortune of the Republican Party. For a large majority of voters, strongly positive national trends trumped all other considerations, leaving them disposed to continue the political status quo by reelecting incumbents of both parties. Prospective challengers who thought it would be a tough year to pry support away from incumbents turned out to be right, although their prophecy was, as always, in large part self-fulfilling. Republicans, trusting that Clinton's disgrace would be their ticket to victory, were left without a viable message to use against Democratic incumbents when the issue fizzled. Democrats were able to squeeze some small advantage from voters' opposition to impeachment and a favorable issue climate and so enjoyed modest but symbolically important gains.[97] Yet the Clinton-Lewinsky scandal probably scared off high-quality challengers in potentially winnable districts, leaving Democrats poorly prepared to take full advantage of their unexpected good fortune. It is worth noting in this regard that four of the five winning Democratic challengers were from that small fraction who had prior experience in elective office (as was the lone successful Republican challenger); all were generously funded.[98]

TABLE 6–12   ISSUES, CHALLENGES, AND TURNOVER IN HOUSE ELECTIONS, 1980–1998

YEAR	ISSUES USEFUL TO CHALLENGERS?	STRONG CHALLENGES?	TURNOVER	INCUMBENTS DEFEATED	NET SWING
1980	Yes—R	Yes—R	74	30	34 R
1982	Yes—D	Yes—D, R	81	23	26 D
1984	Yes—R	No	43	16	14 R
1986	No	No	50	6	5 D
1988	No	No	28	6	2 D
1990	Yes—D, R	No	35	15	9 D
1992	Yes—D, R	Yes—D, R	110	24	10 R
1994	Yes—R	Yes—R	86	34	52 R
1996	Yes—D	No	74	21	9 D
1998	No	No	40	6	6 D

HOUSE ELECTION PATTERNS, 1980–1998

Stepping back from the dramatic details of the most recent elections, we can see the broader patterns that have shaped aggregate House election outcomes over the past two decades. Table 6-12 leaves no doubt about what it takes for elections to change the makeup of the House: Potent issues combined with vigorous challenges. Both are necessary. Issues won't do it by themselves (1984, 1990, 1996); neither will strong challenges (1982 Republicans). But when they are combined, turnover is sharply higher, incumbents become much more vulnerable, and, if the issues favor one party over the other, we observe a large net swing to the favored party.

No matter how favorable the issues are to the challenger's party, a vigorous challenge is almost always necessary to knock off an incumbent. This is evident from Table 6-13, which lists the percentage of winning challengers in years favorable to the challenger's party,[99] depending on whether or not the incumbent was marginal (won more or less than 60 percent of the vote in the last election) and whether the challenge was strong (the challenger had held elec-

TABLE 6–13   SUCCESSFUL CHALLENGES IN ELECTION YEARS FAVORABLE TO THE CHALLENGER'S PARTY, 1972–1998 (IN PERCENTAGES)

CHALLENGE	MARGINAL INCUMBENT	NONMARGINAL INCUMBENT	TOTAL
Strong	34.4 (273)[a]	21.8 (188)	29.3 (461)
Weak	5.5 (110)	1.3 (526)	2.0 (636)
Total	26.1 (383)	6.7 (714)	13.5 (1097)

[a]Number of cases from which percentages were calculated.

Note: Marginal seats are those in which the incumbent won less than 60 percent of the two-party vote in the previous election. Strong challenges are of those in which the challenger spent at least $300,000 (in 1998 dollars) or had previously held elective public office.

tive office or spent at least $300,000 in 1998 dollars). Plainly, the strength of the challenger's candidacy is far more important than the marginality of the incumbent. Even in good years, few challengers merely float in on tidal shifts in votes, while strong challengers have an impressive record of success even against nonmarginal incumbents. Marginal incumbents do attract serious challenges more frequently (71 percent compared to 22 percent for nonmarginal incumbents), which is just what our understanding of careers strategies would lead us to expect. But in the absence of a serious challenge, even marginal incumbents have an excellent prospect of surviving a strong contrary partisan tide.

SENATE ELECTIONS, 1980–1998

Senate elections since 1980 illustrate yet another quirk in the translation of national forces into congressional election outcomes. A final reason why presidential coattails and other national forces can have different aggregate effects in different election years is that the distribution as well as the size of the vote for a party's congressional candidates determines wins and losses. The distribution of votes (and vote shifts) is, of course, strongly affected by local circumstances—candidates, campaigns, and other idiosyncratic factors. Although true of House elections, this is most clearly the case among Senate elections, because of both the great differences in state populations and the underlying competitiveness of nearly every state. The ebb and flow of Senate representation in recent elections offers a particularly striking illustration of how sensitive aggregate election results can be to small changes in voting behavior—and therefore to national or local conditions that influence voters.

In 1980, Republicans took over the Senate in dramatic fashion by winning twenty-two of the thirty-four seats at stake, taking twelve seats from the Democrats and losing none of their own. Yet they did not win a majority of votes cast nationally for U.S. Senator. Republican victories were concentrated in smaller states and were won by narrower margins. Republican candidates won eleven of the fourteen contests in which the winner received 52.1 percent or less of the vote. A shift of only 50,000 votes, properly redistributed, would have given the Democrats seven additional seats and a 54-46 majority.[100] Although strong candidates and campaigns were essential to the Republican victories,[101] with so many cliffhangers even the relatively small coattail effects estimated for Senate contests in 1980 (Reagan supplying about 2 additional percentage points across the electorate) were large enough to have been decisive in producing the Republican majority.[102]

The parties broke even in 1982 Senate contests, each party picking up two seats from the opposition. The Republicans held onto the Senate by once again winning the close ones. They took eight of the ten tightest races; redistribution of fewer than 35,000 votes would have given Democrats control of the Senate. In 1984, Republicans finally won a majority of the votes cast nationwide for senator. The survey evidence examined in this chapter indicates that Reagan's victory added about 4 percentage points to their total. Yet they suffered a net loss of two Senate seats and were defeated in four of the six contests won with less than 55 percent of the two-party vote. The reason is not that Reagan's triumph was unhelpful, but that Republican opportunities were much more limited in 1984 than they had been in 1980. Democrats defended only fourteen seats, and most of the vulnerable incumbents were Republicans.

Considering the number of seats they had at risk, Republicans emerged from the 1984 Senate elections with their prospects for long-term control of the Senate seemingly enhanced. Five of the seven Republican senators whom Democrats had serious hopes of defeating were reelected, all but one (Jesse Helms) by a wide margin. Reagan may have helped Republican Senate candidates as much, if not more, in 1984 as in 1980, but local circumstances were so different that his coattails had a smaller effect on the number of seats changing hands.

In 1986, Democrats recaptured six of the Senate seats they had lost in 1980 and took three others from Republicans, losing only one of their own, for a net pickup of eight seats and a 55-45 majority. Once again, however, a switch of only 55,000 votes, properly redistributed, would have left the Senate in Republican hands. This time the Democrats won the close ones, taking nine of eleven races won with less than 52 percent of the vote. While this might appear to be an instance of surge and decline—Republicans riding in on the Reagan surge in 1980, riding out in the midterm election six years later—these elections hinged largely on the local candidates and campaigns. Some of the surprise Republican victors from 1980 won easy reelection; others were defeated soundly. The difference reflected the variations in the quality of the incumbents (several of the losing Republican incumbents proved themselves to be inept politicians) as well as the challengers.[103] The Democratic challengers won mainly by raising local issues and persuading voters that the Republican incumbents cared more about ideological goals than local interests.[104]

Unlike 1986, the 1988 Senate elections left the partisan balance in the Senate unchanged. Democrats took four seats from Republicans, defeating three incumbents and taking one open seat. Republicans took three seats from Democrats, defeating one incumbent and taking two open seats. The net result was a standoff, leaving a 55-45 Democratic majority, as had the 1986 election before Senator Zorinsky died and a Republican, David Karnes, was appointed in his place. But once again, with changes in only a handful of votes, the net outcome could have been quite different. Four seats were won with less than a 51 percent of the major party vote, three by Republicans. A shift of fewer than 3 percentage points in selected states could have elected three more Republicans or four more Democrats. It would have taken a switch of about 180,000 votes to give Republicans effective control in 1988 (50 seats plus the vice presidency)—about 0.3 percent of the more than 65 million votes cast for Senate candidates.

The 1990 Senate elections further underlined the idiosyncracy of Senate contests. Voters endorsed the status quo to a greater extent than in any election since senators have been chosen by popular vote. Despite a public mood hostile to officeholders and the historically greater vulnerability of Senate incumbents, only a single incumbent—Rudy Boschwitz, a Minnesota Republican—was defeated. No other seat changed party control; thirty-one incumbents were reelected, and Republicans retained control of their three open seats. In contrast to other recent Senate elections, 1990 produced relatively few close contests; only four seats were won with less than 52 percent of the two-party vote, and twenty-two of the thirty-five winners received more than 60 percent. It would have taken a shift of more than 350,000 votes to give Republicans effective control of the Senate.

Some traces of the national trends identified in the House elections did surface. Boschwitz's defeat at the hands of Paul Wellstone, a political novice who spent only $1.3 million against Boschwitz's $6.7 million, was a surprise. So was New Jersey Senator Bill Bradley's narrow victory despite an even greater financial advantage ($12.4 million to $0.8 million). In both cases, many voters appeared to be venting their general disgust with politics on the most available target, the complacent incumbent.[105] A trend against Republicans was also evident—in what the party did *not* achieve. Republicans had hoped to make inroads into the Democratic majority in order to position themselves to retake the Senate in 1992, when the Democrats would have to defend twenty seats. Five Republican House members gave up their seats to run against Senate Democrats thought to be vulnerable; all of them lost, and three of their House seats were taken by Democrats.

The 1992 Senate elections, like the House elections, brought striking demographic changes without altering the partisan balance. Of the twelve newly elected senators, four were women, one of them (Carol Mosely-Braun of Illinois) an African-American; the election tripled the number of women senators from two to six. Another of the entering senators, Ben Nighthorse Campbell of Colorado, was the first Native American ever elected to the Senate. Yet the elections again produced no net partisan change at all, leaving the Democrats with the same 57–43 majority they enjoyed before election day.

As in the House, the advances made by women in the Senate were rooted in the primaries. Three of the four newly elected women—all Democrats—won open Senate seats; the fourth, Diane Feinstein of California, defeated an appointed senator, John Seymour, who was an incumbent in name only. In contrast, the six women (five Democrats, one Republican) who faced elected incumbent Senators in the general election lost. (The lone incumbent woman, Barbara Mikulski of Maryland, won reelection.) All of the victors had previously held elective office, whereas four of the six losers were pursuing their first electoral office.[106]

Only one of the new women senators—Feinstein, who had narrowly lost a race to be California's governor in 1990—would have been a sure bet to win nomination without the special stimulus of the Anita Hill–Clarence Thomas confrontation. Carol Mosely Braun defeated incumbent Democrat Alan Dixon, who had voted to confirm Thomas, in the Illinois primary and then held on to win the general election against a relatively obscure first-time candidate. Patty Murray's self-described status as "a mom in tennis shoes" helped her to emerge on top in Washington's "jungle" primary (in which candidates from all parties run on a single ballot, with the top Democratic and Republican vote-getters winning each party's nomination). Barbara Boxer took the California nomination despite having 143 overdrafts at the House Bank in large part because of the attention and support her gender attracted in the primary.

Apart from putting a record number of women into the upper house, the 1992 Senate elections were not unusual. The average level of competition is always higher in Senate than in House elections—stronger challengers, closer elections, incumbents defeated more frequently—and 1992 was no exception. But neither was it special. The numbers of newcomers (twelve) and successful challengers (four) were about average. The incidence of marginal incumbents—56 percent received less than 60 percent of the vote—was about 10 points higher than it was in the 1980–1990 period, but that is the only sign of unusually intense competition.

The unusual aspect of the 1992 Senate elections was the absence of net partisan change, for the seats at stake in 1992 were the same that had given control of the Senate to the Republicans with a twelve-seat swing in 1980 and to the Democrats with an eight-seat swing in 1986. But this time, they produced no net partisan change at all. The balance of national partisan forces had something to do with this stasis, but the customary idiosyncrasy of Senate elections had more to do with it.

Republicans had initially expected to cash in on both the Gulf War and the fact that the Democrats had more seats to defend (21 of 36), nine of which had been won only narrowly in 1986. Later in the campaign, Democrats anticipated picking up some seats with the help of anger over the Thomas hearings, the faltering economy, and Clinton's coattails. In the end, both parties were probably helped a little by their particular issues, and the net result was a wash. The two Democratic senators who lost (Terry Sanford of North Carolina and Wyche Fowler of Georgia) were among the three southern Democrats who had opposed authorizing the president to use military force against Iraq (Ernest Hollings of South Carolina, the third, won with just 52 percent of the vote). How much this vote contributed to their defeats is uncertain, because both Sanford and Fowler had been narrow victors in 1986 and had other serious electoral problems. Still, if not decisive, their vote against going to war was certainly a political liability.

On the Democratic side, the economy and Clinton's strength probably helped Russ Feingold to defeat Bob Kasten, the Republican incumbent, in Wisconsin. Some of Diane Feinstein's landslide margin over John Seymour in California is attributable to her gender and Clinton's appeal in California, but she was the stronger candidate by almost any standard and would have won in 1992 without any help from national forces. If there was any helpful Democratic trend in 1992, it showed up mainly in the narrowness of some Republican incumbents' escapes and the relative ease with which most of the Democrats who had once seemed vulnerable won reelection. Six of the Republican winners got no more than 52 percent of the two-party vote; all but one of the Democratic winners (Ernest Hollings of North Carolina) enjoyed wider margins of victory. Democrats were aided by the departure of two scandal-ridden incumbents (Alan Cranston of California and Brock Evans of Washington) and their replacement by stronger Democratic nominees. Both parties held on to all of their open Senate seats.

The 1994 Republican tide flowed just as strongly in Senate as in House elections. Republicans took control of the Senate by taking eight seats from the Democrats, immediately adding a party-switching opportunist (Richard Shelby of Alabama) to end up with a 53-47 majority, which grew to 54-46 a few months later when Democrat Ben Nighthorse Campbell of Colorado also switched sides. The Republican Senate victory was less surprising than the House victory, to be sure, because the party had controlled the Senate from 1981 to 1987, and because most Senate seats can be won by either party under the right conditions. But it was just as decisive.

As in the House elections, open seats made the difference. Republicans won all six open seats vacated by Democrats, defeated two of sixteen Democratic incumbents, and kept all the seats they already held (ten incumbents, three open seats). Also as in the House, Senate Democrats tended to retire where constituency voting patterns promised to make life difficult. Democrats vacated six of twelve seats in states where, on average, the two-party vote for Democratic presidential candidates fell below 50.5 percent; they vacated none of the ten seats where the presidential vote exceeded this amount. Strategic retirements thus hurt Democrats in Senate as well as House elections.

It could have been even worse for the Democrats. Three of their winners received less than 52 percent of the vote; only one winning Republican cut it that close. Still, it would not have taken a shift in very many votes to alter the results. A careful redistribution of about 174,000 votes (0.3 percent of those cast) would have let the Democrats retain four seats and thus their majority; but then a shift of only 112,000 votes (0.2 percent of those cast) could have given the Republicans three additional seats.

As usual, experienced candidates both reflected and enhanced the competitiveness of these elections. Although much was made of the victories of two political novices in Tennessee (Fred Thompson, a lawyer and actor, and Bill Frist, a surgeon), no fewer than seven of the eleven new Republican Senators had served in the House, and another had been his state's governor.

In 1996, despite Clinton's victory, the Republicans added two new seats to the majority they had won in 1994, increasing their margin to 55-45. Democrats were hurt by the luck of the draw as well as by retirements. Thirteen senators retired in 1996, the largest number of voluntary departures since 1914, when senators were first directly elected by voters. Eight of the thirteen were Democrats, four of them from the South. The timing of their retirement announcements again suggests strategic withdrawal; all eight of the Democrats, but only one of the Republicans, announced their retirements before Clinton's successful showdown with the Republican Congress in late 1995. Republicans won three of the seats vacated by Democrats, two in the South (Alabama and Arkansas) and one in Nebraska, a state won handily by Bob Dole. Republican Senator Larry Pressler of South Dakota was the only incumbent defeated in the general election and his was the only Republican senate seat lost in 1996.

Democrats were also unlucky in the class of Senate seats up in 1996, for Senate and presidential outcomes tended to coincide. Republicans won fourteen of the seventeen seats at stake in states won by Dole, while Democrats won ten of the seventeen states won by Clinton. The Republicans' good fortune was that states won by Dole were more likely to have Senate contests. Only three of Dole's nineteen states lacked a Senate race, compared to fourteen of Clinton's thirty-one states. By the luck of the draw, the Democrats were poorly positioned to take advantage of whatever help Clinton's victory might have provided their Senate candidates.

More notable than the Senate seat swing in 1996 was the ideological shift within the Republican majority. Not just the three who replaced Democrats, but every one of the nine newly elected Republican senators was more conservative than the senator he or she had replaced.

In 1998, the parties broke even in the Senate, preserving the status quo and the Republicans' 55–45 majoirty. Democrats defeated two Republican incumbents but lost two open seats. Republicans defeated one Democratic incumbent while losing one open seat. Although six Senate seats thus changed hands, the switches were much more a consequence of local issues and personalities than of any general thirst for change. Still, the outcome was disappointing to Republicans, for Democrats were defending most of the vulnerable seats, and Republicans had entertained dreams of winning a filibuster-proof sixty-seat majority.[107] There is some evidence that popular opposition to Clinton's impeachment hurt Republican Senate candidates more than it did Republican House candidates, even though the Senate had not yet addressed the issue.[108] The potential effect of the issue was limited, however, because the number of close elections was comparatively small—only nine were won with less than 55 percent of the two-party vote, compared to fifteen in 1996—and only two contests were won by margins of less than 38,000 votes. In contrast to 1994 and 1996, 1998 disturbed neither the partisan nor the ideological status quo in the Senate.

The Senate has now changed party hands three times since 1980. In two instances, 1980 and 1994, the switch was part of a broader partisan tide visible in other elections as well. However, in the third instance, when the Democrats won control in 1986, the shift was entirely idiosyncratic to the Senate elections. And in the two other years showing some evidence of a significant partisan trend—1982 and 1984—the Senate swings, though small, actually went *against* the trend. Clearly, the close competitive balance in so many states creates a potential for dramatic swings in party fortunes. Yet at the same time, along with the idiosyncratic variety offered by local candidates, campaigns, and issues, it can also allow large swings to occur without strong partisan tides and partisan tides to surge without producing large partisan swings.

ENDNOTES

1. Midterms can be as important as presidential election years in this regard; see Andrew E. Bush, *Horses in Midstream: U.S. Midterm Elections and Their Consequences, 1894–1998* (Pittsburgh: University of Pittsburgh Press, 1999).

2. Gerald H. Kramer, "Short-Term Fluctuations in U.S. Voting Behavior," *American Political Science Review* 65 (1971):131–143; G.J. Stigler, "General Economic Conditions and National Elections," *American Economic Review* 63 (1973):160–167; Francisco Arcelus and Allan H. Meltzer, "The Effects of Aggregate Economic Variables on Congressional Elections," *American Political Science Review* 69 (1975):1232–1239; Howard S. Bloom and H. Douglas Price, "Voter Response to Short-run

Economic Conditions: The Asymmetric Effect of Prosperity and Recession," *American Political Science Review*: 69 (1975):1240-1254; Douglas A. Hibbs, Jr., "President Reagan's Mandate from the 1980 Elections: A Shift to the Right?" *American Politics Quarterly* 10 (1982):387-420. For arguments that the economy makes no difference in midterm elections, see Alberto Alesina and Howard Rosenthal, "Partisan Cycles in Congressional Elections and the Macroeconomy," *American Political Science Review* 83 (1989):373-398; Robert S. Erikson, "Economic Conditions and the Congressional Vote: A Review of the Macrolevel Evidence," *American Journal of Political Science* 34 (1990):373-399; Kenneth Scheve and Michael Tomz, "Electoral Surprise and the Midterm Loss in U.S. Congressional Elections," *British Journal of Political Science* 29 (1999):507-521. For critiques of these arguments, see Gary C. Jacobson, "Does the Economy Matter in Midterm Elections?" *American Journal of Political Science* 34 (1990):400-407, and same author, *The Electoral Origins of Divided Government: Competition in House Elections, 1946-1988* (Boulder, Colorado: Westview Press, 1990), pp. 77-80.

3. Edward R. Tufte, *Political Control of the Economy* (Princeton: Princeton University Press, 1978), Tables 5-2 and 5-4; see also his "Determinants of the Outcomes of Midterm Congressional Elections," *American Political Science Review* 69 (1975):812-826.

4. Bruce I. Oppenheimer, James A. Stimson, and Richard W. Waterman, "Interpreting U.S. Congressional Elections: The Exposure Thesis," *Legislative Studies Quarterly* 11 (1986):227-247.

5. Gary C. Jacobson, "Reversal of Fortune: The Transformation of U.S. House Elections in the 1990s," in *Continuity and Change in Congressional Elections*, ed. David Brady, John Cogan, and Morris P. Fiorina (Stanford, California: Stanford University Press, forthcoming), Table 1. Based on this analysis and updating it through 1998, I estimate that the "expected" number of seats held by House Democrats fell by 42 after 1990. All of the coefficients in the equation remain statistically significant without this adjustment, but with it, the adjusted R^2 rises from .50 to .71.

6. Alan I. Abramowitz and Jeffrey A. Segal, "Determinants of the Outcomes of U.S. Senate Elections," *Journal of Politics* 48 (1986):433-439.

7. Tufte, "Midterm Congressional Elections," p. 826.

8. M. Stephen Weatherford, "Social Class, Economic Conditions, and Political Translation: The 1974 Recession and the Vote for Congress" (Paper delivered at the Annual Meeting of the Western Political Science Association, Portland, March 22-24, 1979), pp. 3-7.

9. Arcelus and Meltzer, "Congressional Elections," p. 1234.

10. See Morris P. Fiorina, "Economic Retrospective Voting in American National Elections," *American Journal of Political Science* 22 (1978):426-443; Donald R. Kinder and D. Roderick Kiewiet, "Economic Discontent and Political Behavior: The Role of Personal Grievances and Collective Economic Judgments in Congressional Voting," *American Journal of Political Science* 23 (1979):495-527; M. Stephen Weatherford, "Economic Conditions and Electoral Outcomes: Class Differences in the Political Response to Recession," *American Journal of Political Sci-*

ence 22(1978):917–938, and Weatherford, "The 1974 Recession and the Vote for Congress"; Gary C. Jacobson, "Reagan, Reaganomics, and Strategic Politics in 1982: A Test of Alternative Theories of Midterm Congressional Elections" (Paper delivered at the Annual Meeting of the American Political Science Association, Chicago, September 1–4, 1983); Alan I. Abramowitz, "Economic Conditions, Presidential Popularity, and Voting Behavior in Midterm Congressional Elections," *Journal of Politics* 47 (1985):31–43; D. Roderick Kiewiet, *Macroeconomics and Micropolitics* (Chicago: University of Chicago Press, 1983), Chapter 6; David W. Romero and Stephen J. Stambaugh, "Personal Economic Well-Being and the Individual Vote for Congress: A Pooled Analysis, 1980–1990," *Political Research Quarterly* 49 (1996):607–616.

11. Samuel Kernell, "Presidential Popularity and Negative Voting: An Alternative Explanation of the Midterm Congressional Decline of the President's Party," *American Political Science Review* 71 (1977):44–66.

12. Robert B. Arseneau and Raymond E. Wolfinger, "Voting Behavior in Congressional Elections" (Paper delivered at the Annual Meeting of the American Political Science Association, New Orleans, September 4–8, 1973); Candice J. Nelson, "The Effects of Incumbency on Voting in Congressional Elections, 1964–1974" (Paper delivered at the Annual Meeting of the American Political Science Association, San Francisco, September 2–5, 1975).

13. Morris P. Fiorina, *Retrospective Voting in American National Elections* (New Haven: Yale University Press, 1981), p. 165; Gary C. Jacobson, "Congressional Elections 1978: The Case of the Vanishing Challengers," in *Congressional Elections*, ed. Louis Sandy Maisel and Joseph Cooper (Beverly Hills: Sage Publications, 1981), p. 238; Jacobson, "Reagan, Reaganomics, and Strategic Politics in 1982, p. 16; Abramowitz, "Voting Behavior in Midterm Congressional Elections," p. 36; Gary C. Jacobson and Samuel Kernell, "National Forces in the 1986 U.S. House Elections," *Legislative Studies Quarterly* 15 (1990):74–82.

14. M. Margaret Conway and Mikel L. Wyckoff, "Vote Choice in the 1974 Congressional Elections: A Test of Competing Explanations" (Paper delivered at the Annual Meeting of the Midwest Political Science Association, Chicago, April 21–23, 1977); Arthur H. Miller and Richard Glass, "Economic Dissatisfaction and Electoral Choice" (Paper, Center for Political Studies, University of Michigan, 1977); Jack M. McLeod, Jane D. Brown, and Lee B. Becker, "Watergate and the 1974 Congressional Elections," *Public Opinion Quarterly* 41 (1977):181–195.

15. Fiorina, *Retrospective Voting*, p. 165; Eric M. Uslaner and M. Margaret Conway, "The Responsible Congressional Electorate: Watergate, the Economy, and Vote Choice in 1974," *American Political Science Review* 79 (1985):788–803; but see the comment on this article by Gary C. Jacobson and Samuel Kernell, "Controversy: The 1974 Midterm Election," *American Political Science Review* 80 (1986):591–592.

16. See Gary C. Jacobson and Samuel Kernell, *Strategy and Choice in Congressional Elections*, 2nd ed. (New Haven: Yale University Press, 1983), pp. 12–13.

17. Morris P. Fiorina, "Short- and Long-term Effects of Economic Conditions on Individual Voting Decisions," in *Contemporary Political Economy*, ed. D.A. Hibbs and H. Fassbender (Amsterdam: North Holland, 1981), pp. 73–100.
18. James A. Stimson, Michael B. MacKuen, and Robert S. Erikson, "Dynamic Representation," *American Political Science Review* 89 (1995):543–565.
19. Walter Dean Burnham, "Insulation and Responsiveness in Congressional Elections," *Political Science Quarterly* 90 (1975):411–435; Randall L. Calvert and John A. Ferejohn, "Coattail Voting in Recent Presidential Elections," *American Political Science Review* 77 (1983):407–419; John A. Ferejohn and Randall L. Calvert, "Presidential Coattails in Historical Perspective," *American Journal of Political Science* 28 (1984):127–146; George C. Edwards III, *Presidential Influence in Congress* (San Francisco: W.H. Freeman, 1980), pp. 74–75; Richard Born, "Reassessing the Decline of Presidential Coattails: U.S. House Elections, 1952–1980," *Journal of Politics* 46 (1984):60–79; James E. Campbell, "Predicting Seat Gains from Presidential Coattails," *American Journal of Political Science* 30 (1986):397–418; Jacobson, *Electoral Origins of Divided Government*, pp. 80–81; Gregory N. Flemming, "Presidential Coattails in Open-Seat Elections," *Legislative Studies Quarterly* 20 (1995):197–212.
20. Gary C. Jacobson, "Party Polarization in National Politics: The Electoral Connection," in *Congress and the President in a Partisan Era*, ed. Jon R. Bond and Richard Fleisher (Washington, DC: Congressional Quarterly Press, 2000), p. 8.
21. Ticket-splitting rates are of course higher in years with substantial independent or third-party presidential candidacies (1968, 1980, 1992, and 1996) if we include these candidates' supporters in the analysis. Such voters are forced to split their tickets if they vote in the House election, because there is no House candidate of their presidential favorites' party to vote for. Even if we include the Perot voters in the 1996 analysis, however, the incidence of ticket splitting is only 22 percent, tying 1988 for the lowest of any year since 1964.
22. For the actual equations, see the second, third, and fourth editions of this book, respectively.
23. Gary C. Jacobson, "Presidential Coattails in 1972," *Public Opinion Quarterly* 40 (1976):194–200; Calvert and Ferejohn, "Coattail Voting," p. 415.
24. Jacobson and Kernell, *Strategy and Choice*," p. 33.
25. Ibid., p. 33.
26. Ibid., pp. 49–59.
27. Ibid., pp. 27–29.
28. "Running Hard in Watergate's Shadow," *Congressional Quarterly Weekly Report* 32 (February 16, 1974):353; "Southern Republicans: Little Hope This Year," *Congressional Quarterly Weekly Report* 32 (October 26, 1974): 2959–2961.
29. Linda L. Fowler, "Candidate Perceptions of Electoral Coalitions: Limits and Possibilities" (Paper delivered at the Conference on Congressional Elections, Rice University and the University of Houston, Houston, January 10–12, 1980), p. 11; Jacobson and Kernell, *Strategy and Choice*, p. 32.

30. Jacobson, *Electoral Origins of Divided Government*, p. 73.
31. Jacobson, "Reversal of Fortune," p. 12.
32. For further evidence to these points, see Gary C. Jacobson, "Strategic Politicians and the Dynamics of U.S. House Elections, 1946-1986," *American Political Science Review* 83 (1989):775-793; Michael Berkman and James Eisenstein, "State Legislators as Congressional Candidates: The Effects of Prior Experience on Legislative Recruitment and Fundraising," *Political Research Quarterly* 52 (1999):481-498.
33. Jacobson, "Strategic Politicians," pp. 787-790; Jacobson, *Electoral Origins of Divided Government*, pp. 55-57; Gary Cox and Jonathan Katz, "Why Did the Incumbency Advantage in U.S. House Elections Grow? *Journal of Politics* 40 (May 1996):478-497.
34. V.O. Key, Jr. (with the assistance of Milton Cummings), *The Responsible Electorate* (Cambridge: Harvard University Press, 1966), p. 7.
35. Morris P. Fiorina, "Who Is Held Responsible? Further Evidence on the Hibbing-Alford Thesis," *American Journal of Political Science* 27 (1983):158-164; Kiewiet, *Macroeconomics and Micropolitics*, pp. 102-108.
36. This estimate is based on the strong linear relationship between the proportions of votes and seats won by parties in postwar House elections:

Percentage of seats won by Democrat $= -42.8 + 1.9 \times$ Percentage of votes
$(.14)$ won by Democrats

$R^2 = .87$ (standard errors are in parentheses)

37. Hibbs, "President Reagan's Mandate," p. 411: Jacobson, "Reagan, Reaganomics, and Strategic Politics in 1982," p. 5.
38. See also Gary C. Jacobson, "Party Organization and Distribution of Campaign Resources: Republicans and Democrats in 1982," *Political Science Quarterly* 100 (1985-1986):603-625.
39. Adam Clymer, "Campaign Costs Up Sharply in 1982," *New York Times*, April 3, 1983.
40. Jacobson, "Party Organization," pp. 616-621.
41. Ibid., p. 616.
42. Adam Clymer, "Campaign Funds Called a Key to Outcome of House Races," *New York Times*, November 5, 1982; Richard E. Cohen, "Giving Till It Hurts: 1982 Campaign Prompts New Look at Financing Races," *National Journal* (December 18, 1982): 2146.
43. Phil Duncan, "Wealthy and Well-Organized GOP Panel Eyes 1984 Elections," *National Journal* (July 2, 1983): 1351.
44. Benjamin Shore, "How Will the Race Change Congress? Not Much," *San Diego Union*, October 28, 1984; C5. See also Alan Ehrenhalt, "GOP Challengers Find PACs Wary This Year," *Congressional Quarterly Weekly Report* 42 (October 20, 1984):2763.
45. Phil Duncan, "House Campaigns Quiet as Few Seek to Run," *Congressional Quarterly Weekly Report* 42 (March 24, 1984):659.
46. "Trial Heats," *Public Opinion* (February/March, 1984):35.
47. Duncan, "House Campaigns Quiet," p. 659.
48. Ehrenhalt, "PACs Wary This Year," p. 2763.

49. Jacobson and Kernell, "National Forces in 1986," pp. 72-85.

50. Samuel Popkin, "Outlook on the Future and Presidential Voting: The 1988 Election and Concerns for the Next Generation" (Paper delivered at the Annual Meeting of the American Political Science Association, Washington, DC, September 1-4, 1988); "Optimism, Pessimism, and Public Policy," *Public Opinion* 11 (November/December 1988):51-55.

51. *The New York Times/CBS News Poll August National Survey* (July 31-August 3, 1988):10.

52. Popkin, "Outlook on the Future"; "Opinion Roundup," *Public Opinion* 11 (November/December 1988):36-37.

53. *The New York times/CBS News Poll Post-Election Survey* (November 10-16, 1988):14.

54. Federal Election Commission, "1990 Congressional Election Spending Drops to Low Point," news release, February 22, 1991.

55. See, for example, Nancy Gibbs, "Keep the Bums In," *Time* 136 (November 19, 1990): 32-42.

56. Deregulation freed savings banks to make risky—and sometimes fraudulent—investments with deposits that were insured by the federal government; many of the investments went sour, and taxpayers were left with a tab in the $100s of billions.

57. Gary C. Jacobson, "Congress: Unusual Year, Unusual Election," in *The Elections of 1992*, ed. Michael Nelson (Washington, DC: Congressional Quarterly Press, 1983), pp. 153-182.

58. John Petrocik, "Divided Government: Is It All in the Campaigns?" in *The Politics of Divided Government*, ed. Gary W. Cox and Samuel Kernell (Boulder, Colorado: Westview Press, 1991), pp. 20-30.

59. Jacobson, "Congress," p. 162-164.

60. *Los Angeles Times*, September 25, 1992, p. A22.

61. *New York Times*, April 2, 1992, p. A1.

62. Gary C. Jacobson and Michael A. Dimock, "Checking Out: The Impact of Bank Overdrafts on the 1992 House Elections," *American Journal of Political Science* 38 (1994): 601-624.

63. Gary C. Jacobson, *The Politics of Congressional Elections* (New York: HarperCollins, 1992), p. 239.

64. Keith Krehbiel, "Institutional and Partisan Sources of Gridlock: A Theory of Divided and Unified Government," *Journal of Theoretical Politics* 8 (1996):7-40.

65. *Los Angeles Times*, January 26, 1995, p. A25.

66. In 1992, 79 percent of the voters (in the national exit poll) thought the economy was in bad shape, and 62 percent of them voted for a Democrat for the House. In 1994, 75 percent said they were no better off financially than they had been two years ago; 57 percent thought the economy was still in bad shape, and 62 percent of this group voted for the Republican. See Gary Langer, "94 Vote: Republicans Seize the Reins of Discontent," ABC News Analysis, reported in *Hotline*, November 11, 1994.

67. In 1992, angry and dissatisfied voters had voted Democratic in House elections 56 percent to 44 percent, in 1994, they voted Republican, 64 percent to 36 percent; see Ibid.

68. Langer, "94 Vote"; *New York Times*, November 13, 1994; A15.

69. The 1988 district presidential vote was recomputed for each district to adjust for redistricting after 1990; the data are from Michael Barone and Grant Ujifusa, *The Almanac of American Politics 1994* (Washington, DC: National Journal, 1993).

70. Gary C. Jacobson, "The 1994 House Elections in Perspective," in *Midterm: the Elections of 1994 in Context*, ed. Philip A. Klinkner (Boulder, Co: Western Press, 1996), p. 8. Jacobson, "Reversal of Fortune"; James E. Campbell, "The Presidential Pulse and the 1994 Congressional Election," *Journal of Politics* 59 (1997):830-857.

71. According to a survey sponsored by the Christian Coalition, 33 percent of the 1994 voters were "religious conservatives," up from 24 percent in 1992 and 18 percent in 1988; see *Congressional Quarterly Weekly Report* 52 (November 19, 1994):3364. In the 1994 exit poll, 38 percent identified themselves as "conservatives," compared with 30 percent in 1992; see *Hotline*, November 12, 1994.

72. The standard deviation of the interelection vote swing across districts between 1992 and 1994 was 7.8 percentage points, compared to an average of 8.8 percentage points for the previous ten elections.

73. Jacobson, "1994 House Elections," p. 15.

74. Ibid., p. 14.

75. Ibid.

76. Against incumbent Democrats in Republican-learning districts, 49 percent (19 of 39) of Republican challengers who spent in excess of $300,000 won, whereas only 6 percent (2 of 32) of the challengers who spent less than this sum managed to defeat the incumbent. If analysis is further confined to Democratic incumbents who supported the Clinton administration on at least two of three key votes, the respective percentages are 52 percent (14 of 27) and 13 percent (2 of 15).

77. George Hager, "GOP Ready to Take Debt Limit to the Brink and Beyond," *Congressional Quarterly Weekly Report* 53 (September 23, 1995): 2865.

78. Gary C. Jacobson, "The 105th Congress: Unprecedented and Unsurprising," in *The Elections of 1996*, ed. Michael Nelson (Washington, DC: Congressional Quarterly Press, 1997), pp. 144-147.

79. Jonathan D. Salant, "House Republicans Stray from the 'Contract' Terms," *Congressional Quarterly Weekly Report* 54 (July 6, 1996): 1929-1933.

80. According to the national exit poll, voters who made their decisions in the last few days before the election went for Dole over Clinton, 40 percent to 35 percent; see *Los Angeles Times*, November 7, 1996, p. 22. An additional 1 percent of the vote would have put the Democratic candidate over 50 percent in eleven House districts; an additional 2 percent would have put them over the top in twenty-two districts. For additional evidence of party balancing in 1996, see Charles E. Smith, Jr., Robert D. Brown, John M. Bruce, and L. Marvin Overby, "Party Balancing and Voting for Congress in the 1996 National Election," *American Journal of Political Science* 43 (1999):737-764.

81. The Democrats picked up seats in 1934 during the New Deal realignment; both parties added seats in 1902 when the House grew by 29 seats,

but the president's Republicans picked up fewer than the opposition Democrats and so were relatively weaker after the election.

82. Bernard Sanders, the lone independent who normally votes with the Democrats, was also reelected.

83. Gary C. Jacobson, "Impeachment Politics in the 1998 Congressional Elections," *Political Science Quarterly* 114 (Spring, 1999): 33–40.

84. The Gallup Poll, October 9-12, 1998 at http://www.gallup.com/POLL _ARCHIVES/981012.htm

85. Gary C. Jacobson, "Public Opinion and the Impeachment of Bill Clinton," *British Elections and Parties Review* 10 (2000), in press.

86. Jeffrey Katz and Dan Carney, "Clinton's Latest, Worst Troubles Put His Whole Agenda on Hold," *Congressional Quarterly Weekly Report* 56 (January 24, 1998): 165.

87. Jacobson, "Impeachment Politics," p. 43.

88. Dan Carney with Carroll J. Doherty, "GOP Struggles to Find Strategy to Deal with Starr Fallout," *Congressional Quarterly Weekly Report* 56 (March 14, 1998): 643-644.

89. "Thrust and Parry: Gingrich v. Clinton," *Congressional Quarterly Weekly Report* 56 (May 2, 1998): 1128.

90. Karen Foerstel, "Clinton's Address Fails to Defuse Ticking Time Bomb of Starr Report," *Congressional Quarterly Weekly Report* 56 (August 22, 1998): 2281.

91. Jacobson, "Public Opinion and Impeachment."

92. Ibid.

93. Ibid.

94. Ibid.

95. Sung to the tune of "Twinkle, Twinkle Little Star," the lyrics were:

> Twinkle, twinkle, Kenneth Starr,
> Now we see how brave you are.
> We could not see which way to go
> If you did not lead us so,
> Twinkle, twinkle Kenneth Starr
> Now we see how brave you are.

New York Times, November 5, 1998, p. B16.

96. Alan I. Abramowitz, "It's Monica, Stupid: Voting Behavior in the 1998 Midterm Election" (Paper presented at the Annual Meeting of the American Political Science Association, Atlanta, September 2-5, 1999), p. 5.

97. Ibid., pp. 6-8.

98. According to Federal Election Commission data, the six successful challengers spent between $954,693 and $1.59 million each.

99. A favorable year is defined as one in which the challenger's party increased its share of the national two-party vote for House candidates by at least 3 percentage points; by this criterion, 1974, 1982, and 1996 were favorable to Democrats, 1980, 1984, and 1994 were favorable to Republicans.

100. Thomas E. Mann and Norman J. Ornstein, "Sending a Message: Voters and Congress in 1982," in *The American Elections of 1982*, ed. Thomas E.

Mann and Norman J. Ornstein (Washington, DC: American Enterprise Institute for Public Policy Research, 1983), p. 136.
101. Jacobson and Kernell, *Strategy and Choice*, p. 82.
102. See also James E. Campbell and Joe A. Sumners, "Presidential Coattails in Senate Elections," *American Political Science Review* 84 (1990):513–524; Campbell and Sumners argue that presidential coattails can be credited with twelve Republican Senate victories since 1972, including four in 1980.
103. The quality of challengers makes an important difference in Senate as well as House elections; see Peverill Squire, "Challengers in Senate Elections," *Legislative Studies Quarterly* 14 (1989):531–547; Gary C. Jacobson and Raymond E. Wolfinger, "Information and Voting in California Senate Elections," *Legislative Studies Quarterly* 14 (1989):509–529.
104. Rob Gurwitt, "Voters Restore Democrats to Senate Control," *Congressional Quarterly Weekly Report* 44 (November 8, 1986):2811–2814; see also Patricia A. Hurley, "Partisan Representation, Realignment, and the Senate in the 1980s" (Paper delivered at the Annual Meeting of the Midwest Political Science Association, Chicago, April 14–16, 1988).
105. Bob Benenson, "Republicans' Net Loss: One Seat and Many Expectations," *Congressional Quarterly Weekly Report* 48 (November 10, 1990): 3824–3825.
106. Jacobson, "Congress," p. 173.
107. Karen Foerstel, "Senate: GOP on the March," *Congressional Quarterly Weekly Report* 56 (October 24, 1998): 2868–2872.
108. Abramowitz, "Monica," p. 8.

CHAPTER SEVEN

Elections and the Politics of Congress

C ongressional elections matter because the U.S. Congress matters. Though often overshadowed in the popular imagination by forceful presidents, Congress retains so much of its institutional autonomy that it remains, in Morris P. Fiorina's apt phrase, the "Keystone of the Washington Establishment."[1] Any lingering doubts have been laid to rest by what has happened since the 1994 elections; Republicans advanced their agenda far more effectively controlling Congress but not the White House than they ever did controlling the White House but not Congress. Congress's performance as an institution therefore has a profound effect on how and how well we are governed.

The workings of Congress, its strengths and weaknesses as a governing institution, are in turn intimately connected to how its members win and hold office. This chapter examines how the system of electoral politics depicted in the first six chapters affects the workings of the House and Senate. Its central point is simple: How members win and hold office powerfully affects both the internal organization of the houses of Congress and the kind of legislation they produce.

The Constitution authorizes the Senate and House to set the rules governing organization and procedure by majority vote. Majorities naturally chose rules that they think will make it easier to achieve their goals. A primary goal for most members is to keep their jobs. But winning reelection is by no means the only objective; making what they think is good public policy, gaining respect and authority in Washington, and, for some, advancing to higher office also make the list.[2] Furthermore, both the desire for reelection and the strategies for pursuing it vary among members and between the parties as well. New members and new majorities with a different mix of goals thus alter congressional procedures and practices to pursue them more effectively. The House and, to a lesser extent, the Senate operate very differently in Republican hands.

One reason that the House and Senate are in Republican hands is the accumulated damage inflicted on congressional Democrats by the unresolved tension between their individual and collective pursuits. This tension is also behind much of the long-term decline in public respect and affection for members of Congress regardless of party. Although members win and hold seats largely through their own personal efforts, it is what they achieve collectively, not individually, that shapes their parties' reputations and the public's level of esteem for Congress. The problem is that the reputations of the parties and of Congress are, for their members, collective goods. Everyone in the majority benefits if their party builds a reputation for governing well, and all members benefit from belonging to a powerful and respected legislative body. Members enjoy these benefits, however, regardless of whether or not they contribute to their achievement.

The electoral needs of individual members and the practices required to make the House and Senate effective governing institutions often generate conflicting demands. The potential cost of ignoring the former is specific and personal: loss of office. The potential cost of ignoring the latter is diffuse and collective: an imperceptible marginal weakening of authority or decline in party stature. It is obvious where the balance of incentives lies. David Mayhew spelled out the danger in his classic book, *Congress: The Electoral Connection*, more than twenty-five years ago: "efficient pursuit of electoral goals by members gives no guarantee of institutional survival. Quite the contrary. It is not too much to say that if all members did nothing but pursue their electoral goals, Congress would decay or collapse."[3] The same holds for the congressional parties.

Congress has not collapsed, though many observers—not all of them Republicans—might argue that it decayed during the two subsequent decades of Democratic rule. Because its members do care about more than reelection, they adopt institutional structures and processes designed to harness individual energies to collectively important ends. These institutional devices necessarily reflect their origins. Under Democratic rule, they were designed to balance conflicting demands for collective effectiveness and individual autonomy, strong leadership and broad participation, coherent policy and particularized benefits. It is not surprising that they often failed to work as expected, were subject to continual criticism from one quarter or another, and were revised from time to time.

The Republican majority assuming power in 1995 faced many of the same tradeoffs, though its members clearly weighed the elements in the mix somewhat differently. During their first year in power, Republicans took great pains to show that they would do things differently, with far more emphasis on collective effectiveness. Still, the electoral processes that put them in power were not so different from those that elected Democratic majorities over the years, so Republican incumbents ended up facing many of the same dilemmas and resolving them in ways not very different from those used by Democrats.

The literature detailing how electoral considerations have shaped and reshaped congressional action is exceptionally rich; I can only touch on some of the highlights here, but they are more than sufficient to make the point. One important aspect of congressional organization intimately tied to electoral politics—the office, staff, travel, and communications resources enjoyed by all members—has already been discussed (see Chapter 3). It therefore requires no further mention other than to note that the new Republican House majority's zeal to reduce House staff and expenses did not extend to personal staff or the franking privilege, which they declined to cut.[4] We can begin, then, with a brief consideration of Congress' two most central institutional pillars: the party and committee systems.

THE CONGRESSIONAL PARTIES

The tension between individual electoral pursuits and the behavior required for Congress to function effectively is brought into sharpest focus in the congressional parties. Parties are the primary institutional devices for organizing collective action. They are responsible for producing policies that bolster the party's collective reputation in the face of persistent incentives for individual members to ride free on the efforts of others.[5] Moreover, the decentralized and specialized legislative system described in the next section could not work effectively without some means for coordinating the activities of its diverse parts. The fragmented activity must be reduced to some order, the diverse membership welded together from time to time into majority coalitions, if Congress is to share in governing. This is what the congressional parties are for—they work to counteract the centrifugal tendencies inherent in the committee system as well as in the candidate-centered system of electoral politics.

Members of Congress recognize that the parties make a vital contribution to partisan and institutional achievement, and not a little of the deference accorded party leaders derives from this knowledge.[6] Still, party leaders face the basic reality that members keep their jobs by pleasing voters, not the congressional party. Leaders can count on loyalty only to the degree that members believe that the ultimate payoff in votes is higher for loyalty than for defection. During the era of Democratic rule, electoral incentives raised formidable barriers to party influence. Members of the Republican majority initially staked their electoral futures squarely on their party's collective performance, and in 1995 they were more responsive to party leadership and discipline than any congressional party since the early part of the century. Subsequently, electoral considerations and internal divisions have since eroded Republican unity somewhat, but the general level of party discipline has remained high.

Democratic leaders had to contend with a fractious membership whose differences were rooted in the diverse constituencies they were elected to represent. Hence they considered it their job not so much to compel members to toe a party line as to discover it, to find and promote policies that party members could willingly support because doing so enhanced their own local reputations as well as their party's image. They were quick to recognize electoral necessity; members were expected to "vote the district first" when conflicts with the party's position arose, and they were encouraged to serve their constituents diligently in order to keep the seat for the party. There was nothing odd about this, for Democratic leaders were chosen to serve their party's members as they wished to be served. Such permissiveness simply reflected a widely acknowledged necessity arising from the diversity of the party's national coalition and its members notions about how to win reelection.

The Democrats were well aware of the costs as well as the benefits of tolerant party leadership. Thus in the 1970s when the Democratic Caucus introduced changes in the committee system (outlined in the next section) that fragmented congressional authority even further, it simultaneously adopted changes designed to strengthen the party. The speaker, who leads the majority party in the House, was given effective control of the Rules Committee, which directs the flow of legislation coming to the floor of the House, and dominant influence on the caucus's Steering and Policy Committee, which, among other things, makes committee assignments. The speaker was also authorized to appoint ad hoc committees to manage specific pieces of legislation, allowing sensitive and controversial bills to be handled by a committee whose members were chosen for their willingness to cooperate. The party's whip organization was enlarged substantially, and the custom of organizing separate task forces to help push through legislation of special importance to the party took root. These changes gave the party leaders more tools to coordinate and combine the work of an increasingly fragmented body.

Democrats could afford to strengthen their party's capacity to act collectively because the division that had threatened to split the New Deal Coalition from the beginning—between northern liberals and southern conservatives—had begun to fade. The southern Democrats' ideological distinctiveness was gradually undermined by the in-migration of northerners, industrial development, the movement of conservative southern white voters from the Democratic into the Republican camp, and the Voting Rights Act, which brought African-American voters into southern Democratic electorates. As the electoral constituencies of Democrats became more similar across regions, their electoral interests became more consonant. The result was greater party cohesion permitting stronger leadership.[7] House Democrats also accepted stronger leadership in the 1980s because they recognized the need to act collectively to make a public record as they contended with hostile Republican presidents and, from 1981 to 1987, a Republican Senate. Still, Democratic leaders rarely found it easy to assemble legislative coalitions on major issues.

Republicans delegated much more authority to their leaders when they took over the House in 1995. Unified by the party's "Contract with America" as well as by their shared conservative ideology, House Republicans made Newt Gingrich the most powerful speaker since the revolt against Joseph Cannon in 1910. Meeting in caucus, the Republicans ignored seniority in appointing committee chairs, ratifying without dissent the slate proposed by Gingrich. Gingrich was also given a strong say in committee assignments, which he used to stack committees with junior allies firmly committed to the contract.

House Republicans gave their leader an unusually strong hand because they believed that his strategy, embodied in the contract but also in the guidance he had given so many of them through GOPAC, had given them their majority, and that their performance on the promises in the contract would determine whether they would keep it. Although the contract's influence on voters was small (see Chapter 6), its impact on the Republican House was enormous, for its promise of quick, focused action made strong leadership indispensable. It did not, however, guarantee that the speaker would always get his way; among the most zealous of the new Republican representatives, commitment to the spirit of the contract was even more powerful than commitment to Gingrich, and they resisted every compromise on the ground that voters would punish them for selling out if they did not. Gingrich had to squash a backbench coup in 1997 and eventually resigned from the speakership and Congress after the Republicans' loss of House seats in 1998 was blamed on his mishandling of the impeachment issue. Still, Republicans retained a comparatively high level of party discipline under new leadership; their near-unanimous vote to impeach Bill Clinton in December 1998 was one important consequence (see Chapter 8).

Even the Senate's tradition of unbridled individualism was disturbed by the winds of change flowing from 1994. In July of 1995 the Republican majority imposed six-year term limits on committee chairs and voted to adopt a formal legislative agenda at the start of each Congress. Committee chairs would also henceforth be subject to ratification by a secret vote of the Republican Conference (all Republican members meeting in caucus). These changes (and several unsuccessful proposals) were intended to make senior members more responsive to party majorities, making it easier for the party to act collectively. In the 104th Congress, even Senate Republicans were acting as if they had an expanded personal stake in their party's collective performance.[8]

THE COMMITTEE SYSTEMS

Most routine legislative activity and all administrative oversight—two major institutional functions of Congress—take place in committees and subcommittees. Authority in Congress is delegated to committees and subcommittees to encourage specialization. The number, variety, and complexity of issues that come before Congress make it essential that members develop specialized knowledge of specific policy areas. This requires a division of labor. Each member needs to focus his or her legislative attention narrowly, because none has the time or energy to become thoroughly knowledgeable about more than a few complex issues and questions. The alternative to developing specialized expertise in Congress is surrender of power to experts in the White House, the administrative agencies, or the private sector. A decentralized system of standing committees with fixed jurisdictions is part of Congress's organizational strategy for survival as a significant policy-making institution.

The committee system certainly serves the collective interests of Congress. But as it actually functions, it also serves the electoral needs of individual members and, at the same time, works to limit the damage this may do to the collective performance of Congress. Some committees do little legislative work while providing a platform for position-taking: making statements and symbolic gestures aimed at pleasing constituent groups. Committees charged with investigating consumer fraud, corruption, or cost overruns on defense contracts are examples; they permit members to speak out bravely against fraud, corruption, and waste. So are committees dealing with issues having a strong ideological tinge, like the House Economic and Educational Opportunities Committee or those dealing with foreign affairs.

Seats on other committees, such as Banking and Financial Services in the House, are noted for attracting campaign contributions from organized interests. Other committees generate benefits for specific states, districts, groups, even individuals: public works, federal installations, development grants, tax breaks, special immigration bills, and the like. Opportunities for doing things for constituents and supporters, for which members can then claim credit, are exploited at every opportunity.

The further subdivision of committees into subcommittees also provides opportunities for claiming credit. "Whatever else it may be, the quest for specialization in Congress is a quest for credit. Every member can aspire to occupy a part of at least one piece of policy turf small enough so that he can claim personal responsibility for some of the things that happen on it."[9] Writing in the early 1970s, Mayhew observed that, "the House may have to create more subcommittees to satisfy its members."[10] That is exactly what it did; the number of standing subcommittees grew from 120 to 151 between 1971 and 1975.

The creation of more subcommittees was only one of many changes in House organization made in the early 1970s. These changes added up to a major transformation in the way Congress did its business. Although they had varied origins, among the most important were developments in the electoral politics of Congress. One essential factor was the influx of a large number of new members who were energetic purveyors of the kind of entrepreneurial politics discussed in Chapter 3. An uptick in voluntary retirements, combined with the 1974 election, which swept seventy-eight new Democrats into the House, produced a host of fresh faces in the early 1970s.

These newcomers were markedly different from their elders. They were more adept at, and more comfortable with, the new styles of electoral politics. This was especially true of Democrats who had replaced Republicans. Their precarious electoral position inspired imaginative cultivation of constituencies and aggressively independent behavior in Washington.[11] They entered Congress at a time when party coalitions were in disrepair and party organizations were moribund in many places. Most of them had come of political age during a decade of assassination, violent protest, the Vietnam War, environmental alarms, energy shortages, political scandal, and a decline in respect for authority of all kinds, but especially that of political institutions and leaders. Like other Americans of their generation, they were typically better educated, more independent of party, and less awed by age and authority than were their predecessors. They shared the conviction that they were elected to lead, not follow.

It is scarcely surprising that this generation refused to wait around docilely until time, electoral security, and the seniority system elevated them to positions of power in Congress. Instead, they helped alter the rules to assure themselves of a solid piece of legislative turf early in their careers. The large classes of new House Democrats provided the votes that effectively undermined the seniority system, dispersed legislative authority from the committee to the subcommittee level, solidified the power of subcommittee chairs, and distributed subcommittee chairs and seats on desirable subcommittees more widely. All of these changes were enacted over the protests of a majority of senior members, who naturally stood to lose much of the power and influence they had patiently accumulated playing by the old rules. Junior members were the chief beneficiaries.[12]

These changes served the immediate needs of individual members, but at the price of fragmenting authority and eroding the Democratic majority's (and Congress's) ability to make coherent national policy. The collective interests of Democratic members were therefore threatened. The threat was met, as we have seen, by changes designed to strengthen the congressional party.

During the 1980s, the decentralizing trend reversed as the pressures of budgetary politics, generated by the growing budget deficits and conflicts between Republican presidents and the Democratic House (and sometimes Senate) majorities, compelled more centralized negotiation of legislative packages. Committee and subcommittee leaders lost influence relative to party leaders, and the number of subcommittees was cut back to about 114 by the 103rd Congress. Committee and subcommittee power fell even more sharply when the new Republican majority revised committee rules to make sure that the agenda outlined in its contract would get swift action. The new rules gave committee chairs greater control over subcommittees by authorizing them to appoint all subcommittee chairs and control the work of all the majority's committee staff. The chairs themselves were, as I noted earlier, subordinated to the speaker. All of these changes served to give the Republican majority more centralized control over its committees than any House majority had exercised since the early years of the 20th century.

The victorious Republicans also rearranged the committee system more to their liking. One of the central themes of their 1994 campaigns was that, under the Democrats, Congress had become bloated and sclerotic. Pruning the committee system was one way of delivering on their promise of reform. They abolished three committees that had catered mainly to Democratic constituencies (Post Office and Civil Service, District of Columbia, and Merchant Marine and Fisheries) by transferring their jurisdictions to other committees. Proposals to disband the Small Business and Veterans Affairs committees failed, however, in response to pleas from their much more Republican clienteles—business and veterans' groups. The number of subcommittees was reduced to fewer than ninety. The Republicans also slashed committee staff by one-third, a politically painless move because it affected only Democratic staffers (the majority party hires two-thirds of committee staff, so the Republicans' newly expanded allotment made it unnecessary for them to fire any of their own).[13]

MAKING POLICY

Particularism

Electoral politics shapes the substance of policy as well as the rules and structures governing the processes by which it is made. Indeed, virtually everything Congress does is permeated by electoral concerns. Electoral incentives establish patterns of congressional attention and responsiveness and have a profound effect on who wins and who loses in the competition for favorable government decisions.

The most notorious example is the traditional interest members have shown in policies that produce particularized benefits.[14] Electoral logic inspires members to promote narrowly targeted programs, projects, and tax breaks for constituents and supporting groups without worrying about their impact on spending or revenues. Recipients notice and appreciate such specific and identifiable benefits and show their gratitude to the legislator responsible at election time. Because the benefits come at the expense of general revenues, no one's share of the cost of any specific project or tax break is large enough to notice. It thus makes political sense for members to pursue local or group benefits that are paid for nationally even if the costs clearly outweigh the benefits. Conversely, there is no obvious payoff for opposing any particular local or group benefit, because the savings are spread so thinly among taxpayers that no one notices.

The influence of Congress's fondness for particularized benefits goes beyond public works and tax breaks. Virtually any proposal will attract more support if the benefits it confers can be sliced up and allocated in identifiable packages to individual states and districts. Since everyone in Washington knows this, policies are deliberately designed to distribute particularized benefits broadly even when this makes no objective sense. If the original proponents of a program do not make the necessary adjustments, Congress will do it for them. Douglas Arnold offers some examples:

> The idea behind model cities was to create a demonstration program pouring massive federal funds into a handful of troubled cities. Congress transformed it completely by providing for 150 cities, making small cities eligible, and limiting any state's share to 15 percent of the total funds. Bureaucrats then selected the cities strategically, for maximum political effect, spreading the benefits among as many of the program's congressional supporters as possible, even selecting a handful of villages with populations under 5,000. Similarly, a water and sewer program (1965) conceived to help rapidly growing areas was transformed so that all areas were eligible. The Appalachian regional development programs (and most other economic development programs) have been broadened to include less distressed areas. The poverty program (1964), conceived as an experiment that would concentrate funds in pockets of poverty, evolved into a program with benefits spread thinly across the country. The list could go on.[15]

Some baneful consequences of particularism are clear from these examples. Resources are not concentrated where they are needed most (or where they can be used most efficiently by any objective criterion). They are wasted and their impact is diluted. Grandly conceived programs emerge in a form that often ensures that they will fail to achieve their objectives, feeding doubts that the federal government can do anything well. Individual members benefit, but at the expense of the reputations of their party—in this case, the Democrats— and Congress more generally.

Arnold identifies similar problems in the formulas that allocate funds under categorical grant programs. After studying the 140 or so formulas then in use, his "most striking discovery is how infrequently formulas are constructed around merit criteria."[16] He found that programs

> ignore legitimate differences in demand. The program whose purpose it is to make railroad crossings safer hands out funds under a formula that counts population, area, and postal-route mileage, but not railroad crossings. Law enforcement grants reflect population, not the incidence of crime. Hunter safety grants ignore the concentration of hunters in rural areas. Urban mass transit grants reflect urban population and density, but not how many people actually use mass transit. New York, a city built around mass transit, receives a subsidy of two cents per transit passenger, while Grand Rapids, a product of the automobile, reaps forty-five cents per passenger.[17]

The search for equitable formulas follows a consistent path. The House prefers formulas using criteria of population; the Senate views things from the perspective of equality among states. The compromise solution is to use the population criterion, but with a minimum and maximum allocation for each state:

> The ceilings usually affect only the largest two or three states and thus do little to diminish House majorities. The floors, which benefit perhaps a dozen small states, contribute generously to Senate majorities. These simple maneuvers, though difficult to defend on policy grounds, consistently yield large, stable majorities.[18]

The fundamental problem with particularized benefits is, of course, that Congress is forever tempted to overproduce them. Individual members gain politically by logrolling, supporting each other's projects or tax breaks in return for support for their own. But when everyone follows such an individually productive strategy, all may end up in worse shape politically when shackled with collective blame for the aggregate consequences. Spending rises, revenues fall, the deficit grows, inefficient government programs proliferate, and the opposition attacks the logrolling coalition—in practice, the majority party—for wastefulness and incompetence.

Attacks on the traffic in particularized benefits, under the more familiar pejorative label "pork," are routinely included in indictments of Congress. In reality, spending for traditional pork barrel projects has been a small and diminishing part of the federal budget for years, and they contributed relatively little to the large deficits of the 1980s and 1990s. As symbols of "waste," however, pork barrel projects are irresistible; witness, for example, the ridicule heaped on a 1991 budget line allocating $500,000 to build a small interpretive center around the North Dakota birthplace of bandleader Lawrence Welk to honor the Volga German immigrant community from which he sprang.[19]

Many of the Republicans first elected in the 1990s portrayed themselves as scourges of pork, but few of them refused to support local projects that would benefit their constituents. For example, Enid Green Waldholtz of Utah, while celebrating her part in a vote to balance the budget, circumvented a Transportation Appropriations Subcommittee rule against earmarked highway projects to secure a $5 million grant for work on Interstate 15 in Salt Lake City.[20] George Nethercutt, who had upset Speaker Tom Foley in 1994, fought hard to spare a $436,000 wheat research facility in his Washington district that had been targeted by Republican budget cutters. And Greg Ganske of Iowa fought to continue funding for local mass transit and recreational projects initiated by an incumbent he had tagged a wasteful spender and defeated in 1994. As Ganske put it, "I see my primary role as trying to [help] government be more fiscally responsible than it has been in the past," but "it's also part of a congressman's job to represent his district."[21] Exactly.

Even when stringent budget constraints limit potential for pork, members care very much about snaring a share of whatever is available. During the 104th Congress, the best opportunity came in military spending, the one area where Republicans wanted to spend more than the Clinton administration. Members made the most of it, adding, for example, projects not requested by the military to the military construction bill for fiscal 1996. When Ed Royce of

California, a self-described "porkbuster," sought to cut $10.4 million earmarked for construction of a new physical fitness center at the Bremerton Puget Sound Naval Shipyard, he was pointedly reminded of his own plea to the chair of the House National Security Military Research and Development Subcommittee for a local project not requested by the Pentagon: "Could you see your way fit to put $34 million in this year's bill, because it will really help me out back in my district?"[22]

With the budget finally back in balance in 1998, members of both houses and both parties reveled in the opportunity provided by authorization of a six-year, $217.9 billion surface transportation bill to deliver particularized benefits to their districts and states. The House version of the bill contained more than 1,500 designated highway and bridge projects, the Senate's version, about 300.[23]

Serving the Organized

Another important consequence of electoral politics is that Congress serves the vocal, organized, and active.[24] The system naturally favors any politically attentive group that is present in significant numbers in a large number of states or districts. The best examples are veterans (widely distributed, well organized) and Social Security recipients (widely distributed, large numbers, consistent voters). Large numbers are not, however, essential for groups to be influential. Organization and money also matter. It is easy to exaggerate the threat that PACs pose to democracy,[25] but their electoral importance is undeniable, and it would be surprising if their political clout were not proportionate. They need not "buy" members with their contributions to be effective. Some of the most successful groups—the National Rifle Association (zealous opponents of gun-control legislation) and anti-abortionists are examples—win by the implicit threat to finance and work for the opponents of members who do not support their positions. A few instances where such groups have helped to defeat seemingly entrenched incumbents are sufficient to keep most members representing districts where such groups are a force from taking them on.

The prospect of being targeted by any group with formidable campaign resources is unsettling; most members prefer to keep a low profile, avoiding votes that consistently offend active, well-organized interests. During the 1970s, for example, Environmental Action, a conservation lobbying group, compiled and publicized a list of the "Dirty Dozen," twelve congressmen who had (by Environmental Action's standards) bad records on environmental issues and who seemed vulnerable. Over five elections, twenty-four of the fifty-two who made the Dirty Dozen list were defeated. A consultant who worked on the campaigns claimed that the tactic "was very effective at making congressmen think twice about certain votes. There were numerous examples of members or their staff calling and saying 'Is the congressman close to being on the list?' or 'Is this vote going to be used to determine the list?'"[26] The League of Conservation Voters (LCV) revived the tactic in 1996, again with considerable success. Seven of the twelve incumbents initially targeted were eventually defeated, as were nine of their "baker's dozen" of thirteen targeted in 1998. The tactic's potential was underlined by the reaction of Bob Dornan, a flamboyant conservative with a career LCV score of about 10 on a 100-point scale, to being put on the list. "In my heart," he confessed, "I'm a Greenpeace kind of guy."[27]

Keeping a low profile to avoid becoming a target became more difficult after the congressional reforms of the 1970s. Rule changes intended to open congressional activities to greater public scrutiny worked; the action became more visible, with more public meetings and more recorded votes. Members were thereby exposed to more pressure from interest and constituency groups. Lobbyists were quick to take advantage; there was a notable increase in the sophistication and effectiveness of Washington lobbyists. Shrewd interest groups learned to combine their work in Washington with work at the grass roots, organizing a stream of messages from the district that, at the very least, encourage members to listen attentively to the pitch made by the group's Washington agent. Conducting such campaigns has become easier with the spread of modern communications technology and the emergence of professionals who organize grass-roots campaigns for a living—if a group has the money to pay for them.

The growth of interest group activity, combined with the expanding financial role of PACs, has transformed Congressional lobbying. Raymond Bauer, Ithiel de Sola Pool, and Lewis A. Dexter's classic study of lobbying in the 1950s described a process dominated by insiders. It was mainly a matter of friends talking to friends. Lobbyists worked through allies in Congress, encouraging them to pursue legislative projects that they were already inclined to favor by helping them do the necessary work. Opponents were ignored; pressure tactics in the insulated social world of Congress were felt to be counterproductive. Not surprisingly, members regarded lobbying as basically benign, lobbyists as a resource to be exploited.[28]

Few members would take such a sanguine view today. Insiders still lobby in the old way, although most of them now supplement their work with outside activities. Some PACs have been created at the behest of Washington lobbyists, who view them as a way to make inside work more effective.[29] But they have been joined by the host of activists and organizations working to influence Congress from the outside. An effective outside strategy does not rely on maintaining friendly relations with incumbents, so outsiders are free to use pressure tactics, including explicit threats of electoral revenge against members who oppose their views.

All of these developments reduced members' political maneuverability. The visibility of action and the growing capacity of organized groups to raise electoral trouble make it harder to engage in a politics of accommodation and compromise. It is not surprising that congressional enthusiasm for sunshine waned in the 1980s and that much of the important legislative action moved back behind closed doors, or that House Democrats became increasingly inclined to adopt more restrictive rules on bills sent to the floor. Nor is it surprising that Republican leaders, having seen how health lobbies mobilized public opposition to help them kill the Clinton health care reforms in 1994, provided only the sketchiest information on their Medicare reforms before bringing them to a vote in 1995.

Immobility

Congress has been known for years to be an exceptionally deliberate deliberative body. As Nelson Polsby once put it, Congress is not "designed to be fast on its 1,070 feet."[30] Its mode of operation, rooted in the system of electoral politics by which its members are chosen, obviously encourages delay and usually frustrates anyone seeking quick and decisive action. Fenno points out that this is not always a bad thing. His persuasive example is the process by which Richard Nixon was forced from office. Lengthy hearings, first by the Ervin Committee in the Senate, then by the House Judiciary Committee considering articles of impeachment, worked slowly but surely to build up a consensus among both political elites and the mass public that Nixon had indeed violated the law (not to mention basic standards of political decency) and should go. What might have been a traumatic source of sharp political conflict—the resignation of a sitting president for the first time in history—was, in the end, greeted with widespread approval and relief. The process as well as the evidence it publicized was essential to making Nixon's expulsion from the White House legitimate.[31]

What is a virtue under some conditions is a defect under others. And there is a distinction between a slow process that builds to consensus and the kind of immobility displayed by Congress in recent years in the face of serious national problems (the energy crisis in the late 1970s, and the budget deficits in the 1980s and 1990s are notorious examples). Even under normal conditions, Congress is weakened by the reality that the work members must do to make the institution strong pays few electoral dividends. Hard legislative work is largely invisible to the folks back home; a successful legislative career is no guarantee of electoral success. Members' resources of time and energy, even staff, are limited; the time spent on legislative work cannot be spent shoring up constituency support. Senators and representatives must recognize the possibility that the more diligently they participate in governing, the greater their electoral risk. The defeat in 1994 of Speaker Tom Foley, along with the chairmen of the Ways and Means, Judiciary, Intelligence committees and a key Appropriations subcommittee, underline the danger.

The new Republican House majority organized itself to act quickly after 1994, but it had to contend with a Senate made up of Republicans who had not signed any contract and enough Democrats to kill any legislation by filibuster if they stuck together, a Democrat in the White House, and their own internal divisions. Although the House met its promised target by voting on every item in the contract within 100 days, their action did not produce any immediate change in important national policies, and work on the 1996 budget, keystone of the entire Republican agenda, dragged on (through two governmental shutdowns in a failed showdown with Bill Clinton) until nearly six months into the new fiscal year. With diminished House margins after 1996 and 1998, the Republicans have found it difficult to reach internal agreement on both policy and strategies for dealing with Bill Clinton, and the Republican Congress has not been notably more nimble than its Democratic predecessors.

Symbolism

The electoral politics of Congress also encourage activity that is heavy on symbolism regardless of its effect on actual results. Members seek (and get) credit for taking the proper positions, making agreeable speeches, and casting correct votes without these actions having any necessary connection to real policy decisions. Mayhew makes the point succinctly: "We can all point to a good many instances in which congressmen seem to have gotten into trouble by being on the *wrong* side in a roll call vote, but who can think of one where a member got into trouble by being on the *losing* side?"[32] Offering as an example a vote on a bill to stop forced busing to integrate schools, he notes that "congressmen had every reason to worry about whether they were voting on the right side but no reason to worry about what passed or was implemented."[33] They are held responsible for taking the right position, not for being successful. Again, it is obvious where the incentives lie. In the short run, making good public policy is rewarded no better than merely talking about it, and it consumes a good deal more time, energy, and staff resources.

Yet in the long run, empty symbolism erodes Congress's public support. Although individual members need only vote "right" to avoid personal blame, their collective reputation suffers when they fail to deliver what the public wants. A profoundly disaffected public eventually punished incumbents of both parties in 1992 and incumbent Democrats in 1994. Since then, manifest accomplishments, including a booming economy, a balanced federal budget, and favorable social trends have lightened the public mood and enhanced Congress's institutional reputation, a trend only partially offset by the Republicans' unpopular effort to impeach and remove Bill Clinton from the presidency in 1998 (see Chapter 8).

Doing the Right Thing

Despite the many disincentives to "do the right thing," members of Congress do sometimes invert their customary practice by enacting policies that impose concentrated costs on specific groups to produce greater, widely shared benefits. If entrenched special interests always won, we would not have the environmental and safety regulations now in place, or deregulated trucking, airline, and telecommunication industries, or the lower marginal tax rates conferred by the Tax Reform Act of 1986. If logrolling coalitions could always protect local benefits, Congress would not have closed military installations all around the United States. Evidently, the electoral payoffs from disregarding special or local interests to the benefit of broader publics sometimes outweigh the costs.

Arnold specifies two conditions that are necessary for this to occur. First, the issue involved must be salient (or potentially salient if an opponent raises it when the next election rolls around) to a large segment of the public. Second, legislative leaders must frame the decision on the issue in a way that forces members to put themselves on the record for or against the general benefits without having an opportunity to amend or modify the policy to serve narrower interests. This requires skillful manipulation of congressional procedures.[34] A third requirement should probably be added: The most powerful potential opponents need to be bought off with special concessions or side deals.

Thus, for example, the success of the Tax Reform Act of 1986, which eliminated a host of special tax favors in order to lower the marginal tax rates across the board, depended heavily on the procedural strategies of its sponsors. Some powerful members whose support was deemed essential received special concessions in the form of *transition rules*—special breaks for specific taxpayers—with support for the bill set as the minimum price for any concession. The package was assembled behind closed doors without recorded votes (no member could be blamed personally for eliminating any particular tax break). It was sent to the floor of the House under a modified closed rule (only three specific amendments could be offered).

In the Senate, which does not use closed rules, the bill's principal sponsor, Senator Packwood, won an agreement that amendments on the floor had to be revenue neutral; this meant that any change producing a tax benefit to some group had to be offset by increased taxes on some other group to make up the difference, precluding the kind distributive logroll among proponents of special tax breaks that would have unraveled the package. Members had to go on record, then, as for or against a substantial cut in taxes for a large majority of taxpayers. They had no opportunity to do any favors behind the scenes for the myriad special interests groups that have traditionally feasted at tax-writing time—and so they could not be blamed for *not* doing the favors. In addition, members on both sides feared for their party's reputation if it could be blamed for scuttling tax reform, and this threat helped to move the legislation through some sticky gates.[35]

Proponents of legislation designed to achieve diffuse, widely shared benefits, then, can sometimes manage to frame the choice in a way that induces members to act contrary to their usual habits because the electoral equation has been altered. The electoral value of avoiding blame for casting a vote against the "public interest" can exceed the payoff from trafficking in particularized benefits.

Instances of this sort are the exception rather than the rule, but they are by no means rare. Congress found a way to close unneeded military bases by authorizing a bipartisan commission of experts to propose a list of closures which then had to be voted up or down together without amendment. The ban on amendments prevented members in districts with targeted bases from cutting deals to save them. Congress also sometimes authorizes the president to negotiate international trade treaties which are then voted up or down without the possibility of amendment. The North American Free Trade Agreement, passed in 1993, is the most important recent example. By committing themselves in advance to take it or leave it, members of Congress bind themselves to forego whatever local or group benefits they might be able to (and thus feel politically compelled to) demand as a condition of their support.

Similarly, the Republican leaders' strategy in 1995 was to roll their entire program of spending and tax cuts into one huge package designed to balance the budget in seven years. This way, in return for voting to impose painful cuts affecting numerous groups, some of them even Republican in their voting habits, Republicans could take credit for enacting a balanced budget and cutting taxes as they had promised.

Building Coalitions

Arnold's more general point is that all of the effective techniques available to presidents, party leaders, and other policy entrepreneurs for building legislative coalitions recognize electoral necessity. The contrast between the approaches taken by the Carter and Reagan administrations in their initial dealings with Congress illustrates this point. Carter's frustration with Congress was reflected in his domestic policy chief's exasperated complaint that "Moses would have difficulty getting the Ten Commandments through [Congress] today."[36] Yet the Reagan administration was remarkably successful in getting Congress to pass its budget and tax program in the first half of 1981.

Why were Reagan's initial dealings with Congress so much more successful than Carter's? One reason is that the Reagan administration was far more sensitive to the electoral connection. Near the end of his second year in office, Carter revealed the breathtaking naivete that lay behind his early efforts to get his programs through Congress. "We had an overly optimistic impression that I could present a bill to Congress which seemed to me patently in the best interest of our country and that the Congress would take it and pretty well pass it. I have been disabused of that expectation."[37] Presidents naturally view things from a national perspective; they are held responsible, by the electorate as well as history, for the national consequences of federal policies and programs. Congressional fates are decided locally, however, and so members are necessarily most attentive to the local impact of national policies. Those who are not are replaced by those who are. Anyone with an adequate grasp of national politics knows this. Nor is how to persuade members of Congress to support a president's programs a great mystery: convince them that their own electoral interests are served by cooperating with the president. Carter never learned to do this effectively; Reagan clearly knew the value of doing it from the start.

One tactic is to support members' local projects and pet programs in return for support for what the administration wants. "Washington is very much a city of 'You scratch my back, I'll scratch your back,'" observed Representative Norman Mineta in 1978. But Carter, he said, dealt "with issues on a vertical plane. He won't say to you 'I need your vote on Mideast arms sales and therefore I will give you the dam you want in your district.'"[38] Reagan had no such scruples; even his budget and tax measures contained compromises that granted concessions to members, many of them Democrats, whose votes were considered crucial.[39]

Reagan also had the advantage that he and his program were initially thought to enjoy strong popular support. The traditional wisdom is that popular presidents have more clout in Congress. An official in the Carter administration involved in congressional liaison put it this way: "When you go up to the Hill and the latest polls show Carter isn't doing well, there isn't much reason for a member to go along with him. There's little we can do if the member is not persuaded on the issue."[40]

The logic of this view is straightforward. If constituents like and support the president, then at least some of them will reward or punish their representatives according to how loyally they support the president's programs. Local activists, campaign contributors, and potential primary and general election opponents will consider support in their strategic calculations. Close association with a popular president will help discourage serious opposition. Conversely, separating oneself from an unpopular president of one's own party may also be a prudent move, as many Democrats learned to their dismay in 1994. Republicans got the same message in 1974, when Richard Nixon's staunchest supporters suffered the consequences at the polls.[41]

Despite its logic, however, the evidence for the view that the president's level of public approval affects his success with Congress is thin. Some studies have reported a significant connection,[42] but the most exhaustive analysis to date reports rather small effects.[43] The Bush administration's experience confirmed that high presidential approval ratings—no president has enjoyed higher ratings than Bush had after leading the allies to victory in the Gulf War—are by no means sufficient to persuade Congress to follow the president's lead. The Reagan administration's experience suggests that a president's popularity must be given a specific district focus if it is to have a major impact. Reagan's operatives did not merely point to his apparent popularity to persuade members of Congress to support his tax and budget policies in 1981; rather, they used it to stimulate an avalanche of messages—letters, telegrams, telephone calls—from the districts of House members who were on the fence. Democratic Representative Dan Glickman of Kansas, for example, reported receiving 1,500 phone calls urging him to support Reagan's tax bill. The technique of grassroots lobbying was convincing in a way that appeals to Gallup Polls or party loyalty or the national interest would never be.[44] An administration that maintains a political organization capable of mobilizing grassroots sentiment after the election or that is led by a president able to galvanize active public support via television is certain to be more successful in its dealings with Congress.[45]

Democratic Speaker Thomas P. "Tip" O'Neill, the public victim of Reagan's early triumphs, made a similar discovery during the Carter administration. O'Neill was, in fact, remarkably successful in pushing Carter's programs, given the difficulties he faced. Among other tactics, he developed unobtrusive methods of party influence. Rather than make direct appeals for party loyalty, the Democratic leadership worked through influential groups in the districts of targeted members (mainly labor unions that had helped finance and conduct their campaigns). Stimulated by the party, these groups then worked to persuade the member to the party's position. Often the member did not suspect party influence at all.[46]

In addition to cutting deals and mobilizing the public, leaders can win support by framing the choice in such a way that electoral necessity induces cooperation. An additional factor in the Reagan administration's initial success was its clever exploitation of the budget process that Congress had, ironically, set up to strengthen itself against encroachments by the executive. The process compels members to cast a few highly visible votes on the whole budget package, providing focal point where the president's persuasive efforts can be efficiently concentrated. Under the old system, which handled budgetary matters in a completely piecemeal fashion, even a popular president enjoying broad public support for his proposals would find it difficult to bring pressure to bear on the many separate decisions that determined the aggregate fiscal product. The connection between any individual program or vote and the aggregate total was relatively easy to obscure. The mechanism Congress adopted, in an attempt to control itself fiscally and to reassert authority over the budget, strengthened the hand of a president who could mobilize district sentiment in support of his policies.

THE BUDGETARY PROCESS

The central themes of this chapter merge in the story of the evolution of congressional budgeting over the past twenty-five years. Budgeting is where individual electoral incentives and collective party and institutional imperatives clash most repeatedly and visibly. The story of Congress' struggle to find a way to manage the conflict shows just how difficult the task can be.

Prior to the reforms of the 1970s, the conflict was managed within the committee system. Committees that raised and spent money were given special status and various legislative privileges in return for saving Congress from the collective effects of its tolerant individualism. Appropriations guarded the treasury, preventing all the pork-barreling and logrolling from sending the national debt into orbit. Tax legislation coming out of Ways and Means was routinely granted a closed rule (forbidding amendments) to prevent a scramble for tax breaks that would sap revenues and remove any final shreds of integrity from the tax structure. Such committees were expected to protect Congress from itself and were given the authority to do so.[47]

These mechanisms of institutional self-control were eroded by the same forces that transformed the committee and party structures in the early 1970s. Newer members of these committees shared neither the electoral security (thus freedom of maneuver) nor the penny-pinching ethos of traditional money committee members. New rules regarding seniority and subcommittee organization weakened committee leadership. The move toward more "openness," which was part of the newer style of operation, made it harder for individual members to forego pushing politically popular projects of dubious worth. Inhibitions against offering floor amendments to fiscal legislation diminished. Aggressively independent junior members, no longer inclined to defer to any institutional authority, became adept at finding ways to circumvent the normal budgetary process to put their favorite programs into action.[48]

More assertive political individualism, growing out of a changed electoral environment, sharpened the conflict between personal and collective congressional goals. Each member has a separate interest in providing programs that please supporters without worrying about the collective impact on the budget of all of them doing the same thing. But the aggregate result is too much spending. That means either raising taxes or having too large a deficit, neither politically desirable. The money committees (especially in the House) worked against this tendency with declining effect after the reforms had taken hold.

The problem was all the more serious because an important external constraint on congressional largess stopped working properly at about the same time. By the early 1970s, Congress had come to rely on the president to save it (and the country) from the aggregate consequences of excessive individual generosity. The president, with congressional acquiescence, took to impounding—refusing to spend—some of the funds authorized and appropriated by Congress in order to keep spending totals from reaching unacceptable levels. Members could still claim credit for enacting programs, but they could avoid the embarrassment of having to present the bill for them to the public.

This comfortable arrangement ended when Richard Nixon, a Republican with no disposition to make life easier for Democratic congressional majorities, entered the White House. Nixon used impoundment to impose his own spending priorities on Congress and to subvert those of the Democratic majority rather than to protect Congress from its own extravagance. He even impounded appropriations passed over his veto. In response to this fundamental challenge to its institutional authority—taxing and spending powers lie at its heart—Congress enacted the 1974 Congressional Budget and Impoundment Control Act. It put presidential impoundment authority under the strict scrutiny and control of Congress. More importantly, it set up internal structures and procedures designed to assure that impoundment would not be necessary to keep the gap between revenue and spending from becoming too wide.

The act established a budget committee in each house, with the assigned task of keeping congressional taxing and spending policies in harmony. It also set procedures and timetables for setting budget targets, supervising the committees' decisions on revenues and spending, and reconciling the tax and spending bills enacted by Congress with the targets. The system was designed to compel members to vote on explicit levels of taxation, expenditures, and deficits, thereby taking greater responsibility for the aggregate fiscal consequences of the myriad separate decisions that are made during a session.

The reformed budget process did not work to constrain members as intended. They quickly learned to use the new system to appear generous and tight-fisted at the same time. "That's the beauty of the budget process," explained one House member shortly after the reform. "You can vote for all your favorite programs, and then vote against deficit."[49] Instead of strengthening congressional control of the budget, the new process made it easier for the president to impose his own budget policies, as Ronald Reagan soon showed. And it failed totally to prevent a string of huge budget deficits through the Reagan and Bush administrations.

During the Reagan years, the president's supply-side economic theories and defense buildup combined with the Democratic House's delight in the distributive politics of spending programs and tax breaks to produce massive budget deficits. In 1981, the administration proposed slashing taxes on the happy theory that doing so would stimulate so much economic growth that total revenues would not actually fall. Congressional Democrats, recognizing the political profit in reducing tax rates and passing out tax breaks, went along despite deep skepticism about "voodoo economics." After imposing some sharp cutbacks in social programs in 1981, Congress resisted further proposals to reduce domestic spending while enacting substantial increases in the defense budget. Despite a tax increase in 1982, deficits on the order of $200 billion per year were projected for the foreseeable future unless drastic changes were made.

Congress had unwittingly intensified the political threat posed by the budget squeeze after 1981 by indexing entitlement spending and tax brackets to inflation. Before entitlements and tax rates were indexed, inflation steadily, quietly, and automatically reduced spending and increased revenues. Inflation eroded the real value of pension and welfare checks; it also increased tax revenues through "bracket creep" as inflated incomes pushed more taxpayers into higher-paying tax brackets. With steady inflation, Congress could allow entitlements to shrink and taxes to rise simply by doing nothing. Better yet, members could please voters by (partially) offsetting inflation-induced changes by voting larger entitlements and lower tax rates. During the 1970s, however, Congress indexed the major entitlements so that they would rise with inflation, and a provision in the 1981 tax legislation did the same with tax brackets. Since then, members of Congress have had to act explicitly to cut entitlement spending or boost taxes, exposing them to sharply greater electoral risk when trying to balance the budget.[50]

The burgeoning deficit after 1981 thus put Congress in a serious bind. Reagan stubbornly refused to consider any serious tax increase and, in view of the drubbing Walter Mondale took in 1984 after proposing new taxes to reduce the deficit, congressional Democrats had no intention of leading the charge to raise taxes. The only alternatives were to tolerate the deficit or cut the budget. Pressure from constituents and rumblings in the financial community made it increasingly difficult to ignore the deficit. But cutting the budget would put Congress in the politically hazardous position of imposing concentrated costs (on the budget losers) in order to produce a diffuse benefit (a lower deficit)—exactly the opposite of what usually makes electoral sense.

In 1985 Congress sought to escape this bind by adopting the Gramm-Rudman-Hollings Deficit Reduction Act (named after its three sponsors, senators Phil Gramm, Warren Rudman, and Ernest Hollings), which required Congress to achieve a balanced budget by 1991 by meeting a series of progressively lower yearly deficit targets. If Congress and the president did not agree on where to make the necessary cuts, they would occur automatically across the board on all programs not explicitly exempted.

The automatic mechanism was one key to the plan's political appeal. Many specific programs could be cut without any member going on record as voting for the cut. Furthermore, members could acquire credit for trying to prevent the otherwise "automatic" cuts in programs their supporters care about most. This returned them to the preferred situation, wherein they could provide concentrated benefits (limiting the damage from Gramm-Rudman-Hollings), while avoiding responsibility for either concentrated or diffuse costs. Even if they voted to cut some programs in order to save others, they could plead the necessity of preventing Gramm-Rudman-Hollings from imposing mindless cuts that would make things even worse.

The cuts were, in a fundamental sense, to be mindless. Programs dear to politically potent constituencies—Social Security recipients and veterans—as well as interest on the national debt, the president's "Star Wars" program, and some welfare programs important to congressional Democrats, were protected. The cuts would have come from remaining discretionary spending, including the defense budget, and would be proportionate across the board if Congress and the president did not agree on some different combination of cuts. In effect, Congress tried to force itself and the president to choose between automatic cuts certain to be painful to important constituencies and making hard, but more considered, choices themselves.

Many who voted for the plan thought it neither wise nor workable; even Senator Rudman called it "a bad idea whose time has come."[51] But it won strong, bipartisan support in both houses, because members anticipated electoral problems if they voted against reducing the deficit, and they could not face the political heat from the interest groups that would be hurt if programs were cut through normal procedures. The measure also passed because no one knew how it would actually work.[52] It was a mark of members' panic that they were willing to tolerate enormous uncertainty, risking budgetary chaos, to deal with the consequences of their inability to inflict pain on identifiable groups in order to cope with a deficit that they believed was a serious threat to the national economy.

Gramm-Rudman-Hollings was revised in 1987 (after the Supreme Court had declared its enforcement mechanism unconstitutional), and the deadline for reaching a balanced budget was extended to 1993. Each year it became more difficult to reach the deficit targets, as the easy moves—changes in accounting procedures and other tricks commonly dismissed as "blue smoke and mirrors"—were exhausted. Both the Democratic Congress and the Republican White House remained strongly disposed to resist spending cuts or tax increases that would impose immediate and palpable costs on their core constituencies to achieve the more indirect and distant benefits of a smaller deficit. As long as both sides saw smaller political damage in deficits than in what they would have to give up to cut a deal, no solution was possible, and most of the maneuvering went into avoiding partisan blame for failure to reach agreement.

Eventually, though, the self-imposed constraints of Gramm-Rudman-Hollings did have some effect. Lengthy and acrimonious negotiations between the administration and congressional leaders over the 1991 budget finally led to a compromise package of painful tax increases and spending cuts that held only because the automatic Gramm-Rudman-Hollings cuts—and the image of abject incompetence the failure to pass a budget would confer on all the participants—promised even greater political retribution. It did not happen easily. Majorities on both sides of the aisle in the House rejected as political poison the initial deficit reduction package proposed by the administration and congressional leaders.[53] Democrats objected to its regressive excise taxes on alcohol and tobacco and cuts in Medicare; Republicans refused to break their talismanic pledge of "no new taxes." A second package, containing a more progressive mix of tax increases and smaller reductions in Medicare, among other changes, won enough additional Democratic support to pass.

Part of the deal was a further extension of the Gramm-Rudman-Hollings deadline; the deficit was rescheduled to reach zero in 1996. Spending ceilings were rendered less draconian: They applied separately to three specific categories (domestic, international, and military), and, initially, automatic cuts were to be imposed only within a category when spending in that category exceeded the permissible limit. The ceilings affected only Congress's own spending initiatives and were not to take effect if the deficit grew from circumstances beyond Congress's control, such as a recession that reduced revenues and raised spending on entitlements or a war.

Although the 1991 deficit reduction package was projected to reduce the deficit by nearly $500 billion over the next five years, it by no means solved the deficit problem. Thus, the new Congress taking office with Bill Clinton in 1993 faced it once again, but with a new partisan configuration: unified Democratic control of the White House and Congress. Clinton initially proposed a quick $30 billion spending package to stimulate the economy, a longer-term $230 billion infrastructure investment package, and a combination of spending cuts ($375 billion) and tax increases ($328 billion) designed to reduce the deficit by $704 billion over five years.[54]

Congressional Republicans, freed of any responsibility for dealing with the deficit themselves, gleefully jumped on the plan, opposing tax increases and demanding deeper spending cuts without, of course, specifying what should be cut. The political play is captured in an exchange between Leon Panetta, Clinton's Director of the Office of Management and Budget, and Republican Senator Trent Lott of Mississippi. Lott

> made the remarkable claim that he had a list of $216 million in "basically painless budget cuts" that could be made in the first year of the Clinton administration. Panetta demanded to see the list. Lott replied, "I'm going to keep it right here," patting his breast pocket, "until I see yours."[55]

Later, Senate Minority Leader Bob Dole refused to offer an alternative on the ground that "Well, we're not the majority party." Instead, he berated Democrats for proposing "the largest tax increase in world history."[56]

The Democrats were the majority party, so they got stuck with the politically dangerous task of doling out the spending cuts and tax increases needed to reduce the deficit. It took all the pressure congressional leaders and the White House could muster, plus numerous concessions to members demands for changes in the legislation, to eke out a victory. As one Senate Democrat said afterward, "Both my arms feel twisted."[57] Every single Republican in Congress voted against the final budget reconciliation bill, which increased taxes by $241 billion and cut spending by $255 billion for a $496 billion reduction in deficit spending over the next five years. It passed the House by a narrow 219-213 margin, and Vice President Al Gore had to cast the decisive vote to win the 50-49 Senate majority. Congressional Democrats were acutely aware of the electoral price they might pay, and only the fear of crippling the first Democratic presidency in twelve years kept enough wavering Democrats on board to pass the bill.[58]

As we saw in Chapter 6, congressional Democrats did pay the price. Without the bipartisan cover that divided government had given members of both parties in previous assaults on the deficit, they took the full brunt of public dismay at the painful adjustments any such assault necessarily requires. The Republicans attacked them for raising taxes, while their reductions in social spending and other programs dampened enthusiasm among their own core supporters.

Despite reducing future deficits by nearly $500 billion, the 1993 budget still failed to put the nation on a path to a balanced budget. The new Republican majority taking office in 1995 had promised to balance the budget while cutting taxes and boosting military spending. Necessarily, balance was to be achieved by drastic reductions in domestic spending. Well aware that balancing the budget was popular but the sacrifices it would take were not, Republicans sought to impose as much of the cost as possible on traditionally Democratic constituencies whose votes they did not expect to get anyway, most notably the beneficiaries of welfare, housing, and job training programs. According to a report by Democratic staffers of Congress's Joint Economic Committee, fully half of the spending cuts in the 1995 plan to balance the budget by 2002 were to be born by families in the poorest fifth of the population, with 75 percent coming from the poorest two-fifths.[59]

The trouble, from the Republican's perspective, was that not nearly enough savings could be squeezed out of programs for poor people and other Democratic constituencies to balance the budget. They had to take on middle-class entitlements as well. Medicare for the elderly, the fastest growing middle-class entitlement program, was an obvious target. It was obviously a dangerous target as well, and Republicans sought to justify their proposed changes in the program by pointing out that they sought only to reduce its rate of growth, not to cut it, and that doing so was necessary to save it. This rhetorical frame came up against the reality that, for recipients, costs would go up and services would be curtailed. When House Republicans made the tactical mistake of putting a $270 billion reduction in the future growth of Medicare funding in the same budget with a $240 billion tax cut plan, Clinton seized the opportunity to cast himself as the protector of Medicare (and other programs) against cutbacks to finance tax breaks for the rich. As we have seen (Chapter 6), the public took his side decisively in the showdown that followed. The Republicans' mistake was in assuming that public support for the goal—smaller, cheaper government—also meant public support for the means—cutbacks in specific programs. They kept their majority in 1996 only by capitulating to Clinton on the budget.

The Republicans in Congress had, however, forced Clinton to accept the goal of balancing the budget by 2002, and in 1997, with a crucial boost from vast new revenues generated by the economic boom, Clinton and Congress finally agreed on a package of modest tax cuts, reductions in future Medicare growth, and short-term spending increases on Clinton's pet projects that promised to meet that goal. Subsequently, the economy grew so vigorously that the budget came into balance in 1998. Budget politics then turn to partisan battles over what to do with the growing surplus: cut taxes, spend more on the military, spend more on social programs, or pay down the national debt. These battles were no less acrimonious, but only because members of both parties were trying to position themselves for the elections of 2000. Electoral politics continue to dominate budget politics even in good times.

In 1998, of course, budget politics—and everything else—was overshadowed by the Lewinsky affair and resulting move to impeach and remove Bill

Clinton from office. The politics of impeachment were also dominated by electoral considerations and will almost certainly have repercussions for the millennial elections of 2000, among the topics I address in the next, and final, chapter.

ENDNOTES

1. Morris P. Fiorina, *Congress: Keystone of the Washington Establishment*, 2nd ed. (New Haven: Yale University Press, 1989).
2. Richard F. Fenno, Jr., *Congressman in Committees* (Boston: Little, Brown, 1973), p. 1.
3. David R. Mayhew, *Congress: The Electoral Connection* (New Haven: Yale University Press, 1974), p. 141.
4. "GOP's House-Cleaning Sweep Changes Rules, Cuts Groups," *Congressional Quarterly Weekly Report* 52 (December 10, 1994): 3487.
5. Gary W. Cox and Mathew D. McCubbins, *Legislative Leviathan: Party Government in the House* (Berkeley, California: University of California Press, 1993), Chapter 5.
6. Mayhew, *Congress*, pp. 145–149.
7. Cox and McCubbins, *Legislative Leviathan*, pp. 153–157.
8. "GOP Senators Limit Chairmen to Six Years Heading Panel," *Congressional Quarterly Weekly Report* 52 (July 22, 1995): 2147.
9. Mayhew, *Congress*, pp. 85–94.
10. Ibid., p. 95.
11. Charles M. Tidmarch, "The Second Time Around: Freshman Democratic House Members' 1976 Reelection Experiences" (Paper delivered at the Annual Meeting of the American Political Science Association, Washington, DC, September 1–4, 1977); William J. Crotty and Gary C. Jacobson, *American Parties in Decline* (Boston: Little, Brown, 1980), pp. 196–201.
12. Ibid., pp. 206–212.
13. "A Republican-Designed House Won't Please All Occupants," *Congressional Quarterly Weekly Report* 52 (December 3, 1994): 3430–3435.
14. Mayhew, *Congress*, pp. 53–54 passim.
15. R. Douglas Arnold, "The Local Roots of Domestic Policy," in *The New Congress*, eds. Thomas E. Mann and Norman J. Ornstein (Washington, DC: American Enterprise Institute, 1981), pp. 272.
16. Ibid., p. 268.
17. Ibid.
18. Ibid., p. 270.
19. "Pyrrhic Victory in the War on Pork," *Congressional Quarterly Weekly Report* 49 (March 9, 1991): 590.
20. "Enid Green Waldholtz," *Congressional Quarterly Weekly Report* 53 (October 28, 1995): 3273.
21. "Freshman Walk Tightrope to Satisfy Voters," *Congressional Quarterly Weekly Report* 53 (May 27, 1995): 1524–1526.
22. "Military Construction Bill Keeps Most Pet Projects," *Congressional Quarterly Weekly Report* 53 (June 24, 1995): 1857.

23. Alan K. Ota,"Senators Pile On the Take-Home Projects after Coaxing House to Reduce Its List," *Congressional Quarterly Weekly Report* 56 (May 30, 1998): 1465.

24. Mayhew, *Congress*, pp. 130-131.

25. Michael J. Malbin, "Of Mountains and Molehills: PACs, Campaigns, and Public Policy," in *Parties, Interest Groups, and Campaign Finance Laws*, ed. Michael J. Malbin (Washington, DC: American Enterprise Institute for Public Policy Research, 1980), pp. 152-210; Frank J. Sorauf, *Money in American Elections* (Glenview, Illinois: Scott, Foresman, 1988), pp. 307-317.

26. "The Trail of the 'Dirty Dozen,'" *Congressional Quarterly Weekly Report* 39 (March 21, 1981): 510.

27. *League of Conservation Voters*, www.lev.org/dirtydozen/callahan_postmt.htm, June 3, 1999.

28. Raymond A. Bauer, Ithiel de Sola Pool, and Lewis Anthony Dexter, *American Business and Public Policy* (New York: Atherton, 1968).

29. Theodore J. Eismeier and Philip H. Pollock, III, "Political Action Committees: Varieties of Organization and Strategy," in *Money and Politics in the United States*, ed. Michael J. Malbin (Washington, DC: American Enterprise Institute for Public Policy Research, 1984), pp. 124-126.

30. Nelson W. Polsby, *Congress and the Presidency*, 3rd ed. (Englewood Cliffs, New Jersey: Prentice-Hall, 1976), p. 16.

31. Richard F. Fenno, Jr., *Home Style: House Members in Their Districts* (Boston: Little, Brown, 1978), p. 245.

32. Mayhew, *Congress*, p. 117.

33. Ibid., p. 115.

34. R. Douglas Arnold, *The Logic of Congressional Action* (New Haven: Yale University Press, 1990), pp. 193-195.

35. For a fascinating account of the politics behind the Tax Reform Act of 1986, see Jeffrey H. Birnbaum and Alan S. Murray, *Showdown at Gucci Gulch: Lawmakers, Lobbyists, and the Unlikely Triumph of Tax Reform* (New York: Vintage Books, 1988); see also Arnold, *Logic of Congressional Action*, pp. 211-223.

36. Quoted in Barbara Sinclair, "Coping with Uncertainty: Building Coalitions in the House and Senate," *The New Congress*, p. 178.

37. Quoted in Joel Havemann, "Will Late-Session Success Spoil Jimmy Carter?" *National Journal* 10 (December 2, 1978): 1943.

38. Quoted in *Congressional Quarterly Weekly Report* 36 (September 2, 1978): 2304.

39. "Reagan Team May Draw Key Lessons from Difficult Struggle over AWACS," *Congressional Quarterly Weekly Report* 39 (October 31, 1981): 2098-2099.

40. Quoted in *Congressional Quarterly Weekly Report* 36 (March 4, 1978): 586.

41. See Gerald C. Wright, Jr., "Constituency Response to Congressional Behavior: The Impact of the House Judiciary Committee Impeachment Votes," *Western Political Quarterly* 30 (1977):401-410.

42. Douglas Rivers and Nancy L. Rose, "Passing the President's Program," *American Journal of Political Science* 29 (1985):192; George C. Edwards, *Presidential Influence in Congress* (San Francisco: W.H. Freeman, 1980).
43. Jon R. Bond and Richard H. Fleisher, *The President in the Legislative Arena* (Chicago: University of Chicago Press, 1990).
44. "Tax Vote Victory," *Congressional Quarterly Weekly Report* 39 (August 1, 1981): 1372.
45. Samuel Kernell, *Going Public: New Strategies of Presidential Leadership* (Washington, DC: Congressional Quarterly Press, 1986), Chapter 5.
46. Lawrence Dodd and Terry Sullivan, "House Leadership Success in the Vote Gathering Process: A Comparative Analysis" (Paper delivered at the Annual Meeting of the Midwest Political Science Association, Chicago, April 24-26, 1980.)
47. Mayhew, *Congress*, pp. 152-156.
48. Allen Schick, "The Three-Ring Budget Process: The Appropriations, Tax, and Budget Committees in Congress," in *The New Congress*, ed. Thomas E. Mann and Norman J. Ornstein (Washington, DC: American Enterprise Institute, 1981), pp. 297-304.
49. Joel Havemann, "Budget Process Nearly Ambushed by Carter and by Congress," *National Journal* 9 (May 21, 1977): 787.
50. Paul E. Peterson, "Vulnerable Politicians and Deficit Politics" (Paper delivered at the Annual Meeting of the American Political Science Association, Chicago, September 1-4, 1995).
51. Elizabeth Wehr, "Congress Enacts Far-Reaching Budget Measure," *Congressional Quarterly Weekly Report* 43 (December 14, 1985):2604.
52. Ibid., p. 2606.
53. The greater their electoral risk for 1990, the more likely were members of both parties to vote against both the initial and final deficit reduction laws. See Gary C. Jacobson, "Deficit Cutting Politics and Congressional Elections," *Political Science Quarterly* 108 (1993):375-402.
54. Paul J. Quirk and Joseph Hinchliffe, "Domestic Policy: The Trials of a Centrist Democrat," in *The Clinton Presidency: First Appraisals*, ed. Colin Campbell and Bert A. Rockman (Chatham, New Jersey: Chatham House, 1996), p. 269.
55. Ibid., p. 270.
56. Ibid., pp. 270-271.
57. Ibid., p. 273.
58. Ibid.
59. "GOP Budget Plans Would Put Burden on the Poor," *Los Angeles Times*, (October 29, 1995), p. A1.

CHAPTER EIGHT

Representation, Responsibility, Impeachment Politics, and the Future of Congressional Elections

C ongress is a representative assembly. Put most simply,[1] it is a representative assembly because its members are chosen in competitive popular elections, and if voters do not like what the members are doing, they can vote them out of office. Voters can hold representatives accountable for their actions as long as members care about their own reelection or their party's future, and nearly every member does. Representation is an effect of electoral politics; the electoral system structures the kind of representation Congress provides. What kind of representation is that?

REPRESENTATION

Political scientists have customarily paid the most attention to one aspect of representation: policy congruence. The central question is the extent to which the policy views of people in a state or district are reflected in the policy stances (usually measured by roll-call votes) of the people they elect to Congress. This has never been an easy question to answer. Information on constituency opinion is scarce and often unreliable, and it is frequently doubtful that there is any "constituency opinion" on a given issue. Measuring constituency attitudes has challenged the ingenuity of a generation of scholars, since the one unquestioned solution—regular, adequately sized sample surveys of a large number of states and districts—is simply too expensive.

Demographic indicators, simulations, referenda voting, and aggregated national survey data have all been used to estimate state and district attitudes. So have small-sample district- and state-level surveys.[2] Each of these approaches has its drawbacks, and there is the additional problem of establishing some kind of comparability between any of these measures and measures of congressional behavior.[3] Still, a number of general conclusions can be drawn from this

work. Most research suggests that congressional roll-call votes are indeed related to estimated district opinion, although the strength of the connection
varies across issue dimensions and is never overwhelmingly large. The relationships are strongest when votes and attitudes are combined and reduced to a
few general dimensions—for example, domestic welfare policy or civil rights
for minorities—and weaker for specific votes on single pieces of legislation.[4]
The connection is also stronger if the constituency is defined as the member's
supporters (defined by voting or partisanship).[5]

All of these findings make sense. Members of Congress develop differentiated images of their constituencies and have a fair notion of who keeps them in
office. It is no surprise that they are more responsive to some groups than to
others. There is no great pressure to vote district (or supporting constituency)
preferences on every vote, especially since on many specific votes constituency preferences are unknown or unformed. Members need only take care
to cast "explainable" votes. On the other hand, anyone who consistently votes
contrary to the wishes of his or her constituents is likely to run into trouble.
Voters, in aggregate, do form passably accurate notions of their representatives' voting patterns, and members who stray too far from home do suffer at
the polls.[6]

Congress is broadly representative on another dimension. As we saw in
Chapter 6, aggregate election results are responsive to national political and
economic conditions. When citizens are unhappy with the government's performance, the administration's party suffers the consequences. The opposing
party picks up more seats, and even those who remain in Congress get the message that they had better recognize new realities. Reagan was able to win budget victories not only because more Republicans sat in the 97th Congress, but
also because the remaining Democrats read the election results as a demand
that something drastic be done about taxes and inflation. The issue in 1981 was
not whether the budget and taxes would be cut, but which package of cuts—
the administration's or the House Democrats'—would be adopted. Similarly,
the influx of new House Republicans in 1994 made balancing the budget and
acting on other items in the Contract for America the top priority for many of
the holdovers as well.

Aggregate representation of this kind is necessarily crude and rests on somewhat shaky foundations, depending, as it does, partly on the self-reinforcing expectations of congressional elites. And it can only operate when there is some
public consensus on the general direction of policy, which is by no means always the case. The energy crisis, designated by Carter as the "moral equivalent
of war," was certainly the dominant national issue when gas lines developed
and energy prices skyrocketed. But Congress could not produce any systematic
plan to cope with it because all of the proposed solutions would impose major
costs on politically powerful groups. Budget politics during the Reagan–Bush
years assumed a similar character, with the public fed up with the problem—
continuing deficits—but badly divided on the solution. The post-1994 political
agreement between Clinton and the Republican Congress to balance the budget in seven years did not extend to a consensus on how to achieve this goal;
luckily, vigorous economic growth allowed the goal to be achieved without a
consensus.

Policy Congruence

The scholarly interest in measuring degrees of policy congruence to assess congressional representation is in itself a consequence of congressional election politics. The question would scarcely arise in a system built around strong programmatic parties. If voters merely expressed a preference for a party's proposals in their vote and the winning party enacted its platform, policy representation would be automatic. Policy congruence is an issue only to the degree that lax party discipline, electoral individualism, and a host of electoral activities that have nothing to do with national policy typify congressional behavior. At the extreme, what kind of representation is provided by those independent political entrepreneurs whose strategy for staying in office emphasizes constituent services and their own personal honesty, sincerity, and availability rather than policies or partisanship?

One of Fenno's important insights is that much of what goes into the cultivation of a personal constituency is in fact essential to meaningful representation in a system without disciplined, programmatic parties.

> There is no way that the act of representing can be separated from the act of getting elected. If the congressman cannot win and hold the votes of some people, he cannot represent any people. Further, he cannot represent any people unless he knows, or makes an effort to know, who they are, what they think, and what they want; and it is by campaigning for electoral support among them that he finds out such things. During the expansionist stage of his constituency career, particularly, he probably knows his various constituencies as well as it is possible to know them. It is, indeed, by such campaigning, by going home a great deal, that a congressman develops a complex and discriminating set of perceptions about his constituents.[8]

This knowledge is the basis for making judgments about what constituents want or need from politics. Two-way communication is essential to representation. The stress members of Congress put on their accessibility invites communication from constituents at the same time it attracts their support. The knowledge and work it takes to win and hold a district not only establish the basis for policy congruence, but also let the member know when it is irrelevant or unnecessary.

Beyond Policy Congruence

There is much more to representation than policy congruence, of course. The work of Fenno and others has made that clear. Members certainly "represent" their constituents in important ways by helping them cope with the federal bureaucracy, by bringing in public works projects, by helping local governments and other groups to take advantage of federal programs, or by helping an overseas relative get permanent resident status. Particularized benefits are still benefits, and an important part of representation is making sure one's constituents get their share.

Representation of still another kind is provided by members who become spokespeople for interests and groups not confined to their constituencies. Some black representatives, for example, try to speak for all African-Americans.

Senator Jesse Helms takes it upon himself to champion the values of the religious right. Representative Henry Hyde leads the legislative fight against abortion for the "Right-to-Life" movement. Senator Barbara Boxer tirelessly promotes the feminist position on women's issues. Opposition to the Vietnam War absorbed the energies of more than a few members some years back. Most members are not so careless that their commitment to a group or cause upsets their supporting constituency; more often it becomes a way of pleasing constituents (especially their core supporters) and so coincides nicely with electoral necessities. But not always. A few members invite consistently strong opposition and regularly court defeat in representing their vision of the national interest. The electoral process, however, tends to weed them out.

On a somewhat more mundane level, the current electoral structure gives representation of a sort to any group that can mobilize people or money to help in campaigns. The views of conservative Christian leaders enjoy much more respectful attention now that they have demonstrated their ability to deliver millions of votes. The corporate PACs, trade associations, labor unions, and ideological groups that supply campaign resources help to elect congenial candidates and to gain access to them; both help to assure that these groups' interests are represented in Congress. It is a matter of debate whether this is a benign or pernicious phenomenon, and the controversy is not likely to die down as long as PACs continue to provide a substantial share of campaign funds. But it would be hard to argue that some mechanism for representing the enormous variety of economic and political interests that cannot be encompassed within the framework of single-member districts is not essential.

Descriptive Representation

In one way Congress does not represent the American public well at all: demographically. It contains a much greater proportion of white, male, college-educated, professional, higher-income people than the population as a whole; the Senate is especially unrepresentative by these criteria. Even the creation of minority-majority districts after 1990 did not eliminate racial underrepresentation in the House, though the gap did narrow. African-Americans comprise 12 percent of the voting age population, 9 percent of the House; Hispanics make up 8 percent of the population, 4 percent of the House. No African-American sat in the Senate after Carol Mosely-Braun's defeat in 1998. And despite the dramatic success of women candidates in 1992, women, who make up a majority of the voting age population (52 percent), held only 13 percent of House seats and 9 percent of Senate seats in the 106th Congress. Occupationally, 37 percent of House members, and 55 percent of Senators, are lawyers; a blue-collar background or an advanced science degree is rare. Congress also boasts a much higher proportion of millionaires than the population at large.

Yet Congress is probably quite representative of the kinds of people who achieve positions of leadership in the great majority of American institutions. It would be unlikely in the extreme for an electoral system like the one described in this book to produce a Congress looking anything like a random sample of the voting age population. What it does produce is a sample of local elites from a remarkably diverse nation. And from this perspective, at times the electoral politics of Congress generates legislative bodies that are *too* representative of the myriad divisions in American society.

Like the members of Congress whom we elect, Americans have wanted to have it both ways. We enjoy the programs and benefits that the federal government provides, but we dislike paying the price in the form of increased taxes, higher inflation, and greater government regulation. Public opinion polls have found, in recent years, solid majorities for national health insurance, government guarantees of jobs, and current or greater levels of spending on the environment, education, the homeless, and health care. Polls have found equally solid majorities believing that the federal government is too large, spends too much money, and is too intrusive in people's lives. We like a balanced budget, but want it to be achieved without increased taxes or reduced services.[9] When Congress is stalemated, produces self-contradictory policies, or tolerates large budget deficits, it accurately reflects our own disagreement, confusion, and self-contradictory preferences. As Mayhew points out, "half the adverse criticism of Congress . . . is an indirect criticism of the public itself."[10]

RESPONSIVENESS WITHOUT RESPONSIBILITY

The dilemmas created by a public demanding mutually contradictory policies reinforces the fundamental danger in the kind of representation encouraged by candidate-centered electoral politics: individual responsiveness without collective responsibility. The safest way to cope with contradictory policy demands is to be acutely sensitive to what constituents and other politically important groups want in taking positions, but to avoid responsibility for the costs they would impose. Voting for Gramm-Rudman-Hollings but against spending cuts or tax increases is the paradigmatic strategy. The pervasive temptation to engage in symbolic position-taking rather than working to find real solutions to national problems is harder to resist when every solution is likely to anger one politically important group or another. It does not help matters when members are rewarded individually for taking pleasing positions but are not punished for failing to turn them into national policy or, when they do become policy, for seeing that they work. As long as members are not held individually responsible for Congress's performance as an institution, a crucial form of representation is missing. Responsiveness is insufficient without responsibility.

The only instruments we have managed to develop for imposing collective responsibility on legislators are political parties. There is nothing original about this observation; it is a home truth to which students of congressional politics inevitably return.[11] Morris Fiorina put the case cogently:

> A strong political party can generate collective responsibility by creating incentives for leaders, followers, and popular supporters to think and act in collective terms. First, by providing party leaders with the capability (e.g., control of institutional patronage, nominations, etc.) to discipline party members, genuine leadership becomes possible. Legislative output is less likely to be a least common denominator—a residue of myriad conflicting proposals—and more likely to consist of a program actually intended to solve a problem or move the nation in a particular direction. Second, the subordination of individual office holders to the party lessens

their ability to separate themselves from party actions. Like it or not their performance becomes identified with the performance of the collectivity to which they belong. Third, with individual candidate variation greatly reduced, voters have less incentive to support individuals and more to support or oppose the party as a whole. And fourth, the circle closes as party-line voting in the electorate provides party leaders with the incentive to propose policies which will earn the support of a national majority, and party backbenchers with the personal incentive to cooperate with leaders in the attempt to compile a good record for the party as a whole.[12]

Pristine party government has never been characteristic of American politics, to be sure, but all of its necessary elements eroded with the electoral changes of the 1960s and 1970s. The emerging issues raised by the civil rights movement, the Vietnam War, the energy crisis, the environmental movement, *Roe* v. *Wade*, and the women's movement initially split both parties, but they cut across people, states, districts, and thus members of Congress in different ways. Coherent and consistent battle lines were absent, so policy coalitions tended to be ad hoc and fluid.[13] Conditions encouraged members to operate as individual political entrepreneurs and rewarded them when they did.

THE REVIVAL OF PARTY COHESION

After the election of Ronald Reagan in 1980, however, partisan divisions began to clarify, reversing the trends of the 1960s and 1970s. The budget crunch deserves a good deal of the credit for the initial change. Congress's electoral and institutional needs mesh most harmoniously when politics can focus on distributing benefits. In periods of prosperity and growth, public and private resources expand together, and members can busy themselves with the happy chore of figuring out how to divide up a growing pie. Universalistic distributive criteria—something for everyone regardless of party—are applicable, and logrolling coalitions are relatively easy to assemble. The 1960s were just such a period. The 1970s, however, brought slower growth, higher inflation, and the need for higher taxes to pay for the benefits so generously provided when the economy was booming. The introduction of indexing made matters worse (see Chapter 7). Instead of the pleasant prospect of distributing benefits, Congress increasingly faced the bleak task of distributing costs.

Constraints on distributive politics drew even tighter in the 1980s, and although many of the newer political cleavages remained, party coherence made a notable comeback. It did so in part because of a development that erected yet another barrier to responsible party government, however: the division of government between a Republican White House and a Democratic Congress. After the brief period in 1981, when the Reagan administration won its major budget initiatives by splitting the House Democrats, divided government helped to unify both parties in both houses. On roll-call votes, Republicans continued to line up loyally behind their president. Democrats became increasingly loyal to their party throughout the 1980s and by the 1990s were achieving the highest party unity scores since *Congressional Quarterly* began keeping track in 1954.

The rise of party cohesion in Congress is documented in Figures 8-1, 8-2, and 8-3. Figure 8-1 traces the percentage of party-unity votes—votes in which

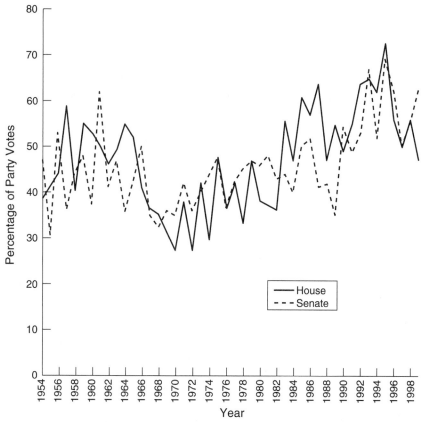

FIGURE 8–1 Party-Unity Votes, 1954–1999
Sources: Norman J. Ornstein, Thomas E. Mann, and Michael J. Mablin, *Vital Statistics on Congress 1997–1998* (Washington, DC: Congressional Quarterly, 1998), Table 8-3; data for 1998 and 1999 are from *Congressional Quarterly Weekly Report* 57 (December 11, 1999):2994.

majorities of Democrats and Republicans took opposite sides—in the House and Senate over the past forty years. Figures 8-2 and 8-3 show the average party-unity scores (percentage of votes in which party members voted with their party's majority on the party-unity votes) of Democrats and Republicans in the House and Senate over this period. In every case, we observe congressional partisanship on roll-call votes falling to a low point in the late 1960s and early 1970s, then rising to new heights by the end of the 1980s. Notice how the majority parties in both the House and Senate have been particularly cohesive in the 1980s and 1990s.

In addition to incentives for the majority party to resist administrations controlled by their rivals and to project an image of party competence, party unity has been enhanced by the structure of decision making under divided government. When the White House and Congress (or one of its houses) are controlled by opposing parties, major policy conflicts have to be worked out

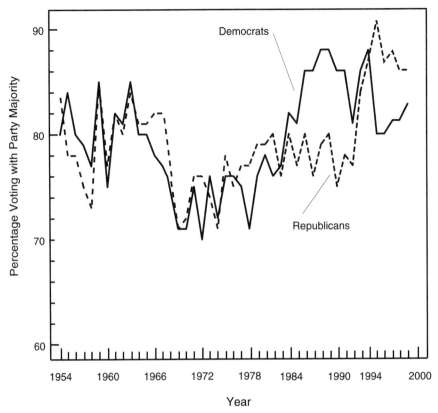

FIGURE 8–2 House Party Unity, 1954–1999

Sources: Norman J. Ornstein, Thomas E. Mann, and Michael J. Malbin, *Vital Statistics on Congress 1997-1998* (Washington, DC: Congressional Quarterly, 1998), Table 8-4; data for 1998 and 1999 are from *Congressional Quarterly Weekly Report* 57 (December 11, 1999):2993.

through high-level negotiation between the president and congressional leaders. The need for high-level negotiation centralizes decision processes, strengthening the hand of the top leadership. Restrictive rules and other procedural devices designed to prevent elaborately negotiated deals from unraveling are easier to justify and enforce. Omnibus legislation leaves only all-or-nothing choices to backbenchers.[14]

Members may have also found it more expedient to be loyal to their parties in the 1980s because of the expanded role of national party committees, leadership PACs such as Newt Gingrich's GOPAC, and other allied PACs in recruiting, training, and financing congressional candidates. Members elected as part of a team, using common campaign themes and issues, and with considerable help from party committees, should be more disposed to cooperate on legislative matters. Members hoping for generous party assistance in future campaigns should be more susceptible to persuasion by leaders who influence the distribution of the party's funds.[15]

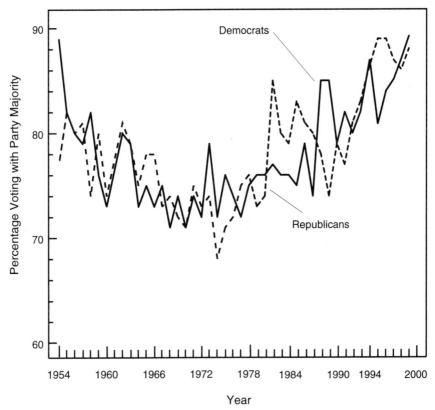

FIGURE 8–3 Senate Party Unity, 1954–1999
Sources: Norman J. Ornstein, Thomas E. Mann, and Michael J. Malbin, *Vital Statistics on Congress 1997-1998* (Washington, DC: Congressional Quarterly, 1998), Table 8-4; data for 1998 and 1999 are from *Congressional Quarterly Weekly Report* 57 (December 11, 1999):2993.

Ideological Polarization in Congress and the Electorate

An even more important source of increased party unity than party money, however, has been the growing ideological homogeneity and polarization of both the congressional parties and their respective electoral coalitions. To appreciate just how sharply the congressional parties have diverged since the 1970s, observe Figures 8–4a through 8–4d, which display the frequency distribution of House members' positions on Poole and Rosenthal's first-dimension D-Nominate score in selected Congresses spanning the past three decades. The scores are calculated from all nonunanimous roll-call votes cast during the 80th through 105th Congresses, locating each member for each Congress on a liberal–conservative scale that ranges from −1.0 to 1.0; the higher the score, the more conservative the member.[16]

In the 93rd Congress, the ideological locations of many House Democrats and Republicans overlapped across the middle half of the scale, and the gap be-

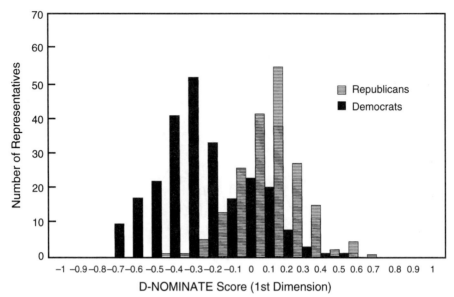

FIGURE 8–4A 93rd Congress (1973–1974)
Source: See text.

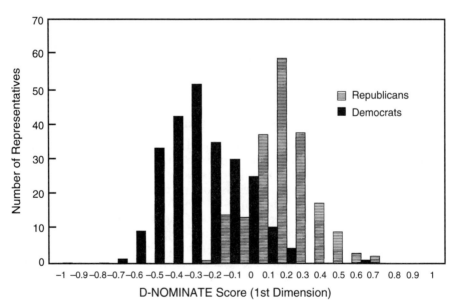

FIGURE 8–4B 97th Congress (1981–1982)
Source: See text.

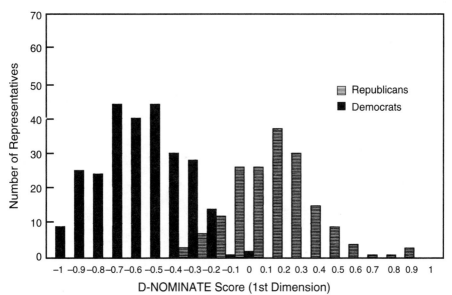

FIGURE 8–4C 101st Congress (1989–1990)
Source: See text.

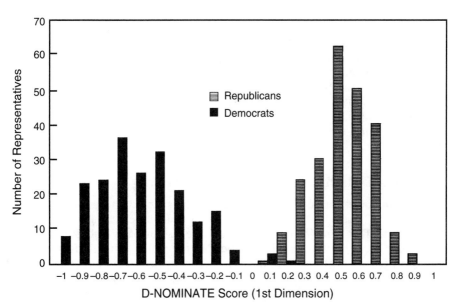

FIGURE 8–4D 105th Congress (1997–1998)
Source: See text.

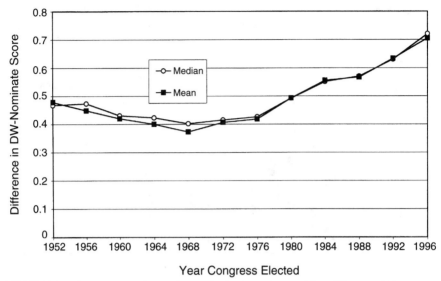

FIGURE 8–5 Difference in Median and Mean D-Nominate Scores of Republicans and Democrats, 83rd through 105th Congresses
Source: See text.

tween the two parties' modal locations was comparatively small. In the 97th Congress, overlap was a bit less extensive but still sizeable. By the 101st Congress, the parties had become noticeably more polarized. The 105th Congress was the most sharply divided of all, with not a single Republican falling below zero on the scale, and only four Democrats with scoring above zero.[17]

Trends in partisan polarization in the House over a somewhat longer period are summarized in Figure 8-5, which displays the difference in mean and median of the two parties' D-Nominate scores in the Congress immediately following each presidential election from 1952 through 1996. Note particularly how dramatically the gap between the parties grew in the 1990s; in the 105th Congress, the parties' medians and means were more than 0.7 points apart on this two-point scale.

Party Polarization: The Electoral Connection

The partisan polarization of Congress has both reflected and encouraged the emergence of distinct and increasingly homogeneous electoral coalitions in both parties. The standard explanation for the rise in party cohesion in Congress since the 1970s is party realignment in the South, which left both congressional parties with more politically homogeneous electoral coalitions, reducing internal disagreements and making stronger party leadership tolerable. This explanation is certainly correct as far as it goes. The realignment of southern political loyalties and electoral habits has been thoroughly documented.[18] Starting from almost nothing in the 1950s, Republican now enjoy parity with the Democrats among voters and hold solid majorities of southern House and Senate seats.[19]

Realignment in the South contributed to the increasing ideological homogeneity of the parties, but it is by no means the whole story. Other forces have also necessarily been at work, for links between ideology and party identification have grown stronger outside the South as well. Since 1972, the National Election Studies (NES) have asked respondents to place themselves on a seven-point ideological scale ranging from extremely liberal to extremely conservative.[20] On average, nearly 80 percent of respondents who say they voted in the House elections are able to locate their position on the scale. As Figure 8-6 shows, tau-b correlations between the voters' positions on the liberal–conservative scale and the NES's seven-point party identification scale have grown noticeably larger since 1972 outside as well as within the South.[21] The increase was steeper for southern voters, and by 1994 they had become indistinguishable on this score from voters elsewhere.

A similar pattern of growing partisan coherence within the electorate is evident in correlations between voters' party identification and positions on several of the NES's seven-point issue scales and the abortion question. On issues ranging from the government's economic role, to race, to women's roles in society, to abortion policy, the trend since 1972 is upward, with correlations reaching their highest levels on four of the five scales in 1998.[22] Back in 1972, a voter's positions on the ideology, jobs, aid to blacks, and women's roles scales predicted party identification (Republican, independent, or Democrat) with only 62 percent accuracy; in 1998, the same four variables predicted party identification with 74 percent accuracy.[23] Clearly, citizens now sort themselves

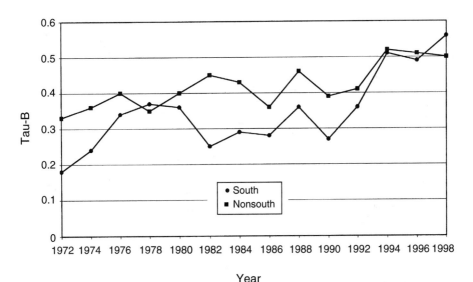

FIGURE 8–6 Correlation between Party Identification and Ideology of House Voters, 1972–1998
Source: American National Election Studies.

into the appropriate party (given their ideological leanings and positions on issues) a good deal more consistently than they did in the 1970s, with the largest
increases in consistency occurring in the 1990s.

Diverging Electoral Constituencies

The growth in partisan coherence, consistency, and loyalty (see Chapter 5)
among voters has made the two parties' respective electoral constituencies—
that is, the voters who support the party's winning candidates—politically
more homogeneous and more dissimilar. And as the parties' respective parties'
electoral constituencies have diverged ideologically since the 1970s, their most
active supporters have moved apart even further. Differences in the ideological
makeup of electoral constituencies can be measured by subtracting the mean
ideological self-placement of NES respondents who voted for one set of winning candidates from the mean for respondents who voted for another set of
winning candidates. Ideological divisions among activist constituents are
gauged by repeating the analysis for respondents who reported engaging in at
least two political acts in addition to voting during the campaign.[24] Figure 8-7
displays the changes in the ideological distinctiveness of the electoral constituencies of House Republicans and Democrats and of southern and non-
southern Democrats since 1972.[25]

In the 1970s, the ideological differences between the two parties' electoral
constituencies were modest and no wider than the gap between southern and

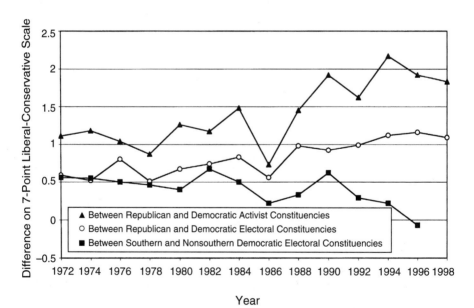

FIGURE 8-7 Difference in Mean Ideological Self-Placement of House Activist and Electoral Constituencies, 1972–1998
Source: American National Election Studies.

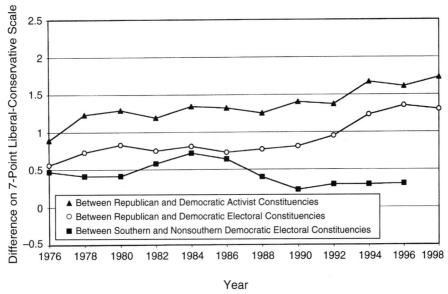

FIGURE 8–8 Difference in Mean Ideological Self-Placement of Senate Activist and Electoral Constituencies, 1976–1998
Source: American National Election Studies.

non-southern Democrats' electoral constituencies.[26] By the 1990s, the difference between the parties' electoral constituencies had more than doubled, to about 1.2 points on the seven-point scale, and the Democrats' regional divergence had entirely disappeared. Realignment in the South again explains only part of this change, for the gap between Republican and Democratic constituencies also grew (from 0.7 to 1.1 points) outside the South. Note also that the mean ideological difference between the parties' most active electoral constituents widened even more, nearly doubling to about 2 points on the scale.

Figure 8-8 presents the equivalent data for Senate electoral constituencies, except that entries are calculated from the three biennial surveys up to and including the year indicated on the chart, so that data from voters electing the entire Senate membership are used to calculate in each observation. The same pattern of ideological polarization between the parties' respective electoral and activist constituencies appears, although somewhat muted, reflecting the greater heterogeneity of the Senate's larger electorates.

Chicken or Egg?

The survey evidence, then, is consistent with the idea that partisan polarization in Congress reflects electoral changes that have left the parties with more homogeneous and more dissimilar electoral coalitions. When the focus of analysis is Congress, electoral change seems to be the independent variable: changes in roll-call voting reflect changes in electoral coalitions. When the focus is on elections, however, it becomes apparent that causality works at least as strongly in the opposite direction: voters sort themselves politically by responding to the alternatives represented by the two parties.

Realignment in the South *followed* the national Democratic party's decision to champion civil rights for African-Americans and the Republican Party's choice of Senator Barry Goldwater, who voted against the Civil Rights Act of 1964, as its standard-bearer that year. Partisan divisions on the abortion issue emerged first in Congress, then in the electorate.[27] Electorates diverged ideologically after the parties had diverged ideologically; the divisions in Congress and among activists during and after the Reagan years left the two parties with more distinctive images, making it easier for voters to recognize their appropriate ideological home. Conservatives moved into the Republican ranks, while liberals remained Democrats.[28] Notice that most of the trends among voters identified in the figures show their largest movement in the 1990s, *after* the firming up of congressional party lines in the 1980s.

This is not to say, however, that members of Congress simply follow their own ideological fancies, leaving voters no choice but to line up accordingly. As vote-seeking politicians, they naturally anticipate voters' potential responses and so are constrained by them. The Republican "southern strategy" emerged because Republican candidates sensed an opportunity to win converts among conservative white southerners. Ambitious Republicans adopted conservative positions on social issues to attract voters alienated by the Democrats' tolerance of nontraditional life styles but indifferent at best to Republican economic policies. Democrats emphasized "choice" on abortion because they recognized its appeal to well-educated, affluent voters who might otherwise think of themselves as Republicans. In the budgetary wars of the past two decades, Democrats have vigorously defended middle-class entitlements such as Social Security and Medicare, while Republicans have championed tax cuts because each position has a large popular constituency. In adopting positions, then, politicians are guided by the opportunities and constraints presented by configurations of public opinion on political issues. Party polarization in Congress depended on the expectation that voters would reward, or at least not punish, voting with one's party's majority.

The relationship between partisan consistency within Congress and within the electorate is thus inherently interactive. Between the 1970s and the 1990s, changes in electoral and congressional politics reinforced one another, encouraging greater partisan consistency and cohesion in both. An important consequence of the increased party loyalty among members of Congress and the ideological polarization of the congressional parties is that the linkage between citizens' decisions on election day and the actions of the winners once they assume office has become much tighter. Indeed, election results predict congressional roll-call voting on issues that fall along the primary liberal–conservative dimension accurately enough to meet one of the fundamental conditions for responsible party government. This is evident when we regress D-Nominate scores on two variables, party and the district-level presidential vote, and observe how much of the variance they explain. The presidential vote stands here as a serviceable if somewhat imprecise measure of district ideology; the higher the Republican share of the vote in any given election, the more conservative the district. The results are summarized in Figure 8-9, which tracks the proportion of variance in first-dimension D-Nominate scores explained by party and presidential vote, individually and in combination, in the congresses immediately following each presidential election since 1952.

As we would expect from the information in Figures 8-4a-d and 8-5, the capacity of party to account for roll-call voting on the liberal–conservative dimension declined from the 1950s to the 1970s but has since risen steeply. The predictive accuracy of the district-level presidential vote remained lower than that of party through most of the period, reaching a low point in 1976 (a consequence of Jimmy Carter's initial appeal to conservative southerners), but then rising to its highest levels in the time series during the 1990s. The *relative* contribution of district ideology to explaining House members' positions on the liberal–conservative dimension tends to be greatest in the 1960s and 1970s, when party's contribution is lowest. Between 1976 and 1996, both variables become increasingly accurate predictors of congressional voting, to the point where by the 105th Congress, party and presidential vote account for a remarkable 91.5 percent of the variance in representatives' positions on the scale.

The voting patterns of House members, then, are increasingly predictable from elementary electoral variables, the party of the winner and the district's ideology as reflected in its presidential leanings (with these two variables themselves correlated in 1996 at the highest level since the 1950s). With this development, voters have a much clearer idea of how their collective choices in national elections will translate into congressional action on national issues. Because party labels are so much more predictive of congressional

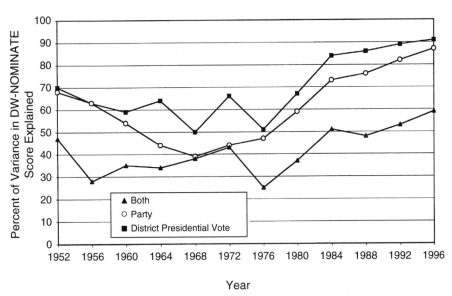

FIGURE 8–9 Variance in Roll Call Ideology Explained by District Presidential Vote and Party, 1952–1996
Source: See text.

behavior, voters have good reason to use them more consistently to guide voting decisions.

In theory, the emergence of more unified parties with distinct policy positions and the strengthened connection between the electorate's decisions and congressional roll-call votes should make it easier for voters to impose collective responsibility on Congress. Fiorina's description of party government looks far less remote from congressional reality than it did when he wrote it. Yet the same circumstances deepen the dilemma faced by moderate voters, bolstering support for divided government, which obscures party responsibility. And, despite the growing divergence between the parties' respective electoral coalitions, most Americans still cluster in the middle of the ideological spectrum. In surveys from the 1990s, about 60 percent of House voters place themselves in one of the middle three positions on the seven-point liberal–conservative scale, down only modestly from about 68 percent in the 1970s. Polarization in Congress has outstripped polarization in the electorate, so the proportion of citizens placing themselves between the two parties has not diminished.[29] Thus although the 1998 NES survey found party-line voting to be near its highest level in thirty years, it also found that

- only 45 percent of voters preferred the continuation of the two-party system to elections without party labels (29 percent) or new parties to challenge the Republicans and Democrats (26 percent);
- 84 percent thought that the phrase, "too involved in partisan politics" described Congress quite (40 percent) or extremely (44 percent) well;
- 56 percent preferred control of the presidency and Congress to be split between the parties, while only 24 percent preferred one party to control both institutions (the rest did not care).

With elite polarization outstripping mass polarization, the advent of a central component of responsible party government—unified parties with distinct policy positions—may have had the paradoxical effect of strengthening support for divided government. The more divergent the parties' modal ideological positions, the more reason the remaining centrist voters have to welcome the moderating effect of divided government.[30] But under divided government, the more divergent the parties, the more rancorous the conflict between the president and Congress, and rancorous political conflict is welcomed by almost no one.

PARTY POLARIZATION AND THE POLITICS OF IMPEACHMENT

The Republican Congress's attempt to impeach and remove Bill Clinton from the presidency epitomizes the sharp partisan divisions that now split both the Congress and the public and sets the stage for the 2000 election. In December 1998, when the House of Representatives voted to impeach President Bill Clinton, all but four Republicans voted for at least one of the four articles of impeachment; only five Democrats voted for any of them. On what everyone claimed was a conscience vote, 98 percent of Republican consciences dictated a vote to impeach the president, while 98 percent of Democratic consciences dictated the opposite. The Senate's verdict after the impeachment trial was only slightly less partisan. Every Democrat voted for acquittal, while 91 percent of the Republicans voted for conviction on at least one article.

Although the public as a whole steadfastly opposed the impeachment and conviction of Clinton in every national poll taken on the question, typically by margins of nearly two-to-one, it was, we saw in Chapter 6, sharply divided along partisan lines as well. In a dozen CBS News/*New York Times* Polls between September 1998 and February 1999 asking respondents, "Are Bill Clinton's actions enough to warrant impeachment and removal," an average of 86 percent of the self-identified Democrats said "no," while an average of 61 percent of self-identified Republicans said "yes."[31] Virtually identical partisan splits appeared in responses to questions about special prosecutor Kenneth Starr's impartiality and whether Clinton's transgressions were a public or private matter.[32]

Furthermore, the more politically active the respondents, the wider the partisan division on the issue. As Figures 8-10a–8-10d reveal, among Republican respondents to the 1998 NES survey, those who said they voted were more supportive of impeachment than those who did not, and the most active Republicans were most supportive of all. Among Democrats, the opposite pattern appears, so that, for example, the difference between opinions of Democrats and Republicans on impeachment who did not vote was 37 percentage points, between those who voted, 57 percentage points, and between activists, 72 percentage points.[33]

The stark partisan division among voters on the impeachment issue goes a long way toward explaining partisan polarization on the issue in Congress. The strong pro-Clinton consensus among Democratic identifiers was instrumental in keeping Democrats in Congress from deserting him. Clinton's relationship with his party's congressional delegation has never been particularly close. Many of them blamed him for their loss of majority status in 1994 and felt abandoned by his strategy of "triangulation"—moving to positions between the Republicans and traditional Democrats on issues such as welfare reform and balancing the budget—for winning reelection in 1996. No Democrat could (or wished to) defend his behavior in the Lewinsky scandal, and many reasonably feared that his downfall would take them down with him. Thus in August when Clinton was finally forced to admit to having the affair and lying about it, more than a few congressional Democrats prepared to abandon ship. According to journalist Bob Woodward, Senate Minority Leader Tom Daschle "counted as many as seven Democrats who were running around with speeches or statements in various states of completion calling for Clinton to resign for the good of the party."[34] Woodward estimates that as many as half of the Senate's Democrats privately hoped that Clinton would resign.

Had Clinton's public support evaporated, and, especially, had Democratic voters turned against him, Democrats in Congress, facing reelection in November, would almost certainly have deserted him en masse. But as polls continued to show widespread public approval of Clinton's presidency and opposition to

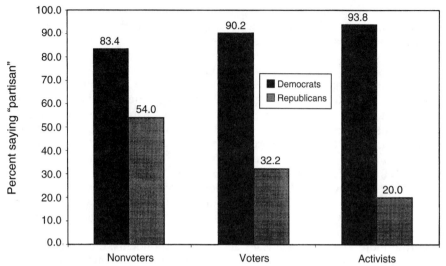

FIGURE 8–10A "What comes closer to your view: that Starr's investigation was impartial, or that it was partisan?"
Source: 1998 American National Election Study.

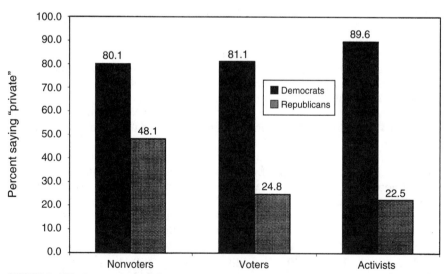

FIGURE 8–10B "Do you think of this whole situation more as a matter having to do with Bill Clinton's personal life, or more a public matter having to do with Bill Clinton's job as president?"
Source: 1998 American National Election Study.

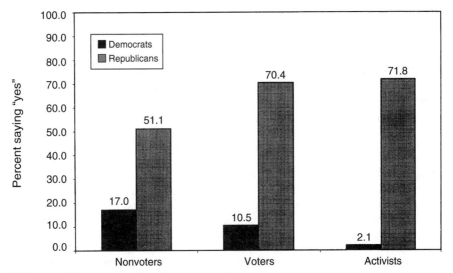

FIGURE 8–10C "Should President Clinton resign?"
Source: 1998 American National Election Study.

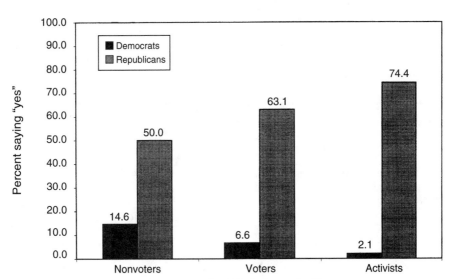

FIGURE 8–10D "If Clinton does not resign, should he be impeached?"
Source: 1998 American National Election Study.

his impeachment, so Democrats warily returned to the fold. In September, 138 of the 206 House Democrats had joined the unanimous Republicans in voting to release the full text of Kenneth Starr's salaciously detailed report recommending impeachment to the public. In October, thirty-one House Democrats voted to authorize impeachment hearings. And as we have seen, in December, only five Democrats voted for any one of the four articles of impeachment. In February, not a single Democratic Senator voted for conviction on any article of impeachment. Clearly, constituency opinion powerfully influenced Democratic politicians' actions on impeachment. All but a handful of congressional Democrats ended up expressing the same position taken by most citizens and an overwhelming majority of Democratic identifiers, that Clinton's behavior deserved condemnation but not impeachment and removal from office.[35]

Congressional Republicans, on the other hand, doggedly pursued impeachment despite its continuing unpopularity with the general public. Even the November election, in which the strategy of focusing on Clinton's disgrace flopped (see Chapter 6), did not stop them. Neither did the near certainty that the effort to remove Clinton would fail. Although their determination might be explained by the visceral hatred many of them felt toward the president, their actions were also in line with the preferences of a strong majority of their core supporters, and particularly their activists. We can see from Table 8-1 how partisan differences on the impeachment issue translated into differences in the views of each congressional party's electoral coalition. Although a majority of voters in districts won by Republicans in 1998 opposed impeachment, more than two-thirds of those who said they had voted for the Republican candidate favored impeachment. More than two-thirds of the voters in districts represented by Democrats opposed impeachment, with 87 percent of those who said they voted for the Democrat taking that position.

Republicans, then, in pursuing Clinton's impeachment and conviction, may have ignored most Americans and even most of their constituents, but they were certainly acting as large majorities of their own partisans and their own voters desired. Forced into the unhappy choice between offending their core

TABLE 8-1   OPINIONS ON IMPEACHMENT OF HOUSE REPUBLICAN AND DEMOCRATIC ELECTORAL COALITIONS

"Just from the way you feel right now, do you think President Clinton's actions are serious enough to warrant his being impeached and removed from the Presidency, or not?" (voters only)

	REPUBLICAN DISTRICTS		DEMOCRATIC DISTRICTS	
	All constituents	Republican voters	All constituents	Democratic voters
Yes	45.3%	**67.2%**	32.8%	12.8%
No	54.7%	32.8%	67.2%	**87.2%**
N	1792	1051	1473	939

Sources: CBS News and CBS News/New York Times surveys completed November 17, 1998, December 15, 1998, December 17, 1998, January 4, 1999, and February 7, 1999.

supporters and offending the broader public, they chose the second option. Strong pressure from party leaders encouraged them to take this course, for the Republican leadership in the House treated the impeachment vote as a party-defining event—anyone who opposed impeachment was not a real Republican—and refused to permit a vote on a resolution of censure that would have given backbenchers an alternative to voting for impeachment or no sanction at all.

The public's strongly partisan reaction to the Lewinsky scandal and Clinton's impeachment echoed the intense partisan conflict that dominated national politics during the Clinton years. Responding to this echo and thus the preferences of their core supporters, members of Congress split nearly perfectly along party lines, reinforcing the impression that the move to impeach Clinton was merely a particularly nasty case of ordinary party politics. This reaction made it impossible for Republicans to turn the impeachment of Bill Clinton into a bipartisan enterprise, dooming the effort to failure and setting the stage for a millennial electoral showdown in 2000, about which I will have more to say at the end of this chapter.

DIVIDED GOVERNMENT IN THE 1990S

A recurring theme in this book is how in the 1990s elections have become more partisan, more nationally focused, and more issue oriented than they have been in decades. Incumbency is no longer as potent an electoral advantage as it was in the 1970s and 1980s; all politics is no longer local; district electorates are voting more consistently across offices. House members are more ideologically polarized along party lines, more loyal to their parties and less attached to the institution; fewer envision lifetime careers in Congress. Coinciding with these mostly modest and incremental changes is one decisive historical departure: the Republicans' rise to durable majorities in the House and Senate, with the party finally approaching the level of success in congressional elections that they have displayed for years in presidential elections.

Yet despite these changes, divided government—Democrats controlling one branch of the federal government, Republicans the other—persists. To be sure, divided government reemerged, transposed, after a two-year hiatus only because Bill Clinton was not on the ticket in 1994, but in 1996 voters chose a Democratic president and a Republican Congress on the same ticket. The transposition raises the question of whether divided government in the 1990s has the same electoral roots as it had in the 1970s and 1980s. In some important respects, the answer is yes. But there are major differences as well.

Insofar as divided government reflects the public's own divided and self-contradictory preferences, nothing fundamental has changed. Most voters continue to desire a balanced budget, low tax rates, low inflation, a less intrusive government, greater economic efficiency, and a strong national defense. At the same time, they continue to dislike paying the necessary price: cuts in middle-class entitlements and other popular domestic spending programs, greater exposure to market forces, and greater environmental risk. In the 1980s, voters expressed both sets of preferences at the polls by electing Republican presidents committed to low taxes, economic efficiency, and a strong national defense, and for congressional Democrats who promised to minimize the price they had to pay for these goods in forgone benefits and greater exposure to market or environmental harm.[36] George Bush's failure to deliver on the economy or hold the line on taxes (supposedly Republican strong suits) put a Democrat in the White House in 1993. When Clinton's deficit reduction program included a large tax increase and his proposed restructuring of the health care system looked like big government run amok, Republican congressional candidates were able to use (among other things) their presidential themes of low taxes and smaller government to win control of Congress. In this transposed version of divided government, partisan roles remained the same, but institutional bases were exchanged. After 1994, it was the Republican Congress that sought lower spending, lower taxes, and a less intrusive government, and it was the Democratic president who championed the ordinary people targeted to pay the costs of the Republican "revolution." Indeed, the chance to redefine himself as defender of popular domestic programs threatened by the Republican Congress saved Bill Clinton's presidency.

Despite Clinton's comeback, voters continued to endorse the Republican goal of a smaller, cheaper government, and they refused, albeit narrowly, to hand the Congress back to the "tax-and-spend Democrats." In this sense, 1996 looked like the 1980s all over again, only with the branches of government switched. This outcome is also, however, consistent with the argument that divided government arises because some moderate voters deliberately split their tickets to give each party control of one branch in order to ensure that government policy takes the form of centrist compromises.[37]

Still, it is by no means certain that government remains divided only because some voters wanted to keep the Congress Republican to restrain the president on the usual issues of taxes, spending, and big government (or, indeed that he needed much restraining after the lessons of 1994). A more immediate consideration may well have been the administration's odor of scandal and widespread doubts about Clinton's personal character, which gave suspicious voters sufficient reason to want Republicans to remain in a position to keep an eye on him. Moreover, Clinton won reelection not only by what he resisted, but also by what he conceded to the Republican Congress. While defending programs popular with the middle class, he signed a bill to end welfare entitlements that had been part of the social safety net since the New Deal, agreed to balance the budget by 2002, and conceded that "the era of big government is over." He also opposed gay marriages, supported prayer in school, and advocated the v-chip, school uniforms, and curfews for young people. Clinton sought and won reelection by mutating, effectively, into a moderate Republican. Congressional Republicans saved their House majority by beating a tactical retreat back toward the center as well: giving into Clinton on the budget, supporting modest health insurance reforms, even providing enough votes to raise the minimum wage.

Indeed, considering that the Democrats kept the White House only because Clinton moved so far toward the center that he practically became the median voter himself, and that the Republicans retained the House only by moderating their revolutionary fervor, the underlying basis of divided government after 1996 seems far more reminiscent of the Eisenhower era than of the Reagan-Bush years. Eisenhower won election as a "modern Republican" who was willing to concede that the New Deal was here to stay and was, as president, content merely to curb its excesses. His stance invited congressional Democrats to adopt a strategy of cooperation rather than confrontation, and they accepted. Clinton won reelection by conceding that "the era of big government is over" and moderating, but not resisting, the conservative thrust of Republican policies. Both Eisenhower and Clinton were far more popular than their opponents and ran well ahead of their party's congressional candidates in total votes, partly because both could claim credit for peace and prosperity. Yet in both cases, congressional and presidential voting was highly correlated at the district level (recall Figure 6-1), suggesting that the vote for both offices lined up on a common dimension.

The reversal of institutional roles undercuts one explanation for divided government during the Reagan-Bush years. I had argued that voters, to borrow Fiorina's concise summary of the point, "matched party strengths with institutional responsibilities," viewing Congress as better suited to the distributive politics relished by Democrats, and regarding the president as having primary responsibility for the macro economy and the nation's defense.[38] Plainly such institutional expectations, if they have any force at all, turn out to be of decidedly secondary importance. Of course, voters had no opportunity to put a Republican back in the White House in 1994; those who wanted government to pursue the good things commonly associated with Republicans had no option but to elect Republicans to the House and Senate.

REFORMING CONGRESS

The Republicans took over Congress in 1994 by persuading voters to hold Democrats collectively responsible for the sorry state of Congress as well as of the nation. By the early 1990s, Congress had become more widely distrusted and disdained than at any time since the advent of scientific polling. Politicians by trade, members of Congress have never inspired much respect as a class, but the degree of suspicion and contempt expressed in polls and other venues (call-in talk shows, focus groups, letters to editors) was extraordinary by any standard. Solid majorities of citizens believed that most members were financially corrupt, misused their office to enrich themselves, and lied when the truth would hurt them politically. Even larger majorities believed that the people they elected to Congress quickly lost touch and cared more about keeping power and serving themselves than about the welfare of the nation or their constituents.[39]

The public's image of members of Congress as indifferent and out of touch was deeply ironic to anyone aware of the enormous investment of effort most members put into keeping in touch with constituents, their devotion to casework, and their sensitivity to district opinion on policy issues. Yet individual responsiveness of this sort evidently failed to penetrate deeply enough to counteract the general image of members as a bunch of self-serving, pampered, overpaid, arrogant hacks. Republicans took advantage of this image in their 1994 campaigns, making internal reforms of Congress "aimed at restoring the faith and trust of the American people in their government" the first element in their "Contract with America."[40] The proposed reforms included ending Congress's exemption from workplace laws, reducing the number of committees and committee staff, limiting terms of committee chairs, and banning the casting of proxy votes in committee, all of which were quickly adopted.

Term Limits

The most radical reform, limiting House and Senate terms, failed to win enough votes to move forward, however. Although the contract promised only a vote on a constitutional amendment limiting terms, the idea had been an official part of the 1988 and 1992 Republican platforms, and many Republican candidates had campaigned in 1994 as avid supporters of congressional term limits, so the distinction between "voting on" and "voting for" was probably lost on most of the public. However, many senior House Republicans as well as a majority of Democrats opposed term limits, and the only option of the four voted upon to get even a simple majority of votes (twelve-year limits for both the House and Senate) still fell sixty-one votes short of the required two-thirds.

There is no mystery why so many Republican candidates championed term limits in 1994. The public loves the idea. Opinion surveys typically find overwhelming majorities in favor of limiting legislative terms, and term limit measures have passed in every state where they have been put up to a popular vote. By 1995, when the Supreme Court struck down state-imposed term limits on federal officials as unconstitutional, twenty-two states had adopted them.[41]

The logic behind the idea is curious. Its supporters claim that the high success rates of incumbent House candidates has given us an ossified ruling clique, out of touch with voters and responsive only to the special interests whose money keeps them in office. The only way to ensure change is to limit tenure. But Congress has scarcely been starved for new blood; more than half of the representatives in the 104th Congress (1995–1996) had served less than three terms, and more than half of the senators were in their first or second term. Moreover, in 1992 and 1994, voters demonstrated that they could limit terms the old-fashioned way, by voting out incumbents or compelling them to retire in the face of almost certain defeat.

Beyond that, it seems strange to expect better representation from members who must give up their seats regardless of how well they perform; what quality of work should be expected from an employee who is sure to be fired no matter how well he or she does the job? Moreover, it strains credulity to imagine that someone who will soon be looking for a new job, probably in the private sector, will be less solicitous of "special interests" than someone whose future is controlled by voters. It seems equally doubtful that we would receive better representation from elected officials inferior in knowledge and experience to unelected bureaucrats, congressional staff, and professional lobbyists. Boosting the number of open seats, which beget the most expensive campaigns, seems an odd way to reduce the electoral importance of money (and hence the political clout of donors). Finally, it seems unlikely that representatives would be more responsive to district sentiments when casting votes or taking positions in Washington if the political cost of ignoring constituents were reduced. Indeed, for some proponents, the chief virtue of term limits lies in freeing members to do the right thing regardless of what constituents want.[42] Members would, of course, become equally free to do the wrong thing.

Term limits would have their most profound effect on representation, however, by diminishing members' opportunities and incentives for developing strong ties with constituents. As Fenno has so vividly shown, it takes years of time and effort simply to learn who one's constituents are, what they want, what they need. Even after this has been accomplished, keeping in touch is an endless, labor-intensive chore. Only the prospect of a lengthy series of future elections makes the effort worthwhile. Given the size (averaging more than 600,000 citizens) and diversity of most present-day House districts, authentic "citizen legislators" would begin with little knowledge of the opinions, lives, and values of most of their constituents. With a limited electoral future in the district, they would have little reason to invest in learning more. The only "people" they would perhaps be closer to are those in their own limited social or occupational circles. This hardly seems a recipe for better representation for everyone else.

Constituents, from their side, would know even less about their representatives than they do now, in part because the faces would change more often, in part because incumbents would put less effort into making themselves known. Voting decisions would thus be, on average, less informed than they are today. Jeffrey Mondak and Carl McCurley have shown that elections now tend to filter out the more incompetent and corrupt incumbents over time; the average quality of members remaining in each electoral class increases with each election they survive. Truncating House careers would interrupt this filtering process, reducing the aggregate quality of House members significantly.[43] This hardly seems a recipe for better representation, either.

These are obvious points, but they do little to undermine support for term limits because it rests on emotion, not analysis. The idea provided a focus for public anger at members of Congress as a class and at the more general failure of the political establishment in Washington to solve major national problems. It is no accident that the movement arose at a time when responsibility was blurred by divided government. In an ironic inversion of the usual pattern, even people who continued to like and support their own representative could still back a move to punish politicians wholesale by automatically firing them after a fixed period.

After 1995, the drive toward congressional term limits was not sustained. The Supreme Court declared state-level action imposing term limits on federal officials to be unconstitutional. Improving economic and other social conditions reduced voters' anger at politicians; by 1998, political experience was an electoral plus once more. Republicans' enthusiasm for term limits faded with their enjoyment of majority status, and several from the class of 1994 who had promised to serve only three terms renounced their pledges and sought reelection in 2000. Term limit advocacy groups vowed to campaign heavily against them, so the election will provide a test of the issue's current potency.[44] Even if public support for term limits remains high, however, amending the Constitution is never easy, particularly when the prime victims of the amendment would have to provide two-thirds majorities.

If the term limits were ever imposed, it is doubtful that either the public or their proponents would like the consequences. Term limits would probably make the parties much more important in congressional elections and politics than they are today. The irony is, of course, that most term limit advocates despise political parties as much as they despise career politicians. With less information about incumbents and with a larger number of open seats to contend with, voters would rely more heavily on cheap information shortcuts, the readiest of which is the party label, to sort out the candidates. With higher turnover, interest groups would see less advantage in cultivating individual members and more in cultivating parties and factions, redeploying their resources accordingly. With weaker ties to constituents, representatives would be freer to follow the party line; and with less time to develop their own sophisticated understanding of policy issues, they would be more open to party or ideological guidance. It would be a fine irony indeed if a populist movement inspired by fantasies of government by citizen legislators finally ushered in something like the British-inspired "responsible two-party system" advocated by an earlier generation of political scientists.[45]

THE PUBLIC'S EVALUATIONS OF CONGRESS

While failing on term limits, the zealous Republicans of the class of '94 did succeed in forcing votes on a rule banning all manner of gifts from lobbyists and legislation tightening up their registration and reporting requirements, which then passed overwhelmingly. Some of them also agitated for campaign finance reform, though without success. There is no reason, however, to think that gestures of this sort, along with the internal reforms adopted at the beginning of the 104th Congress, would restore public faith in Congress. In the most thorough study of congressional unpopularity to date, John Hibbing and Elizabeth Theiss-Morse argue that the public objects chiefly to the way Congress does its normal business.

People want legislators to be fair and efficient. Fairness means looking out for the interests of "the people," not "special interests." Efficiency means making policy without the posturing, haggling, threatening, and compromise it normally entails—that is, without the politics.[46] Insofar as internal reforms, staff reductions, gift bans, campaign finance reform, or term limits are thought to make members of Congress less insulated, more responsive to ordinary people, they should improve Congress's public image. But if Hibbing and Theiss-Morse are right, as long as Congress remains the venue in which intense political disagreements are thrashed out in public view, Congress will continue to be unpopular. "Just as people want governmental services without the pain of taxes, they also want democratic procedures without the pain of witnessing what comes along with those procedures."[47]

Thus

a major part of [the public's] distaste for Congress is endemic to an open legislative body in a large and complicated modern democratic polity. When the issues are complex and far-reaching, and when interests are diverse and specialized, the democratic process will be characterized by disagreements and a pace that can be charitably described as deliberate. And these disagreements will likely be played out by surrogates rather than by ordinary people.

The public performs no useful purpose by adopting the attitude that these surrogates, whether they be members of Congress, leaders of the parties, or officials of interest groups, have messed everything up and all would be right if they would only listen to ordinary people again. The truth is that ordinary people disagree fundamentally on vital issues. The noise and acrimony we despise so much in politics is a reflection of our own diversity and occasional convictions.[48]

From this perspective, Congress's standing is bound to suffer from the inevitable conflicts that arise when it tries to make national policy.[49] Moreover, the very things people don't like about Congress are exacerbated by divided government, which popular majorities consistently say they do like.

TOWARD THE MILLENNIUM

Whether voters will continue to choose divided government, and, if so, in what form, remain key questions as we look forward to the election of 2000. The issue may well be decided by the lingering effects of impeachment politics.

Competition for control of both Congress and the presidency is now closely balanced. Neither congressional Republicans nor presidential Democrats have as firm an electoral grip on their respective institutions as their counterparts did prior to the 1990s. The Republican House majorities elected between 1994 and 1998 have all been smaller than any of the majorities held by the Democrats between 1954 and 1994; Democrats need to gain only six seats in 2000 to take over (assuming Bernard Sanders of Vermont, a left-leaning independent, votes with them). And despite Clinton's two solid victories in the 1990s, Democrats have not won more than 50 percent of the total presidential vote since Jimmy Carter's 50.1 percent in 1976. Only the Senate Republican majority (55–45) seems secure. But Republicans must defend nineteen of the thirty-three Senate seats up in 2000, and Senate elections have delivered major surprises before. The House of Representatives and the White House are therefore clearly up for grabs in 2000, and even the Senate could conceivably come into play.

Whatever the outcome, the results will offer a unique test of competing theories of the connection between congressional and presidential elections. The traditional conception of presidential coattails, underlined by the recent decline in ticket splitting and rise in partisan coherence, suggests that whichever party wins the presidency should also win the House. If, in this view, a Republican were to win the presidency, the party would also certainly retain control of the Senate; a Democratic presidential victory could also give the party the Senate, but this is less likely without extraordinarily long coattails or some unanticipated breaks.

As of this writing (December 1999), the Republican frontrunner for the nomination, Texas Governor George W. Bush, enjoys a wide lead in the horse-race polls over both Vice President Al Gore and his rival for the Democratic nomination, former Senator Bill Bradley. If the lead holds—by no means a sure thing—then according to the coattails scenario, the election of 2000 should produce a Republican victory of great historic import. For the first time since the 83rd Congress (1953–1954), the Republican party would enjoy full control of the federal government. The consequences for national policy are potentially enormous.

But that very potential could work against its realization. The prospect of a Republican Congress unrestrained by a Democratic president might prove unsettling to some centrist voters. According to balancing models of divided government, an expected Republican presidential victory should throw moderate support to Democratic congressional candidates. The outcome would again be divided government, restoring (assuming the Republicans hold onto the Senate) the arrangement that prevailed from 1981 through 1987, with Republicans in control of the White House and Senate, and Democrats in control of the House. Again, at this writing, Democrats are ahead in most of the generic House election polls, so if both these and the presidential polls are predictive, the pre-Clinton version of divided government will be the outcome.

Intriguingly, the political aftermath of Clinton's impeachment and acquittal point to such an outcome as well. Although the move to impeach Clinton was popular with a majority of Republicans, it was unpopular with even larger majorities of independents and Democrats. Republicans in Democratic-leaning districts who voted to impeach the president clearly displeased most of their constituents, provoking an early mobilization of high-quality opponents and campaign money to challenge many of them in 2000. Twenty-eight of the House Republicans who voted to impeach Clinton represent districts in which the president won at least 55 percent of the two-party vote in 1996, so there are more than enough Republicans potentially vulnerable on the issue to give Democrats hope of regaining the House. Even if impeachment is old news by the time the election takes place, such Republicans may still suffer from the formidable opposition their impeachment votes stimulated. A Democratic challenger need not extol or defend Clinton to use the impeachment vote to portray the Republican as ill-fitted to the district. The challenger could simply point out that a representative whose conscience compels a vote contrary to the clear preferences of a solid majority of constituents on the most important issue of the day is not the appropriate person to represent the district. With the party balance in the House so close, it would not take a very strong anti-impeachment backlash to return control to the Democrats.

Ironically, the same issue may help Republicans at the presidential level. "Impeachment fatigue" was one popular explanation for Al Gore's continuing weakness in the early presidential polls. Although most people did not want Clinton to be driven from office, and his approval ratings remained high over the year after his trial, some observers argue that the public's dim view of his honesty and morality and disgust with his personal behavior made changing regimes an attractive prospect. Instead of campaigning squarely on the glowing economy, the budget surplus, and progress on crime, welfare dependency, and other social problems during the Clinton–Gore administration, the president's heir-apparent has had to manage the delicate process of separating himself from the moral squalor that is also part of the administration's legacy.

The astonishingly robust economy, with strong growth, low inflation, and low unemployment, combined with the other favorable social trends, raises yet another possible outcome in 2000. As in 1996 and 1998, voters might be content to endorse the status quo. Barring unforeseen disaster, Al Gore will have a strong case, based on peace and prosperity, for keeping the White House in Democratic hands; no doubt his campaign will let no one forget the comparatively sorry economic performance of the previous Bush administration. But, as always under divided government, congressional Republicans can claim their share of credit for good times, and a national campaign by Democrats calling for continuity and affirmation would give voters little reason to turn Republicans out of Congress. Republicans will certainly have more than abundant resources to make this argument and otherwise to defend threatened incumbents, so they could conceivably hold onto Congress even if a Democrat wins the presidency.

That *any* combination of unified or divided government remains a plausible outcome of the 2000 election stands as eloquent testimony to the close partisan balance prevailing in the United States at the beginning of the 21st century. With everything at stake, we can anticipate appropriately millennial contests for control of both Congress and the White House. The results will tell us much about the balance between electoral forces that have created more unified, cohesive, ideologically consistent parties (in both Congress and the electorate), and the consequently greater incentive for centrist voters to moderate the partisan extremes by giving neither party full control of the levers of government.

ENDNOTES

1. It is a complicated concept. See Hanna Pitkin, *The Concept of Representation* (Berkeley: University of California Press, 1967).
2. For an account of this literature, see Walter J. Stone, "Measuring Constituency-Representative Linkages: Problems and Prospects," *Legislative Studies Quarterly* 4 (1979):624.
3. Ibid., pp. 624–626; Catherine Shapiro, David W. Brady, Richard Brody, and John A. Ferejohn, "Linking Constituency Opinion and Senate Voting Scores: A Hybrid Explanation," *Legislative Studies Quarterly* 15 (1990):599–622; Larry M. Bartels, "Constituency Opinion and Congressional Policy Making: The Reagan Defense Buildup," *American Political Science Review* 84 (1991):457–474.
4. Compare Stone, "Linkages," with Gillian Dean, John Siegfried, and Leslie Ward, "Constituency Preference and Potential Economic Gain: Cues for Senate Voting on the Family Assistance Plan," *American Politics Quarterly* 9 (1981):341–356.
5. Stone, "Linkages," pp. 632–634.
6. Robert S. Erikson, "Roll Calls, Reputations, and Representation in the U.S. Senate," *Legislative Studies Quarterly* 15 (1990):623–642; Patricia Hurley, "Partisan Representation, Realignment, and the Senate in the 1980s," *Jour-*

nal of Politics 53 (1991):3-33; Robert A. Bernstein, "Limited Ideological Accountability in House Races: The Conditioning Effect of Party," *American Political Quarterly* 20 (1992):192-204; Amy B. Schmidt, Lawrence W. Kenny, and Rebecca B. Morton, "Evidence on Electoral Accountability in the U.S. Senate: Are Unfaithful Agents Really Punished?" *Economic Inquiry* 34 (July 1996):545-567.

7. Barbara Sinclair, "Agenda Control and Policy Success: Ronald Reagan and the 97th House," *Legislative Studies Quarterly* 10 (August 1985):291-314.

8. Richard F. Fenno, Jr., *Home Style: House Members in Their Districts* (Boston: Little, Brown, 1978), p. 233.

9. Gary C. Jacobson, *The Electoral Origins of Divided Government* (Boulder, Colorado: Westview Press, 1990), pp. 106-112.

10. David R. Mayhew, *Congress: The Electoral Connection* (New Haven: Yale University Press, 1974), p. 140.

11. Mayhew, *Electoral Connection*, pp. 174-177; Morris P. Fiorina, "The Decline of Collective Responsibility in American Politics," *Daedalus* 109 (Summer, 1980):25-45.

12. Fiorina, "Decline of Collective Responsibility," pp. 26-27.

13. Barbara Sinclair, "Coping with Uncertainty: Building Coalitions in the House and Senate," in *The New Congress*, ed. Thomas E. Mann and Norman J. Ornstein (Washington, DC: American Enterprise Institute for Public Policy Research, 1981), p. 215.

14. Barbara Sinclair, *Unorthodox Lawmaking: New Legislative Processes in the U.S. Congress* (Washington, DC: Congressional Quarterly Press, 1997), Chapter 5.

15. Paul S. Herrnson, *Party Campaigning in the 1980s* (Cambridge, Massachusetts: Harvard University Press, 1988); Kevin Leyden and Stephen A. Borelli, "An Investment in Good Will: Party Contributions and Party Unity among U.S. House Members in the 1980s," *American Politics Quarterly* 22 (1994):421-452.

16. For an explanation of the methodology for computing these scores and justification for their interpretation as measures of liberal-conservative ideology, see Nolan M. McCarty, Keith T. Poole, and Howard Rosenthal, *Income Redistribution and the Realignment of American Politics* (Washington, DC: AEI Press, 1997); Keith T. Poole and Howard Rosenthal, *Congress: A Political History of Roll Call Voting* (New York: Oxford University Press, 1997), Chapters 3 and 11.

17. The pattern for the 105th Congress is not merely a consequence of the Republican takeover of the House in 1994, for polarization was nearly as sharp in the 103rd Congress (1993-1994).

18. Earle Black and Merle Black, *Politics and Society in the South* (Cambridge, Massachusetts: Harvard University Press, 1987); Paul Frymer, "The 1994 Aftershock: Dealignment or Realignment in the South," in *Midterm: The Elections of 1994 in Context*, ed. Philip A. Klinkner (Boulder, Colorado: Westview Press, 1995); Richard Nadeau and Harold W. Stanley, "Class Polarization among Native Southern Whites, 1952-1990," *American Journal of Political Science* 37 (August 1993):900-919; Harold W. Stanley, "Southern Partisan Changes: Dealignment, Realign-

ment, or Both?" *Journal of Politics* 50 (February 1988):64–88; Martin P. Wattenberg, "The Building of a Republican Regional Base in the South: The Elephant Crosses the Mason-Dixon Line," *Public Opinion Quarterly* 55 (1991):424–431; M.V. Hood, III, Quentin Kidd, and Iriwin L. Morris, "Of Byrd[s] and Bumpers: Using Democratic Senators to Analyze Political Change in the South, 1960–1995," *American Journal of Political Science* 43 (1999):456–487.

19. Gary C. Jacobson, "Party Polarization in National Politics: The Electoral Connection," in *Polarized Politics: Congress and the President in a Partisan Era*, ed. Jon R. Bond and Richard Fleisher (Washington, DC: Congressional Quarterly Press, 2000), p. 16.

20. The categories are extremely liberal, liberal, slightly liberal, moderate or middle of the road, slightly conservative, conservative, and extremely conservative.

21. I use the tau-b statistic to measure the relationship because the analysis is of ordinal variables; alternative measures of association, including the product-moment correlation, reveal precisely the same trends; all of these analyses are confined to respondents who reported voting for one of the major party candidates in the House election. For details on the tau-b statistic, see Hubert M. Blalock, *Social Statistics* (New York: McGraw-Hill, 1960), pp. 232–234.

22. Jacobson, "Party Polarization."

23. Based on logit equations, with the three-point party identification scale as the dependent variable; leaners treated as partisans; the baseline (null) predictive accuracy for 1972 was 49 percent, for 1998, 50 percent.

24. The acts include trying to persuade others to vote for a candidate, going to political meetings or rallies, working for a party or candidate, wearing a campaign button or putting a bumper sticker on a car, and donating money to a party or candidate's campaign; about one in five voters is an activist by this measure.

25. The 1998 survey contained too few southern voters for winning Democrats to permit meaningful analysis.

26. Indeed, for four of the six election years prior to 1984, the difference in mean ideological self-placement of southern Democratic and Republican constituencies was statistically insignificant at $p < .05$.

27. Greg D. Adams, "Abortion: Evidence of an Issue Evolution," *American Journal of Political Science* 41 (1997):718–773.

28. Alan I. Abramowitz and Kyle L. Saunders, "Ideological Realignment in the U.S. Electorate," *Journal of Politics* 60 (1998):634–652; Edward G. Carmines and Geoffry C. Layman, "Issue Evolution in Postwar American Politics: Old Certainties and Fresh Tensions," in *Present Discontents: American Politics in the Very Late Twentieth Century*, ed. Byron E. Shafer (Chatham, New Jersey: Chatham House, 1997).

29. The share of voters placing themselves between the points where they place the parties on the seven-point liberal–conservative scale has not changed appreciably since the 1970s, remaining at about 30 percent.

30. Morris P. Fiorina, *Divided Government*, 2nd ed. (Boston: Allyn and Bacon, 1996), pp. 72–91.

31. The partisan gap actually grew over time; in the final February poll, 90 percent of Democrats opposed impeachment, while 60 percent of Republican supported it. See Gary C. Jacobson, "Public Opinion and the Impeachment of Bill Clinton," *British Elections & Parties Review* 10 (2000): Figure 10d.
32. Ibid., Figures 10b and 10c.
33. Activists are defined as for Figure 8-8.
34. Bob Woodward, *Shadow: Five Presidents and the Legacy of Watergate, 1974-1999* (New York: Simon & Shuster, 1999), p. 469.
35. Jacobson, "Impeachment Politics and the 1998 Congressional Elections," *Political Science Quarterly* 114 (1999):46.
36. Jacobson, *Divided Government*, Chapter 6.
37. Fiorina, *Divided Government*, pp. 72-81.
38. Fiorina, *Divided Government*, p. 65.
39. *The Public Perspective* 3 (November/December 1992):82.
40. Clide Wilcox, *The Latest American Revolution?: The 1994 Elections and Their Implications for Governance* (New York: St. Martin's Press, 1995), p. 69.
41. *U.S. Term Limits v. Thornton*, May 22, 1995.
42. George F. Will, *Restoration: Congress Term Limits, and the Recovery of Deliberative Democracy* (New York: The Free Press, 1992).
43. Jeffrey Mondak, "Competence, Integrity, and the Electoral Success of Congressional Incumbents," *Journal of Politics* 57 (1995):1043-1069; Jeffrey Mondak and Carl McCurley, "Inspected by #118406313: The Influence of Incumbents' Competence and Integrity in U.S. House Elections," *American Journal of Political Science* 39 (1995):864-885.
44. Kristian Brainerd, "Several Term Limit Supporters Recant Vows to Leave the House, Saying Their Work Is Not Yet Done," *Congressional Quarterly Weekly Report*, (June 19, 1999):1444.
45. Committee on Political Parties of the American Political Science Association, "Towards a More Responsible Two-Party System," *American Political Science Review* 44 (1950); Part 2.
46. John R. Hibbing and Elizabeth Theiss-Morse, *Congress as Public Enemy: Political Attitudes toward American Political Institutions* (New York: Cambridge University Press, 1995), pp. 14-20.
47. Ibid., p. 19.
48. Ibid., p. 82.
49. See also Robert H. Durr, John B. Gilmour, and Christina Wolbrecht, "Explaining Congressional Approval Association," *American Journal of Political Science* 41 (1997):175-207.

BIBLIOGRAPHY

Abramowitz, Alan I. "A Comparison of Voting for U.S. Senator and Representative." *American Political Science Review* 74 (1980):633–640.

———. "Choices and Echoes in the 1978 U.S. Senate Elections: A Research Note." *American Journal of Political Science* 25 (1981):112–118.

———. "Economic Conditions, Presidential Popularity, and Voting Behavior in Midterm Congressional Elections." *Journal of Politics* 47 (1985):31–43.

———. "The End of the Democratic Era? 1994 and the Future of Congressional Elections." *Political Research Quarterly* 48 (1995):873–889.

———. "Explaining Senate Election Outcomes." *American Political Science Review* 82 (1988):385–403.

———. "It's Monica, Stupid: Voting Behavior in the 1998 Midterm Election." Paper delivered at the Annual Meeting of the American Political Science Association, Atlanta, September 2–5, 1999.

———. "Name Familiarity, Reputation, and the Incumbency Effect in a Congressional Election." *Western Political Quarterly* 28 (1975):668–684.

———. "National Issues, Strategic Politicians, and Voting Behavior in the 1980 and 1982 Elections." *American Journal of Political Science* 28 (1984):710–721.

———. "Partisan Redistricting and the 1982 Congressional Elections." *Journal of Politics* 45 (1983):767–770.

Abramowitz, Alan I., and Cribbs, Kenneth J. "Don't Worry, Be Happy: Evaluations of Senate and House Incumbents in 1988." Paper delivered at the Annual Meeting of the American Political Science Association, Atlanta, August 31–September 3, 1989.

Abramowitz, Alan I., and Segal, Jeffrey A. "Determinants of the Outcomes of U.S. Senate Elections." *Journal of Politics* 48 (1986):433–439.

Achen, Christopher H. "Measuring Representation." *American Journal of Political Science* 22 (1978):475–510.

Ahuja, Sunil; Beavers, Staci L.; Berreau, Cynthia; Dodson, Anthony; Hourigan, Patrick; Showalter, Steven; Waltz, Jeff; and Hibbing, John R. "Modern Congressional Election Theory Meets the 1992 House Elections," *Political Research Quarterly* 47 (1994):909–921.

Alesina, Alberto, and Rosenthal, Howard. "Partisan Cycles in Congressional Elections and the Macroeconomy." *American Political Science Review* 83 (1989):373–398.

Alford, John R., and Hibbing, John R. "The Disparate Electoral Security of House and Senate Incumbents." Paper delivered at the Annual Meeting of the American Political Science Association, Atlanta, August 31–September 3, 1989.

Anagnoson, J. Theodore. "Federal Grant Agencies and Congressional Election Campaigns." *American Journal of Political Science* 26 (1982):547–561.

Ansolabeher, Stephen, and Gerber, Alan. "The Mismeasure of Campaign Spending: Evidence from the 1990 U.S. House Elections," *Journal of Politics* 56 (1994):1106-1118.

———. "The Effects of Filing Fees and Petition Requirements on U.S. House Elections." *Legislative Studies Quarterly* 21 (1996):249-264.

Arcelus, Francisco, and Meltzer, Allan H. "The Effects of Aggregate Economic Variables on Congressional Elections." *American Political Science Review* 69 (1975):232-239.

Arnold, R. Douglas. *The Logic of Congressional Action*. New Haven: Yale University Press, 1990.

Banks, Jeffrey S., and D. Roderick Kiewiet. "Explaining Patterns of Candidate Competition in Congressional Elections." *American Journal of Political Science* 33 (1989):997-1015.

Bauer, Monica, and Hibbing, John R. "Which Incumbents Lose in House Elections: A Reply to Jacobson's The Marginals Never Vanished," *American Journal of Political Science* 33 (1989):262-271.

Berch, Neil. "The 'Year of the Woman' in Context." *American Politics Quarterly* 24 (1996):169-193.

Berkman, Michael, and Eisenstein, James. "State Legislators as Congressional Candidates: The Effects of Prior Experience on Legislative Recruitment and Fundraising." *Political Research Quarterly* 52 (1999):481-498.

Bianco, William T. "Party Campaign Committees and the Distribution of Tally Program Funds." *Legislative Studies Quarterly* 24 (1999):451-469.

———. "Strategic Decisions on Candidacy in U.S. Congressional Districts." *Legislative Studies Quarterly* 9 (1984):351-364.

Biersack, Robert; Herrnson, Paul S.; and Wilcox, Clyde. "Seeds for Success: Early Money in Congressional Elections." *Legislative Studies Quarterly* 18 (1993):535-551.

Bloom, Howard S., and Price, H. Douglas. "Voter Response to Short-Run Economic Conditions: The Asymmetric Effect of Prosperity and Recession." *American Political Science Review* 69 (1975):1240-1254.

Bond, Jon R. "The Influence of Constituency Diversity on Electoral Competition in Voting for Congress, 1974-1978." *Legislative Studies Quarterly* 8 (1983):201-218.

Bond, Jon R.; Covington, Cary; and Fleisher, Richard. "Explaining Challenger Quality in Congressional Elections." *Journal of Politics* 47 (1985):510-529.

Bond, Jon R., and Fleisher, Richard H. *The President in the Legislative Arena*. Chicago: University of Chicago Press, 1990.

Bond, Jon R.; Fleisher, Richard H.; and Talbert, Jeffrey C. "Partisan Differences in Candidate Quality in Open Seat House Races, 1976-1994." *Political Research Quarterly* 50 (1997):281-299.

Born, Richard. "Assessing the Impact of Institutional and Election Forces on the Evaluations of Congressional Incumbents." *Journal of Politics* 53 (1991):764-799.

———. "House Incumbents and Inter-Election Vote Change." *Journal of Politics* 39 (1977):1008-1034.

———. "Partisan Intentions and Election Day Realities in the Congressional Redistricting Process." *American Political Science Review* 79 (1985):305-319.

————. "Reassessing the Decline of Presidential Coattails: U.S. House Elections, 1952-1980." *Journal of Politics* 46 (1984):60-79.

————. "Strategic Politicians and Unresponsive Voters." *American Political Science Review* 80 (1986):599-612.

————. "Surge and Decline, Negative Voting, and the Midterm Loss Phenomenon: A Simultaneous Choice Model." *American Journal of Political Science* 34 (1990):615-645.

Brady, David W. "A Reevaluation of Realignments in American Politics: Evidence from the House of Representatives." *American Political Science Review* 79 (1985):28-49.

Brunell, Thomas L. "Partisan Bias in U.S. Congressional Elections: Why the Senate Is Usually More Republican Than the House of Representatives." *American Politics Quarterly* 27 (1999):316-337.

Bullock, Charles S., III. "The Impact of Changing the Racial Composition of Congressional Districts on Legislators' Roll Call Behavior." *American Politics Quarterly* 23 (1995):141-158.

————. "Redistricting and Congressional Stability." *Journal of Politics* 37 (1975):569-575.

Burnham, Walter Dean. "Insulation and Responsiveness in Congressional Elections." *Political Science Quarterly* 90 (1975):411-435.

Busch, Andrew E. *Horses in Midstream: U.S. Midterm Elections and their Consequences, 1894-1998.* Pittsburgh: University of Pittsburgh Press, 1999.

Cain, Bruce E. "Assessing the Partisan Effects of Redistricting." *American Political Science Review* 79 (1985):320-333.

————. *The Reapportionment Puzzle.* Berkeley: University of California Press, 1984.

Caldeira, Gregory A.; Patterson, Samuel C.; and Markko, Gregory A. "The Mobilization of Voters in Congressional Elections." *Journal of Politics* 47 (1985):490-509.

Calvert, Randall L., and Ferejohn, John A. "Coattail Voting in Recent Presidential Elections." *American Political Science Review* 77 (1983):407-419.

Campbell, Angus; Converse, Philip E.; Miller, Warren E.; and Stokes, Donald E. *Elections and the Political Order.* New York: John Wiley, 1966.

————. "Predicting Seat Gains from Presidential Coattails." *American Journal of Political Science* 30 (1986):397-418.

————. "The Presidential Pulse and the 1994 Midterm Congressional Election." *Journal of Politics* 59 (1997):830-857.

————. *The Presidential Pulse of Congressional Elections.* Lexington: University of Kentucky Press, 1993.

————. "The Presidential Surge and Its Midterm Decline in Congressional Elections." *Journal of Politics* 53 (1991):477-487.

Campbell, James E. "The Return of the Incumbents: The Nature of the Incumbency Advantage." *Western Political Quarterly* 36 (1983):434-444.

Campbell, James E.; Alford, John R.; and Henry, Keith. "Television Markets and Congressional Elections." *Legislative Studies Quarterly* 9 (1984):665-678.

Campbell, James E., and Sumners, Joe A. "Presidential Coattails in Senate Elections." *American Political Science Review* 84 (1990):513-524.

Canon, David T. *Actors, Athletes, and Astronauts: Political Amateurs in the United States Congress*. Chicago: University of Chicago Press, 1990.

———. *Race, Redistricting, and Representation*. Chicago: University of Chicago Press, 1999.

———. "Sacrificial Lambs or Strategic Politicians? Political Amateurs in U.S. House Elections." *American Journal of Political Science* 37 (1993):1119–1141.

Clarke, Harold D.; Feigert, Frank B.; Seldon, Barry J.; and Stewart, Marianne C. "More Time with My Money: Leaving the House and Going Home in 1992 and 1994." *Political Research Quarterly* 52 (1999):67–85.

Clarke, Peter, and Evans, Susan. *Covering Campaigns: Journalism in Congressional Elections*. Stanford, California: Stanford University Press, 1983.

Clem, Alan L., ed. *The Making of Congressmen: Seven Campaigns of 1974*. North Scituate, Massachusetts: Duxbury Press, 1976.

Cnudde, Charles F., and McCrone, Donald J. "The Linkage between Constituency Attitudes and Congressional Voting Behavior: A Causal Model." *American Political Science Review* 60 (1966):66–72.

Coleman, John J. "The Importance of Being Republican: Forecasting Party Fortunes in House Midterm Elections." *Journal of Politics* 59 (1997):497–519.

Collie, Melissa P. "Incumbency, Electoral Safety, and Turnover in the House of Representatives, 1952–1976." *American Political Science Review* 75 (1981):119–131.

Conway, M. Margaret, and Wyckoff, Mikel L. "Voter Choice in the 1974 Congressional Elections." *American Politics Quarterly* 8 (1980):3–14.

Copeland, Gary. "Activating Voters in Congressional Elections." *Political Behavior* 5 (1983):391–402.

Cover, Albert D. "One Good Term Deserves Another: The Advantage of Incumbency in Congressional Elections." *American Journal of Political Science* 21 (1977):523–542.

———. "Contacting Congressional Constituents: Some Patterns of Perquisite Use." *American Journal of Political Science* 24 (1980):125–135.

Cover, Albert D., and Brumberg, Bruce S. "Baby Books and Ballots: The Impact of Congressional Mail on Constituency Opinion." *American Political Science Review* 76 (1982):347–359.

Cover, Albert D., and Mayhew, David R. "Congressional Dynamics and the Decline of Competitive Congressional Elections." In *Congress Reconsidered*, 2nd ed., ed. Lawrence C. Dodd and Bruce I. Oppenheimer. Washington, DC: Congressional Quarterly Press, 1981.

Cox, Gary W., and Katz, Jonathan. "The Reapportionment Revolution and Bias in U.S. Congressional Elections." *American Journal of Political Science* 43 (1999):812–840.

———. "Why Did the Incumbency Advantage in U.S. House Elections Grow?" *American Journal of Political Science* 40 (1996):478–497.

Cox, Gary, and Kernell, Samuel, eds. *Divided Government*. Boulder, Colorado: Westview Press, 1991.

Cox, Gary W., and Magar, Eric. "How Much Is Majority Status in the U.S. Congress Worth?" *American Political Science Review* 93 (1999):299–309.

Cox, Gary, and McCubbins, Mathew. *Legislature Leviathan: Party Government in the House*. Berkeley, California: University of California Press, 1993.

Cummings, Milton C., Jr. *Congressmen and the Electorate*. New York: The Free Press, 1966.

Dabelko, Kristen la Cour, and Herrnson, Paul S. "Women's and Men's Campaigns for the U.S. House of Representatives." *Political Research Quarterly* 50 (1997):121-135.

Damore, David F., and Hansford, Thomas G. "The Allocation of Party Controlled Campaign Resources in the House of Representatives, 1989-1996." *Political Research Quarterly* 52 (1999):371-385.

De Boef, Suzanna, and Stimson, James A. "The Dynamic Structure of Congressional Elections." *Journal of Politics* 57 (1995):630-648.

Dimock, Michael A., and Jacobson, Gary C. "Checks and Choices: The House Bank Scandal's Impact on Voters in 1992." *Journal of Politics* 57 (1995):1143-1159.

Dwyre, Diana. "Spinning Straw into Gold: Soft Money and U.S. House Elections." *Legislative Studies Quarterly* 21 (1996):409-424.

Edwards, George C., III. *Presidential Influence in Congress*. San Francisco: W. H. Freeman, 1980.

Ehrenhalt, Alan, ed. *Politics in America: Members of Congress in Washington and at Home 1990*. Washington, DC: Congressional Quarterly Press, 1989.

Eismeier, Theodore J., and Pollack, Philip H., III. *Business, Money, and the Rise of Corporate PACs in American Elections*. New York: Quantum Books, 1988.

Elling, Richard C. "Ideological Change in the U.S. Senate: Time and Electoral Responsiveness." *Legislative Studies Quarterly* 7 (1982):75-92.

Epstein, David, and O'Halloran, Sharon. "Measuring the Electoral Impact of Majority-Minority Voting Districts." *American Journal of Political Science* 43 (1999):367-395.

Erikson, Robert S. "The Advantage of Incumbency in Congressional Elections." *Polity* 3 (1971):395-405.

———. "Constituency Opinion and Congressional Behavior: A Reexamination of the Miller-Stokes Representation Data." *American Journal of Political Science* 22 (1978):511-535.

———. "Economic Conditions and the Congressional Vote: A Review of the Macrolevel Evidence." *American Journal of Political Science* 34 (1990):373-399.

———. "The Electoral Impact of Congressional Roll Call Voting." *American Political Science Review* 65 (1971):1018-1032.

———. "Is There Such a Thing as a Safe Seat?" *Polity* 9 (1976):623-632.

———. "Malapportionment, Gerrymandering, and Party Fortunes in Congressional Elections." *American Political Science Review* 66 (1972):1234-1245.

———. "Measuring Constituency Opinion: The 1978 U.S. Congressional Election Survey." *Legislative Studies Quarterly* 6 (1981):235-246.

Erikson, Robert S., and Palfrey, Thomas R. "Campaign Spending and Incumbency: An Alternative Simultaneous Equations Approach." *Journal of Politics* 60 (1998):355-373.

Erikson, Robert S., and Sigelman, Lee. "Poll-Based Forecasts of the House Vote in Presidential Election Years, 1952-1992 and 1996." *American Politics Quarterly* 24 (1996):520-531.

Erikson, Robert S., and Wright, Gerald F., Jr. "Policy Representation of Constituency Interests." *Political Behavior* 1 (1980):91-106.

Eubank, Robert E. "Incumbent Effects on Individual Level Voting Behavior in Congressional Elections: A Decade of Exaggeration." *Journal of Politics* 47 (1985):958-967.

Eulau, Heinz, and Karps, Paul D. "The Puzzle of Representation: Specifying Components of Responsiveness." *Legislative Studies Quarterly* 2 (1977):233-254.

Feldman, Paul, and Jondrow, James. "Congressional Elections and Local Federal Spending." *American Journal of Political Science* 28 (1984):147-163.

Fenno, Richard F., Jr. *Congressmen in Committees*. Boston: Little, Brown, 1973.

———. *Home Style: House Members in Their Districts*. Boston: Little, Brown, 1978.

———. *The United States Senate: A Bicameral Perspective*. Washington, DC: American Enterprise Institute, 1982.

Ferejohn, John A. "On the Decline of Competition in Congressional Elections." *American Political Science Review* 71 (1977):166-176.

Ferejohn, John A., and Calvert, Randall L. "Presidential Coattails in Historical Perspective." *American Journal of Political Science* 28 (1984):127-146.

Ferejohn, John A., and Fiorina, Morris P. "Incumbency and Realignment in Congressional Elections." In *The New Direction in American Politics*, ed. John E. Chubb and Paul E. Peterson. Washington, DC: The Brookings Institution, 1985.

Fiorina, Morris, P. "The Case of the Vanishing Marginals: The Bureaucracy Did It." *American Political Science Review* 71 (1977):177-181.

———. *Congress: Keystone of the Washington Establishment*. 2nd ed. New Haven: Yale University Press, 1989.

———. *Divided Government*. 2nd ed. Boston: Allyn and Bacon, 1996.

———. "Economic Restrospective Voting in American National Elections: A Micro Analysis." *American Journal of Political Science* 22 (1978):426-443.

———. *Representatives, Roll Calls, and Constituencies*. Lexington, Massachusetts: DC Heath, 1974.

———. *Retrospective Voting in American National Elections*. New Haven: Yale University Press, 1981.

———. "Short- and Long-Term Effects of Economic Conditions on Individual Voting Decisions." In *Contemporary Political Economy*, ed. D. A. Hibbs and H. Fassbender. Amsterdam: North Holland, 1981.

———. "Some Problems in Studying the Effects of Resource Allocation in Congressional Elections." *American Journal of Political Science* 25 (1981):543-567.

———. "Who Is Held Responsible? Further Evidence on the Hibbing-Alford Thesis." *American Journal of Political Science* 27 (1983):158-164.

Fiorina, Morris P., and Rohde, David, eds. *Home Style and Congressional Work*. Ann Arbor, Michigan: University of Michigan Press, 1989.

Fishel, Jeff. *Party and Opposition: Congressional Challengers in American Politics.* New York: David McKay, 1973.

Flemming, Gregory H. "Presidential Coattails in Open Seat Elections." *Legislative Studies Quarterly* 20 (1995):197-211.

Fowler, Linda L. "Candidates' Perceptions of Electoral Coalitions." *American Politics Quarterly* 8 (1980):483-494.

Fowler, Linda L., and McClure, Robert D. *Political Ambition: Who Decides to Run for Congress.* New Haven: Yale University Press, 1989.

Franklin, Charles H. "Eschewing Obfuscation? Campaigns and the Perception of U.S. Senate Incumbents." *American Political Science Review* 85 (1991):1193-1214.

Frantzich, Stephen. "Opting Out: Retirement from the House of Representatives, 1966-1974." *American Politics Quarterly* 6 (1978):251-273.

Froman, Lewis A., Jr. *Congressmen and Their Constituencies.* Chicago: Rand McNally, 1963.

Frymer, Paul; Kim, Thomas P.; and Bimes, Terri L. "Party Elites, Ideological Voters, and Divided Government." *Legislative Studies Quarterly* 22 (1997):195-216.

Gaddie, Ronald Keith. "Congressional Seat Swings: Revisiting Exposure in House Elections." *Political Research Quarterly* 50 (1997):699-710.

"Economic Interest Group Allocations in Open-Seat Senate Elections." *American Politics Quarterly* 25 (1997):347-362.

———. "Investing in the Future: Economic Political Action Committee Contributions to Open-Seat House Candidates." *American Politics Quarterly* 23 (1995):339-354.

Gelman, Andrew, and King, Gary. "Estimating the Incumbency Advantage without Bias." *American Journal of Political Science* 34 (1990):1142-1164.

Gerber, Alan. "Estimating the Effects of Campaign Spending on Senate Election Outcomes Using Instrumental Variables." *American Political Science Review* 92 (1998):401-411.

Gilliam, Franklin D., Jr. "Influences on Voter Turnout for U.S. House Elections in Non-Presidential Years." *Legislative Studies Quarterly* 10 (1985):339-352.

Gilmour, John B., and Rothstein, Paul. "A Dynamic Model of Loss, Retirement, and Tenure in the U.S. House of Representatives." *Journal of Politics* 58 (1996):54-68.

Glazer, Amihai, and Robbins, Marc. "Congressional Responsiveness to Constituency Change." *American Journal of Political Science* 29 (1985):259-273.

———. "Voters and Roll Call Voting: The Effect on Congressional Elections." *Political Behavior* 4 (1983):377-390.

Goidel, Robert K., and Gross, Donald A. "A Systems Approach to Campaign Finance in U.S. House Elections." *American Politics Quarterly* 22 (1994):125-153.

———. "Reconsidering the 'Myths and Realities' of Campaign Finance Reform." *Legislative Studies Quarterly* 21 (1996):129-149.

Goldenberg, Edie, and Traugott, Michael. *Campaigning for Congress.* Washington, DC: Congressional Quarterly Press, 1984.

———. "Congressional Campaign Effects on Candidate Recognition and Evaluation." *Political Behavior* 1 (1980):61-90.

———. "Normal Vote Analysis of U.S. Congressional Elections." *Legislative Studies Quarterly* 6 (1981):247-258.

Goodman, Saul, and Kramer, Gerald H. "Comment on Arcelus and Meltzer, The Effect of Aggregate Economic Conditions on Congressional Elections." *American Political Science Review* 69 (1975):255-265.

Green, Donald P., and Jonathan S. Krasno. "Salvation for the Spendthrift Incumbent." *American Journal of Political Science* 32 (1988):844-907.

———. "Rebuttal to Jacobson's 'New Evidence for Old Arguments.'" *American Journal of Political Science* 34 (1990):363-372.

Grofman, Bernard; Brunell, Thomas L.; and Koetzle, William. "Why Gain in the Senate But Midterm Loss in the House? Evidence from a Natural Experiment." *Legislative Studies Quarterly* 23 (1998):79-89.

Gronke, Paul. *Settings, Institutions, Campaigns, and the Vote.* Ann Arbor: University of Michigan Press, forthcoming.

Groseclose, Timothy, and Krehbiel, Keith. "Golden Parachutes, Rubber Checks, and Strategic Retirements from the 102nd House." *American Journal of Political Science* 38 (1994):75-99.

Herrick, Rebekah. "Is There a Gender Gap in the Value of Campaign Resources?" *American Politics Quarterly* 24 (1996):68-80.

Herndon, James F. "Access, Record and Competition as Influences on Interest Group Contributions to Congressional Campaigns." *Journal of Politics* 44 (1982):996-1019.

Herrnson, Paul S. *Congressional Elections: Campaigning at Home and in Washington,* 2nd ed. Washington, DC: Congressional Quarterly Press, 1998.

———. "Do Parties Matter? The Role of Party Organizations in Congressional Elections." *Journal of Politics* 48 (1986):612-613.

———. *Party Campaigning in the 1980s.* Cambridge: Harvard University Press, 1988.

Hershey, Marjorie Randon. "Incumbency and the Minimum Winning Coalition." *American Journal of Political Science* 17 (1973):631-637.

———. *The Making of Campaign Strategy.* Lexington, Massachusetts: Lexington Books, 1974.

———. *Running for Office: The Political Education of Campaigners.* Chatham, New Jersey: Chatham House, 1984.

Hibbing, John R. "The Liberal Hour: Electoral Pressures and Transfer Payment Voting in the U.S. Congress." *Journal of Politics* 46 (1984):846-865.

———. "Voluntary Retirements from the House in the Twentieth Century." *Journal of Politics* 44 (1982):1020-1034.

Hibbing, John R., and Alford, John R. "Constituency Population and Representation in the United States Senate." *Legislative Studies Quarterly* 15 (1990):581-598.

———. "The Electoral Impact of Economic Conditions: Who Is Held Responsible?" *American Journal of Political Science* 25 (1981):423-439.

Hibbing, John R., and Brandes, Sara L. "State Population and the Electoral Success of U.S. Senators." *American Journal of Political Science* 27 (1983):808-819.

Hibbing, John, and Theiss-Morse, Elizabeth. *Congress as Public Enemy: Public Attitudes Toward American Political Institutions*. Cambridge, UK: Cambridge University Press, 1995.

Hill, Keven A. "Does the Creation of Majority Black Districts Aid Republicans? An Analysis of the 1992 Congressional Elections in Eight Southern States." *Journal of Politics* 57 (1995): 384–401.

Hinckley, Barbara. "The American Voter in Congressional Elections." *American Political Science Review* 74 (1980):641–650.

———. *Congressional Elections*. Washington, DC: Congressional Quarterly Press, 1981.

———. "House Re-Elections and Senate Defeats: The Role of The Challenger." *British Journal of Political Science* 10 (1980):441–460.

———. "Incumbency and the Presidential Vote in Senate Elections: Defining Parameters of Subpresidential Voting." *American Political Science Review* 64 (1970):836–842.

———. "Issues, Information Costs, and Congressional Elections." *American Politics Quarterly* 4 (1976):131–152.

Hinckley, Barbara; Hofstetter, Richard; and Kessel, John. "Information and the Vote: A Comparative Election Study." *American Politics Quarterly* 2 (1974):131–158.

Huckshorn, Robert J., and Spencer, Robert C. *The Politics of Defeat*. Amherst, Massachusetts: University of Massachusetts Press, 1971.

Hurley, Patricia A. "Electoral Change and Policy Consequences: Representation in the 97th Congress." *American Politics Quarterly* 12 (1984):177–194.

———. "Partisan Representation, Realignment, and the Senate in the 1980s." Paper delivered at the Annual Meeting of the Midwest Political Science Association, Chicago, April 14–16, 1988.

Hurley, Patricia A., and Hill, Kim Quaile. "The Prospects for Issue Voting in Contemporary Congressional Elections: An Assessment of Citizen Awareness and Representation." *American Politics Quarterly* 8 (1980):425–449.

Hutcheson, Richard G., III. "The Inertial Effect of Incumbency and Two-Party Politics: Elections to the House of Representatives from the South, 1952–1974." *American Political Science Review* 69 (1975):1399–1401.

Jackson, Brooks. *Honest Graft: Big Money and the American Political Process*, updated ed. Washington, DC: Farragut Publishing Company, 1990.

Jackson, Robert A. "The Mobilization of Congressional Electorates." *Legislative Studies Quarterly* 21 (1996):425–445.

Jacobson, Gary C. "Congress: A Singular Continuity." In *The Elections of 1988*, ed. Michael Nelson. Washington, DC: Congressional Quarterly Press, 1989.

———. "Congress: Politics after a Landslide without Coattails." In *The Elections of 1984*, ed. Michael Nelson. Washington, DC: Congressional Quarterly Press, 1985.

———. "Congress: Unusual Year, Unusual Election." In *The Elections of 1992*, ed. Michael Nelson. Washington, DC: Congressional Quarterly Press, 1993.

———. "Deficit Cutting Politics and Congressional Elections." *Political Science Quarterly* 108 (1993):375–402.

———. "The Effect of the AFL-CIO's 'Voter Education' Campaigns on the 1996 House Elections." *Journal of Politics* 61 (1999):185–194.

————. "The Effects of Campaign Spending in Congressional Elections." *American Political Science Review* 72 (1978):469-491.

————. "The Effects of Campaign Spending in House Elections: New Evidence for Old Arguments." *American Journal of Political Science* 34 (1990):334-362.

————. *The Electoral Origins of Divided Government: Competition in U.S. House Elections, 1946-1988*. Boulder, Colorado: Westview Press, 1990.

————. "Enough Is Too Much: Money and Competition in House Elections, 1972-1984." In *Elections in America*, ed. Kay L. Schlozman. New York: Allen and Unwin, 1987.

————. "Impeachment Politics and the 1998 Congressional Elections." *Political Science Quarterly* 114 (1999):31-51.

————. "The Marginals Never Vanished: Incumbency and Competition in Elections to the U.S. House of Representatives, 1952-1982." *American Journal of Political Science* 31 (1987):126-141.

————. "Measuring Campaign Spending Effects in U.S. House Elections." In *Capturing Campaign Effects*, ed. Henry Brady and Richard Johnston. Ann Arbor: University of Michigan Press, forthcoming.

————. "Money and Votes Reconsidered: Congressional Elections, 1972-1982." *Public Choice* 47 (1985):7-62.

————. *Money in Congressional Elections*. New Haven: Yale University Press, 1980.

————. "The 1994 House Elections in Perspective." *In Midterm: The Elections of 1994*, ed. Philip A. Klinkner. Boulder, Colorado: Westview Press, 1996.

————. "The 105th Congress: Unprecedented and Unsurprising." In *The Elections of 1996*, ed. Michael Nelson. Washington, DC: Congressional Quarterly Press, 1997.

————. "Parties and PACs in Congressional Elections." In *Congress Reconsidered*, 4th ed., ed. Lawrence C. Dodd and Bruce I. Oppenheimer. Washington, DC: Congressional Quarterly Press, 1989.

————. "Party Organization and Distribution of Campaign Resources: Republicans and Democrats in 1982." *Political Science Quarterly* 100 (1985-1986):603-625.

————. "Party Polarization in National Politics: The Electoral Connection." In *Polarized Politics: Congress and the President in a Partisan Era*, ed. Jon R. Bond and Richard Fleisher. Washington, DC: Congressional Quarterly Press, 2000.

————. "Presidential Coattails in 1972." *Public Opinion Quarterly* 40 (1976):194-200.

————. "Reversal of Fortune: The Transformation of U.S. House Elections in the 1990s." In *Continuity and Change in Congressional Elections*, ed. David W. Brady, John Cogan, and Morris P. Fiorina. Stanford: Stanford University Press, 2000.

————. "Running Scared: Elections and Congressional Politics in the 1980s." In *Congress: Structure and Policy*, ed. Mathew McCubbins and Terry Sullivan. New York: Cambridge University Press, 1987.

————. "Strategic Politicians and the Dynamics of House Elections, 1946-86." *American Political Science Review* 83 (1989):773-793.

Jacobson, Gary C., and Dimock, Michael A. "Checking Out: The Effects of Over-drafts on the 1992 House Elections." *American Journal of Political Science* 38 (1994):601-624.

Jacobson, Gary C., and Kernell, Samuel. "National Forces in the 1986 U.S. House Elections." *Legislative Studies Quarterly* 15 (1990):72-85.

———. *Strategy and Choice in Congressional Elections*, 2nd ed. New Haven: Yale University Press, 1983.

Jacobson, Gary C., and Wolfinger, Raymond E. "Information and Voting in California Senate Elections." *Legislative Studies Quarterly* 14 (1989):509-524.

Johannes, John R. *To Serve the People: Congress and Constituency Service.* Lincoln, Nebraska: University of Nebraska Press, 1984.

Johannes, John R., and McAdams, John C. "The Congressional Incumbency Effect: Is It Casework, Policy Compatibility, or Something Else?" *American Journal of Political Science* 25 (1981):512-542.

Jones, Charles O. *Every Second Year.* Washington, DC: Brookings Institution, 1967.

———. "Inter-Party Competition for Congressional Seats." *Western Political Quarterly* 17 (1964):461-476.

———. "A Suggested Scheme for Classifying Congressional Campaigns." *Public Opinion Quarterly* 26 (1962):126-132.

Kahn, Kim Fridkin. "Does Being Male Help? An Investigation of the Effects of Candidate Gender and Campaign Coverage on Evaluations of U.S. Senate Candidates." *Journal of Politics* 54 (1992):497-517.

———. "Senate Elections in the News: Examining Campaign Coverage." *Legislative Studies Quarterly* 16 (1991):349-374.

Kahn, Kim Fridkin, and Kenney, Patrick J. "A Model of Candidate Evaluations in Senate Elections: The Impact of Campaign Intensity." *Journal of Politics* 59 (1997):1173-1205.

Kayden, Xandra. *Campaign Organization.* Lexington, Massachusetts: D.C. Heath, 1978.

Kazee, Thomas A., ed. *Who Runs for Congress? Ambition, Context, and Candidate Emergence.* Washington, DC: Congressional Quarterly Press, 1994.

Kazee, Thomas A., and Thornberry, Mary C. "Where's the Party? Congressional Candidate Recruitment and American Party Organization." *Western Political Quarterly* 43 (1990):61-80.

Kenny, Christopher, and McBurnett, Michael. "Up Close and Personal: Campaign Contact and Candidate Spending in U.S. House Elections." *Political Research Quarterly* 50 (1997):75-96.

Kernell, Samuel. "Presidential Popularity and Negative Voting: An Alternative Explanation of the Midterm Congressional Decline of the President's Party." *American Political Science Review* 71 (1977):44-66.

Kiewiet, D. Roderick. *Macroeconomics and Micropolitics.* Chicago: University of Chicago Press, 1983.

———. "Policy-Oriented Voting in Response to Economic Issues." *American Political Science Review* 75 (1981):448-459.

Kiewiet, D. Roderick, and McCubbins, Mathew D. "Congressional Appropriations and the Electoral Connection." *Journal of Politics* 47 (1985):59-82.

Kim, Thomas P. "Clarence Thomas and the Politicization of Candidate Gender in the 1992 Senate Elections." *Legislative Studies Quarterly* 23 (1998):399-418.

Kinder, Donald R., and Kiewiet, D. Roderick. "Economic Discontent and Political Behavior: The Role of Personal Grievances and Collective Economic Judgments in Congressional Voting." *American Journal of Political Science* 23 (1979):495-527.

King, Gary, and Browning, Robert X. "Democratic Representation and Partisan Bias in Congressional Elections." *American Political Science Review* 81 (1987):1251-1273.

Kingdon, John W. *Candidates for Office: Beliefs and Strategies.* New York: Random House, 1968.

Koetzle, William. "The Impact of Constituency Diversity upon the Competitiveness of U.S. House Elections, 1962-1996." *Legislative Studies Quarterly* 23 (1998):561-573.

Kostroski, Warren Lee. "Party and Incumbency in Post-war Senate Elections: Trends, Patterns, and Models." *American Political Science Review* 67 (1973):1213-1234.

Kramer, Gerald H. "Short-Term Fluctuations in U.S. Voting Behavior, 1896-1964." *American Political Science Review* 65 (1971):131-143.

Krasno, Jonathan S. *Challengers, Competition, and Reelection: Comparing Senate and House Elections.* New Haven: Yale University Press, 1994.

Kritzer, Herbert M., and Eubank, Robert B. "Presidential Coattails Revisited: Partisanship and Incumbency Effects." *American Journal of Political Science* 23 (1979):615-626.

Kuklinski, James H., and McCrone, Donald J. "Policy Salience and the Causal Structure of Representation." *American Politics Quarterly* 8 (1980):139-164.

Kuklinski, James H., and West, Darrell M. "Economic Expectations and Mass Voting in United States House and Senate Elections." *American Political Science Review* 75 (1981):436-447.

Lee, Frances E., and Oppenheimer, Bruce I. "Senate Apportionment: Competitiveness and Partisan Advantage." *Legislative Studies Quarterly* 22 (1997):3-24.

Leuthold, David A. *Electioneering in a Democracy: Campaigns for Congress.* New York: John Wiley, 1968.

Lewis-Beck, Michael, and Rice, Tom W. "Forecasting U.S. House Elections." *Legislative Studies Quarterly* 9 (1984):475-486.

Lockerbie, Brad. "Prospective Economic Voting in U.S. House Elections." *Legislative Studies Quarterly* 16 (1991):239-262.

Lublin, David. "The Election of African Americans and Latinos to the U.S. House of Representatives, 1972-1994." *American Politics Quarterly* 25 (1997):269-286.

———. "Quality, Not Quantity: Strategic Politicians in U.S. Senate Elections, 1952-1990." *Journal of Politics* 56 (1994):228-241.

Lyons, Michael, and Galderisi, Peter F. "Incumbency, Reapportionment, and U.S. House Redistricting." *Political Research Quarterly* 48 (1995):857-871.

Mattei, Laura Winsky, and Mattei, Franco. "If Men Stayed Home . . . The Gender Gap in Recent Congressional Elections." *Political Research Quarterly* 51 (1998):411–436.

McAdams, John C., and Johannes, John R. "The 1980 House Elections: Reexamining Some Theories in a Republican Year." *Journal of Politics* 45 (1983):143–162.

———. "The Voter in the 1982 House Elections." *American Journal of Political Science* 28 (1984):778–781.

McLeod, Jack M.; Brown, Jane D.; and Becker, Lee B. "Watergate and the 1974 Congressional Elections." *Public Opinion Quarterly* 41 (1977):181–195.

McPhee, William, and Glaser, William A., eds. *Public Opinion and Congressional Elections*. New York: The Free Press, 1962.

Magleby, David B., and Nelson, Candice J. *The Money Chase: Congressional Campaign Finance Reform*. Washington, DC: The Brookings Institution, 1990.

Maisel, Louis Sandy. "Congressional Elections in 1978: The Road to Nomination, the Road to Election." *American Politics Quarterly* 8 (1981):23–48.

———. *From Obscurity to Oblivion: Running in the Congressional Primaries*. Knoxville, Tennessee: University of Tennessee Press, 1982.

Maisel, Louis Sandy, and Cooper, Joseph, eds. *Congressional Elections*. Beverly Hills, California: Sage Publications, 1981.

Maisel, L. Sandy, and Stone, Walter P. "Determinants of Candidate Emergence in U.S. House Elections: An Exploratory Study." *Legislative Studies Quarterly* 22 (1997):72–96.

Malbin, Michael J., ed. *Parties, Interest Groups, and Campaign Finance Laws*. Washington, DC: American Enterprise Institute, 1980.

———. ed. *Money and Politics in the United States: Financing Elections in the 1980s*. Washington, DC: American Enterprise Institute, and Chatham, New Jersey: Chatham House, 1984.

Mann, Thomas E. *Unsafe at Any Margin: Interpreting Congressional Elections*. Washington, DC: American Enterprise Institute, 1977.

———. *The American Elections of 1982*. Washington, DC: American Enterprise Institute, 1983.

Mann, Thomas E., and Wolfinger, Raymond E. "Candidates and Parties in Congressional Elections." *American Political Science Review* 74 (1980):617–632.

Mayhew, David R. *Congress: The Electoral Connection*. New Haven: Yale University Press, 1974.

———. "Congressional Elections: The Case of the Vanishing Marginals." *Polity* 6 (1974):295–317.

Miller, Warren E., and Stokes, Donald E. "Constituency Influence in Congress." *American Political Science Review* 57 (1963):45–57.

Mondak, Jeffrey. "Presidential Coattails in Open Seats: The District-Level Impact of Heuristic Processing." *American Politics Quarterly* 21 (1993):307–319.

Mondak, Jeffrey, and McCurley, Carl. "Cognitive Efficiency and the Congressional Vote: The Psychology of Coattail Voting." *Political Research Quarterly* 47 (1994):151–175.

Nelson, Candice. "The Effects of Incumbency on Voting in Congressional Elections." *Political Science Quarterly* 93 (1978/1979):665–678.

Nice, David. "Competitiveness in House and Senate Elections with Identical Constituencies." *Political Behavior* 6 (1984):95–102.

Nicholson, Stephen P., and Miller, Ross A. "Prior Beliefs and Voter Turnout in the 1986 and 1988 Congressional Elections." *Political Research Quarterly* 50 (1997):199–213.

Niemi, Richard G., and Abramowitz, Alan I. "Partisan Redistricting and the 1992 Congressional Elections." *Journal of Politics* 56 (1994):811–817.

Oppenheimer, Bruce I.; Stimson, James A.; and Waterman, Richard W. "Interpreting U.S. Congressional Elections: The Exposure Thesis." *Legislative Studies Quarterly* 11 (1986):227–247.

Ornstein, Norman J.; Mann, Thomas E.; Malbin, Michael J. *Vital Statistics on Congress 1997–1998.* Washington, DC: Congressional Quarterly, 1997.

Owens, John R. "Economic Influences on Elections to the U.S. Congress." *Legislative Studies Quarterly* 9 (1984):123–150.

Paletz, David, "The Neglected Context of Congressional Campaigns." *Polity* 3 (1971):195–218.

Paolini, Philip. "Group-Salient Issues and Group Representation: Support for Women Candidates in the 1992 Senate Elections." *American Journal of Political Science* 39 (1995):294–313.

Parker, Glenn R. "The Advantage of Incumbency in House Elections." *American Politics Quarterly* 8 (1980):449–464.

———. *Homeward Bound: Explaining Changes in Congressional Behavior.* Pittsburgh: University of Pittsburgh Press, 1986.

———. "Interpreting Candidate Awareness in U.S. Congressional Elections." *Legislative Studies Quarterly* 6 (1981):219–234.

———. "Some Themes in Congressional Unpopularity." *American Journal of Political Science* 21 (1977):93–109.

Parker, Glenn R., and Davidson, Roger H. "Why Do Americans Love Their Congressmen So Much More than Their Congress?" *Legislative Studies Quarterly* 4 (1979):53–61.

Parker, Glenn R., and Parker, Suzanne L. "Correlates and Effects of Attention to District by U.S. House Members." *Legislative Studies Quarterly* 10 (1985):223–242.

Payne, James L. "The Personal Electoral Advantage of House Incumbents, 1936–1976." *American Politics Quarterly* 8 (1980):465–482.

Peters, John G., and Welch, Susan. "The Effects of Charges of Corruption on Voting Behavior in Congressional Elections." *American Political Science Review* 74 (1980):697–708.

Petrocik, John R., and Desposato, Scott W. "The Partisan Consequences of Majority-Minority Redistricting in the South, 1992 and 1994." *Journal of Politics* 60 (1998):613–633.

Pierson, James E. "Presidential Popularity and Midterm Voting at Different Electoral Levels." *American Journal of Political Science* 19 (1975):683–693.

Pothier, John T. "The Partisan Bias in Senate Elections." *American Politics Quarterly* 12 (1984):89–100.

Powell, Lynda W. "Issue Representation in Congress." *Journal of Politics* 44 (1982):658–678.

Ragsdale, Lyn. "The Fiction of Congressional Elections as Presidential Events." *American Politics Quarterly* 8 (1980):375-398.

———. "Incumbent Popularity, Challenger Invisibility, and Congressional Voters." *Legislative Studies Quarterly* 6 (1981):201-218.

Robeck, Bruce W. "State Legislator Candidates for the U.S. House: Prospects for Success." *Legislative Studies Quarterly* 7 (1982):507-514.

Robertson, Andrew W. "American Redistricting in the 1980s: The Effect on Midterm Elections." *Electoral Studies* 2 (1983):113-129.

Romero, David W. "The Case of the Missing Reciprocal Influence: Incumbent Reputation and the Vote." *Journal of Politics* 58 (1996):1198-1207.

Romero, David W., and Sanders, Francine. "Loosened Partisan Attachments and Receptivity to Incumbent Behaviors: A Panel Analysis, 1972-1976." *Political Research Quarterly* 47 (1994):177-192.

Romero, David W., and Stambough, Stephen J. "Personal Economic Well-Being and the Individual Vote for Congress: A Pooled Analysis, 1980-1990." *Political Research Quarterly* 49 (1996):607-616.

Schantz, Harvey L. "Contested and Uncontested Primaries for the U.S. House." *Legislative Studies Quarterly* 5 (1980):545-562.

Scheve, Kenneth, and Michael Tomz. "Electoral Surprise and the Midterm Loss in U.S. Congressional Elections." *British Journal of Political Science* 29 (1999):507-521.

Schoenberger, Robert A. "Campaign Strategy and Party Loyalty: The Electoral Relevance of Candidate Decision Making in the 1964 Congressional Elections." *American Political Science Review* 63 (1969):515-520.

Segura, Gary M., and Nicholson, Stephen P. "Sequential Choices and Partisan Transitions in U.S. Senate Delegations, 1972-1988." *Journal of Politics* 57 (1995):86-100.

Serra, George. "What's In It for Me?" *American Politics Quarterly* 22 (1994):403-420.

Serra, George, and Cover, Albert D. "The Electoral Consequences of Perquisite Use: The Casework Case." *Legislative Studies Quarterly* 17 (1992):233-246.

Shields, Todd G.; Goidel, Robert K.; and Tadlock, Barry. "The Net Impact of Media Exposure on Individual Voting Decisions in U.S. Senate and House Elections." *Legislative Studies Quarterly* 20 (1995):415-430.

Simon, Dennis M.; Ostrom, Charles W., Jr.; and Marra, Robin F. "The President, Referendum Voting, and Subnational Elections in the United States." *American Political Science Review* 85 (1991):1177-1192.

Sinclair, Barbara. "Agenda Control and Policy Success: Ronald Reagan and the 97th House." *Legislative Studies Quarterly* 10 (1985):291-314.

———. "Washington Behavior and Home-State Reputation: The Impact of National Prominence on Senators' Visibility and Likability." *Legislative Studies Quarterly* 15 (1990):475-494.

Sorauf, Frank J. *Money in American Elections.* Glenview, Illinois: Scott, Foresman, 1988.

Squire, Peverill. "Challenger Quality and Voting Behavior in U.S. Senate Elections." *Legislative Studies Quarterly* 17 (1992):247-264.

———. "Challengers in Senate Elections." *Legislative Studies Quarterly* 14 (1989):531-547.

————. "Preemptive Fund-raising and Challenger Profile in Senate Elections." *Journal of Politics* 53 (1991):1150-1164.

Squire, Peverill, and Smith, Eric R.A.N. "Repeat Challengers in Congressional Elections." *American Politics Quarterly* 12 (1984):51-70.

Stimson, James A.; MacKuen, Michael B.; and Erikson, Robert S. "Dynamic Representation." *American Political Science Review* 89 (1995):543-565.

Stein, Robert, and Bickers, Kenneth N. "Congressional Elections and the Pork Barrel." *Journal of Politics* 56 (1994): 349-376.

Stewart, Charles, III, and Reynolds, Mark. "Television Markets and U.S. Senate Elections." *Legislative Studies Quarterly* 15 (1990):495-524.

Stone, Walter J. "The Dynamics of Constituency: Electoral Control in the House." *American Politics Quarterly* 8 (1980):399-424.

————. "Measuring Constituency-Representative Linkages: Problems and Prospects." *Legislative Studies Quarterly* 4 (1979):623-639.

Sullivan, John L., and Uslaner, Eric M. "Congressional Behavior and Electoral Marginality." *American Journal of Political Science* 22 (1978):536-553.

Swain, John W.; Borrelli, Stephen A.; and Reed, Brian C. "Partisan Consequences of the Post-1990 Redistricting for the U.S. House of Representatives." *Political Research Quarterly* 51 (1998):945-967.

Thomas, Martin. "Election Proximity and Senatorial Roll Call Voting." *American Journal of Political Science* 29 (1985):96-111.

Tidmarch, Charles M., and Karp, Brad S. "The Missing Beat: Press Coverage of Congressional Elections in Eight Metropolitan Areas." *Congress and the Presidency* 10 (1983):47-61.

Tufte, Edward R. "Determinants of the Outcomes of Midterm Congressional Elections." *American Political Science Review* 69 (1975):812-826.

————. *Political Control of the Economy*. Princeton, New Jersey: Princeton University Press, 1978.

————. "The Relationship between Seats and Votes in Two-Party Systems." *American Political Science Review* 67 (1973):540-554.

Uslaner, Eric. "'Ain't Misbehavin': The Logic of Defensive Issue Strategies in Congressional Elections." *American Politics Quarterly* 9 (1981):3-22.

Uslaner, Eric M., and Conway, M. Margaret. "The Responsible Electorate: Watergate, the Economy, and Vote Choice in 1974." *American Political Science Review* 79 (1985):788-803.

Waterman, Richard. "Comparing Senate and House Electoral Outcomes: The Exposure Thesis." *Legislative Studies Quarterly* 15 (1990):99-114.

Weatherford, M. Stephen. "Economic Conditions and Electoral Outcomes: Class Differences in the Political Response to Recession." *American Journal of Political Science* 22 (1978):917-938.

Welch, Susan, and Hibbing, John R. "The Effects of Charges of Corruption on Voting Behavior in Congressional Elections, 1982-1990." *Journal of Politics* 59 (1997):226-239.

Westlye, Mark C. "Competitiveness of Senate Seats and Voting Behavior in Senate Elections." *American Journal of Political Science* 27 (1983):253-283.

————. *Senate Elections and Campaign Intensity*. Baltimore: Johns Hopkins University Press, 1991.

Wilcox, Clyde. "I Owe It All to Me: Candidates' Investments in Their Own Campaigns." *American Politics Quarterly* 16 (1988):266-279.

Wolfinger, Raymond E., and Rosenstone, Steven J. *Who Votes?* New Haven: Yale University Press, 1980.

Wolfinger, Raymond E.; Rosenstone, Steven J.; and McIntosh, Richard A. "Presidential and Congressional Voters Compared." *American Politics Quarterly* 9 (1981):245-255.

Wolpert, Robin M., and Gimpel, James G. "Information, Recall, and Accountability: The Electorate's Response to the Clarence Thomas Nomination." *Legislative Studies Quarterly* 22 (1997):535-550.

Wright, Gerald C., Jr. "Candidates' Policy Positions and Voting in U.S. Congressional Elections." *Legislative Studies Quarterly* 3 (1978):445-464.

————. "Constituency Response to Congressional Behavior: The Impact of the House Judiciary Committee Impeachment Votes." *Western Political Quarterly* 30 (1977):401-410.

————. *Electoral Choice in America*. Chapel Hill, North Carolina: Institute for Research in Social Science, 1974.

Wright, Gerald C., and Berkman, Michael B. "Candidates and Policy in U.S. Senate Elections." *American Political Science Review* 80 (1986):567-588.

Yiannakis, Diana Evans. "The Grateful Electorate: Casework and Congressional Elections." *American Journal of Political Science* 25 (1981):568-580.

INDEX